MINUTES
OF THE
SEVENTH ANNUAL CONFERENCE
OF THE
YOUNG PEOPLE'S SOCIETY OF CHRISTIAN ENDEAVOR

HELD IN

HELD IN BATTERY D ARMORY, CHICAGO,

ILL.,

July 5 - 8, 1888.

WITH PAPERS READ AT THE CONFERENCE.

First Fruits Press
Wilmore, Kentucky
c2015

First Fruits Press
The Academic Open Press of Asbury Theological Seminary
204 N. Lexington Ave., Wilmore, KY 40390
859-858-2236
first.fruits@asburyseminary.edu
asbury.to/firstfruits

MINUTES

—OF THE—

SEVENTH ANNUAL CONFERENCE

—OF THE—

YOUNG PEOPLE'S SOCIETY

—OF—

CHRISTIAN ENDEAVOR,

HELD IN BATTERY D ARMORY, CHICAGO, ILL.,

Thursday, Friday, Saturday and Sunday, July 5, 6, 7 and 8, 1888

WITH PAPERS READ AT THE CONFERENCE

PUBLISHED BY
The United Society of Christian Endeavor,
No. 50 BROMFIELD STREET, BOSTON

PREFACE.

Carlyle says there are in the British Museum enormous folios, many of which have been printed, but never edited, except "As you edit wagon loads of broken bricks and dry mortar simply by tumbling up the wagon." To attempt to edit the account of the proceedings of the Seventh Annual Conference of the Societies of Christian Endeavor is an undertaking your Secretary finds almost an impossibility.

I would that all could have been present at this, the greatest and grandest of all the national meetings ever held under the auspices of our Society. While this, of course, could not be, we realize that to the prayers for the convention's success sent up by many of those who were prevented by various reasons from being in attendance, a great share of the blessings which attended the meetings was due. It is therefore the object of this printed report to attempt to compensate, in a small degree, those who were absent, for their loss, by presenting to them an account, (brief and faulty though it be) of all that was done at Chicago.

May it yield to all a blessing and may the perusal of its pages furnish to all its readers a small portion at least of the inspiration and encouragement our delegates received, and may a more thorough study of its contents tend to make God's presence as near and real to all as it was to those who were present at the convention in Chicago.

GEORGE M WARD.
General Secretary.

MINUTES.

THURSDAY, JULY 5 — 1888

The Conference was called to order at 9 A. M. President Van Patten in the chair. After prayer by Rev. H. W. Pope, Palmer, Mass., Alexander McConnell, Evanston, Ill., was elected scribe, Roger Leavitt, Cedar Falls, Iowa, assistant scribe, and A. L. Winship, Lynn, Mass., time keeper.

The rules of the last Conference were adopted and the chairman was, on motion, instructed to appoint the usual standing committees.

After the devotional exercises, which were led by Rev. Asher Anderson, Bristol, Conn., addresses of welcome were delivered by Rev. E. D. Burr, representing the Churches of Chicago; C. B. Holdrege, Bloomington, Ill., for the Chicago C. E. Union, and L. W. Messer, Secretary of the Young Men's Christian Association of Chicago.

Response was made in fitting terms by Mr. Van Patten.

After singing "All Hail the Power of Jesus' Name," short addresses were made concerning the progress of the work; Rev. S. W. Adriance, Lowell, Mass , speaking for New England; Rev. H. B. Grose, Pittsburg, Pa., for the Middle States; Rev. E. M. Noyes, Duluth, Minn., for the Northwest; C. M. Perkins, St. Louis, Mo., for the Southwest; J. W. Hedges, San Diego, Cal., for the Pacific Coast; and Mrs. Seldon for Florida. The hymn "Tell it to Jesus" was then sung, after which J. W. Howell, Evanston, Ill., read a paper on "The duties and opportunities of State Unions."

After singing "At the Cross," the moderator announced the following committees, viz. :

On Credentials—J. W. Howell, Evanston, Ill., Roger Leavitt, Cedar Falls, Iowa, A. Olson, Longwood, Fla., A. H. Warner, Bridgeport, Conn., Ralph Emerson, Jr., Rockford, Ill.

On Resolutions—The Rev. J. L. Hill, Medford, Mass. ; the Rev. J. T. Kerr, Elizabeth, N. J. ; S. B. Smith, Esq , Boston, Mass., the Rev. C. F. Carter, Burlington, Vt. ; the Rev. Edward M. Noyes, Duluth, Minn.

On Business—F. J. Harwood, Appleton, Wis,; J. W Hedges, San Diego, Cal. ; F. G. Pratt, Boston, Mass. ; E. M. Revell, Rockford, Ill. ; H. M. Bowers, Philadelphia.

On Nominations—The Rev. S. W. Adriance, Lowell, Mass. ; the

Rev. W. G. Poor, Paola, Kan.; E. A. West, Decatur, Ill.; Edward Douglas, Middleton, Conn.; George B. Graff, St. Louis, Mo

On Reports and Papers—The Rev. C. A. Dickinson, Boston, Mass.; the Rev. H. B. Grose, Pittsburg, Pa.; the Rev Mr. Faville, Appleton, Wis.; the Rev. Norman Plass, Detroit, Mich.; G. W. Bassett, Rochester, N. Y.

The session was closed with prayer by Rev. N. Boynton, D. D., Boston, Mass.

THURSDAY AFTERNOON.

The Conference re-assembled at 2 o'clock.

The Scriptures were read by Rev. F. T. Lee, Whitewater, Wis., from 5th chapter Matthew. Prayer was offered by Rev. C. P. Mills, Newburyport, Mass.

The general subject for discussion was "How the Society Aids the Church." Papers were read by Rev. J. L. Sewell, Milton, Vt., on "The Society in Country Towns," Rev. R. W Brokaw, Belleville, N. J., and W. H. Pennell, Portland, Me., on "The United Society an Aid to every Church," Rev. James L. Hill, Medford, Mass., on "The Society a Training-school for the Church," Rev. C. A. Dickinson, Boston, Mass., on "Opening Fresh Fields to Young Christian Workers." Rev. A. E. Winship, Boston, Mass., made a short address on the necessity which exists for the Society in order to meet the changing conditions of our church life.

A letter was read from Mr. Chas. Burch, announcing that at the convention of Young People's Unions of Missouri, recently held, it was decided to dissolve the organization for the purpose of uniting with the Endeavor movement.

The session closed with the recitation in concert of the Lord's Prayer, and the Christian Endeavor Benediction, "The Lord watch between me and thee when we are absent one from another."

THURSDAY EVENING.

The evening session was opened at 7.30 o'clock by reading of Scriptures by Rev. Mr. Brooks, Fitchburg Mass., and prayer by Deacon Choate Burnham, of Phillips Church, Boston, Mass.

Secretary Ward made an address reviewing the work of the year which was listened to with marked attention and received with frequent hearty applause.

Mr W. G. Heinrich of Boston then sang a solo.

Rev. H. B. Grose, Pittsburg, on behalf of the New York delegation presented a magnificent floral piece to Rev. F. E. Clark, which was gracefully acknowledged. Mr. Clark then gave an address on the general work of the society in the past and the duties devolving on it for the future.

In closing Mr. Clark proposed an amendment to the model constitution in reference to the older active members. No action was taken on this proposed amendment at this time, the matter coming properly before the conference through its committee on Reports and Papers.

The conference sermon was then preached by Rev. James H. Brookes, D. D , St. Louis, Mo. A discourse full of earnest and eloquent exhortation, urging the thorough study of God's word that they might work in the power of the Spirit and thus help forward to a glorious fulfilment of the promised outpouring of the Holy Spirit upon our sons and daughters which seemed to be foreshadowed by the marvelous growth and deep earnestness of these societies of Christian Endeavor.

After singing the doxology, the session closed with the benediction.

FRIDAY MORNING.

At 6.30 o'clock a prayer-meeting was held in charge of Ralph C Goodwin, of Thomaston, Conn. The attendance was about 2,000, and much earnest spiritual emotion was manifested.

At 9 o'clock the conference reassembled with Rev. E. Blakeslee, Spencer, Mass., in the chair.

After singing "Holy, Holy, Lord God Almighty," and "Revive us Again,' Scriptures were read by Rev. Judson Titsworth, Milwaukee, Wis., from Isaiah, 6th Chapter. Prayer was offered by Rev. Mr. Boller, Sedalia, Mo. "Keep your colors flying" was then sung, after which Mr. W. H. Childs, No. Manchester, Conn., read a paper on the prayer-meeting and how it may be improved.

Rev. W. G. Poor, Paola, Kan , spoke on the Consecration meeting, after which Mr. B. F. Jacobs of Chicago, chairman of the International Sunday School committee, made a short address referring to the enthusiasm evinced in the conference and urging the necessity for a spirit of consecration, the fuel that was to support the movement.

"Christian Endeavor in England" was the subject of the next address by President Clark. He told of the enthusiasm with which he was received and of the general desire to learn fully of the plans of work which seemed to the speaker, to be even more needed in England than in this Country.

Mr. Shaw, treasurer of the society, then made his report, which was on motion received and accepted with a vote of thanks for his untiring efforts. Mr.Shaw then made an appeal for the consecration of more means and proceeded to call the roll of societies by States for pledges for the work of the United Society. Pledges to the amount of $6,433.00 were received.

The session having been prolonged beyond the usual time, the Christian Endeavor story by "Pansy," was, by a vote of the conference, postponed until the opening hour of the afternoon session.

After the benediction by Rev. Asher Anderson, Conn., the Conference adjourned.

FRIDAY AFTERNOON.

The Conference reassembled at 2 o'clock and was opened with singing "Oh scatter seeds of loving deeds." Scriptures were read by Rev. C. A. Towle, Cedar Rapids, Iowa, from 6th Chapter Ephesians. Prayer was offered by Rev. J. T. Kerr, Elizabeth, N. J.

After singing "I will follow Jesus," Rev. J. L. Hill in most fitting terms introduced "Pansy," (Mrs. G. R. Alden), who read her short story of "Chrissy's Endeavor" to a large and delighted audience.

"At the cross," was then sung and was followed by Rev. J. F. Brant, Sandusky, Ohio, who spoke on "Every prayer meeting a place for decision," and was followed by Rev. J. B. Wilson, Muskegon, Mich., on "Our Associate Members, how can we reach them?"

Benediction was pronounced by Rev. R. W. Brokaw, New Jersey.

FRIDAY EVENING.

Notwithstanding the intense heat the hall was filled to its utmost capacity. The session was opened at 7.30 o'clock with reading of scriptures by Rev. H. W. Pope, Palmer, Mass., from Acts, 8th chapter, and prayer by Rev. J. W. Savage, Lake Linden, Mich.

"Tell it to Jesus" was then sung, after which Moderator Van Patten introduced Rev. John H. Barrows, D D of Chicago, who delivered a most eloquent address on "America for Christ."

Mr. Heinrich then sang a solo which was heartily applauded.

Bishop Samuel Fallows of Chicago then made an address on the Y. P. S. C. E. and Christian Union. After singing "The Saviour is Calling," the Benediction was pronounced by Bishop Fallows

SATURDAY MORNING.

The usual prayer meeting was held at 6.30 o'clock, and was led by Mrs. J. L. Hill, and was attended by even larger numbers than the first meeting. It awakened a deep spiritual influence.

The Conference reassembled at 9 o'clock. Scriptures were read by Rev. Mr. Faville, Appleton, Wis., and prayer offered by Rev. S. I. Briant of Vermont. The hymn "I Will Follow Jesus," was sung.

A despatch was read from the Central Christian Endeavor Union of Philadelphia, sending greeting.

Seven minute addresses followed by Miss Mary Houghtaling, St Paul, Minn., on the Lookout Committee; M. A Hudson, Syracuse, N. Y., on the Prayer Meeting Committee; Miss Hattie Brown, Decatur, Ill., on the Social Committee; Rev. J. C. Cromer, Fort Wayne. Ind., the Temperance Committee; Frank W. Ruggles. Worcester, Mass., the Sunday School Committee; Edward S. Niles,

Boston, Mass., the Missionary Committee; Rev. H. N. Kinney, Winsted, Conn., on other helpful committees.

Mr. E. O. Excell sang "The Handwriting on the Wall." The question drawer was then opened and replies given in a very happy manner, by Rev. J. L. Hill.

W. H. Childs read a call signed by a large number of delegates for a conference of gentlemen at the close of the session in respect to raising funds for the work of the United Society, the State pledges not being sufficient to meet the wants of the Society for the coming year. Miss Hattie Brown, on behalf of the ladies, announced a similar meeting.

"Come thou Fount of Every Blessing," was then sung, after which Rev. E. Blakeslee, Spencer, Mass., addressed the Conference on the subject of "Our Literature." He spoke in warm terms of the Golden Rule, and of the great benefit it had been to the United Society.

Rev. E. Blakeslee then offered the following resolutions, which were seconded by Rev. E. M. Noyes, Minn., and unanimously adopted, viz. : —

Resolved, That this Convention extend its hearty thanks to The Golden Rule for its exceedingly valuable service to the Christian Endeavor cause during the past two years.

Resolved, That we congratulate it on the high order of excellence it has attained, and gladly reaffirm our adoption of it as the official organ of the Christian Endeavor Societies.

Resolved, That we regard this paper of paramount importance as a means of disseminating information on Christian Endeavor matters, of cultivating a proper *esprit de corps* in Christian Endeavor Societies, and of enforcing and conserving the essential Christian Endeavor principles, and therefore that we express our earnest desire that it find its way into the hands of every Christian Endeavor worker in the land.

Resolved, That while thus emphasizing its Christian Endeavor character at this time we would not forget its still wider scope as a thoroughly good, undenominational, religious paper, and would specially commend it for its helpfulness to the Sunday School, its devotion to the best forms of our common church life and work, and for its warm sympathy with all that aids in the Christian nurture of the family.

It was announced that invitations to hold the next Conference had been received from St. Louis, Omaha, Minneapolis, and other places, but the committee were not able at this time to decide the question. A letter was read from the Omaha Board of Trade, inviting the Conference to hold its next meeting at that point, and guaranteeing on behalf of its 120,000 citizens, a hearty welcome and the fulfilment of all the usual obligations and pledges required by the Society.

Rev. F. W. McMillen, Oberlin, Ohio, next addressed the meeting on the subject of Junior Societies.

A greeting was read from the Second Congregational Church of Exeter, N. H.

Adjourned with benediction by Rev. C. A. Towle, Cedar Rapids, Iowa.

SATURDAY AFTERNOON.

Conference was in session at 2 o'clock. The devotional exercises were led by Rev. J. T. Kerr, N. J. Scriptures were read by Rev. W. G. Bassett, N. Y., from 15th chapter John. Rev. Mr. Westervelt, Omaha, Neb., offered prayer. "Am I a Soldier of the Cross," was sung.

Rev. S W. Adriance from the Committee on Nominations reported the following named persons for officers (the scribe and assistant scribe having already been elected), and suggested that the filling of vacancies be left with the Board of Trustees: —

Moderator of the Conference—W. J. Van Patten, of Burlington, Vt.

Vice Presidents—The Revs J. W. Cooper, D. D., New Britain, Conn.; Wayland Hoyt, D. D., Philadelphia, Pa.; Charles F. Deems, D. D., New York; S. J. Niccolls, D. D., St. Louis, Mo.; Bishop Samuel Fallows, D. D., Chicago, Ill.; Robert Christie, D. D., St. Paul, Minn.; Charles D. Barrows, D. D., San Francisco, Cal.

State Officers—Oregon, the Rev. Dr. Landon; Washington Territory, S. M. Hanson, Seattle; Nevada, —— ——; Wyoming, Marcus M. Mason, Cheyenne; Montana, the Rev. George C. Tilly, Helena; Dakota, —— ——; Minnesota, the Rev. Edward M. Noyes, Duluth; Wisconsin, F. J. Harwood, Appleton; Michigan, the Rev. H. P. Welton, Grand Rapids; Iowa, the Rev. C. A, Towle, Cedar Rapids; Nebraska, the Rev. Willard Scott, Omaha; Kansas, the Rev. William G. Poor, Paola; Texas, D. W. Bailey, Groveton; Utah, the Rev. J. B. Thrall, Salt Lake City; Arizona, —— ——; New Mexico, —— ——; Louisiana, Edward Shute, New Orleans; Kansas, —— ——; Missouri, George B. Graff, St. Louis; Colorado, the Rev. W. D. Westervelt, Denver; Illinois, C B. Holdrege, Bloomington; Indiana, the Rev. J. C. Cromer, Fort Wayne; Ohio, the Rev. F. W. McMillen, Oberlin; Kentucky, the Rev. S. S. Waltz, Lousiville; Tennessee, E. A. Palmer, Grand View; North Carolina, —— ——; South Carolina, J. L. Wilson, Society Hill; Georgia, the Rev. William Shaw, Atlanta; Florida, F. E. Nettleton, Lake Helen; Alabama, —— ——; Mississippi, —— ——; Virginia, —— ——; Maryland, —— ——; New York, W. G. Bassett, Rochester; the Rev. H W. Sherwood, Syracuse; C. J. Frye, New York; New Jersey, the Rev. J. T. Kerr, Elizabeth; Pennsylvania, the Rev. H. B. Grose, Pittsburg; Maine, V. R. Foss, Portland; New Hampshire, the Rev. W. G. Sperry, Manchester; Vermont, the Rev. J. L. Sewell, Milton; Rhode Island, H. Edward Thurston, Providence; Massachusetts, the Rev. Erastus Blakeslee, Spencer; Connecticut, Eli Manchester, Jr., New Haven; Delaware, E. M. Richmond, Wilmington.

On motion of President Clark the report was received and adopted.

Mr. Van Patten responded gracefully, accepting the trust reposed in him.

Mr. J. W. Howell, for the Committee on Credentials, reported an attendance of 4,000 delegates, representing 1,800 societies, 700 towns, thirty-three States.

The report of the Committee on Reports and Papers was read by Rev. C. P. Mills, of Newburyport, in the absence of the chairman of the committee, Rev. C. A. Dickinson. On motion the report was received and adopted, the adoption of the report carrying the adoption of the amendment to the model constitution The report is as follows:

MR. CHAIRMAN AND MEMBERS OF THE UNITED SOCIETY OF CHRISTIAN ENDEAVOR:

Your Committee on reports and papers, had they time, would be glad to emphasize a good many important points which have been brought to their notice in the papers presented during this convention. So many good things have been said that it is somewhat difficult for them to single out for special comment the suggestions and facts which in their judgment have the most important bearing upon the well-being of the United Society. In reading over our General Secretary's report we are impressed with three things : 1st, The vastness of the work; 2d, The limitations of our agencies, and 3d, The large results reached by these limited agencies.

We say with all confidence that it would probably be impossible to find any other organization whose agent in the field has accomplished more with a comparatively small expenditure of money than our Secretary has accomplished during the past year. Seldom have money and energy been more immediately fruitful in results; and we are convinced that every dollar which is put into the work this coming year will bring even a larger income than it did last year.

In reading over our President's paper, we notice two suggestions which we desire to commend especially to the consideration of the United Society and Board of Trustees.

1st, The recommendations that the State Unions and Conventions refrain from levying taxes or demanding fees for membership, and that the small amounts needed for current expenses be raised by free gifts at the State Conventions. This same thought is emphasized in Mr. Howell's excellent paper on "The State Unions," and the reasons which are there given for keeping, not only the State expenditures, but those of the United Society as small as possible, seem to us worthy of the careful study of all who are engaged in our work.

The second and to our minds the most important recommendation in our President's address is the proposed amendment to the model constitution, which provides for the transference of the older members of the Society to the affiliated membership, with the understanding that the prayer meeting pledge of each affiliated member shall be binding upon him for faithful attendance and participation in the usual Church prayer meeting instead of the Society meeting.

This plan seems to us to solve one of the most perplexing difficulties which has presented itself in the development of the Christian Endeavor work, and, if adopted, will weld Church and Society together in such a way that even the careless observer must see that they are one and undivisible. We therefore strongly recommend that the United Society, at its next regular meeting, introduce this amendment into the model constitution.

Respectfully submitted,

CHAS. A. DICKINSON.
H. B. GROSE,
NORMAN PLASS.

Rev. Arthur Mitchell, D. D., Secretary of the Presbyterian Board of Foreign Missions, was introduced and delivered an able address on the relations of young people to the subject of foreign missions.

Treasurer William Shaw made a report of the pledges received from representatives of the societies, giving a total of $6,433 00.

Rev. J. L. Sewell, Vermont, announced: The result of the caucuses which were held this morning revealed the following feeling on the part of many delegates in this convention—a desire to hand in to the Treasurer of this society personal pledges of funds for the coming year. In accordance with this wide-spread desire manifested by the members of the convention, by permission of the trustees and by courtesy of the business committee, the hats are now to be passed around to give an opportunity for any one to deposit therein either a personal pledge or cash for the above purpose. While the collection proceeded the audience engaged in singing.

After the collection, Rev. H. A. Schauffler, of Cleveland, Ohio, was introduced and made an earnest plea for our foreign population.

Rev. E. P. Goodwin, D. D, of Chicago, then made a short address. He wanted to see the society grow and develop the young Christians. He felt that with an eye single to the service of God and a heart loyal to His cause, the Y. P. S. C. E. had before it a grand future.

After singing "Bringing in the Sheaves," Rev. J. C. Thrall, of Utah, spoke of the value of the society, and especially in Utah, whose only hope was in her young people.

S. L Mershon, Evanston, Ill, then made an address on "How to raise money for missions."

Rev. J. L. Hill continued the question drawer topics, the time allotted in the morning session not being sufficient for a reply to all of the important questions propounded.

After singing the "The Gloria," the Benediction was pronounced by Rev. Mr. Boller, Sedalia, Mo.

SATURDAY EVENING.

The Conference was opened at 7:30 o'clock with reading of the Scriptures by Rev. Mr. Sanborn, and prayer by Rev. Mr. Alden, Mr. Shaw reported that the pledges and cash received from the collection amounted to $1077, making a total offering of $,7500. A telegram from members of Christian Endeavor Societies, assembled at Mr. Moody's summer school, at Northfield, sending greetings, was read.

Prof. W. R. Harper, of Yale College, was then introduced and delivered an able address on systematic study of the Bible. He made an earnest appeal to the societies to undertake as a part of its prescribed work the systematic study of the Bible. Prof. Harper closed by announcing that he had prepared a course of studies according to the ideas he had presented, and that they would be published in successive numbers of the Golden Rule, beginning about September 12.

President Clark in a few words characterized this as one of the most important matters that had come before the Conference, and hoped the societies would adopt the plan.

Miss Katharine Willard then sang "More holiness give me," and in response to a hearty encore, sang "My ain Countrie."

Miss Frances E. Willard was then introduced and greeted her younger sisters and brothers as second only, if indeed second in the affection she bore to her own "white ribboners" of the W. C. T U. Miss Willard spoke earnestly for temperance and social purity, and was frequently and loudly applauded. At the close she was presented with a cluster of Calla lilies, on behalf of the Springfield, Bloomington and Decatur, Illinois, delegations. Adjourned with the benediction.

SUNDAY EVENING.

The closing meeting of the Conference was held at 7:30 o'clock. After singing, the Scriptures were read by Rev. J. T. Kerr, from 2 Kings chap. 6, and the closing verses of the 11th chapter of Hebrews. Prayer was offered by Bishop Fallows, of Chicago, followed with a response service of Scripture, with song, which was led by Roger Leavitt, Iowa.

Rev. J. L. Hill, of the Committee on Resolutions, read his report, which was as follows: —

WHEREAS, Appeals from various organizations, Christian in character, and in themselves worthy of general sympathy and support, have been made to the United Society of Christian Endeavor for indorsement and aid; and,

WHEREAS, The Young People's Society of Christian Endeavor is an organization in the church, and having as its specific object the development of spiritual life among the young people of the churches; therefore be it

Resolved, That it is essential to the highest interests and permanency of the Young People's Society of Christian Endeavor, that it hold strictly to its own lines of effort, as they are laid down in its constitution, and be not in any wise diverted therefrom; that all special appeals for contributions to any outside cause be referred to the church officers as responsible for the general benevolence of the church; that the United Society be advised to deal uniformly with all applicants, declaring its adherence to its own great objects, and its conviction of duty to take upon itself no other burdens.

Resolved, That it is inexpedient to allow this Society to be made auxiliary to any other, or to be used to further any object other than its own.

WHEREAS, As at the last convention the board of trustees were instructed, "for the sake of uniformity, beauty and economy," to provide a society badge, and inasmuch as this has been done, therefore be it

Resolved, That we express our gratification at the result, and commend the badge universally to members of societies.

WHEREAS, We believe that the use of uniform topics will advance the interests of the prayer meeting work of the Young People's Societies of the Christian Endeavor.

Resolved, That this Conference recommend to all the societies the adoption of those topics whenever it shall be expedient so to do.

WHEREAS, Repeated evidence has appeared testifying to the efficiency of our various State organizations; by means of which, for example, in New York alone the Societies now number 947, and the growth of societies has been, for example, in Missouri, 400 per cent. therefore,

Resolved, That for the propagation of societies we commend these organizations where they exist for their efficient and fruitful service, and we recommend the formation of State unions as soon as practicable in all localities not as yet pre-empted.

WHEREAS, The systematic study of the Bible must be the basis of intelligent Christian growth, and

WHEREAS, Prof. W. R. Harper, of Yale University, has, at the request of our officers, prepared a series of Bible studies, to be published in our society paper, *The Golden Rule.*

Resolved, That we commend these Bible studies to the thoughtful and prayerful consideration of the members of the societies.

WHEREAS, Intemperance recruits its ranks constantly from the youth of our land, therefore,

Resolved, That the Societies of Christian Endeavor commit themselves definitely and unreservedly to the cause of personal abstinence from intoxicants, and to the work of undoing the power of the drunkeries that line the streets in many of our cities and towns.

WHEREAS, The observance of United Society Day has greatly promoted unity among us and a most desirable *esprit de corps*, and has been attended incidentally with an augment of $8,000 to our needy treasury; therefore,

Resolved, That the United Society Day be recommended for our societies in the years that are to come.

WHEREAS, Each Society of Christian Endeavor comes of some specific church, being of it, is indebted to it, and always to be identified with it, and is to be recognized as having no separate existence whatever; therefore,

Resolved, That we pledge our loyalty to the pastor of that particular church with which we are severally connected, and that we regard it as no part of our work to break down denominational ideas, but that we go into that church with which we are allied, and there abide. doing our work in that place in the best way that may be disclosed to our united wisdom.

WHEREAS, The Society of Christian Endeavor is in its very spirit an aggressive missionary organization; therefore it is

Resolved, That we commit ourselves to co-operation with the missionary organizations of our respective churches, and that we work through them in expressing our spirit and in applying our methods.

On motion the report was received and adopted.

Mr. Hill announced that the committee did not think it advisable to fix the place for the next meeting at this time, and the matter would be left to the trustees of the United Society to determine and announce in due time

Rev. Wayland Hoyt, D. D., of Philadelphia, was next on the programme for an address, but was unable to be present. Mr. Van Patten read the following dispatch: "To my immense disappointment, cannot reach you. My warmest greetings to the convention. Am more than ever enthusiastic for Christian Endeavor Wayland Hoyt."

Rev. Arthur Little, D. D., was introduced and made an able address on the topic, "Some of the conditions of spiritual power." He was followed by Rev. N. Boynton, D. D., of Boston, who delivered an earnest address, and closed by showing that by purity of life we should learn to see God, and it was in teaching this purity of life that the great work of the society lay.

Mr. Van Patten, in making the closing address, impressed the hope that the conference had been beneficial to all who attended it, and especially to those of the vast North West, in whose interest it had been here convened. He seconded the suggestion of President Clark that our motto for the coming year be "Not to be ministered unto, but to minister." After thanking the delegates and all their friends for their unwearied attendance upon the meetings, he announced that after singing the hymn, "God be with you till we meet again," the Conference would be adjourned subject to the call of the trustees of the United Society. Mr Van Patten announced that after adjournment there would be a consecration meeting lasting one-half hour.

The audience then joined in singing and the benediction was pronounced by Rev. Arthur Little, D. D., of Chicago. After the benediction nearly all of the vast audience remained for the consecration meeting, which was led by Mr. Van Patten.

At the close all joined hands and sang, "Blest be the tie that binds." The benediction was pronounced by Rev. F. E. Clark, closing the Seventh Annual Conference of the Young People's Societies of Christian Endeavor.

ALEXANDER McCONNELL, *Scribe*.

FINANCIAL STATEMENT.

SOCIETY PLEDGES.

CALIFORNIA.—1st Presbyterian, San Diego,	$15 00
COLORADO.—1st Congregational, Denver.	25 00
2nd Congregational, Denver	10 00
CONNECTICUT.—So. Congregational, Bridgeport,	40 00
Park Street Congregational, Bridgeport,	10 00
Congregational, Bristol,	20 00
1st Presbyterian, Bridgeport,	10 00
Congregational, East Hartford,	10 00
Congregational, Enfield,	20 00
Center Congregational, Hartford,	10 00
Windsor Avenue, Hartford,	10 00
4th Congregational, Hartford,	15 00
So. Baptist, Hartford,	5 00
So. Congregational, Hartford	5 00
Congregational, Kensington	5 00
Congregational, Kent,	5 00
So Congregational, Middletown,	50 00
1st Congregational, Manchester,	20 00
1st Congregational, Norwich,	20 00
2nd Congregational, Norwich,	10 00
No. Congregational, Manchester,	30 00
United, New Haven,	20 00
3rd M. E., New Haven,	5 00
2nd Congregational, New Haven,	25 00
Dwight Place, Congregational, New Haven,	10 00
Grand Avenue Baptist, New Haven,	15 00
Congregational, New Britain,	5 00
Congregational, New Milford,	5 00
No. Congregational, New Hartford,	10 00
Congregational, Plantsville,	5 00
Congregational, Plainville,	10 00
Congregational, Riverton,	5 00

OF CHRISTIAN ENDEAVOR.

Congregational, Rocky Hill,	2 00
Congregational, Salisbury,	5 00
Congregational, Simsbury,	20 00
2nd Baptist, Suffield,	10 00
1st Congregational, Suffield,	10 00
Congregational, So. Norwalk,	5 00
Congregational, Terryville,	10 00
1st Congregational, Thomaston,	25 00
1st Congregational, Winsted,	13 00
Congregational, Windham,	5 00
2nd Congregational, West Cornwall,	5 00
Methodist Episcopal, Windsor,	2 00
Congregational, Windsor,	10 00
DAKOTA.—Methodist Episcopal and Presbyterian, Roscoe,	5 00
1st Congregational, Yankton,	25 00
1st Presbyterian, Gainsville,	10 00
FLORIDA.—Congregational, Winter Park,	10 00
ILLINOIS.—1st Presbyterian, Aurora,	5 00
N. E. Congregational, Aurora,	10 00
1st Congregational, Aurora,	10 00
1st Presbyterian, Aledo,	10 00
So. Baptist, Belvidere,	10 00
1st Presbyterian, Belvidere,	10 00
2nd Presbyterian, Bloomington,	100 00
Congregational, Bloomington,	10 00
1st Baptist, Bloomington,	10 00
Congregational, Bunker Hill,	10 00
Congregational, Buda,	10 00
Union Park Congregational, Chicago,	40 00
St. Pauls R. E., Chicago,	20 00
Grace M. E , Chicago,	15 00
Western Avenue C of C., Chicago,	10 00
M. E. Congregational, Chicago,	25 00
Chicago Avenue, Chicago,	10 00
Bethany, Chicago,	10 00
8th Presbterian, Chicago,	5 00
1st Presbyterinan, Chicago,	25 00
Presbyterian, Carbondale,	5 00
Presbyterian, Clinton,	5 00
Presbyterian, Carthage,	10 00
Union Congregational, Cobden,	5 00
Duncan Avenue Congregational, Cheltenham,	5 00
Congregational, Canton,	10 00
Presbyterian, Carrollton,	2 00
Presbyterian, Cairo,	5 00
1st Presbyterian, Decatur,	20 00
Church of God, Decatur,	4 00

YOUNG PEOPLE'S SOCIETY

1st Baptist, Decatur,	5 00
Christian, Decatur,	5 00
1st Congregational, Dwight,	25 00
Union, Dover,	5 00
Methodist Episcopal, Dixon,	5 00
Presbyterian, Danville,	5 00
1st Congregational, Evanston,	50 00
1st Presbyterian, Evanston,	50 00
1st Congregational, Elgin,	10 00
1st Congregational, Englewood.	10 00
Presbyterian, Grand Crossing,	5 00
1st Church of Christ, Galesburg,	10 00
1st Presbyterian, Gibson City,	5 00
Brooklyn Presbyterian, Grand Crossing,	5 00
1st Congregational, Galesburg,	5 00
1st Presbyterian, Hyde Park,	10 00
Baptist, Hyde Park,	2 00
Congregational, Lake View,	5 00
Congregational, La Grange,	25 00
Congregational, Millburn,	5 00
Congregational, Maywood,	5 00
Presbyterian, Mason City,	5 00
Baptist, Morris,	5 00
Congregational, Normal,	5 00
American Reformed, Norwood Park,	10 00
Presbyterian, Oregon,	5 00
2nd Presbyterian, Peoria,	10 00
C. E. Union, Peoria,	100 00
Congregational, Paxton,	5 00
Grace, Peoria,	5 00
1st Congregational, Rockford,	25 00
2nd Congregational, Rockford,	20 00
1st Presbyterian, Rockford,	5 00
State Street Baptist, Rockford,	15 00
2nd Presbyterian, Springfield,	5 00
1st Presbyterian, Springfield,	10 00
C. E. Union, Springfield,	100 00
96th Street Congregational Mission, South Chicago,	5 00
Congregational, South Chicago,	5 00
1st Evangelical, South Chicago,	5 00
Presbyterian, South Evanston,	5 00
Congregational, Stillman Valley.	5 00
Christian, Sterling,	1 00
1st Congregational, Sterling,	5 00
Presbyterian, Tamaroa,	5 00
Congregational, Toulon,	5 00
Bethany Union, Washington Heights,	10 00

Congregational and friends, Western Springs,	50 00
INDIANA.—1st C. P., Evansville,	5 00
Grace Presbyterian, Evansville,	10 00
Plymouth Congregational, Fort Wayne,	5 00
Tabernacle, Indianapolis,	5 00
Mayflower Congregational, Indianapolis,	5 00
1st Baptist, Indianapolis,	5 00
1st Presbyterian, Indianapolis,	5 00
Congregational, Michigan City,	20 00
Presbyterian, Mishawaka,	5 00
1st Presbyterian, Richmond,	10 00
Baptist, South Bend,	5 00
2nd Presbyterian, South Bend,	5 00
1st Presbyterian, South Bend,	10 00
Presbyterian, Valparaiso,	5 00
Presbyterian, Warsaw,	5 00
IOWA.—Union, Anamosa,	5 00
1st Presbyterian, Burlington,	5 00
1st Presbyterian, Cedar Falls,	3 00
Congregational, Cedar Falls,	5 00
Rev. C. A. Towle,	5 00
Presbyterian, Des Moines,	5 00
North Park Congregational, Des Moines,	5 00
Congregational, Dunlap,	5 00
Congregational, Earlville,	5 00
Congregational, Hampton,	5 00
Iowa Union, Mrs. E. H. Slocum,	25 00
1st Congregational, Le Mars,	5 00
Congregational, Monticello,	10 00
Congregational, Miles,	5 00
Congregational, Mount Pleasant,	5 00
Congregational, Nashua,	5 00
Congregational, Tabor,	10 00
Congregational, Shenandoah,	5 00
Presbyterian, Wyoming,	5 00
Presbyterian, Waterloo,	5 00
Congregational, Waterloo,	5 00
KANSAS.—1st Congregational, Kansas City,	10 00
1st Presbyterian, Wichita,	10 90
Plymouth Congregational, Wichita,	5 00
MAINE.—Union Congregational, Kennebunk,	20 00
Williston Congregational, Portland,	25 00
1st Parish, Yarmouth,	10 00
MASSACHUSETTS.—West Congregational, Andover,	15 00
South Congregational, Andover,	10 00
Congregational, Ashfield,	10 00
Congregational, Ashfield,	10 00

Congregational, Auburndale,	20 00
Congregational, Allston,	10 00
Pleasant Street Congregational, Arlington,	20 00
Clarendon Street Baptist, Boston,	25 00
Park Street Baptist, Boston,	35 00
Berkeley Temple, Boston,	50 00
Evangelical, Brighton,	25 00
1st Congregational, Bradford,	10 00
Congregational, Chesterfield,	5 00
3rd Congregational, Chicopee,	20 00
Congregational, Concord,	20 00
Congregational, Dalton,	20 00
Pilgrim Congregational, Dorchester,	10 00
Congregational, Everett,	10 00
Congregational, Florence,	10 00
Central Congregational, Fall River,	10 00
Central Congregational, Fitchburg,	10 00
Rollstone Congregational, Fitchburg,	25 00
1st Baptist, Fitchburg,	15 00
1st Congregational, Gardner,	35 00
West Congregational, Grafton,	5 00
Congregational, Housatonic,	10 00
Congregational, Hatfield,	5 00
2nd Congregational, Holyoke,	15 00
Congregational, Hinsdale,	25 00
1st Congregational, Hadley,	5 00
1st Congregational, Hyde Park,	10 00
North Congregational, Haverhill,	100 00
Centre Congregational, Haverhill,	100 00
Winter Street Free Baptist, Haverhill,	20 00
Congregational, Haydenville,	15 00
1st Congregational, Leverett,	5 00
Eliot Congregational, Lowell,	25 00
Kirk Street Congregational, Lowell,	100 00
North Congregational, Lynn,	35 00
Central Congregational, Lynn,	25 00
Chestnut Street Congregational, Lynn,	25 00
Congregational, Marion,	10 00
Mystic Congregational, Medford,	125 00
1st Congregational, Malden,	50 00
1st Congregational, Middleboro,	5 00
Congregational, Northboro,	5 00
Grace Union, No. Wilbraham,	25 00
Edwards Congregational, Northampton,	10 00
1st Congregational, Northampton,	25 00
Baptist, Pittsfield,	20 00
South Congregational, Peabody,	25 00

Congregational, Palmer,	25 00
1st Baptist, Roslindale,	3 00
Immanuel Congregational, Roxbury,	15 00
Congregational, Rockland,	5 00
Trinity. M. E., Springfield,	10 00
South Congregational, Springfield,	25 00
Memorial, Springfield,	25 00
North Congregational, Springfield,	50 00
Hope, Springfield,	10 00
1st Congregational, Springfield,	50 00
State Street M. E., Springfield,	25 00
State Street Baptist, Springfield,	25 00
1st Baptist, Springfield,	50 00
Congregational, South Deerfield,	10 00
Franklin county, H. A. Field,	125 00
Broadway Congregational, Somerville,	5 00
Phillips Congregational, South Boston,	100 00
Congregational, Shelburne Falls,	15 00
Crombie Street, Salem,	25 00
Methodist Episcopal, Spencer,	5 00
1st Congregational, Spencer,	50 00
Congregational, Saundersville,	10 00
Congregational, Shrewsbury,	5 00
Congregational, South Amherst,	5 00
Park Street, West Springfield,	15 00
Congregational, West Hampton,	5 00
1st Congregational, Williamstown,	10 00
Salem Street, Worcester,	10 00
Park Congregational, Worcester,	5 00
West Stockbridge,	5 00
1st Congregational, Westfield,	16 00
2nd Congregational, Westfield,	25 00
1st Congregational, Warren,	10 00
Congregational, West Mdford,	5 00
Congregational, Wakefield,	25 00
Congregational, West Newton,	25 00
MICHIGAN — Congregational, Allegan,	5 00
Congregational, Bridgman,	3 00
Congregational, Benzonia,	5 00
Presbyterian, Corunna,	10 00
Congregational, Covert,	5 00
Warren Avenue Baptist, Detroit,	10 00
Washington Avenue Presbyterian, East Saginaw.	10 00
Baptist, East Saginaw,	5 00
South Congregational, Grand Rapids,	5 00
1st Presbyterian, Grand Rapids,	10 00
Congregational, Grand Haven,	3 00

Congregational, Galesburg,	2 00
1st Congregational, Kalamazoo,	10 00
1st Presbyterian, Kalamazoo,	10 00
Congregational, Lake Linden,	5 00
Oak Street Congregational, Manistee,	5 00
Maple Street Baptist, Manistee,	5 00
1st Presbyterian, Marquette,	10 00
1st Congregational, Muskegon,	25 00
Presbyterian, Niles,	5 00
Overisel, Presbyterian,	5 00
Congregational, St. Joseph,	5 00
Congregational, Traverse City,	5 00
MINNESOTA.—Congregational, Clearwater,	5 00
Pilgrim Congregational, Duluth,	10 00
Union, Glyndon,	5 00
Central Baptist, Minneapolis,	10 00
Westminster Presbyterian, Minneapolis,	25 00
Riverside Mission, Minneapolis,	5 00
Highland Park Presbyterian,	5 00
Franklin Avenue Presbyterian, Minneapolis,	5 00
Hennepin Avenue M. E., Minneapolis,	10 00
Plymouth Congregational, Minneapolis,	100 00
1st Free Baptist, Minneapolis,	10 00
1st Presbyterian, Minneapolis,	15 00
Congregational, Lake City,	10 00
Presbyterian, Rush City,	5 00
Reformed Episcopal, St. Paul	20 00
House of Hope, Presbyterian, St. Paul,	50 00
St. Anthony Pk., St. Paul,	5 00
1st Congregational, Spring Valley,	5 00
1st Congregational, Sauk Center,	5 00
MISSOURI.—Congregational, Carthage,	5 00
1st Presbyterian, Hannibal,	5 00
McCausland Avenue, St. Louis,	5 00
Pilgrim Congregational, St. Louis,	25 00
2nd Baptist, St. Louis,	20 00
Lafayette Park Presbyterian,	25 00
2nd Presbyterian,	10 00
Lucus Avenue C. P., St. Louis,	5 00
Glasgow Avenue Presbyterian, St. Louis,	10 00
Aubert Place Mission, St. Louis,	10 00
Soulard Market Missions, St. Louis,	10 00
Westminster Presbyterian, St. Louis,	10 00
1st Christian, St. Louis,	7 00
Compton Hill, St. Louis,	20 00
1st Baptist. St. Louis,	2 00
North Presbyterian, St. Louis,	23 15

1st Methodist Episcopal, St. Louis,	10 00
Westminster Presbyterian, St. Joseph,	10 00
Congregational, St. Joseph,	10 00
Broadway Presbyterian, Sedalia,	10 00
1st Congregational, Sedalia,	10 00
Calvary Presbyterian, Springfield,	25 00
NEBRASKA.—Congregational, Ashland,	10 00
1st Presbyterian, Beatrice,	10 00
Congregational, Chadron,	5 00
Congregational, Fullerton,	25 00
1st Presbyterian, Omaha,	10 00
St. Mary's Avenue Congregational, Omaha,	5 00
1st Congregational, Omaha,	5 00
Calvary Baptist, Omaha,	5 00
3rd Congregational, Omaha,	5 00
1st Congregational, York,	10 00
NEW HAMPSHIRE.—1st Congregational, Concord,	50 00
Congregational, Hampstead,	5 00
1st Congregational, Exeter,	5 00
1st Congregational, Manchester,	20 00
Franklin Street Congregational, Manchester,	20 00
1st Congregational, Milford,	20 00
NEW JERSEY.—Reformed, Belleville,	15 00
Presbyterian, Camden,	5 00
Calvary Baptist, Cape May,	10 00
3rd Presbyterian, Elizabeth,	10 00
1st Congregational, Jersey City,	40 00
Bergen Baptist, Jersey City,	10 00
Trinity Reformed, Plainfield,	5 00
NEW YORK —Central Presbyterian, Avon,	3 00
Congregational, Bridgewater,	5 00
1st Presbyterian, Baldwinsville,	10 00
Presbyterian, Bath,	10 00
West Presbyterian, Binghampton,	10 00
Clinton Avenue Congregational, Brooklyn,	10 00
Classon Avenue, Brooklyn,	10 00
1st Presbyterian, Buffalo,	10 00
Washington Street Baptist, Buffalo,	20 00
1st Congregational, Buffalo,	20 00
Lafayette Presbyterian, Buffalo,	20 00
East Presbyterian, Buffalo,	5 00
Pilgrim Congregational, Buffalo,	5 00
Cedar Street Baptist, Buffalo,	3 00
Hudson Street Baptist, Buffalo,	10 00
Union Congregational, Churchville,	10 00
Presbyterian, Greenport,	10 00
Union, Holland Patent,	2 91

Congregational, Honeoye,	10 00
Baptist, Ilion,	10 00
1st Presbyterian, Lockport,	10 00
Presbyterian, Newark,	10 00
Congregational, Norwood,	5 00
1st Reformed, Fordham, New York,	10 00
Presbyterian, Olean,	5 00
W. D. Summers, Oswego,	100 00
Grace Presbyterian, Oswego,	25 00
South Congregational, Rochester,	5 00
1st Presbyterian, Rochester,	25 00
2nd Baptist, Rochester,	5 00
Brick Church, Rochester,	25 00
Central, Rochester,	50 00
North Presbyterian, Rochester,	10 00
Park Presbyterian, Syracuse,	10 00
1st Baptist, Syracuse,	8 50
2nd Presbyterian, Saratoga,	25 00
Presbyterian, Sodus,	3 00
1st Presbyterian, Schenectady,	10 00
Presbyterian, Verona,	5 00
Jermain Memorial, West Troy,	25 00
Congregational, West Winfield,	5 00
OHIO.—Walnut Hill Congregational, Cincinnati,	10 00
Plymouth Congregational, Cleveland,	10 00
1st Baptist, Cleveland,	5 00
Presbyterian, Central College,	5 00
Memorial, Dayton,	20 00
Congregational, Hudson,	10 00
Congregational Medina,	10 00
Central Congregational, Madison,	5 00
1st Congregational, Springfield,	20 00
Lagonda Avenue Congregational, Springfield,	5 00
U. P., Steubenville,	10 00
Congregational, Sandusky,	10 00
1st Congregational, Toledo,	20 00
Congregational, Tallmadge,	5 00
PENNSYLVANIA.—Bally,	5 00
Betchtelsville,	5 00
1st Presbyterian, Easton,	30 00
Central Presbyterian, Erie,	5 00
Presbyterian, Franklin,	10 00
Methodist Episcopal, Franklin,	10 00
Menonite, Hereford,	5 00
Presbyterian, Kingston,	10 00
Presbyterian, Moosic,	50 00
Belmont Methodist Episcopal, Philadelphia,	5 00

W. Spruce St. Presbyterian, Philadelphia, ... 50 00
North Presbyterian, Philadelphia, ... 10 00
Bethlehem Eden Baptist, Philadelphia, ... 15 00
2nd R. E., Philadelphia, ... 10 00
Pourlton Avenue Baptist, Philadelphia, ... 10 00
Memorial Baptist, Philadelphia, ... 50 00
Spring Garden Methodist Episcopal, Philadelphia, ... 5 00
Central Congregational, Philadelphia, ... 10 00
10th Presbyterian, Philadelphia, ... 10 00
2nd Presbyterian, Scranton, ... 15 00
Grace R. E., Scranton, ... 10 00
Washburn Street Presbyterian, Scranton, ... 10 00
1st Presbyterian, Scranton, ... 10 00
Plymouth Congregational, Scranton, ... 10 00
1st Presbyterian, Susquehanna, ... 5 00
RHODE ISLAND.—Broad Street Baptist, Central Falls, . . . 10 00
Congregational, Central Falls, ... 50 00
Union Congregational, Providence, ... 25 00
Pilgrim, Providence, ... 25 00
Central, Providence, ... 25 00
Cranston Street Baptist Church, Providence, ... 15 00
2nd Congregational, Providence, ... 20 00
Park Place Congregational, Pawtucket, ... 25 00
Congregational, Pawtucket, ... 25 00
VERMONT.—1st Congregational, Burlington, ... 50 00
College Street, Burlington, ... 20 00
Congregational, Chester, ... 10 00
Congregational, Charlotte, ... 5 00
Congregational, Hartford, ... 10 00
Union, Jericho, ... 5 00
Congregational, Montpelier, ... 10 00
Congregational, Milton, ... 10 00
Congregational, Rutland, ... 10 00
Baptist, St. Albans, ... 10 00
1st Congregational, St. Albans, ... 15 00
Congregational, West Westminster, ... 5 00
WISCONSIN.—Memorial Presbyterian, Appleton, ... 25 00
1st Presbyterian, Baraboo, ... 10 00
Congregational, Columbus, ... 10 00
Presbyterian, Chippewa Falls, ... 10 00
1st Congregational, Eau Claire, ... 15 00
Congregational, Ft. Atkinson, ... 10 00
Congregational, Grand Rapids, ... 2 00
Presbyterian, Jamesville, ... 10 00
Baptist, Presbyterian and Congregational, Kenosha, . . . 10 00
Congregational, Lake Mills, ... 3 00
Baptist, La Crosse, ... 10 00
1st Congregational, Manwatosa 5 00

26 YOUNG PEOPLE'S SOCIETY

Pioneer Presbyterian, Mannette,	10 00
Presbyterian, Manitowoc,	10 00
Asbury Methodist Episcopal, Milwaukee,	5 00
Algonia St. Methodist Episcopal, Oshkosh,	5 00
Methodist Episcopal, Pewaukee,	5 00
Congregational, Plattsville,	5 00
Methodist Episcopal, Whitewater,	5 00
ONTARIO.—Central, Hamilton,	5 00
Zion Congregational, Toronto,	5 00
Total,	$6,793 56

PERSONAL PLEDGES.

CONNECTICUT.—A. W. Dickey, Norwich,	5 00
John T. Manson, New Haven,	5 00
W. E. Staver, West Milford,	5 00
W. J. Mutch, New Haven,	5 00
C. E. House, South Manchester,	5 00
Mary C. Holbrook, Norwich,	3 00
Mary A. Phipps, Norwich,	3 00
F. H. Thayer, Collinsville,	5 00
Mrs. Ely, Norwalk,	20 00
Theo. I. Pease, Thompsonville,	50 00
Hart T. Dexter, Talcottville,	5 00
ILLINOIS.—Frances B Patterson, Chicago,	30 00
Addie E. Hawley, Springfield,	5 00
Marion C. Prentiss, Aurora,	2 00
Annie L. Howell, Aurora,	2 00
Minnie W. Mershon, Chicago,	50
Flora B. Mershon, Chicago,	50
Gertie S. Hayes, Chicago,	50
A. L. Warner, M. D., Kankakee,	1 00
Nettie Dunn, Chicago,	5 00
John N. Hyde, Carthage,	3 00
J. W. Conley, Joliet,	2 00
W. B. Pinkerton, Chicago,	1 00
Chas. H. Sterling, Sterling,	5 00
Nellie H. Robinson, Chicago,	5 00
Katie C. Rising, Lima,	1 00
Mrs. Eva R. Dickinson, Galva,	5 00
Geneveive I. Stevens, Chicago,	5 00

OF CHRISTIAN ENDEAVOR. 27

INDIANA.—Katherine R. Williams, Lima,	2 00
Lida O. Murray, South Bend,	5 00
Lottie J. Roberts, South Bend,	1 00
Mary Gates, South Bend,	1 00
Mrs. G. L. McNutt, Indianapolis,	1 00
Mary Lyon, St. Joseph,	1 00
Adah and Marcia Bittinger, Ft. Wayne,	5 00
IOWA.—T. E. Armstrong, New Providence,	5 00
Roger Leavitte, Cedar Falls,	10 00
Rev. B. St. John, Des Moines,	1 00
Edw. N. Prouty, Tabor,	2 00
Margaret R. George, Des Moines,	5 00
Mrs. E. H. Slocum, Rockford,	5 00
Alonzo Allen, Belle Plains,	5 00
KANSAS.—W. R. McClane, Wichita,	5 00
Josie Jamison, Paola,	1 00
MAINE.—Harris M. Barnes, Portland,	5 00
MASS.—Mrs. Alvan Simonds, Roxbury,	10 00
H. W. Cutler, No. Wilbraham,	25 00
Frank H. Chase, Haverhill,	5 00
Carrie M. Evans, Merrimack,	5 00
Eva E. Lewis, Florence,	5 00
Chas. T. James, So. Boston,	2 00
James M. Marsh, Lynn,	5 00
W. E. Lewis, Lynn,	5 00
Alfred J. Hunter, Boston,	10 00
C. F. Reed, Haydenville,	5 00
John A. Squire, Arlington,	5 00
Robert D. Maynard, Springfield,	1 00
Geo. E. Day, Westfield,	5 00
Robert W. Mathews. Boston,	2 00
A. H. Whipple, Northbridge,	5 00
E. F. Pearce, Fall River,	10 00
Fred. T. Shedd, Haverhill,	10 00
Henry B. Gifford, Springfield,	5 00
MICHIGAN.—W. D. Barnard, Manistee,	5 00
Elsie D. Kellogg, Grand Rapids,	2 00
Francis Line, Detroit,	5 00
Emma D. Moore, Niles,	2 00
Kate E. Sherwood, St. Joseph,	2 00
Minnie Sherwood, St. Joseph,	5 00
Belle Hammond, Traverse City,	5 00
MINNESOTA.—J. L. Keough, Minneapolis,	2 00
Cady Ellis, Minneapolis,	1 00
L. Peters, Howard Lake,	5 00
Mrs. F. L. Hoxise, St. Paul,	2 00
MISSOURI.—S. L. Biggers, St. Louis,	5 00
May J. Stevenson, St. Louis,	1 00

YOUNG PEOPLE'S SOCIETY

Alice C. White, Potosi,	1 00
Albert L. Cross, Kansas City,	10 00
John W Davis, Independence,	5 00
Mrs. L. G. Hammever	2 00
H. Coon, Kansas City,	2 00
Edward E. Israel, St. Louis,	5 00
George B. Graff, "	10 00
NEW HAMPSHIRE.—F. W. Mason, Concord,	2 00
NEW YORK.—Mary Nion, Rochester,	2 00
J. E. Hale, Seneca Falls,	5 00
D. C. Perkins, Castile,	10 00
D. L Bardwell, Greenport,	25 00
Henry McV. Smith, Olean,	5 00
Otis W. Barker, Brooklyn,	10 00
W. B. Taylor, Buffalo,	1 00
OHIO.—Annette Hooker, Defiance,	1 00
N. Stanley Lewis, Cleveland,	5 00
ONTARIO.—Fred. J. Gould, Toronto,	2 00
PENNSYLVANIA,— Euclid B. Rogers, Franklin,	5 00
William N. Tucker, Susquehanna,	5 00
G. S. Benson Jr., Philadelphia,	10 00
Carrie B. Leonard, Mauch Chunk,	2 00
E. Boyd Weitsel, Scranton,	5 00
Lizzie A. Sterling, Mauch Chunk,	1 00
VERMONT.—Mrs. J. S. Sewell, Milton,	5 00
Lillie D. Thompson, Burlington,	1 00
WISCONSIN,—Frank Strassburger, Racine,	2 00
A. E. Matherson, Elkhorn,	1 00
Wm. B Humphrey, Beloit,	1 00
C. L. Harwood, Ripon,	5 00
G. D. Smalley, Manitowoc,	1 50
Hattie M. Baldwin, Ripon,	3 00
Charles Flatt, Somers,	10 00
Mrs. Harriet E. Williams, Indian Ford,	5 00
Total,	$572 00
Cash Received at Convention,	$192 48
	$764 48

ADDRESSES OF WELCOME.

Address of Welcome By the Rev. E. D. Burr, Representing the Churches of Chicago.

I feel myself, dear Brothers and Sisters, in almost an anomalous position this morning because you placed me to represent the churches of Chicago I have all that I can do, I think, a little man like myself, to represent the one small church of which I have the honor of being pastor, and more than that, I am almost the most recent comer in Chicago among the pastors I think, therefore, that you should have gathered to your platform some representative of the older churches, or those who have been in Chicago longer. You might have had perhaps a more royal welcome, but if enthusiasm of heart and if joy of service in the Lord can add any emphasis to the words that I can say to you, I shall be very glad.

You have come to our City at a very opportune moment; we have just recovered from the Republican Convention. We have heard such melodies as "Marching through Georgia", and "John Brown's body lies a-moulding", and we have seen the waving of banners and we have heard a great deal of eloquence, and we have wondered what in the world was going to be done. There has been, in a word, a great deal of commotion in our City, commotion in the hotels, commotion in our homes, commotion on our Board of Trade, commotion everywhere; and then we have just gotten over the Fourth of July. We have heard all of our boys, every-one of them throughout the city, with all the enthusiasm and firecrackers that they could hold, celebrating mercy knows what. I sometime wish that underneath all this noise we could be sure that there was one or two thoughts at least for our noble country. At least, it is true that we must give them the credit, these noisy urchins, of having some emotions in their hearts. We must believe that there is in their hearts some feeling of patriotism, some love of country, some real, earnest thought,—so we have had commotion and we have had emotion; we have had politics and patriotism; and now we come right back to the sensible place for all the people to be, this real, common, ordinary, every day motion, and here you have come to our city just at a time when we feel as though we were in the track of a cyclone. You know out in this Western country—some of you have come from the East, so I can talk as a Westerner—we do get up a cyclone once in a while. There are mighty whirls of earth, and there are convulsions of mountains, and there are meetings of contending winds, and the storm gathers silently and quickly, taking from every mountain a breeze, from every hill a zephyr, from every lake a shower, and from every brooklet a drop, until it comes with a mighty flood and torrent and noise, and rush, and it leaves a wreck in its train, but I think that after the clouds have vanished away, after the storm has ceased, that the wind blows quietly in the valleys, and the wave splashes against the quiet shore, when the noise and tumultuous tempest has gone away,—and so you have brought to us the quiet ripple of Christian thought; you have brought to us the South wind of Christian love and Christian hope and Christian devotion to our common cause, and it is time that this noble side of so many be brought at the feet of our common Saviour,—and therefore I welcome you to this City of the Lake, because you have come bringing to us the message of quiet, the message of peace, and you can open your convention with the best song of all, "What a Friend we have," not in a party, but "in Jesus" and it is that you may have the power and the privilege of bringing this city to know and realize that there is a potency in the mighty agencies of Christian work far greater than this world has yet known; and then perhaps we can find another motion that will be the result at least of our convention, and that will be promotion. I think that you will promote not only the interests of our city, but the interests of our churches.

I somehow stand in awe of the Society of Christian Endeavor, I am a little in the attitude of the mother of three boys, who, after Sunday School service one afternoon, was greeted at the front door by the smallest of the three who raised his hands, opened his mouth, and with all kind of gesticulation said, "Oh, Ma! Oh, Ma!" "Well, well well what is going to happen?" "Well, the Superintendent told us to listen hard, and I don't know exactly what he said, but we all had to wait and all had to listen, and he said, 'they are going to christianize the devil.'" Well, she was perfectly confounded; she didn't know what in the world was going to happen, until finally the next oldest son went home, and she said, "Charlie, what in the world are they going to do with the church? What are they going to do with the Sunday School? Baby comes and says, 'you are going to christianize the devil'." "Oh, that is all nonsense; they are going to educate the devil". Finally, the oldest boy came home, and she says, "Now, Henry, what are they going to do with the Sunday School; Baby says, they are going to Christianize the devil, and Charlie says they are going to educate the devil. Now, what is it?" "Why, Mamma, they are going to do nothing but organize a Society of Christian Endeavor."

Well, God bless you if you will do both, and do it right here in this Town of Chicago, and that is the reason that I come with all my heart to welcome you, as a representative of the churches. We have in this City of the west, a mighty enterprise before us We have indeed, a great thing to be done. If ever the devil shows his cloven foot he does it in Chicago; if ever we feel the whisk of his tail, we do it in Chicago; if ever we have met the devil face to face we have to do it in Chicago. We have him here in all forms. We have him here in everything. We have the saloons, we have him here in mercy knows what. Well, now, if you can add your power to the power of the churches, and leave here some effect that shall promote the work of the churches, in the name of our Lord Jesus Christ, then in the name of the churches, and in the name of our Lord, I bid you welcome

Then, too, we can promote the interest of the churches in this city, in this one great fact, that you know how, as no other people know how, to demonstrate to the churches, and to every young man and young woman, and old man and old woman, individually, and collectively, that in the Church of Christ there is something for everyone to do. That is your power, that is where your potency lies, in giving somebody, everybody, something to do, so you must teach us Chicago people a very great lesson.

Why, do you know that the people in Chicago are so that the only way we can get them to work—I take it that none of my people are here, so I can talk about them, and about others to—the only way we can get anybody to work, is this: we just have to think over what is to be done, then look all over the congregation and see if we can discern some one individual who will suit that work. After a good deal of prayer and a good deal of thought, we select a man to do the work. Then we have to ask him, "will you do it?" He says "yes." Then I have to make him pledge to me he will do so, and he says, "yes." Then I have to take out a Bible and say, "will you swear on the word of God that you will do it?" He says "yes". Well, then I have to go half a dozen times to see that he does it, and finally I have to do it myself.

So if you can teach us this lesson, giving everybody something to do, you will, indeed have a large share in the promotion of the greatest necessity in our city and in our churches.

I bid you therefore, welcome; I bid you welcome in the hearty Saxon way, no formality about it. I would just like to shake your palm with both hands, and say "you are welcome."

And before I sit down I would like to put in a single word, one thought in my heart, and it is this; I would like to have you put it in words by singing again the first verse of the old hymn that you have just sung, and that is "Blest be the tie that binds." Now, if there is a tie, and it does not bind, we can afford to sing that hymn more than once, and I would like to have you sing it to the old tune of Boylston, not to the tune of Dennis. And I would like to sing it to that old fashioned tune, because I want the old fashioned church folks---that is an old fashioned hymn---I want the old fashioned church folks to be lieve and to know that there is no chasm between the church and the Society for Christian Endeavor. So that on behalf of the churches, I ask you to join with me—I am the churches and you are the Society of Christian Endeavor,—and let us rise and sing, " Blest be the tie that binds ", to " Boylston."

Address of Welcome By Mr. C. B. Holdredge, Representing the Illinois Union.

Mr President and Members of the Convention : To be able to say what should be said on any occasion like this requires men who are poets and orators. I regret to say that I am neither, but we have in this convention this morning both orators and poets, the first of whom we have just listened to, and the poet follows.

Dear friends, Illinois has long looked forward to this day when you so kindly accepted her invitation of last year to Chicago. We began preparing in our hearts and minds, and in every way possible, so that this day might be long remembered by you, and we have looked forward to it, and now it has come. I regret indeed, that I cannot say to you in language fitting for this occasion, those words which came to my mind last night. My heart was full, as I sat in my room last night after an evening service, a closing evening service with the Connecticut delegation, and my heart went back and mind reverted to that convention of last year in Saratoga. We all thought last year that was the best convention that ever could be held, and those of us of Illinois, the few of us who were there, came home from there with blessed memories, and we shall never forget those sweet days. So the convention at Saratoga was the best we ever had, and now let us one and all say this was the best we ever had. Dear Friends, how many from this convention will say that this convention was the best we ever had. May God help us.

Dear Friends from Maine, we welcome you, we are glad to have with us to-day Brother Pennell, the first one to sign the first Christian Endeavor pledge We welcome the pastor of that church ; we welcome brother Dickinson, who was the pastor of the Second Parish Church that formed the second Society of Christian Endeavor, and we welcome all the members from Maine, all the members hearts from Massachussetts, God bless Massachussetts ; how our throbbed last year when she came up to the rescue and cleaned up the debt in that noble way. Oh, how it did our hearts good. From that moment Massachussetts was dear to me, but not less dear was Connecticut. Connecticut led the way, and how blessed to us it was in that great time. How blessed that which one of our Brethren put in language that came out in the "Golden Rule", and how we kept it in our memories.

Connecticut comes up with a penny badge That little penny badge represents not only a penny pledge, but a blessed pledge. I need not tell you how much of a pledge beyond that, of warm friends They are working together for the Christian Endeavor movement, and it will please you all to know to-day that 150 of them are with us in this Convention. God bless them all. And they are all from New England,—they are here to-day, and we welcome you all. Those from the Empire State,—God bless the progress that has been made in New York. What a wonderful showing she will have here in this convention when the reports will be read. We are sorry to-day that Dr. Deems and others that were with us last year will not be present now, but we know that there are others who will take their places here to-day and during the sessions of this convention.

And we welcome those from New Jersey and Pennsylvania. Thank God we shall hear the voice of Dr. Hoyt before this convention ceases and there are others coming.

And from the South we welcome them, and those from beyond the Mississippi, how we shall welcome them, and we do welcome you all here to-day. There are many that shall come yet, many that are coming this afternoon, those from St. Louis. St. Louis sends the banner delegation of all City delegations, and we shall right royally welcome them, and we welcome this pastor who is now a citizen of Chicago. We welcome those from the Northwest, we welcome those from the Pacific Coast. There are delegates away from California, and we welcome them. Oh, how we welcome you all; how our hearts throb with gratitude when we think that the day has come when so many of us Christian Endeavorers can meet together, in the name of the Lord Jesus Christ, our Blessed Master.

There is just one thought in connection with that, it gives me an idea of discretion; we stop just right; that is the way with us Christian Endeavorers. Did you ever see a Christian Endeavorer but was discreet? They always stop just right, and those dear pastors who are afraid there is some mistake going to be made by the young people, let them feel what our motto is, "For Christ and the Church"; let them think that when young people take such a motto as that there must not be any peril, for we have Christ to guide us.

I remember a little trip that I took with my wife up through the Connecticut Valley into Vermont,—the southern part,—and as we got there toward evening, late in the afternoon, just in front of the home of our friends, there is an an immense hill known as " Minister Hill". The impulse seized me that I must ascend that hill that I might take in the beautful view there was, and so after tea, suiting the action to the word, or the impulse, I took my way up that hill by the pathway made by the sheep and the cattle as they had walked up the hillside, and I did not look out until I had reached the summit, and when I got there a view met my eye that I shall never forget. All those beautiful valleys spread before my eye, and away in the distance I could see Mount Washington towering up through the clouds.

My dear friends, to-day we come up to this summit; Oh, may we look from the summit of this convention up to that mount, the City of our God, where we shall be gathered in that great convention, that blessed convention, with Christian Endeavorers, and with our Master Jesus Christ, for our Commander and for our President.

Mr. President, we welcome you most heartily; we thank you for the manner in which you conducted the last convention of our Society, and we thank you again for being president here to-day. We know that you will conduct the exercises of this convention in the admirable manner in which you have always conducted them.

We welcome the trustees; God bless them all We thank God for such an able body of men to guide and manage the affairs of the United Society.

Address of Welcome By Mr. C. W. French.
Representing the Chicago Union.

Brethren of the Convention, I would I had the silvery tongue of a Cicero, or the golden accent of a Demosthenes, that I might tell you how gladly we welcome you all into our midst. For the last few months we of Chicago have been looking forward to the first week in July with the greatest pleasure and enthusiasm, when we should have the pleasure of meeting this Christian convention, and Christian Endeavor Societies in our midst, and now that you are here, it devolves upon me in behalf of the Christian Endeavor Societies of Chicago and vicinity, to extend to you each and all the most hearty greeting.

The cause of Christian Endeavor in our midst is young, but it is developing with a remarkable rapidity. Two years ago we scarce had heard the name. A year ago the Chicago Union was organized, with about twelve Societies. To-day we stand here as representing seventy societies, which had grown from the number of twelve within one year and we do not propose to stop here, because we expect to receive so much inspiration, so much impetus from our work in this convention that next year, if God shall spare our lives, in the coming convention, with ripened experience and deeper activity, we hope to reward them. Chicago has come to be Christian Endeavor to the very core, I believe our Union here is the largest City Union in the world, and if it is so, it is well.

Chicago—you will pardon me if I say just a word in regard to our beloved City—Chicago sits to-day the uncrowned queen of religious and business America. The sweet waters of yonder blue sea which ripple upon the shores at our feet and extend northward to the confines of the country are dotted with the white sails of a fleet larger than that which made Carthage the Mistress of the Mediterranean;

radiating from us in every direction are lines of steel rails which connect this city with all quarters of the country. And all the world hastens to do homage to the city sitting upon the throne by the sea, and pours the treasures of earth, land and sea into the lap of our city, and Chicago, in turn, sends forth to all quarters of the world the product of her industries, and her mighty influence for good or for bad. It has come to be common saying that as Chicago goes so goes the Northwest, and I believe that the time is coming in the future when it will be true that as Chicago is so shall America be. If this is true in the business world, and in all the multiform transactions of life, it certainly will be in the religious world, and going forth from the city of Chicago to-day are religious influences, and influences which are not religious, that are making the lives and existence of these miles on miles around us. As in ancient times, all the cities of Imperial Rome looked towards their Queen City, and aspired, each one, to become a miniature Rome, so is the religious life of Chicago to-day reflected in the existence of these hamlets and villages and cities which stretch out over our western prairies to the hills and mountains, and sea beyond. Well, it is indeed, that Chicago be strongly intrenched behind Christian Endeavor ramparts; that we have in this great host of Christian workers one division eager to be in the van of battle which is marching underneath the shadow of the White Banner of the Cross, upon whose glistening folds are emblazoned in letters of living life these words, "The Young People All for Christ."

We have around us a mighty conflict to-day. There are forces of evil rampant in our city which, unrestrained, will bring nothing but ruin and destruction and anarchy, and the young people must band together, and we must work and deal as hard blows as those who are against us.

My friends, I welcome you to-day not as strangers. You from the far New England shore where first in dewy freshness the sun smiles upon the New World, those of you from the golden slopes of the Pacific where his rays linger before going from the boundless West, those of you from the South, whose fragrant breezes are wafted sometimes to our doors—we welcome you. We have read something of your trials, and we profit by them, and we come together to-day, and we extend our hands and we greet you as brethren in our work. Our aim is one, and we are all of us marching along in the same grand division of the Lord, working towards the same end, and looking for the same reward. I welcome you as friends who have long been separated; I welcome you to our beautiful and busy city; I welcome you to our Christian Endeavor household, for we are in our household; I welcome you to share in our trials, and to be a party in our work. May Christ welcome us all above to our everlasting victory, for "after the contest comes the crown." May God's blessing rest upon this assembly, and may His spirit move us, sanctify us, in all our deliberations, in every thing that we shall say, in every prayer that shall be uttered, in every song that shall be sung, so that it may all be done in his good, and by and bye, in future years, we shall look back over the course of life and see this assembly as one of the hallowed spots in our lives, and one of the land-marks in the grand career of the Young People's Society of Christian Endeavor.

Address of Welcome By Mr. L. W. Messer, Representing the Y. M. C. A.

Mr. President and Members of the Convention. It is an honor and a privilege, and a very great pleasure, for me to bring to this convention this morning the most hearty greetings and welcome of the Chicago Young Men's Christian Association. It is with added pleasure that I extend this word of welcome, when I recognize on this platform, and among the delegates on the floor, so many loyal, true, steadfast members of the Young Men's Christian Association, which organization I have the pleasure of representing.

The Young Men's Christian Association, and the Young People's Society of Christian Endeavor are both the children of the church. Their motto is identical; First, "Loyalty to Christ; second, Loyalty to the Church; third, Loyalty to our respective Societies." These organizations have sprung up to meet the need of the times. There have been new departures in these channels; some of them we believe, are builded upon the sand, and when the winds and storms beat about them, they will fall to the ground and pass away. Others there are which are builded upon the rock, and upon that rock they will abide and remain, and we believe that both of these Societies to-day are founded upon that rock, Jesus Christ, that rock which shall stand through the ages and through Eternity. These Societies have not been organized by man. Man very often forgets the needs of humanity; God never does. Away back in the very commencement of the history of the human family, when man had sinned and had raised a barrier between himself and God, there came a promise from our Heavenly Father of a mighty delivery, that the seed of a woman should bruise the serpent's head, and down through the ages the people of God looked forward to the coming of that deliverer, and he has come, he has fulfilled his mission on earth, he has set the captives free, and under his banner together these two organizations march to-day, When the great Commander of the Children of Israel, the host of the Lord, gave up his work and was called on high. Joshua came to the front to lead those forces into the promised land; and down later in the history of the Church, when superstition was so prevalent, there came a Luther raised by God to bring about a mighty revolution that should bring light where there was darkness and happiness where there was sorrow. And so in this time, God looking down upon our people, put it in the hands of that great leader in London, who organized the first Young Men's Christian Association, and from that small beginning we have seen the mighty growth of this organization, in which you are always interested; and later on the same Divine hand, the same Divine thought was seen in this movement to organize this Society and reach out to an important sphere of usefulness and bless the young people of the Churches. These Societies to-day have with them the blessing of God, and in this organization which you represent this morning, I see the haud of God, in the development and the training and the inspiring of Christian young people to send men into this mighty conflict. We know that the young people of the Churches to-day should be fed with the right food; that food is the word of God, which is taught in the Bible classes and in the gatherings which you have. We know they shonld take the right food into the system, that should cause them to develop into Christian lives, and this opportunity is given to you in this organization, by conducting meetings of various kinds, by Committee work, by the assistance of each man and woman as a Christian worker, and through it to have an agency for mighty use in future. And as I look into your faces this morning I think I can almost see here those who, through the development you can get in this Society, shall go out and teach the Gospel of Jesus Christ which shall be commited to you. I think I see here men who will stand foremost on earth; I think I see here men who shall be sent out to these Cities as Secretaries of the Young Men's Christian Associations, and so out of this organization will spring Christian workers, who will be blessed in God, in holding high aloft the banner of the Lord Jesus Christ.

Reterence has also been made this morning to the convention which has been recently assembled in this city. There came up to this great City of Chicago and convened in this wonderful Auditorium that we have here, delegates of one of the greatest parties of the country. They came here for the specific purpose of nominating a leader—rather two leaders, men who should command the confidence, the united support and the enthusiasm of the party which placed them to the front. After due deliberation their choice was made, and those men have returned to their homes, and in every paper we see to-day the notices of enthusiastic gatherings ratifying those nominations, and of the loyal pledges of support from all branches of that party. Men hitherto who were perhaps enemies to the candidates are now their avowed supporters, interested in their election and victory.

Members of the Society of Christian Endeavor assembled here to-day, ycu come not to Chicago to nominate a leader, thank God. You have a leader who has been named from the foundation ot the world, the Lord Jesus Christ. You come here not to ratify, if I may use that word, the choice of this leader. You come here to attest your loyalty to Him, your devotion to His services; you come here to meet Him face to tace, and to show such enthusiasm and loyalty and devotion to His support that will enable you, as a body of men, to be even more enthusiastic, even more loyal, even more true to your Commander, as you certainly should, than are the politicians of any political party.

May God bless you all while you remain here in the City. We regret that our Association building at present is not in just the best possible condition to welcome you there. However, such as we have we gladly offer you, and we ask you to come and see us, and we shall be sure to give you the right-hand of welcome on your mission, and a hearty Godspeed in your future work.

Address By Mr. W. T. Van Patten
President of the Convention.

Dear friends, the task has been assigned to me to respond to these words of welcome. I would it might have been given to some one of readier speech, for these welcoming words have gone to the hearts of every one, and they should be responded to in a manner that should show the feeling that we have for them, but whatever my speech would be, the feeling of thanks in my heart is as strong as they could wish it to be

I thank these representatives of the religious activity of Chicago, for our Societies, for the words that they have spoken to us.

We remember a year ago at Saratoga how strong and urgent the invitation was to come West, the invitation from Illinois, from Wisconsin, from Iowa and the other States, how they represented that we were needed in this great West; that this great convention could do much for the cause of Christian Endeavor here. We recognized the position they took, we recognized that this great broad country here, in which already the Christian Endeavor was taking such a hold, was entitled to what aid and help it might receive from our meeting together, and so after due deliberation our Trustees voted that the next convention should be held in Chicago, and so we are assembled here in this building to-day.

We have been looking and planning for this meeting ever since we went home from Saratoga. What question has been oftener on our lips to what question have we oftener been obliged to respond than this: "Are you going to Chicago," and haven't we said every time "we mean to."

We are sorry that many that thought that they were coming, that intended to be with us here to-day, have been unavoidably detained, but we are glad that we have rallied in such numbers as we have, and we hope that this convention meeting in Chicago will do much good, will promote the cause of Christian Endeavor in a way that was anticipated and the way for which we longed.

We have found, dear friends, that in coming to Chicago in one respect it is like old Rome. Perhaps old Rome did not lead to Chicago, but we have found that all railroads lead there, haven't we. And so on these steel roads from North and West, and South and East we have come over hundreds and thousands of miles that we might sit together in this convention, to learn, to be inspired, to renew our consecration to remember once more that it is for Christ and His Church that we are banded together, for Him and for the work that He has given His Church to do, and so dear friends, we are met here, a company of young people.

For many of us this is the first visit to Chicago, and I esteem it a good thing for such of us, that our first impressions of this great City are to be the impressions that we shall get in such a gathering as this, enforced as they will be, with the words of welcome we have had from the representative of Chicago, and may we carry home this impression; that in Chicago, while there may be things that are wicked here, while there may be much to overcome—that we have found here a great company of strong Christian people, of young people that are banded together with us in striving to overthrow the sin and evil, in striving to lift higher the banner of the Cross, striving in the name of Christ to carry forward the work that He has given us to do. We have not come here as others come. We know the fame of Chicago; it has gone out over all the world. Men listen to what is said and what is done here. The markets of Chicago are listened for by the commercial world everywhere, and its pulse beats faster or slower in order to conform to what is done here. The great political convention meets, and partisans everywhere are listening to the latest words from it. You have the great social problems here to deal with, and all the country is bound up with you in that; it is of the greatest interest for us everywhere to know what Chicago is doing to solve these great questions.

But as I said, we come here for a different purpose; we did not come to buy or sell or get gain. We have no candidates for office. We do not think to solve the social problems of the age, but we do come to strive to lift higher the banner of the Cross, we come to learn and in meeting in this way we shall accomplish this great end. We recognize more and more as we carry forward this work of Christian Endeavor that we are at work in the Church and for the Church, that we are of the Church; and so it gives us the greatest pleasure to have these words of appreciation from this representative of the Chicago Churches. May we ever remember the words that have come to us; may we carry forward in all our grand work in connection with these Societies the thoughts that were given us; that we hold fast to the Church, and that it may be the means of building it up to greater and greater activity and greater and greater good in the Master's cause. And to the words of welcome from Illinois—I cannot say much to them. I can manage to respond to those words of welcome from Illinois, as you know how Connecticut and Illinois are bound together in bonds of Christian Endeavor love. And these words of welcome from the Chicago Union, do they not go to your hearts? Are they not our friends in a special degree? Oh, we give them thanks for these words that they have spoken to us. We rejoice that they feel that they are welcoming those that are bound together with them in this work, and we recognize what they have done in the year past in increasing the number of their Societies to almost four-score. And these representatives of Christian activity of Chicago who gave such words of welcome, we recognize the great work that they are doing; we know that we are all bound together in one cause, and what helps one particular church's work, helps all, and so we rejoice that we are together with them for the one great end, the salvation of the world.

And now, dear friends, I will speak a word of welcome to you on behalf of your officers We thank you that so many have responded to our call for this convention, and at a large expense of money, of time, of labor, have come together here to sit in the deliberations of this convention, and we trust that the result will be that you will go home, as our friend Holdrege says, and say, "well, the last impressions are the best of all".

Let us strive together, dear friends, that we may realize this. As much depends upon the delegates, as much depends upon those that are in the seats as those that are upon the platform, as to whether such a meeting as this shall be a success or not, and let us strive together that we may make it a success, that we can say when we go home, "well, the *Chicago* convention was the best of all".

And there are some here no doubt that have come up to this convention that they may know of its principles, of what it has accomplished, and I hope they will listen to what is to be said They will learn that we are working not for our own aggrandisement, as Brother Burr has said, but that we are working to make the labor of the church more uniform; that it is young people working for young people, that that they may be one to Christ and the Church. That is our work. It is in building up our Christian cause. That is the work that we are striving to do, and those that have come here to learn will find that our program is so arranged that all the different methods of Society work, of committee work, are brought out in such manner, that I am sure you can go home from this Convention, and start a society of Christian Endeavor anywhere without any further help than you can get from what you hear here and from the literature that we so gladly supply.

You would be glad to have heard from others than myself, I am sure, and I wish our program could have been so arranged that you could have.

I have noticed since I have been here with Secretary Ward through these last few days that he was ready with a shake of the hand and a recognition for almost every one that came to this convention, and I wish that I might have done the same. I wish that I might know you as he has known you

You have seen the father of our Societies here, Father Clark, and you will be glad to hear from him, and glad that we are met together in this way, and I ask you once more that we shall strive by all the means we can, to have this meeting of the greatest possible profit to each one that is here.

REPORT OF THE GENERAL SECRETARY OF THE U. S. C. E.

Since the earliest days of its history, it has been a time-honored custom in the annual reports of the secretaries of the societies of Christian Endeavor, to consolidate the entire year's record under the one word *Progress*.

The history of the movement in years past has justified the use of this term. Year by year, with a more than seven-league stride, the cause has traveled westward from the city of its birth on the eastern coast, until a few days ago, with the arrival of the steamship *Etruria*, it landed again on its native shore, after completing the circuit of the globe.

Year by year its ranks have increased in numbers, from the day of that first convention, in 1882, when forty or fifty members answered to the roll-call, until to-day in 1888, like England's drum-beat, which calls to duty her loyal soldiers, its roll-call, on consecration night is heard around the globe, calling to each one of its hundreds of thousands of members to answer to his name, with a renewed consecration of his powers and service to the King of kings, and to the Country to which all else is tributary.

Year by year it has gained the confidence of the Lord's people, from that time when the pastor and members of the one devoted church realized the benefit it was doing their friends, until to-day, in this vast assemblage, thousands upon thousands of Christian people of all denominations, and creeds, and classes, have arisen and journeyed over hundreds of miles, from the North and from the South, from the East and from the West, to come here together and lend their testimony to its claim to be called "Blessed."

Best of all, year by year, it has called to its associate members: " Remember now thy Creator in the days of thy youth " and, as each twelve months have passed, the unconverted in its ranks have answered to its appeal; from the time of the first revival in which it had its birth, to the present day, when the records brought before you to-night prove that its converts are numbered by thousands, yea, until every one in our midst is ready to exclaim, " This is the Lord's work and it is marvelous in our eyes."

The term is rightly applied; progress not only in numbers and territory, progress not simply in power and enthusiasm, but progress in all that is good. Progress in the Lord's work, progress in training up workers for His Kingdom, progress in uplifting His cross, progress in performing the labors He has placed upon us, and for the completion of which at our hands He will require an account.

Since last we met together in convention, your secretary has lived the life of a wanderer Out from the home office the start was made in September last; month by month the journey has continued, with no pause, save the Christmas holidays, when the churches were too busy in other matters to attend to our case—until to-day, this national convention has put an end to his trip here in Chicago.

During the ten months thus passed, every State and Territory in the Union has been traversed, and the cause presented in almost every city and town of any size in the country.

To sum it all up in figures, the trip has covered over forty thousand miles, while the cause of Christian Endeavor has been publicly presented on over three hundred and sixty different separate occasions, as many as there are days in the year.

What the results of this trip have been, it is, of course, impossible to determine, even from an unprejudiced standpoint.

Its design has been to spread the work into fields where it was not thoroughly understood; to disseminate a more thorough understanding of the true significance of Christian Endeavor; to gain a knowledge of the work and workers as they appear in the various parts of this vast country: and to gain, by studying the work in all possible circumstances and surroundings, an intimate knowledge of all that goes to insure its best welfare.

In a word, the aim of the trip was like the object of the United Society, a missionary one.

We believe that, to a degree, all of these purposes have been served by this trip, but, for a knowledge of its actual and full results, we must await the verdict of the judgment day, and the decision of Him who rules all destinies.

If nothing else has been gained, one fact, at least, your secretary has learned and learned thoroughly, namely, that this is a great country, that there are a great many stations to visit, and that it is a great way between the stations.

I cannot better express my own impressions of the extent of Uncle Sam's possessions than by telling you of a little incident that occured during a trip in Florida. Squatted on a claim near Kissimee, a town situated a few miles west of the St. John's river, there is a family of native-born Minorcans, known in slavery days as "poor white trash," and more lately as "Crackers."

The entire period of their lives had been spent within a radius of ten miles of Kissimee, and, in consequence their views of matters and things in general were somewhat biased and limited by the boundaries of their observations.

The sudden rise in land consequent upon the boom in Florida, brought to our friends what, to them, constituted unbounded riches. A portion of the claim was sold to speculators, and the family found themselves in possession of five thousand dollars.

It was at once decided that John, the eldest, should travel; great preparations were made, farewells were said as if the young man were leaving for a life-time and then he set out on his trip of four hours to Jacksonville

On his return, several days after, the young man was looked upon by his fellows as a great traveler, and one who had risen above the level of the common herd. He appeared dazed, however, and more quiet than when he started out; said nothing, and, in fact, was a great disappointment to his friends. Finally, after repeated questioning as to his travels, the cause of his wonder was traced to the extent of territory he had seen and, being pushed for an answer to the oft-repeated question as to what kind of country there was above Kissimee, he delivered himself of the following pearls of wisdom: "Yes, boys, it's a great country up there, it must be. Why, boys, if the world the other side of Jacksonville is as big as the world between here and Jacksonville, I tell you, it's a mighty big world!"

To-night, friends, I stand here ready to vouch for John's words. It *is* a big world beyond Jacksonville, and to those of you who think you have come "way out West to Chicago," let me say it's a very big big world west of Chicago.

You heard this morning of the work in the different sections of the country from the Superintendents. I shall speak of it as it looks to one who moves from place to place over the entire field.

In New England, Christian Endeavor is to-day an established fact. Under its own or some other name it has become one of the features, I had almost said a necessary feature, in the churches of all denominations.

Here, where it first saw the light of day, it is doing better work than ever before For this reason, we find here an answer to the oft repeated question, "Is Christian Endeavor a *permanent* thing?"

If greater growth, more blessed results, and firmer loyalty to the church, as the years go by, is any proof of its lasting qualities, then the societies of New England have settled the question.

Of the Middle Atlantic, almost the same could be said. With the Empire State of New York in the lead in number of societies, not only in her own division of States, but in the world, and with Pennsylvania and little New Jersey to second her efforts in the glorious way they have done, the success of Christian Endeavor is here assured.

In the middle belt of States, we find the centre of the movement. Friends from the East, do not fancy that you have come out *West* to attend the annual convention. You have simply come a little more than half way toward the centre of the country, and find yourselves at the centre of the movement. In the South, the cause has gained the least headway of any portion of the country. This is perfectly natural, the climate, the poverty of portions of this district, the unwillingness which seems to exist to assume religious responsibility, and many other obvious reasons, all have contributed to render progress in Christian Endeavor, like progress in all else, extremely slow.

During the last year, however, an entering wedge has been driven. Florida is well advanced and is rapidly waking up to the advantages of our cause; the Carolinas, Tennessee and Alabama are beginning to realize that they have been asleep, and, altogether, since our last meeting at Saratoga, a vast step forward has been taken by the South.

West of the Mississippi, we will make use of the natural and usual divisions, the Rocky Mountains.

East of these great giants, every State and Territory is busily engaged in the cause. In Iowa, one of the first societies founded in the entire history of the movement still flourishes, and looks on with pride at the growth of its many branches. Through this belt of country the greatest activity is to-day to be found in all that pertains to the movement.

West of the Rockies, in that much boomed land, where a golden haze seems to surround and envelop everything, we look for great things in Christian Endeavor, as in everything else, nor are we disappointed.

All the way from San Diego, the southernmost city of California, up through the wheat and fruit lands to San Francisco, thence northward through the beautiful Shasta Mountain region, and across the famous Oregon Valley of the Williamette, clear up to the top of the Puget Sound and the boundaries of Canada, the work of Christian Endeavor has steadily pushed its way.

Here in these new countries, where all the citizens are young people, where business, society, politics and religion as well, all seem in a formative period, Christian Endeavor has, to-day, its most fertile and, to my own mind, its most important field.

To-day it can, by training up the youth of that country, put an impress on that Western coast, which shall mark it as the Lord's.

To-day, as never again, when years have shaped and moulded this region, so rich in all that goes to make up a most important section of our domain, the society can and *is* making itself felt for eternity.

Thus, briefly, I have tried to sketch in a general way the cause, as it appears to one who has visited it in all its departments.

The work is ever new, it differs as sections differ; everywhere you can, of course, trace in its members and in its workings the characteristics of the country where it dwells.

For example, when we pass the Mississippi the members are, as a rule, more outspoken; trouble is not met with in inducing the members to take part; if they have acknowledged their Master they are willing to speak out for him.

On the other hand, the question of amusement is ofttimes a mooted point, and one that requires frequent and earnest study.

Thus, had I time, I might point out to you the peculiarities of the work as it is found in various sections.

Everywhere it is gaining, it is no longer an experiment, it is a fact, gaining in numbers, gaining in popularity, and gaining in a more thorough knowledge of what Christian Endeavor means.

Long since, such abuses as were formerly found at times under our standard have been corrected, and Christian Endeavorer to-day means to all, what it means to us here to-night, devoted, loyal service to Christ and the church.

Over the whole country it has traveled; out across the sea it has taken its way; into foreign lands it has journeyed, only to he adopted and to bring a blessing wherever it makes its abiding place.

Our societies differ in locality, differ even in nationality, differ to a degree, in methods and means, but, the world over, one motto expresses the object, "For Christ and the Church."

It is said that through all cordage used by the British navy there runs a scarlet silk thread, so that wherever, the world over, a piece of this cordage is found, running through its centre is this scarlet thread that marks it as the Queen's.

So on all societies, whether they are North or South, whether they are East or West, whatever their nationality, or color, or denomination, through them all runs the scarlet thread of Christ's atoning blood, marking them as the King's. I have said that God has blessed us and so prospered us, and He has done so right heartily.

In territory, the society has encircled the globe; every State and Territory long since yielded to its sway; Canada, Nova Scotia, Prince Edward's Island, New Brunswick, Newfoundland, England, Scotland, Spain, Syria, Burmah, India, Ceylon, South Africa and China were but lately added to our provinces.

It has been a question of great interest each year, where is the centre of the movement? In our answer to-night to this question, we find that a strange thing has happened. The first year the centre remained in Portland; the next two or three years it swerved around from place to place in New England; last year we found it had gone out to Buffalo, but this year, wonder of wonders, the centre is back again in Portland or Boston.

Nor is this a retograde step. No, it is the greatest stride of all, for in the past year, our cause has gone completely around the globe, and we may select our centre, and what spot so appropriate as the starting point, or the home-office?

In our own country the central point has moved still further westward, and, to be anywhere near it, we had to come out here to Chicago, where the centre had located itself.

As regards growth by States, New York leads with over nine hundred societies, closely followed by Massachusetts with nearly six hundred societies.

As the domain has increased, the recruits have come pouring in, and, to-day, the loud battle cry, "For Christ and the Church," is raised from the throats of three hundred and ten thousand loyal members of Christian Endeavor.

We have passed the day when the question, "Is the Christian Endeavor confined to any one denomination?"

That question is answered far more forcibly than words of mine could handle it, by simply pointing to the records which prove that every denomination in the country has joined hands in training its youth and is gladly answering in the words of Paul; for all our young people, though they may have distinct church homes, though they shall remain loyal to those church homes, yet for one and all there is but one Lord and one faith, one God and one Father of all, who is above all, and through all and in all.

"For Christ and the Church" has been our cry, and for Christ and the church our best records are reserved this evening.

Pleased as you are with the grand showing just read you, how much more fervently shall we thank God that during the past year, twenty-two thousand of our membership, hearing our Great Commander's call to service and seeing the honor and glory of that service, have bravely answered, "Here am I, O Lord, take me," boldly taken their stand for Jesus, and added themselves to the membership of the parent churches.

This is our most glorious record; this it is that gives us courage to press onward and that makes us certain of God's blessing: twenty-two thousand people won for the Master, twenty-two thousand recruits added to His army, twenty-two thousand souls entered upon a pathway illuminated by that shining light whose radiance shall grow brighter and brighter unto the perfect day.

Such is the record of the past, such is the history of Christian Endeavor. Not such history as Napoleon described, as that which wise men had agreed upon, but history of the work that God in His wisdom has allowed the comparatively untrained hands of the young people to do.

Burke says, "Man does not know himself until he has had a chance to do the worst thing," but the history of Christian Endeavor has shown that man did not know what the youth could do for their Master until they had a chance to do the best thing. All this has become history and consequently over it we of to-day can have no further control or influence, even if we would. As Phillips Brooks has said, "We have had nothing to do with the past but to get a future out of it." The future is then to a measure in our hands.

You do not question that we are responsible.

Is it asking too much of those of us who have reaped the benefits that Christian Endeavor can so readily bestow, to ask that we in our turn assume the responsibility of giving to others the same great blessings?

We cannot refuse the call. Could you for one day sit at my desk in the central office and read the appeals as they come from all over the world asking for help in the Lord's name, you would hear again and again the "Come over into Macedonia and help us," that is steadily ringing in our ears.

Do you doubt the urgency of the appeal? Think you anything but an urgent appeal would have drawn our beloved president from his happy pastorate? Think you anything but an urgent call would have sent your secretary to live the life of an Arab? The call *is* urgent, never more so.

Mr. Clark will tell you to-morrow how England is looking to you for help. The foreign missionaries are urging that their fields receive the much needed attention. Shall we not do our best to aid them?

In one of the recent Art Exhibitions in London under the auspices of the Royal Acadmy, the principal place in all the hanging, the most noteworthy position in the entire building, was given to a picture painted by the latest elected member of the Academy, the youngest artist in that talented assembly.

It portrayed a group of young people returning from a revel through the streets of an Italian city. Their faces are flushed with pleasure and happiness, and they are gayly singing as they move along. As they pass through an arch that spans the roadway, the leader of that gay company, the handsomest and proudest of them all, sees before him on the ground a beggar pleading for alms and help, and holding up to his gaze a crucifix; asking for help in the name of the Crucified.

The youth stops, the color fades from his face, the song dies from his lips, and every sense is steadied and silenced as he realizes that he is facing the symbol of Christ's suffering and His atoning love.

Beneath the picture the artist has simply painted the words, "The Symbol," and underneath that quotation from Lamentation, "Is it nothing to you, all ye that pass by?"

Friends, in a few days, from this blessed gathering we to, like the youth in the picture, shall be wending our way homeward.

Happy and joyous we too shall doubtless be, as we realize all that this cause and meeting has been to us; but, friends, there will always be facing us the appeal from all over the world in the name of the Crucified, " Iu the name of the Saviour, help us "

From all sections the cry is still coming, " In Christ's name, help."

From many points in our own land, from England and her provinces, from foreign mission fields in particular the cry is, " In the name of the crucified Saviour, we ask you for help for our youth."

You who have enjoyed these great blessings, you who have pledged yourselves to the Master's service, " Is it nothing to you, all ye that pass by " that our young people should perish? What shall our answer be?

TREASURER'S REPORT.

BY WILLIAM SHAW, TREASURER.

The year that has just closed has been a remarkable one in the history of our society. We entered upon it with $153.58 in our treasury, but with bills unpaid amounting to $739.55, leaving an actual deficit of $585.97. During the year, our general secretary has given his whole time to the South and West, travelling thousands of miles, and visiting hundreds of churches and societies. This accounts for the large increase in the item of travelling expenses.

Our president, at the earnest request of Christian workers in England and France, and acting under the advice of the trustees, raised the Christian Endeavor banner in those two countries. The demands upon the United Society for literature, and information concerning the work, have been unusually large, taxing to the utmost the time and strength of the workers there. Our literature has gone literally to the ends of the earth, and in the mission fields the societies are multiplying rapidly, and are proving their worth as training-schools for Christian workers. But all this aggressive work meant large expense, and depending, as we do, upon voluntary contributions from the societies, the question was raised, "Can we do it?" Will the societies accept the responsibility and furnish the money? The report just read grandly justifies the faith we had in you. One year ago our president, in his address, called for $15,000. You have answered his call, and given good honest measure. The business department has been managed in such a way that the profits very nearly paid the actual office expenses. Every cent that is made on our badges, hymn-books and general literature is used in the spread of our work. The strictest economy has been observed in all our work. The hundreds of addresses delivered by the president, trustees, and other faithful workers during the year, have not cost the United Society a single cent. These friends have freely given of their time and thought, and the local societies have met their traveling expenses.

The United Society Day, which was celebrated in February with so much enthusiasm, added over $8,000 to our treasury, and with the nearly $7,000 paid on the Saratoga pledges, gives us the sum of over $15,000 as the contribution of the young people to this part of the Lord's work. May I thank you for your hearty and generous support, and rejoice with you in the completion of our seventh year of work with all bills paid and $2,034,19 in the treasury.

50 BROMFIELD ST., BOSTON, July 1st, 1888.

WM. SHAW, Treasurer, in account with the United Society of Christian Endeavor for the year ending July 1st, 1888.

DR.

To balance from old account,	$153.58
" Annual membership fees,	200.00
" Sustaining membership fees,	40.00
" Societies and individuals for life membership,	5,160.00
" Office sales, literature, badges, etc.,	3,343.43
" Contributions from Societies and individuals,	9,993.04
	$18,890.05

CR.

By Conference expenses 1887,	$467.14
" Literature, Printing, etc.	6,174.76
" Salaries account 1887,	566.66
" Salaries,	2,836.00
" Travelling expenses Gen. Sec.,	2,685.25
" " " Pres. Eng. trip,	350.00
" " " Trust. & Treas.,	116.55
" Office expenses, postage, etc.,	1,575.75
" Cost of badges,	1,158.23
" Office supplies, repairs, furniture, etc.,	210.47
" Safe,	90.00
" Rent,	326.10
" Copyrights and patent,	108.45
" Engrossing and mailing life certificates,	66.50
" Conference expenses on account 1888,	125.00
Total,	$16,855.86
" Balance on hand,	2,034.19
	$18,890.05

I have examined the foregoing account, and find it correctly cast and properly vouched.

ALBERT W. BURNHAM, *Auditor.*

Lowell, Mass., June 28, 1888.

Address of the President of the United Society of Christian Endeavor.

MEMBERS OF THE SOCIETY OF CHRISTIAN ENDEAVOR:

When, a year ago at this time, you called me to leave a beloved and devoted church, and to give my time wholly to the interests of the Society of Christian Endeavor, it was a very serious problem in which direction lay the path of duty. After much prayerful consideration I decided that your call could not be disregarded, and, nine months ago, I closed my pastorate to take up your work. If you knew fully the affectionate relations of the people of Phillips Church and myself, you would know that it was no slight thing for me to say to-day, that I am not sorry that the Lord has guided me in this way. It was a movement which I now see had been ripening for many months and years, and, owing to my previous relations to the society, was inevitable.

Let me tell you the great problem which has confronted us during the past year, and, which, during the coming years, will assume larger and larger dimensions. It is this: *How to so guide this mighty agency, which God has raised up in our land, that it shall promote to th utmost personal piety among our members, and the prosperity ofe the Church for which it lives.* The very size of the society and marvelous rapidity of its growth pressed this problem upon us. Before we knew it. a score of delicate questions, all arising from our rapid growth, were demanding settlement. The puny, sickly child, while giving its parents solicitude, does not require them to provide outlets for its superfluous vitality It is the young giant, lusty, and strong of lung and limb, who has come into the world to stay a hundred years, who needs attention, that he may not only do no harm, but the utmost possible good in the world. So with this young Christian Endeavor giant, that he may be wholly consecrated, and used of the Master to the building up of His kingdom, this is the great anxiety which should burden our hearts. To secure the best results from this rapidly accumulating strength, to conserve through it, just as far as possible, every righteous cause, to keep single-eyed, to be true to our motto, "For Christ and His Church," this has been the object of our honored general secretary, and board of trustees, of your president, and no less of every leader in every local society; and because of this, I believe God, through His good grace, has given us such abundant fruits during the past year.

"But why the need of any haste in spreading a knowledge of this work?" says some one. "Societies were being formed fast enough." Very true, and the rapidity of their multiplication was the very reason for the utmost haste to anticipate their formation by a knowledge of our true principles.

Had the societies not multiplied so rapidly the problems of the past year would have been few and simple, as in the early years of the movement.

It was very evident, a year ago, and it has become increasingly evident since, that there was only one way to meet the requirements of the situation, and that was the abundant dissemination of our literature. Our general secretary has done all that one could do, and his labors have been as valuable as they have been abundant, but even were he ten times as ubiquitous as he has been the past year, he could not speak to one Christian Endeavor Society in twenty; your president and board of trustees, and other leaders in the work, though giving every spare moment of their busy lives, could only touch the fringe of the work in this country, to say nothing of all the world lying beyond America.

There was only one thing to do, and that was to thank God for Guttenberg and the printing-press, and make the most of the printer's ink. This has been done to the best of our ability; much thought and much time have been put into these publications, and, as a result, in part at least, of these labors, two thousand five hundred and seventy-three societies have been added to the previously long list, an increase in one year of over one hundred per cent. This method of preaching by the use of "white paper and black type" has the advantage of being accurate, swift. capable of reaching a universal audience, and being comparatively inexpensive. One of these missionaries can be equipped and sent, at a moment's notice, to California for two cents, to China for five cents, or to South Africa or Australia for another nickel. These silent missionaries have been nine in number, and have been called the THE GOLDEN RULE, "The Model Constitution," "The Society of C. E., What It Is and How It Works," "The Beginnings of a Society," "Junior Societies," "The United Society and Local Unions," A Short History of the Society," "Reorganization," "What the Pastor's say," besides various other cards and leaflets. To these missionary forces can be added others as our needs develop, but the above have been sent forth by the hundred thousand, all over the world, during the past year, and, except where carelessness in Uncle Sam's mail department has stopped them on the way, they have swiftly and, we hope, thoroughly accomplished their mission.

We have looked backward long enough, perhaps. For a few minutes let us look toward the future, the rising sun of Christian Endeavor. Hardly, as yet, does the first rim of his disk show above the horizon. What shall it be at midday? Whether glorious and powerful for the advancement of the cause of God, or obscured by mists and cloud, depends largely upon those who make up this Convention to-day. If we are humble, wise, open-eyed to catch the beckoning of the divine finger, open-eared to hear the divine voice, I believe that numbers and blessings, of which none of us dare to dream, await our society. In looking forward to the future, four duties, which, after all, are one duty, claim our serious consideration.

The first duty is the further vigorous advancement of our society in all proper ways. By this I do not mean any forcing of it upon the churches, or even knocking for admission at any barred doors, but simply a proclamation of our real principles and aims to the hundreds of thousands who are willing and eager to know about them. This is a necessary and logical result of our belief in the Christian Endeavor Society. If we are convinced that it has been useful in one church, yes, in five thousand churches, then we must believe that we have a message for the other eighty thousand churches, more or less, in the United States, which have, as yet, no Societies of Christian Endeavor, I recall a phrase which you received with the utmost favor at the last convention. It was something like: "Our motto, 'for Christ and the Church,' logically carried out, means a church in every hamlet, and a Christian Endeavor Society in every church." Our commission is none other and no less than the one which Christ our Lord Himself gave to his own disciples. "Go ye into all the world and preach the gospel to every creature." The torch has been handed down from hand to hand until now it is handed to you, my brother and sister. It has been called by different names, in your hands it is called the Society of Christian Endeavor, but it is the same old gospel torch. Trace it back from hand to hand, and we find that at last it is from the hand of Him who is the "Light of the World," and who "lighteth every man that cometh into the world" Therefore, the very fact that this society has been blessed of God to the conversion of young people and the strengthening of His church, imposes upon us an obligation which we cannot ignore.

The second obvious duty of the coming year is to spread the society in its purity. The Society of Christian Endeavor was established for certain *definite, specific* purposes, and these purposes were and are of a purely religious and spiritual nature. It can never too strongly be impressed upon our hearts, that if our society fails of its *highest* mission it is an *utter and total* failure. However successful it may be as a literary or social organization, yet, if it loses its grasp on spiritual things, if its eye becomes dull and bleared to heavenly glories, and its ear dim to heavenly music, it were good for it that it had never been born. The world is not pining for more social clubs, or for more literary centres. Our society has no mission along these lines except to make them subservient to higher and better things. The world *is* dying for a lack of a knowledge of Christ, and for lack of *heroic enthusiasm* in proclaiming Christ, and this is the aim of the Society of Christian Endeavor. By the prayer-meeting, with its stringent rules, by the committee work, in all its multifarious lines of activity, by the contact of earnest soul with soul, must Christ be proclaimed. If this is not done by our society, nothing worth doing is done Because I feel this so profoundly, I ask you, fellow-members of the society, to support us in every effort to keep the helm steady and to hold on in our course. There are always numerous efforts to capture a vigirous organization and to carry it into the camp of some hobby, or some one reform, or some one denomination or sect, and when such hobby, or reform, or denomination sees that it cannot be captured or bought, it is very apt to denounce the movement, or to start a rival which it is thought will divide and destroy it. These efforts have been tried, these ambuscades very likely await our society. I appeal now for your support in attempting to keep the Christian Endeavor Society a *Christian Endeavor Society*. We can only serve all reform movements by not coming under the denomination of any one idea. We can only serve the cause of Christ in all denominations by not being narrowed to one denomination. While each society owes allegiance only to the local church and denomination with which it is connected, the idea, the movement, the society as a whole, owes allegiance only to evangelical, biblical Christianity. I urge upon you, brethren, in all your different denominations, hearty devotion to your own creed, to your own religious order, to your own local church. I also urge you to resist the efforts of zealots who would divide the Young People's Society into denomination clans. As Sunday schools are practically the same in all denominations, though adapted to the needs of every church, so let our societies of young people, in all denominations, have common aims and common methods, thus forming one mighty army of the living God.

The third duty before us in the years to come is to accomplish all this at a small expense. We are not so situated as to obtain large sums from the churches, nor do we wish to obtain such sums. All the marvelous growth of the past year has been accomplished at an expense of from $15,000 to $16,000, and the society asks no more for the coming year. To demand or expect hundreds of thousands of dollars, such sums as our great denominational missionary societies expect, would be unwise, if not impossible. To levy any tax or assessment we are convinced would be equally unwise, as we would put no barrier whatever to the formation of new societies. On that account the United Society asks for a very modest sum, and asks for it as a free-will offering from the societies represented here, who will especially feel the impetus and realize the importance of spreading the work. Let it be remembered that the United Society is working towards self-support, that it performs its large duties with the greatest economy, and you will not fail gladly to contribute what is necessary for the spread of a knowledge of our cause. Let it be proclaimed again and again. *There is no tax involved in joining the United Society.* It is simply, as its name indicates, the enrolment of all the societies, and is supported by free-will offerings solely. But all this may be defeated, and the cause greatly retarded, if the State unions and conventions levy taxes or demand fees for membership. Most earnestly would I advise that this plan be abandoned, and that the money raised for current expenses be raised by free gifts at the State conventions.

But, after all the most important duty of the society is the training of the individual member for usefulness in the church. Let us always bear in mind that the society does not exist for its own aggrandizement. Its mission will be ended, its grave will be dug, and its funeral oration pronounced when it departs from its early traditions and seeks its own glory, and not the glory of Christ and the church In our constitution the object of the society is expressed in simple language : "To promote an earnest Christian life among the members, and to make them more useful in the service of God." This was the object of the first society. It is equally the object of all the societies throughout the world to-day. To secure this result for all the future ; to make good our motto, or rather to make it sure that this motto shall represent the society in days to come. it is necessary, I think, that we should take one advance step to-day ; and that step is to answer the question, *What shall we do with our graduates?* The Christian Endeavor Society is primarily *a training school.* The very idea of a school involves graduation some time. It may not be for many years, but some time it must come. We are not only in training ; we are in training *for something* ; and that something is the work of the church. Moreover, it is an undeniable fact that we are all growing older. The boys and girls who began in the society seven years ago are no longer boys and girls, and when seven times seven more years have shall have passed, we shall all, to say the least, be old boys and old girls ; but even then, and for seventy times seven years, we hope our society will be a *young people's* society of Christian Endeavor. To be sure, within some of us there may be such a fountain of perpetual youth, that for fifty years to come we may still be eligible for active membership, but before the next half century shall have passed away most of us will have graduated from active membership. When shall this graduation occur? At a certain age limit? That were hardly wise, because the mere accident of *years* is such an uncertain thing in determining a person's age. Many a boy of sixteen is much older, you know, then when he is six-and-twenty. Or shall we say that the graduation must occur when one has has been so many years in the society? That would still be more unfortunate, for some need a much longer course of training than others. The boy of ten would be likely to need the society longer than the man of thirty. We see but one solution. There can be no fixed and arbitrary rule, but when the time comes, as it often will come to our older members, that they must choose between the society meeting and the weekly church meeting, then they should choose the church meeting. Then will come the proper time for graduation. So long as these older members can be faithful to both meetings, let them remain in the active membership, but no longer.

In order that the United Society, through its president, may go on record on this important subject, which I believe will affect the whole future of our organization for good, if it is wisely and promptly handled,

I would propose this amendment or addition to the model constitution. Since it would in the end defeat the very object of our organization if the older active members, who have been trained in ths society for usefulness in the church, should remain content with fullfilling their pledge to the society only, therefore it is expected that these older members, when it shall become impossible for them to attend to weekly prayer-meetings, shall be transferred to the honorary membership of the society; if prev ously faithful to their vows as active members. This transfer, however, shall be made with the understanding that the prayer-meeting pledge of each honorary member shall be binding upon him for faithful attendance and participation in the usual church prayer-meeting, instead of the society meeting. It shall be left to the lookout comm.ttee, in conjunction with the pastor, to see that this transfer of membership is made as occasion requires. Special pains shall also be taken to see that a share of the duties and responsibilities both of the prayer-meeting, and of the general work of the society, shall be borne by the younger members.

This plan requires no hasty exit, no dangerous uprooting, no unnecessary reorganization of the society. Gradually and naturally, and one by one, not in classes or ranks, shall we come to our graduation day as active members, but we need never sever our connection with the society as honorary members, while faithful to our church vows. So long as we are especially needed to help and guide the new members, as many of us will be for many a year to come, so long shall we remain active members, but gradually will the duties and responsibilities be shifted to the shoulders of the younger and less experienced, and thus the society will always remain in fact, as in name, a Young People's Society of Christian Endeavor. But what will most commend some such plan to you is this, that thus our organization remains true to its first principles as a humble helper and hand-maid to the local church with which it is connected. Thus we make it plain in our very constitution that our one purpose is, not to magnify the society, but to make each individual " more useful in the service of God" in the church where God has placed him. The whole idea of the society naturally leads us on to this issue, and I commend it most seriously to your attention. Such are the matters of vital importance which I would present to you. The work of the past year and a wide outlook over the whole field have forced them upon my attention. Brethren and sisters, it is a glorious vista which opens before us to-day, as we look to the coming years of the Christian Endeavor.

I dare to use only the light of the past blessings in interpreting the future. But, reading by that light, I see nearly ten new Societies of Christian Endeavor established every day during the coming year. I see tens of thousands of young people coming into the kingdom of Christ; I see millions of prayers ascending from young hearts, like incense to the throne; I hear millions of testimonies to the love of Christ; I see pastors' faces glowing with gratitude to God, and many a feeble church taking on new courage and strength by means of the young blood in its veins; I see the old waste places rebuilt, and the desert blossoming as the rose. Is this an empty prophecy, or will you help to make it true, first in your own lives, and then in your own society? We have already heard recently of one of our Christian Endeavor Societies in Burma, whose name, literally translated into English, is "The Society which tries." That is what every Society of Christian Endeavor is, " The Society which Tries." Make that name true of yonr society, and my vision of the coming year is a reality. Last year, at this time, we took for our motto the one which we will always, perhaps, write upon our society banners: " For Christ and the Church " To-day I would propose an individual motto for the coming year. As the Israelites bound the Scripture upon their foreheads, may we engrave this upon our hearts: "NOT TO BE MINISTERED UNTO, BUT TO MINISTER." O societies that try! O individuals who try! This was His motto whose we are, and whom we serve: NOT TO BE MINISTERED UNTO, BUT TO MINISTER.

REPORTS.

REPORT FROM NEW ENGLAND.

BY REV. S. W. ADRIANCE.

It is always the correct thing for a minister to begin his address with a text, and my text is a forcible one. It is as follows: Massachusetts, 578 societies of Christian Endeavor; Connecticut 220; Maine 142; Vermont 110; New Hampshire 102; Rhode Island 65; in all 1,217. This text represents a vast rank and file of earnest workers. After the text it is always necessary to unfold, and in this case there are vital truths underneath which explain the work in New England. In the first place, this text means progress, to some of you, that may not seem surprising or noticeable. You are just at the beginning, here in the West Societies are springing up everywhere. But in New England it has been growing all the time. Societies have multiplied rapidly. Now when I say there is just the same advance all along the line, it means that the people of New England having watched the growth these years, are abundantly satisfied with it, and propose to keep on.

The work in New England has proved that this work is not a temporary matter but permanent. The question has often been asked whether this movement is not merely in the hour? But the first days of new enthusiasm have gone by in New England, and yet the insignificant thing is that in these oldest societies the work this past year has assumed proportions never known before. Many who began with a fear lest the full pledge is to strong, have found the necessity of reorganization on the "cast-iron pledge," that "they will be there every time and take part every time." I note the aggressiveness of this work. We in New England are supposed to be cold-blooded and slow, but I want you to understand that we have trains called the "Flying-Yankee," and both in business and religious work, there is a tremendous earnestness. I wish I could tell you some of the romances of Christian Endeavor work, of the constant help in all branches of church work, of the controlling desire that the lost shall be gathered in Christ. I must speak briefly, and so note once more the close connection between the Societies and the church. It was noteworthy that in the Maine State Conference the Secretary reported from church after church testimonies from pastors and officers of the great worth of the Society in the church. In another State Association of churches, a special resolution of approval of the work was introduced by one of the oldest and most influential clergymen. Pastors have found everywhere that the societies can be relied on in all kinds of work. So these are the points: first, great growth; second, perseverance; third, aggressiveness; fourth, closeness of connection with the local church.

REPORT FOR THE MIDDLE AND INTERIOR STATES.

BY REV. H. B. GROSE, PITTSBURG, PA.

Mr. President, and Delegates of the Conference: You have heard a good deal about Chicago this morning, but I must add one thing more. I believe it was a Chicagoan, talking with one of the New England delegates when they had this little bit of a tilt. The New Englander said, " you will please to remember that the wise men came from the East." "Oh, yes," said the Chicagoan, " They were wise men because they came from the East." "Yes," again, said the New Englander, for he would not give up so easily—a Yankee never gives up until he has to—" but you will remember they went back." " Oh, well," said the Chicagoan, " that was almost 1900 years ago."

I have just a few figures to give you, but it is very difficult to get the accurate figures about Christian Endeavor, to get at the statistics. For a work that will not for one single moment stay, how are you going to get the statistics?

Now, I am a New Yorker from Pennsylvania, a Christian Endeavorer in New York, and just now over the line in Pennsylvania. When I left Pittsburg - it only takes twelve hours to come from there here—New York State had about 600 Christian Endeavor Societies, but twenty-four hours later she had nearly a thousand. I will give you my text for the Middle States, Indiana,—Indiana, a Middle State? Well, I found out when I got out there they said it was I did not expect to speak for Indiana or Michigan, or Ohio, for when I was a boy our geography didn't put them in the Middle States, but I find out here that they are the Middle States. First, Indiana, 80 Societies with 5200 members; Michigan 180 Societies with 10,700 members; Ohio 245 Societies; with 15,900 members; Pennsylvania 249 Societies with 16,000 members; New Jersey—they said the work had gone into foreign lands, but New Jersey will never be a foreign land any more now that

Christian Endeavor has gone in there. Why, New Jersey has 178 Societies with nearly 12,000 members. There were only 18 Societies in New Jersey two years ago, a growth of 85 per cent in that State. New York, 947 Societies, 61,500 members.

I think that is a good text, that we have a total in six of the Middle States of 1899 reported Societies with a membership of more than 120,000, and if you add two more states that should be added, Maryland and Delaware, it gives us a grand total of 125,000 members in those eight States in the middle section of our land.

Now, if I should seem to say a little more about New York than any other State you will please to remember that it is because I know more about New York than any other State, and though it is unpopular with some to talk about that which they know the best, yet I find it is the safest thing to do, and it is not immodest; the New York delegates needn't listen while I am talking a little about the work in that great State.

First, let me say that in every one of these large States there is a State Union or a State Conference, and I believe that we can say from the reports of these conferences that it is since our States have taken up the work of Christian Endeavor in the State conferences and have pushed it through, that the marvelous growth has come.

Two years ago at Saratoga, New York State could report only sixty-four societies with a total membership, so far as we knew, of 2400, and now I ask you to look at the change in just two years; from 64 societies to 947, and from 2400 members to over 60,000. You say "how has it come about"? Well, first, we thank God it has come about through that which is in the work itself, not through the United Society, not through the State Conference, not through the Local Union, but because of the power of the spirit of God which is in the work itself. Let us not fail to recognize, amid all our gratitude for the progress of the work, that it has been made because the hand of God is upon the work and the power of God has been with the young people in it. Why, there is no record we read that proves to me the mission we have as Christian Endeavor Societies, like this; that at the last State conference in New York, there were more than 1000 conversions during the year from among our associate members, and that our Secretary informs me that since last November, having received reports from less than 250 societies, he already has reports of more than 1500 conversions and uniting with the churches; and whenever I speak for Christian Endeavor, and whenever any one raises the least voice of criticism about it, I say to him "read our record of the thousands upon thousands of our conversions that are reported," and if that does not satisfy criticism, then nothing will.

Now, we have one feature in New York State that I think is somewhat peculiar, and I believe that to it is due very much of our great progress. The State is large in territory and in population. We felt that no organization could reach every part of it if it had simply a secretary and the usual officers, and so we districted the State, at first into twenty districts. Now, I think we have thirty, and put a district secretary in each district, who shall look after the extension of the work there. We made each district comparatively small so that one man can keep his eye over that field, and I speak of this to-day because I believe in this large territory of the west, in your States of vast extent, if you want to spread the work in a judicious way, you will spread it by districting your States and thus dividing the responsibility for carrying on an extension of the work.

Our local Unions have in some places been remarkable for the work they have done in elevating the entire Christian life of a community. Why, I know one city where the Christian life has been fairly revolutionized in fifteen months by the united efforts of the Young People's Society of Christian Endeavor. Now, in every Protestant church in the city there is not only life, but there is zeal, there is movement. In New York City, we have had a local Union that promises to move our work forward as it ought to be. In Brooklyn we have a most flourishing Union, and in the Cities of Syracuse and Rochester, their work speaks so loud for what they have done through their united efforts, that it only needs to be mentioned here.

Now, one word more, we have been growing rapidly in the middle States; in every one of these six States the increase in the last two years has been remarkable. It has averaged over 80 per cent in every one of them, and we have got to realize that we have more members in a single State to-day than we had in the whole United States only two years ago. No wonder we are amazed when we stand in the presence of such figures and facts as these. Christian Endeavor has grown. Let us see to it that it ever does grow of its own inherent power; that is my point. Let no one in over-zeal try for one instant to push Christian Endeavor where it is not welcome, where, as yet it is not wanted; that is the only mistake we can make. Why, we do not need to push it; we only need to *live* it. Let every Christian Endeavorer *live* the principles of his society. This is the way for him to do, and let every society be true to itself and to its pledge, and that is the way to extend the knowledge of it; not in the spirit of rivalry, not in the spirit of trying to hasten the work which God is hastening for us, as rapidly as we can wisely take care of it. Don't let's imitate the man who was told about by one of the eminent pastors of this city, and since it is his story I have a right to tell it here. He said that one very hot day in August, a very long man with a satchel in one hand and an umbrella in the other, and his hat pushed back on his head, was rushing down 34th St. in New York for the Ferry. He had heard the boat whistle, and it was the last boat for his train, and he thought he would lose it, so down he went, the satchel flying one way and his umbrella another, and his hat flying off behind, and he went for that boat, and as he got near the Ferry house looking through the big crowd, he saw a gap there, and it seemed to be at least five feet over it, but rushing past the gateman on he went, down went his umbrella and satchel and off went his hat and he gave a gigantic leap for that boat and landed square in the stomach of a fat man who stood on the front of it, and as soon as he could get his breath the fat man blubbered out "you sacred fool, this boat is coming in." And so it was.

And the Christian Endeavor boat is coming in, and don't let anybody try to jump, or hasten things, but just trust the God who thus far has guided us, and he will surely lead us on, not to any victories that are temporary, but to victories for Christ and for the church that shall be eternal.

REPORT FOR THE NORTHWEST.

BY REV. E. M. NOYES, DULUTH, MINN.

It was at first something of a puzzle to me why my name should be selected to represent the Northwest, but since coming into this hall I have discovered the reason of it. I think perhaps one was that I might bring to this convention at least a satchel full of lakeside air. I should be very glad if I could. I think it would be grateful to-day. Another reason has been suggested by the gentleman who spoke from England, that those who represent the districts should be able to appreciate both sides of the question. Now, I reciprocate, for I was born New England, and I am proud of the wooden nutmeg state and of its record.

You will appreciate perhaps, the embarrassment under which I labor in endeavoring to report from the Northwest, when I state to you that when I came to Minnesota five years ago I found myself the only Congregational minister in a county as large as the whole state of Connecticut. It is somewhat difficult to report for a territory magnificent in distance.

I have been reminded here of the story of the old farmer who was asked about his son's politics. His son had a somewhat variable political career. The old man was asked one afternoon which way John was going to vote, with the Democrats, Republicans, or with the Greenbackers. Well, the old man wiped his brow and says, "I don't know, I am sure; I have not seen him since breakfast."

My friend who has spoken from Pittsburgh relates the phenomenal increase of the number of societies in New York. I have been having a somewhat similar experience, since I arrived here this morning, in finding that the societies have grown faster than I could report them. I will give you a few faulty figures. We held our first Christian Endeavor convention in Minnesota a year ago last April. Three years ago there were to my knowledge not more than a dozen at the outside. At our first convention, when we organized, there were reported something like thirty. At Saratoga last year our report was 49. We have to-day in the State, those that are known to the Secretary, an even 100 societies. Wisconsin last year reported something like 100 societies; Wisconsin reports to-day 150 societies. For Iowa I have not the full data to give you a complete report, but their growth has been in equal ratio, 130 up to 200 or more,—195, I believe, are the exact figures. Dakota has only just begun this work. Last year there were but five societies reported. Now, I understand there are fifty at least in Dakota, and they are about to complete—shall I say a "state organization," or "Territorial organization?" "State organization!" Dakota has tried her hand at territorial organization I hope that the State organization will be permanent.

And what can I say about the Northwest that stretches out far beyond us?

President Northrup of Minnesota State University, formerly of Yale, told me that he went out in Montana, and there he discovered a little log school house. He asked the boys, when he was called upon to address the school—it was on the western slopes of Montana—"What are you going to do when you grow up?" Every hand went up immediately. "Well, what are you going to do?" "Going to the Northwest". He said he thought he was pretty well to the Northwest, but then you must remember that the "Northwest" stands, not only for Wisconsin, Minnesota, Dakota, and Iowa and Northern Illinois, but it stands also for Montana and for Idaho and for Washington Territory and for Alaska too, and you must remember that when you get to Sacramento or San Francisco, California, you have only got to the centre of this country, as it reaches West, that Alaska reaches way out beyond.

Mr. President, I have been reminded since I came here of that text in the Scriptures where the Master is represented as going into a far country and leaving to every man his share of talents and opportunities, and it seems to me it represents this Christian Endeavor movement as we find it in the Northwest, and as you find it in the East. We have the raw material in abundance. We have this material to develope for product, a material which the world needs. We find the need up in the Northwest where the men are occupied so much, perhaps more than any other section of country—the need of having men and women to work with their minds and their hearts. We need consecrated men and women. Now we have the raw material in abundance. There are, in the State of Minnesota, and I speak of that for I know it best, only about fifty per cent of our children in Sabbath Schools. We have the raw material in abundance there, and that is the population. We have in our State some ten thousand Scandinavians. We have among them a Free Scandinavian Church and a Congregational Church. A pastor came to me, a young man, in great trouble. He said, "There is a member of my church I want to expel". I said, "What is the matter with him?" "O, he bad man." "Why," I said, "What does he do?" Does he steal?" " O, no, he no steal, I don't tink." "Well, does he abuse his wife?"—some Scandinavians do, among the lower classes— "No, he don't do that." "Is he dishonest in his business?" "No," "Does he drink alcohol?" "No." "What does he do?" "O, he bad man." "What is the matter with him?" "Why, he no come to prayer-meeting, and I tink he no read his bible every day." He was going to expel him. Mr. President, is not that good material to make Christian Endeavor Societies out of? In this movement among the Scandinavians I expect to see develope in the next few years Scandinavian Societies of Christian Endeavor.

And so among all our foreign population, we need not try to limit the Societies to the lines we have been working on. They are working in this land as well as in other lands. I said we have the raw material in abundance; we have this material which has proved effectual in producing warm-hearted and earnest working Christian men and women, but we must know that the work is valueless unless we have the power, and I thank God that the power in this movement is the power of the spirit of God, and that is bringing us in the Northwest, as well as in the East and the South, young men and women whose hearts are in the work, and with the love of Jesus Christ are not afraid to do good work for the Lord Jesus Christ, and so I bring the greetings of the Northwest, and I ask your prayers that after we have passed the first stage that we may have the guidance of God in the training the young men and women in the aggressive work, " For Christ and for the Church."

REPORT FROM FLORIDA.

BY MRS. SHELDON.

Mr. Hill, about one moment ago, asked me if I would not speak for Florida. Now, Florida is my native State, and I am always glad to speak for her, especially in such a cause, but certainly I had not anticipated this. I had hoped that our Superintendent, Mr. Nettleton, who, by the way, is from Scranton, Pennsylvania, and I met some of his friends in this Convention,—I hoped that he would be here. I wrote to him a few days ago asking if he would send his statistics in regard to our work in Florida; I would gladly present them to the Convention. I have not heard from him yet but I hope I shall before the convention is over.

I can only say that our State, though far away, is very much interested in this work. I represent a society in Central Florida, Gainsville. We have about seventy members, and we think we are a very active society. We are enthusiastic and we certainly are a happy society.

I was very much encouraged personally, and I am sure we all were, by a visit from our Secretary, Mr. Ward, last winter.

There are, I believe, about fifty societies in the State. Next winter we intend to organize a State Union. We will meet in our City, and at our next Convention I hope we shall be able to present a full report and a great many more societies.

REPORT FROM THE SOUTH.

BY MRS. PERKINS OF MISSOURI.

In the absence of our friend from St. Louis, Mr Graff, the President of the Missouri delegation and of the Missouri Union I shall have to make a very brief report. In Missouri the work did not fairly start until about a year ago, but since that time under the good influence of Brother Williams and Mr. Graff, we have come rapidly to the front, until Chicago beat us, as it does in most everything. We had the largest local State Union in Missouri there was in the country. Lately Chicago has come to the front and laid us out. But we are getting warm down there; the thermometer down there day before yesterday was close to 100, and we are working with all our might and main to bring you down there in about two years to warm you up in the work of Christian Endeavor. We have got a fine large hall, and I was informed a day or two ago by the managers that they would guarantee in July to keep the Convention in a state of exceedingly warm enthusiasm all the time there were visitors, but some one has got the best of us by putting in a whole lot of improved machinery and guaranteeing to cool us off to about 12 or 15 degrees less than it is outside the building,—but we have got a good large country town, and can accomodate you in the hotels and in the fields, and we hope to see the Convention coming down there and push the work where it needs it. There is a section across the river in the neighboring State of Illinois called Egypt, from its dark ages, and they need a little help in that country, and we have to help Illinois once in a while.

While I cannot make as complete an address as our President would, we will assure you all a warm welcome there in 1889, if not, in 1890 sure.

CHRISTIAN ENDEAVOR IN CALIFORNIA.

MR. HEDGES OF CALIFORNIA WAS UNEXPECTEDLY CALLED UPON TO REPORT CONCERNING THE PACIFIC COAST, AND SPOKE AS FOLLOWS:

Mr. President and kind Christian Friends, I am very sorry indeed that I am the only representative of the large State we have out there, but it seems that such is the case. I have no statistics that I can give you, but I can tell you that we are well up to the work. I come myself from the Southern part of California, San Diego. We are having, as I suppose you all know, quite a boom down there; and although the majority are booming land and real estate, a few of us there are booming the Christian Endeavor. A society was started, the first one, in the Presbyterian Church on February 20th, 1886, with twelve charter members. We now have some fifty-five members in that Society, active, and I think about seven associate members. Altogether we have eleven societies reported and we have two hundred and ninety members, of which two hundred and thirty-four are active, and the rest associate, and we have lately organized a Union there. The work is going grandly on. I have heard from there since I came here. In the consecration meeting, a similar interest was taken, everyone coming up and taking part. That is what we want of you. We have a large field to work in there, and we need your prayers in our behalf; and we hope to do a grand and glorious work the coming year. I thank you all kindly.

CHRISTIAN ENDEAVOR IN UTAH.

BY REV. J. C. THRALL, SALT LAKE CITY.

It is a pleasure, I assure you, to tell you something about the Christian Endeavor work in Utah. Although the Society is not very old, still there is some interest taken in it, and the pastors are coming forward and taking hold in a right spirit.

In this meeting the pastors are to give testimony as to their experience in regard to the value of the Young People's Society of Christian Endeavor, and certainly if any are justified in giving this experience it must be the pastors of the churches, We have the floor; I am asked to bring tidings. I might bring tidings from my parish in Connecticut where I had the privilege of organizing a Young People's Society of Christian Endeavor some time, I think, early in 1883, and which was of great assistance to me there, but I bring tidings from a far more difficult, and a far more hopeless field; hopeless in one sense, hopeful in another, for the hope of Utah is not in her old; the hope of Utah is in her young. If you cannot reach the old in Utah, it is certain from experience that you can reach the young.

I will not attempt to say what the Young People's Society of Christian Endeavor may or may not do elsewhere, but with us it is a positive success. I might speak of my own church. A few weeks ago I laid the hands of baptism upon the heads of four young ladies, girls just budding into womanhood. I suppose I never should at that time have laid the hands of baptism upon their heads had it not been for their previous training as active members of the Young People's Society of Christian Endeavor.

When I left that church for an extended trip in the east, I left the sick I left the care of the strangers with my young people, and I know that the flowers will bloom in the sick chamber while I am gone, as they have bloomed through the long cold days of winter, as they have bloomed upon my desk every Sunday during the nearly two years that our Society has been in existence. I know that the Bible will he read at the pillow of the sick and of the dying while I am gone, because we have a Young People's Society of Christian Endeavor. Other pastors to whom I wrote before coming away, Utah pastors through all parts of the territory, testified to the same effect. One said "tell them that it is the biggest helper that I ever had in my work".

I spoke by invitation in the City of Ogden, a few weeks ago to over 100 of these young people. I asked them what they thought of organizing territorial unions for Salt Lake City next fall. They answered "we will come if we have to walk the 37 miles!"

Mrs Bailey, whom some of those present probably know, and knowing her, know her favorably, the wife of the Congregational minister in Ogden, told me a little story which I must tell to-day. Said she, "last night at our meeting the daughter of a saloon keeper, an active member of our Young People's Society rose, and prayed in these words; 'Oh, Lord, Oh, Lord, help us to boom this Society of Christian Endeavor until it shall be the biggest thing in town". It was to be bigger than her own father's saloon.

I might say that in Utah, probably, above all other territories, the Society of Christian Endeavor is applicable, not merely as a nursery of the church. There are two kinds of nurseries; one is a nursery where you go and take a little shoot and trans-plant it into your orchard, or trans-plant it as a beautiful shade tree in your front yard, and it grows and is beautiful, and it bears fruit. The other is a nursery where the mother sends her little children whom God gave to her to take care of, —puts them in charge, night and day, of a hireling,—the most cursed thing that was ever done in a home.

There are two kinds of nurseries, my friends, but the kind of nursery of the Christian church that I refer to is the first.

There are Societies of Christian Endeavor in Utah to-day. One year from now they may possbily be churches. One Society of Christian Endeavor that I know of grew into a church. We are peculiarly situated there, Remember that many are preaching against the very name of the church; they have had enough of ecclesiasticism; they have tried that in the past. They have had enough of that, but they have not had enough of religion; they have not had enough of faith ;they have not had enough of prayer; they have not had enough of love; they have not had enough of hope in immortality, and therefore when they hear of a Society of Christian Endeavor very many of them will not only allow their children to come, but will come themselves.

It is a peculiar pleasure to me to-day to speak of one Society of Christian Endeavor which is named—I speak of it with especial pleasure for two or three reasons,—one of those reasons will be apparent to you

—for the Society is named after the Phillips Church in South Boston of which our honored President was pastor when you called him to this work.

In that Society let me speak of four girls of whom I know. These four girls, do not tell it, it would hurt their feelings; but I must tell it to you to-day. These four girls are daughters of a polygamist; they are not allowed, by their parents, to join the church, but they are active members in the Young People's Society of Christian Endeavor. The oldest of those four girls is a teacher in one of the new West schools, and graduate of another. The second a poor girl who may die of consumption, is nevertheless trusting sweetly in Christ. The third, attending school, the librarian of the Sunday School; the fourth, a girl of only 13 has, in that Sunday School, a class of fourteen children. Do you suppose that that girl is any ordinary teacher? By no means. She takes her large Bible in her hand, she stands up among those fourteen children, and she tells them of Jesus Christ. They gather around her, they hang upon her lips; they love her as only children can love. They go to the librarian; they ask for quarterlies, "because Ethel wants us to learn our lesson well". The influence of that one girl of 13 upon those fourteen children, who shall measure? Who shall measure? I will not say. In the destiny of the territory of Utah who should say "measure as we bring in the sheaves, sum up the harvest at the last".

There is another Society of which I would gladly speak, also for a peculiar reason, that Society is named after the Church of Burlington, Vermont, of which our presiding officer is a member, and of which our well beloved friend and former pastor is the leader- In that church is a young man. Two or three years ago I organized or started a daily prayer meeting in one of our academies. I remember that young man; I could not get him to take part; I could not get him to say a word for Christ, to pray, but they organized a Young People's Society of Christian Endeavor. The rest took part, and that young man's first prayer was this: "Lord forgive my sins, and bless my father and mother." Measured by the prayer which our Lord commended, who shall say that this young publican did not pray well when first he prayed? He to-day is the President of that Society.

Well, I am speaking of members There are over eighty schools in the territory of Utah to-day that are maintained by you, over eighty of those schools, and every one of them ought eventually to have a society of Christian Endeavor; every one of them ought to become a church of Christ: Send them literature, send them bibles, send them your *Golden Rule*.

Let me speak of your Golden Rule, for my young people told me to do so. They love *The Golden Rule*. There are mothers there that I know of, who read that *Golden Rule* whom you can never get to read a denominational paper. Why? Because Utah Territory is a peculiar territory, with peculiar conditions. Send them *The Golden Rule*. It will never be wasted. Put your money there, it will bear fruit in the hereafter. There are other things that you might do, but I will not specify.

There will be young men, there will be young women who will be wanting to come East, who will be wanting to get an education at our Eastern seminaries and college,. Who will educate them? Their fathers and mothers probably will not. Who shall give them that education? Who shall fit them to go back and carry the tidings to those whom they know?

I said a few weeks ago in an address which I was called upon to deliver at a Christian convention of all denominations,— I was asked to say a word of encouragement for the future to our workers out there, and I spoke of the future in this way, that we were undermining the hell gates of the West just as General Newton undermined the hell-gate of the East which obstructed navigation. I said that the gospel ship and the ship of State needed to move over these waters; I told them at last the mines would be completed, the dynamite would be laid, the wires would be stretched and some one would touch the electric button. It was General Newton's little five year old girl who touched the button, and Hell-gate was in the air, and I said to them they were doing the mining. but it was not for them to say who should touch the button, they should leave that with God : it is for you away there in the Bay State, you away there in the Granite State, you away there in the Nutmeg State, you away there in the Green Mountain State, to touch the electric button, and the hell-gate of the west shall be in the air, for the hope of Utah is in her youth. Above all places, above all localities I ever knew, it is not in the old.

But I want to see this spirit spread. I believe that you represent not mottoes; I never want to see the Society represent merely mottoes. I want to see it represent the spirit which can take hold of and use any motto. I want to see you like Sargeant McWade at the Siege of Sebastopol, who, when a boy in front of him, a little fellow not more than 18 or 20 years old, was carrying the colors over the parapet to sure death and glory, threw him back, took his place and said, "no, you are to young to die".

There are hopes there that are too young to die. It is on that principle, it is on that idea that this Society is founded. From top to bottom they are too young to die.

That is what the church says. Why, do you know what church means? Church means Ecclesia. That was the meaning of the word. They were called out of the world. Well, now I want these Young People's Societies to go to the church and call them out of this; I want them called out of their ecclesiasticism; I want them called out of their old methods; I want them called out of the ruts; I want them called out for Christ's sake ; for the sake of Christ and humanity I want them called out. That is the spirit of vicariousness. "Take his place he is too young to die." That is what Christ said when he came into the world. That is just what this society says ; it is just what the churches say to this society, it is just what ought to be said everywhere. I like the iron-clad pledge ; I like nothing better in your society unless it be its enthusiasm, which I see everywhere, unless it be the principle, which I know is next to prayer, unless it be the character that is built up and that takes its shape in the form of gratitude, that gratitude which Luther had when he took his place and said "I cannot do otherwise". It is not until our disposition, it is not until our good will has passed over the line that separates us, that we can help them, that we can help the youth. I like that iron-clad pledge. I like your applause; I like your symbolism; I know that Constantine himself fought, conquered and died in that sign; I know that the Old World's battle has been fought and is to be conquered in that sign. I know that you can take the clouds as Constantine took them, the mists and the vapors, and you can weave them into those clouds—circles, and then the clouds and mists shall disappear, and we shall all be bound together in societies, United Societies of Christian Endeavor.

NOTE.

The remaining papers and addresses are arranged in the following general order:

1st. Those relating to Committee Work.
2d. Special Features of Society Work.
3d. Relation of the Society to the Church.
4th.   "   "   "   "   Mission Work.
5th. Addresses and Sermon.

Committee Work.

THE LOOKOUT COMMITTEE.

BY MISS MARY HOUGHTALING.

When our Christian Endeavor Society was in its infancy, the Lookout committee was viewed in a peculiar light. None of us understood the aims and objects of this uniquely named committee; but those who have served upon it since that time have learned that important, serious and continuous work is peculiar to the committee. Could the workings of the model lookout committee be portrayed to our minds, we might be able to reach a higher standard of excellence in each of our own societies. But what a task! Certainly, ignorance of the work expected of the members of this committee is their only salvation when they enter upon its work. The duties of this committee are defined as fourfold, but they unfold, until they become manifold.

The Lookout committee shall, first, bring new members into the society; second, introduce members to other members and to the work; third, affectionately look after and reclaim any who may seem indifferent to their duties; fourth, satisfy themselves of the fitness of young persons to become members. Who is sufficient for this? Truly the work is great. Through Christ's strengthening power alone it can be accomplished, even in a small degree.

Great wisdom must be exercised in effecting good results. This committee has special work, and no member upon it can be excused from the performance of it. I confess, it is a trying task to approach him who has been neglectful of his pledge, and, in a kindly, affectionate way, seek the reason for it. Yet this is a part of the required work, and all members must realize that the lookout committee is only doing that for which it was appointed to do. The members are not prying into the private doings of any one, but only performing the requirements of the committee upon which they serve. A systematic marking plan should be adopted. Each member should have a record book, in which all names are placed, with blank spaces for the attendance mark. The names should be alphabetically divided among the members of the committee, and each one held responsible for the names in his list. The chairman must keep a record of the attendance at each regular meeting. A uniform system of marking should be agreed upon, and the different books compared at least once a month, as, ∕ present, ∕ present and participated,⫽ present and interviewed, Ā absent and interviewed, so that a complete record may be kept.

The chairman will find it necessary to take a few minutes at home the same day of the meeting, to mark the number who participated, and when one habitually comes, and fails to keep his pledge, he should be waited upon by the one upon whose list he is, and the reason learned and reported to the chairman. This interchange of interviews is helpful, and all learn ways to meet objections when presented.

After each consecration meeting, at least, the chairman should make three lists of names. First, of those present who failed to participate. Second, of those who were absent. Third, of those who have three consecutive absent marks against their names, upon consecration nights. This list should go where the chairman goes, and abide where the chairman abides, until each member whose name appears in it has been interviewed. Then, too, the other members should keep a list of their own absentees, and, in a week, each one will have been casually or by design, met and questioned, not only once, but twice. No one but a member of the lookout committee can know the continuousness of this task. Indeed, if the absentees could for a short time be placed upon this committee, they would be more prompt in sending an excuse to the society. Ever and anon, we shall find members of other committees doing the work which seems to belong to the lookout committee, but this apparent conflict is the secret of the success of this, the grandest movement of our day.

We cannot draw a line at which the functions of one committee ends and another begins, but we can work together with such a unanimity of feeling and action that only good results will follow, and all will be instrumental in accomplishing that for which we are endeavoring.

The members of the lookout committee ought to be devoted to the Master's work. They ought to be interested in all young people, and not be easily discouraged, when, after repeated efforts, failures to comply with pledge requirements exist. This committee is the President's Cabinet to the society. The power vested therein is certainly important. The members should ever be on the alert, and watchful of the best interests of each active and associate member of the society. This committee should work harmoniously with the president as to the best ways and means of carrying on the work. It should be in direct sympathy and communication with the other equally important committees. All the chairmen and the president should have frequent conferences on the needs and progress of the society. Plans for work should be considered, and the best decided upon.

A common list of names of those interested in, but not a part of the society should be in the hands of each chairman, and it should not remain folded from month to month, but should be looked over often, and as opportunities present themselves, or are made, the persons should be assured that a welcome word and friendly hand will be extended to them if they desire to attend the Christian Endeavor meetings. When this concentrated action is brought to bear upon these individuals, it is astonishing to see how, one by one, the list of names will be checked off and added to the membership.

Through the lookout committee the members gain entrance to the society. How needful for this committee to be composed of those who are faithful to their profession, mindful of their example, and devoted to the work which is of all work the most lasting and fruitful, labor for souls! We need Christian help and sympathy quite as much after we become Christians as before, and in no other way can our growth in this direction be so well sustained and strengthened as in the Society of Christian Endeavor.

> "Let us then be up and doing,
> With a heart for any fate;
> Still achieving, still pursuing,
> Learn to labor and to wait."

THE PRAYER-MEETING COMMITTEE.

BY M. A HUDSON.

The "Gospel of Work," or "Good Tidings of Work," has come to the young people, and they have come to love their prayer-meeting as one of the places in which to do their work. This love of the prayer-meeting has largely come about by the faithful work of the prayer-meeting committee. It has justly been said that "the prayer-meeting committee is the captain of our companies of Christian Endeavor." No campaign can be successful unless there be not only the wise and able commander-in-chief, but skilful and loyal captains.

"This committee shall have charge of the weekly prayer-meeting, see that a leader and topic are provided for each meeting; and shall do what it can to secure faithfulness to the prayer-meeting pledge."

The important work of choosing leaders and topics should be the first duty of this committee after it has organized, held a short prayer-meeting and elected a secretary. As far as possible, in choosing leaders those who have never led before should be selected. A committee should then visit them, and get their consent. To do this will require tact, but very little difficulty will be found, if this committee will assure them of hearty support at the meeting they are to lead. Their preference as to the date and the topic should be consulted. As for topics, there are none better than those issued by *The Golden Rule*, although local needs may occasionally require one of a different character. For instance, to have the meetings varied, the music, temperance, or missionary committee should be invited to take charge of a meeting, and may have a special topic. In some societies, the Bible trainers' classes take one evening for a Bible reading.

After the leaders and topics are arranged, have them printed in a neat and attractive manner. The topic cards should be placed within easy reach of every member of the society, at least one week before the first meeting. A good plan by which to help and encourage the leader, and also to notify him that his time to lead has arrived, is to have the chairman of the committee write him a letter a week before his meeting, assuring him of the committee's prayers and support. Scripture helps upon the topic and hymns bearing upon the subject should be given him. He should be assured of the prayers and support of the other committees. The social committee should be seen and asked to provide an usher and singing-books for the strangers and new members. The music committee should be invited to gather promptly around the organ with their leader. A series of short sentence prayers can be arranged for the leader, and several who always wait until the last to testify can be invited to the first. A list of the active members placed upon two small memorandum-books, and left with two members of the prayer-meeting committee, is of great service in helping this committee to "do what it can to secure faithfulness to the prayer-meeting pledge." These books can be quietly marked during the meeting, *e. g.*, **A** for absence, No. 1 for present, and 2 for took part. In this manner a record of the faithfulness of each member is placed on file.

At the close of the month, when the chairman presents his written report, he can take the names of those who do not attend, and give them to the lookout committee, "that they may again interest them in the work." A list of those who have not been faithful to their pledge ("to take some part") should be made, and after much prayer, and with the pastor's advice, they should be visited, with a view to their future faithfulness. If you are successful, encourage them with your sympathy and thanks for their faithfulness. The leader, after each meeting, should be encouraged by some kindly mention of the meeting he has just led.

The duties of this committee should not end with the endeavor prayer-meeting; for the regular services of the church claim our support. So let us try to induce more of the Endeavor members to attend the church prayer-meetings, and let their voices be heard there. Several committees have provided subjects for prayer for every day in the week; others have provided daily Bible readings and Bible trainers' classes. We have come to love our prayer-meetings; let us learn to love our bibles. The class of which I have been a member two and a half years has been a source of strength to all the members. Children's and cottage prayer-meetings have been held by this committee, and have been the means of great good. With all our plans, let us not forget the source of all our help, and in closing I would urge upon this committee in the words of another: "Pray for the meeting. Pray for the pastor. Pray for the active and associate members. Pray, pray, keep up the praying, and God will bless you and your meetings."

THE SOCIAL COMMITTEE.

BY MISS HATTIE J. BROWN.

Ever since the creation we find that man, by nature, is a social being, for, after God had created man in His own image, He said, "It is not good that man should be alone; I will make him an helpmeet." Man seeks naturally the society of those of congenial minds. But what is congenial to him is largely a matter of education. Heredity has much to do in the peculiar structure of the mind, but education has a great deal more to do in shaping the development of that mind. Because man is naturally a social being, the associations of childhood and early life are important factors in shaping the thoughts, in developing the tastes, and quickening the desires. Hence the importance of throwing around the early life, when impressions are readily made on the tender mind, those associations whose influences are not simply negatively good, but positively so. He must not only "cease to do evil, but learn to do well." The evil trait that begins to manifest itself must be counteracted by the vigorous cultivation of the corresponding good trait. The first school into which he is introduced is naturally the *home*. And in this day and age of the world we are in sorrow constrained to agree too often with the man who said, "There is *no* place like home, and I am glad there is not." And yet there is not, as a general thing, the positive evil teaching of the parents in the home that tends to make the boy or the girl bad, but it is the carelessness of such parents as to the earliest associations which they permit their children to have. They cannot expect to raise wheat among briars and thorns any more than upon the beaten highway.

Next to the parent the *teacher* is responsible, and especially the teacher in the Sabbath school. Can any one give a sound, solid reason why a room in a schoolhouse should be deemed amply furnished that had four white walls, and as many combination desks as could be conveniently crowded into it? If association has such a powerful influence over the mind, why not make every square yard of those walls suggestive to the pupil of something pure, noble and good, uplifting and outreaching; something bright, happifying and attractive? And, as a rule, how much more attractive is the Sunday school room? You don't have much trouble in getting a full school out on Children's Day, or at a

Christmas Festival, and prolonging the service twice the usual time. And why? Simply because you make all the surroundings in the school-room that day attractive to the children, and, oftentimes to the parents as well. God did not make this world so wondrous in its beauty and attractions, that man might shut it out of doors, lest the minds of the children should be diverted from his too often sombre and dyspeptic presentations of religious truth. Jesus strikes the hardest kind of blows upon the time-serving, money-loving heart with no other weapon than the lilies of the field. He made the fall of the sparrow eloquent in teaching how minute are the providences of God. And amid such surroundings as these, with what greater facility could the conscientious, Christ-loving teacher perform the duty assigned. If it contributes inspiration to the pupil, how much more so to the teacher.

But next to the teacher comes the great *school of society*. As a general thing, when we speak of society, we speak of that which is separate and distinct from the church, and yet, in the formation of which, Christian and worldling are found mingling together, and, oftentimes, in scenes of questionable Christian propriety. In this promiscuous mingling together, which of the two is doing the work of the real educator?

Is the Christian bringing up the worldling to his standard of what a young man and woman ought to be, or is the worldling bringing the Christian down to his standard? If you were to seek for genuine, every day spirituality for the devoted, conscientious, self-denying Christian, would your judgement prompt you to seek such in the ball-room, at the theatre, at the card-table, or on the boulevards of a Sabbath? I leave this for the ministers and for more experienced Christians than I to answer. It is in these schools that the social life is largely formed and cultivated. What provision has the church to control these, or to render the evil tendencies of some of them null and void.

The great need in our churches to-day is more sociability, more hand-shaking, more interest in the welfare of those around us, more of a willingness to brighten the lives of those who are less fortunate than ourselves, more of the Christ-spirit for the weary and heavy-laden, less of thought about our comfort and gratification. To this end we have the Social Committee. The first duty of this committee is to cultivate this social nature in themselves. If your pastor has preached a helpful sermon to you, don't hesitate to tell him so. If the music has touched a chord in your heart, tell the choir how much you enjoyed their selections. If you see any one in the congregation that looks weary and sad, give them a welcome smile, and a kind invitation to meet with you again. Above all things do not neglect the children, especially the boys, they are the hope of the church. When we accept a young person as a member of the Endeavor Society, it is just as necessary to cultivate and foster their social nature as it is their religious nature. Show them that you are interested in them by being friendly yourself; this sociability is contagious, it spreads rapidly. Real sociability, however, is a plant that is better cultivated in the *home* than any where else. It is there we gain more of the true character, the talents, the tastes and the availability of the person for some department of Christian work, than in any other way. The aim and object is not to have young men and women join the society simply to swell the numbers, or to keep them from temptation, by the social influence which the society throws around them and over them, but to give them *something to do* in some one of the various departments of Christian work mapped out by the society. How can we wisely direct the steps of the young Christians unless we become familiar with their home life and their school life? I would urge the importance of visiting these young people in their homes. Don't feel that your work is completed when you have visited each member of your society. Manifest an interest in them whenever you have an opportunity. God wants us to be cheerful and happy together. He has promised to pour out His Spirit upon us. Let us be emptied vessels that He may fill us and use us to the pulling down of Satan's strongholds, and the bringing in of the kingdom of our Lord, whose we are and whom we serve.

THE TEMPERANCE COMMITTEE.

BY REV. J. C. CROMER

At its last convention, our society put itself on record for temperance in the following words; "Whereas, the evils of intemperance are the most momentous and gigantic that now impede our work among young men, therefore, Resolved: That we express ourselves as intensely opposed to this evil, and pledge our labors and our prayers to its banishment from among us." These are noble, strong words They at once set our faces against the foe. They put prayers into our hearts, and weapons into our hands, and send us out, thus equipped, to do valiantly for humanity. It perhaps remains only for me to indicate a few doors of usefulness that stand open before us; to point out a few elements of power that belong to us as a Young People's Society of Christian Endeavor.

First, then, we are strong for this work on behalf of humanity, because we are *Christian*. Let it be accepted at once that we cannot do the work of a regularly organized temperance society. This exists for temperance alone. But cannot we do a work for temperance which such a society cannot accomplish? Have we not a vantage-ground of power which it does not possess? We are distinctively a Christian body. Whatever we do for temperance will be winged with the love of Christ for men. It will have these *two characteristics, the vision of Christ in its methods, and the power of Christ in its performance.* We will ever tenaciously hold the Christian view of the essential evil of intemperance. Men may come to us and say, "See yonder home,—what squalor and wretchedness, what misery and woe! Can we do nothing to relieve it?" They will take down their lightning calculators, and strive to set before us in figures the cost of the traffic in liquors. They will point us to the asylums and almshouses, to the prisons and penitentiaries, kept constantly full because of this evil. They will show us the rum power in politics,—to all of which things we shall have our eyes open. But, from this thought of things external, we of the Christian Endeavor Society turn to that of the things internal. From the effects of the evil outward and visible, we look to the cause inner and invisible. And we must say that, so long as the souls of men are enslaved by sin, it is but natural that the sin should find an outward expression. So long as the reason of man is dethroned, and passion and appetite set up in its stead, we must expect to see misery and wretchedness. And the essential evil after all, for the cure of which we must look, is the *sin* which reigns within the heart.

Keeping thus within the vision of Christ, we shall ever remain loyal to the power of Christ. We shall learn to put less emphasis upon methods human, and more upon power divine. We shall have, I hope, a just appreciation of all efforts looking toward the removal of the temptations. And if men can show that methods of restriction have done good, we shall be ready to approve. If local option has lessened the power of the saloon, then we shall rejoice in local option. If prohibition, State or national, can be achieved, whether by third party, old party, or no party whatever, then we shall say, in the name of Christ and the church, let us achieve it. But we shall have too much knowledge of the depravity of the human heart and of the fertility of suggestion in the arch-enemy of our race, to even dare hope that, after every saloon has been banished, and every distillery has gone out of business, we shall have a temperate race. With reference to physical things, it has been said:

> "The earth around is full of evil,
> And so is the wide sea;
> Diseases as well by day and also by night
> Approach unbidden, and bring ills to mortals."

But this fertility of source leading to physical evil is more than overmatched by the infinite variety and form of temptation to moral evil. If we go to a corrupt people and kill their corrupt ruler, he will at once be replaced by another of like character. And when the saloon shall have been brought down from its throne of power, the tobacco and opium habits will remain. When they are gone, something else will be forthcoming. And so, while we shall rejoice in all that is done, and can be done, to sweep the world of temptation until it is clean, we must ever regard this work somewhat as we think of the boy who stands by the mighty ocean trying to dip it dry with his bucket. And whilst we turn not away from these fields of noble endeavor, we shall give our best efforts, our young enthusiasm, our most loyal devotion, not to the work of taking away temptation from men, but that of making the men superior to the temptations. We shall not refuse to go to men, and upon the low plane of morality, or even of decency, entreat them to be temperate; but all this will give way to that better work, which looks to the giving to men of that power within which, being "born of God, overcometh the world."

Again, we are strong for this work for humanity because we are young. Being young, we have a position of power, because we stand just where we can fight hand to hand with the enemy. I need not here state what we all know to be true, that the great majority of the recruits to the ranks of intemperance comes from the young, and that the most efficient work for temperance can be done among young men. For an old man, the chances of reformation have decreased inversely as the square of the distance that he has come down in life. In young manhood character is forming, habits are forming, streams are starting from their sources. Now think of these three hundred and twenty-five thousand Christian Endeavorers throughout the world. They stand as young men among young men,—aye, as young women among young men, with power imperial. Fired with zeal and love for Christ, with hands ready and willing, and with hearts full of sympathy for their fellows, who shall be able to set bounds to their power and influence in staying the tides of intemperance just here where they begin to flow?

To do this work successfully, much depends upon a wide-awake efficient temperance committee. First of all, by pledge or otherwise, the committee should bring the society itself to the position of total abstinence; for to stand in any other position will be to lose the very crown of its glory and power. Afterwards, plans and methods of work which will reach out to the world can be devised. The saloon should be equalled, if possible surpassed, for social attractions. Individual young men should be prayed for and gone after. At times the whole thought, prayer and endeavor of the society should be directed, for weeks and months, towards some one young man, until he is brought in and saved.

But does some one remark that this work is necessarily slow and hopeless? That while one is snatched as a brand from the burning, hundreds are being caught of the fire? Then we reply that, so long as our banner floats on the breezes, bearing the inscription, "For Christ and the Church," we can undertake none other than this practical, Christian temperance work; that for these talents, distinctively and peculiarly our own, we shall be held accountable in the end; and that for hopefulness and promise in the future, we shall find, in their use and development, that the darkest skies above us will be streaked through with light, because of Him whose are the eternal years of God, and who has said, "Lo, I am with you alway, even unto the end of the world."

THE MISSIONARY COMMITTEE.

DR. EDWARD S. NILES.

The Missionary Field for the Young People's Society of Christian Endeavor, both home and foreign is the United States of America. According to our best reports from our missionary authorities, and from other sources, there are coming to our shores every month, 10,000 infidels and idol worshippers. Here, then, in our large cities and towns, is abundant field for missionary labor. And I must say that this work is presented to us at the outset of our existence, for I believe this present condition of the Society of Christian Endeavor is but the outset; we have but passed over the threshold of our usefulness.

Let us for a moment look at the field which is before us. Boston has to-day 400,000 inhabitants; only 50,000 can we count as regular attendants of Protestant churches. New York has a population of 2,000,000; only 90,000 attend her Protestant churches. Chicago has 800,000, of whom only about 100,000 are church-goers. Here, then, in three cities alone we have 2,860,000 that do not attend our churches. Do we need to go to Africa, do we need to go to Italy, do we need to go to Ireland, do we need to go to Germany to preach the gospel to foreign people? No. We have them here under the eaves of our very churches. I do not mean that there is no need of foreign missionary work, but I do mean that those of us who stay at home have a great field at our very doors. Let us for a moment, in the view of the gospel, take a look at this vast army of non-church-goers. If this Bible is true, those who finally reject the Lord Jesus Christ have nothing before them except eternal punishment. Need I say that a large proportion in the least calculation of this 2,860,000 are in everlasting and terrible danger! Can it be said that this is not true? I lay this upon the hearts of you young people. You are strong, you have not the complex and diverting influences of large business cares and responsibilities upon you. You are free. Now, while you choose for your pursuits in life, do not forget these great truths; leave a place for the gospel, leave a place in your life where the Lord can use you in His service.

In my committee we have fifty members; we go out every Sunday in Boston to preach the Gospel. Last Sunday in one of the car stables I called around my committee, twelve young men, conductors and drivers. We said, "Have you accepted Christ!" "Have you accepted Christ!" "Have you accepted Christ?" and they said they believed in Christ. "Have you accepted Him for your personal Saviour?" "No, I don't know that we have; if we have, the sins of the world are breaking us down, we cannot resist them." We said, "Will you look to God in prayer with us for help?" Every man took off his hat, twelve of them, and we led them to God in prayer, to deliver them from temptation. We also distributed tracts and religious reading among them, and as a result of this personal work, scores of those men have been brought to our church services, and many of them have accepted Christ. Next Sunday we are going to do that work in Chicago. How many will go with us? We are going to the Stock Yards, we are going to the Rolling Mills, we are going to see the sailors out here on your rivers. We are going to the Car Stations. How many will meet us at the Young Men's Christian Association at half past seven o'clock and go out with us: I assure you you will have an opportunity to speak for Christ.

[Dr. E. S. Niles organized an efficient corps of workers who did good service the following Sunday in the streets, and on the wharves, and at the stock yards of Chicago.]

VARIOUS HELPFUL COMMITTEES

BY REV. HENRY N. KINNEY.

The Lookout, Prayer-meeting and Social Committees show that you have a Society of Christian Endeavor; the Temperance, Sunday School and Missionary Committees, that you probably have a good one; the number and character of your other helpful committees show whether in your sphere of labor you have just the society you ought to have. How many committees should a society have? As many as there are davits to swing these life-boats from; as many as there are crews to man them; as many as are needed to save the drowning men around you. We have not half committees enough for our own good; for half our members are not on any committee. Satan finds mischief still even in an Endeavor Society for idle hands to do. We are a training school, but there ought to be no opportunity for members to "train" in a bad sense. To every man his work, then; let every Stephen be a stevedore. Let every member be on some committee.

We need more committees. Wherever, in society, church, or community, there is in a religious sense a cry heard from Macedonia, a sparrow fallen to the ground, a man among thieves by the wayside, a cup of cold water unlifted, a beckoning or a pointing finger,—wherever there is a felt want, a neglected duty, a forgotten command of Christ, an unused opportunity, a stone unturned, a cobweb unbrushed; wherever Christ would be, there should be the Society of Christian Endeavor, to prepare the way for His coming into many hearts.

Spain thought Gibraltar ended the world, sailed back and forth in its busy, petty Mediterranean, crept timidly down towards Africa, *terra incognita*, and darted back again, and complacently stamped on her coin, "No more beyond." Spain discovered America, and wrote

"*More beyond.*" A good Christian Endeavor motto. Add, then, to your committees at least those mentioned in the model constitution. Add to the Missionary Committee a Flower; to the Flower a Calling, to the Calling Relief; to the Relief a White Cross; to the White Cross a Music Committee, and over all an Executive Committee. "For if these things be in you and abound, they make you that ye shall neither be barren nor unfruitful."

Sylvanus Stall says there is room in every church at work for thirteen committees, namely, on District Visitation, Highways and Hedges, Bible School, Social Visitation, Prayer-Meeting Absentees, Strangers, the Sick, Tract Distribution, the Poor, Lectures, Missions, Temperance, Finance.

The following committees are, or might well be, at least in local use in our societies:

Emergency.—To provide for sudden exigencies that may arise, funerals, special meetings, etc., covered by no other committee.

Pastor's Aid.—To report to the pastor daily or weekly for special service, personal work, errands, etc., in his behalf. Tired pastors welcome this committee.

Study.—To interest young people of the society and community in self-improvement, good reading, and an education.

Newspaper.—To ascertain what papers are taken in the community. To see that there is some good religious paper in every house. To secure the subscription of every member to the GOLDEN RULE. To collect newspapers and magazines after a first reading for use elsewhere, in hospitals, on mission fields, or in families too poor to subscribe.

Home Department.—To have charge of the Home Department, of the Sunday School—canvass the parish for members; keep rolls and register; distribute and collect papers, books, etc.

Personal Work. To co-operate with the pastor in seeing that every unconverted person in the community has some Christian or Christians working and praying for his conversion.

District Prayer-Meeting.—To conduct Evangelistic prayer-meetings in outlying districts, and "cottage-meetings."

Junior Endeavor.—To have charge of the Junior Endeavor Society.

Church Prayer-Meeting.—To aid the regular prayer-meeting of the church, especially by seeing that every member of the Endeavor Society also attends and participates in this service.

Assistant Lookout.—Consisting of every faithful, active member, each one a separate committee, agreeing to watch over in Christian love from three to five other members of the society, including pastor officers and lookout committee.

"Smile 'Em Up."—To be at the door of the prayer-meeting to "smile up" people to the front seats.

"Put 'Em Out."—To "put out" unruly boys from the back seats, preserve order, etc.

Observations.—The duty of this committee is to keep their eyes open, especially to see what goes on in church. Let them notice strangers and find out who they are. Let them see who has no hymn-book, and pass one Let them see to it that the old lady in the back seat who cannot hear gets a good seat in front. Let them inspect the thermometer, open the windows on the proper side of the church when too warm, and close them when one evidently feels the draft. Let them promptly shut the blind when the light strikes some one disagreeably. This committee acts during the service, and may be very useful to pastor and congregation alike.

The Church Edifice Committee.—Sees that the audience room and edifice is in good condition for worship. They act as conscience to the sexton, and aid and abet the trustees or the society's committee. They insist on the audience-room being aired during the week and between services; suggest repairs needed; speak of the dust in the corner and the finger-marks on the paint; see that the hymn-books are in order in every pew, and erase the scribbling and comic illustrations on the lids inside. In winter they see that the church sidewalk is not the last to be cleared of snow, or to be covered with ashes when icy. In summer they pick up those "droppings of the santuary," the old bottles, hoop-skirts and debris that find a refuge under the eaves of the church. They remove noisy boys from the church steps on week days, and also disturb the lovers cooing there. Committees like this may be made use of *ad libitum*. The work of the Flower, Calling and Relief Committees is important, because they lock arms with the community, and may do much to give the church a good name among those who are prejudiced against it. They co-operate with the committees of the church. Their duties may sometimes be combined.

Flower.—Somebody on it should love Christ, His little ones and the flowers. The rest should learn to. 1, Get your flowers. Find, beg, buy, borrow—or better burrow, that is, plant. Societies should have money in the treasury for this committee. In summer, pack mosses and ferns for winter use. Have a Y. P. S. C. E. garden or conservatory. Get the members to seal a pansy-bed or consecrate a rose-bush to the Master. On Flower Sunday, give out seeds or potted plants, to be raised for Christ. 2, Take the flowers somewhere,—to the church, to the prayer-meeting room, the parsonage, the grave. Take them to the sick-room, the hospital, and take them there before the petals drop off. It is time to stop sending second-hand flowers to the sick. Living plants are better for the sick-room. 3, Try to make the members of the Society love flowers, and have them on the breakfast table.

Relief.—Visit the sick and poor, and often enough to become a friend. Carry smiles, potatoes, cheer, clothing, prayers, toys, jelly, consolation, or the gospel, as the immediate necessity may be. Read to the blind and aged; watch with the sick, speak a loud word in kindness into deaf ears; take some notice of the half-witted boy; put a slipper on Cinderella. Get some of the church-members who have horses to take to ride some of those who have not,—the tired women who hardly stir out of the house or kitchen from one week's end to the other. Bring the infirm, or those at a distance, to church, on a pleasant Sunday. Take care of the baby sometimes and let the mother go.

Calling.—Know every stranger in the parish, and register facts about them. Get others to call. Get members of the Society to call on each other. Call again. Follow up acquaintances until they are secure in church and Sunday School. Look after the hotels, to invite transient visitors to church. District the parish, to systematize the work. Report to the pastor.

White Cross.—Inculcate social purity. Seek to check profanity and vulgarity. Burn the *Police Gazette*. Stop on the street to erase from fence or sidewalk offensive marking. Complain of corner loafers. Help Anthony Comstock.

Music.—Turn the musical ability of the Society to account on all religious occasions. 1, In meetings of the Society, provide organist, leader, choir, chorus, orchestra,—provide *good singing*. 2, Induce members of the Society to do their part in the singing of the Sunday School and church. 3, Offer the services of an Endeavor chorus or quartette—or soloist for any other service of the church.

These committees are not to do the work for the Society, but to see that the Society does the work. To make sure of this every society should consider itself a *committee of the whole*. In legislative assemblies this committee has three peculiarities. 1, Every member is on it 2, No sub-committee can do its work. 3, It cannot adjourn until its work is done.

THE SUNDAY SCHOOL COMMITTEE.

BY FRANK W. RUGGLES.

The Sunday School Committee should exist for the benefit of the Sunday School. It should be a large Committee. The necessity of this is obvious from the nature and extent of the work it has to perform. It should be composed of at least twenty persons. Do not place on this committee those who are disqualified for every other committee, simply to give them a place somewhere: but bring to it the young men and young women who possess agreeable address, quick, clear perception, perseverance and the habit of success. The first organization of this committee should be so arranged that one-half of the members shall serve one term, and one-half serve two terms. Then on each successive election, one-half only, of this committee will have to be newly appointed. This will leave a sufficient number of persons on the committee who are familiar with the details of the work; the new members will thus be quickly assimilated, and the work will suffer a minimum of the hindrance and interruption, incident to the surrender of old committees and the introduction of new ones. The chairman of this committee should be selected from among those who have served one term. The importance of these provisions is obvious from the nature and duration of the work of this committee.

Do not try to do the entire work of the Sunday School; leave something for the organized workers of the School to do The duties of this committee should consist mainly of securing new members for the Sunday School. There are two departments of work to this end, namely: "Auditorium and Vestibule work," and "district" or "parish" work. First, the "Auditorium and Vestibule" Work. This applies more particularly to those Sunday Schools whose exercises occur directly after the morning worship, of which there are not a few. This work must be done with dispatch and precision, for the time is short in which it can be conducted Have your committee distributed through the congregation, as uniformly as possible, and have them in their seats early. Let each one note minutely those in his or her vicinity who are not members of the Sunday School, also all visitors. The moment the benediction is pronounced, lose no time in extending an invitation to some of these persons to come into the Sunday School with you. When a person accepts your invitation, *make that person your guest* in the School for that day. If you can take care of two or three guests, secure them if possible. Better have but one than leave any without ample attention. When a person says, "Yes. I should like to go into Sunday School," do not consider your duty ended, and leave your guest to get in as best he can, or even to walk in unattended, if you do he will be more likely to walk out than to walk in. But *stick to your guest* to the very end of the service; invite him to come again ; invite him to join a class : see that he is called on during the week by as many of your friends as can make opportunity to do so. Call yourself, and invite him to come next Sunday. If by any circumstance you should be prevented from calling before the next Sunday, write your guest a note, expressing your hope to see him in Church and Sunday School next Sunday. Take pains to introduce these guests to the Superintendent, and arrange to have them introduced to a suitable class. If you are called to another class than the one to which they are assigned, first go with them and introduce them, then be sure to give them a parting greeting as they pass out, and take this time particularly, to introduce them to your friends.

If from among those in your vicinity in the congregation, no one accepts your invitation, pause in the vestibule and there continue your work until you secure some one, or until the bell calls you into School. Every member of the committee should act in like manner. As soon as you secure a guest, start with him for the School room, entertaining him with agreeable conversation, though he be a stranger to you. If, as you pass, you have opportunity to give another invitation, give it. More often than otherwise, however, one guest is all that one person can successfully attend to Hence the need of a large committee. You will find that your knowledge of the *personel* of the School will increase marvelously as you pursue this work.

Second. The "District, or Parish" work. District the parish, and detail your committee for visitation. We are going to know why so many are out of the Sunday School; they are not going to stay out from lack of an invitation. This work requires a large Committee, and it requires that tact, discrimination and good judgement be exercised by each member. Obtain all the information you can, bearing on the purpose in hand, concerning the residents in each district, before beginning the first round of visitation. The first visit will enable you to make the acquaintance and secure the names of those who do not attend Sunday School, and to give them an invitation to attend your School—subsequent visits will be for the purposes of thorough supervision of the field.

Study carefully your mode of approaching and conducting this work. Great skill and tact is necessary, likewise prayerfulness. Avoid obtrusiveness, use care on this point. Make yourself a welcome, though brief visitor. Carry greetings from your School—The purpose is to know your parish, aud to get its residents into your Sunday School. In case teachers are unable to look after absent members, that work may be delegated to this Committee by the Superintendent or the proper officer of the School. This Committee may also be helpful by providing the Superintendent with a list of substitute teachers. This would be an invaluable resource for the Superintendent to rely on. Finally let this Committee place itself at the service of the Superintendent for such work as he may wish to delegate to it, inside the School.

Special Features of Society Work.

THE PRAYER-MEETING—HOW IT MAY BE IMPROVED.

BY W. H. CHILDS.

This subject implies at the outset that we have a prayer-meeting, but it does not state what kind of a meeting it is that we are to try to improve. I will presume then that it is an Endeavor meeting, and that the Society has been but recently organized. It is obviously impossible in the ten minutes allotted to this discussion to give the details of many methods. The desire, rather, is to suggest topics that may be brought out in detail in the discussion which follows. My remarks, then, will bear the same relation to the discussion that the headlines do to a newspaper article, simply to attract your attention and give you a foretaste of the good things that are to follow.

I shall not mention many original or perhaps new things, to many of you, but rather those methods which have been tested, and which have demonstrated their practical value in different localities. Let us always have ushers at the doors of our prayer-meeting room, not alone to welcome strangers, but to seat our own members near the leader. A Society in Middletown, Connecticut, call the ushers their "Smile them-up Committee," because it is their duty to smile up the members into the front seats. Let your members understand that the front seats are reserved for them, not alone to help the leader, but so that those who are not members may not be crowded into the very back seats or perhaps out of the room into the street. Have a five or ten-minute singing service before the opening hour. Nothing attracts young people from the outside like good, lively music, wafted to them through the open windows of our prayer-meeting room. Private prayer at home by individual members, just before coming to the meeting, and also a five or ten-minute preliminary prayer-meeting of a half dozen or so, always including the leader, in some ante-room of the chruch, give a sure inspiration to the service. In the prayer-meeting the church custom of bowing the head a moment in silent prayer just after taking the seats is beneficial, not only to those who do it, but to those who see it.

Upon the blackboard to one side of the leader is printed the subject of the meeting, with perhaps added a verse of Scripture, or a free translation of the subject for the benefit of the younger members. We hear constant exhortations upon the use of the blackboard in our Sunday Schools. We should be keen enough to use these same advantages for our prayer-meetings.

Our meeting opens with a young lady in the chair, as should be the case at least half the time in an Endeavor meeting, let her give out clearly the hymn, so that all may hear it. Let her read the Scripture, making such remarks as she chooses upon the subject, and then lead personally in prayer, asking others, if she chooses, to follow. The courage thus displayed is sure to be effective upon the meeting. Let the singing during the meeting be started often from the floor, without the use of the organ. An unexpected quartette of chorus song appropriate to the subject is effective. The repeating of the Lord's Prayer, the Apostles' Creed, or the First Psalm near the opening of a meeting helps members to accustom themselves to the sound of their own voices. Now, the service is thrown open, and the responsibility is shifted from the shoulders of the leader to those of the members present. Don't let us make a mistake right at this point over a misconception of what a good Endeavor Prayer-meeting is. Upon the wall, back of the leader, is printed in bold type our Prayer-meeting pledge which says, "That every active member should take some part in every meeting." No Endeavor Prayer-meeting, however spiritual, however uplifting, is a good Endeavor Prayer-meeting, if a quarter or a half of the members present have broken that pledge.

The primary object of an Endeavor meeting is the growth resulting to each individual member from a regular participation in each service. You ask if an insistence upon this principle might not sometimes lessen the tone and earnestness of our meetings. You say, "Is it not better for the society, as a whole, that Deacon A., who can pray with such power, who can speak in such an interesting and instructive manner, should speak or pray for five minutes, than that Jimmie C. over yonder should say his verse, which, perhaps, has no application to the subject whatever?" I say No, emphatically No. The prime aim of the Endeavor Prayer-meeting is not to have a spiritual or even pleasing service, but to make Deacon A's out of Jimmie C's. As a fact of actual experience, this system deepens, rather than lessens, the spirituality of our meetings, and constantly and steadily increases their earnestness and power. Anything, then, which helps towards this result improves the prayer-meeting. Brevity on the part of every member is required, that all may have an opportunity to take part. When the leader says, "In the next five minutes let us have ten or fifteen short prayers," don't get up and pray for seven minutes.

Let the prayer-meeting committee be ready to take part at the very beginning, so that none may be crowded out at the end of the meeting for want of time. Let the lookout committee check the attendance and participation of every member so that a few earnest words may prevent the failure of the few becoming by natural accretion the silence of the many. This disease is one which spreads rapidly, and one which strikes the very heat, that very life of our organization, and this system has been as practically successful in stopping it as anything yet tried. No meeting should close without, if there is time, an opportunity being given to those who are not members to confess Christ. There is no better way to close a meeting than, after rising and singing, to have the pastor lead in a few earnest words of prayer, to enable the members to carry the thought of the meeting home with them. In some societies when the Endeavor meeting precedes the evening service, the following plan of united service has been successfully used. After a forty or fifty-minute Endeavor service, led by one of the members who sit in the front seats, the pastor and the leader, without any break in the service change places. The pastor then preaches for ten, fifteen, not to exceed twenty minutes, upon the subject of the prayer-meeting. In country towns this has, in many localities, solved the Sunday evening service problem, uniting as it does the old, young, and strangers in one service, and giving the pastors a fine opportunity to make more forcible the points brought out in the Endeavor service, and also to present Christ directly to those who are not Christians, and to follow it up when opportunity offers, with an inquiry meeting, with an abundance of workers right at hand.

I have given you hastily a few of the tested ways of improving Endeavor prayer-meetings, and in closing, to put it in a nutshell, the way to improve our prayer-meeting is to improve *ourselves*. Dr. Abbott says the service of the church should be "one-tenth worship and nine-tenths work."

I had a prayer-meeting card sent me once with the topic on it, and with this motto upon it, "Deeds, not Words," an excellent motto, but what its application was to a prayer-meeting I could not see. I would like to change it to this, "Words *and* Deeds." In our prayer-meeting we should gain an inspiration to go out and do service for Christ. The better we serve God in our prayer-meeting, the better we shall serve Him in our committee work, the better we shall serve Him in our every-day life and again, the be'ter we serve Him in these things, the better and more helpful services shall we render in our prayer-meetings. There should be a constant advance, step by step, week by week, from the prayer-meeting to every-day service, and from service back again to worship. "The goal of yesterday is but the starting place of to-day." The Christian race begins with "Lord, what wilt thou have me to do?" but it does not consist in standing all life long in the roadway asking that question. "It is a pursuit: a pursuit of an ever receding ideal; an ideal that ever beckons and ever flees before that we may follow after." Dr. Horace Bushnell says, "The grandest attribute of the human minds, one that belongs to no other finite creature whatever, is that they have the gift of a growth everlasting." Prof. Henry Drummond says, "What the churches of Christ need to-day is not more men, but a better brand of men." That is what our Endeavor prayer-meetings are for. Through the power and the guidance of the Holy Spirit may they accomplish it.

THE CONSECRATION MEETING.

BY REV. W. G. POOR.

The central reason for the success of our great Society is expressed in the letters that were presented last night. We might read them backwards, it seems to me, for, though we have called the Society one of Christian Endeavor, it has become a God-blest Society, because it exalts Christ, and that is the thought about which all the prayer-meetings and the discussions tend, to exalt Christ. We are told by one of those loving apostles, "Sanctify in your hearts Christ as Lord," and we are guided further by many an illustration from the other apostles, and from Christ himself, to understand that we are to seek to have the very mind of Christ Jesus. The principle of consecration stands as the power at the centre to hold the other two forces that are natural to young manhood and young womanhood, to hold those forces from becoming tangential, the force of enthusiasm, and the force of energy, through natural, youthful perseverance. Either one of those by itself might lead us into danger, if not into peril, and peril to our very institution. Consecration stands not only as the power which holds those forces true, but it is the power which helps us to further understand that the power of Christ is His own life. The consecration meeting in its first sense becomes something like that gathering which was held when a small band of Israelites were preparing to go forth against an unnumbered force of Midianites. The consecration service acts just the way it did then, to take out those who have chronic toothache, or chronic colds, or chronic sore throats on the prayer-meeting night, and to send them somewhere else until they can endeavor to exalt Christ continually. And that very principle which would weed out that which is not true and constant, will also give, by the blessing of the Lord Jesus, a new power. That principle is the first thought in the consideration of the consecration meeting, that it determines who are the ones who mean what they say in their pledges, and who will keep their vows to the Lord It also discovers the unfaithful ones and sets them one side, still continuing to pray for them, however, that they may come back and try again to become fully consecrated And right there is the thought from the Scripture that shows what is the test sometimes for every one of us; we learn only from the Lord that we have to pass an examination in order to become his followers. "He that will not take up his cross daily and follow after me cannot be my disciple;" and that enters into the thought of the consecration meeting. Once more, the consecration meeting brings us to the point when we put aside ourselves, not alone in the way of repeating Scripture passages, not alone in the way of learning, for the first time perhaps, what those hymns that we sing mean, not alone in trying to come nearer to Christ by our weak efforts in the beginning, but by having Christ come into us. I believe that the world, at least our country and all its churches, is learning for the first time what it means to receive the Christian's full inheritance. Those men who wrote this New Testament could not have been mistaken, that beloved Peter could not have been mistaken when he wrote, "Hereby are given unto us great and precious promises," in order that we might become partakers of the Divine nature. Christ was not mistaken when he said to His disciples, "As the Father hath sent me, so have I sent you." The consecration meeting brings that thought out more and more, and the continual blessing of it comes in the fact that it makes the next meeting, the second meeting and the third, up to another consecration meeting more and more like the consecration meeting that preceded it. It teaches us that we need not think that we have many troubles, and it teaches a great many timid Christians that they are sacrificing themselves, and that they are showing their love to Christ just as truly by being willing to fail for Christ's sake in leading the meeting, or in speaking in the meeting, as if it were positive they would say something to the edification of all present.

You will pardon a personal reminiscence on that point. It has touched me more deeply than anything else that I have seen, even in Christian Endeavor. A young person who had an impediment in speech had felt for some weeks that the Lord had called upon her to try to lead the meeting, but she had continually urged this difficulty, until at last, with tears in her eyes and in her voice too, she said, "I will fail for Jesus' sake, if, by doing that, I can serve Him better." Of course the meeting was a very decided drawing of us all unto the Lord, and of course she didn't fail, because she was willing to try.

Once more this power of the Lord Jesus by which He reaches forth and holds us from making mistakes on either the one hand or the other, is the central part of our Christian Endeavor work, but, after all, it teaches through the Scriptures, through the communion with Himself in our prayers, to study, not the meaning of the name of Christ, not the pathways He trod, it teaches not even to try to sift out His different statements except as we do all this, that we may gain within ourselves the vitality of Jesus Christ himself. That is what Christian Endeavor has shown to many of us for the first time, that we are to study the secret of Christ's life, that we are to understand that unknown food that kept Him sustained by the well of Samaria, that could make Him, not alone on the cross, not alone in Pilate's judgment hall, but everywhere, so tranquil and full of thoughtfulness and tender love for everyone. That vitality of His is what the Christian Endeavorer is studying, and, of course, having studied this—for out of the abundance of the heart the mouth must speak—his life becomes more and more shaped by that consciousness of Christ within him. What a motto it is for one who is following Christ in our Christian Endeavor ranks to have written all through his spiritual circulation this determination, "For me to live is Christ," "For me to live is Christ." And the life which we now live in the flesh we live not by our inheritance from our parents or by our own power to make ourselves successful, but we live that life by the blessing of the Son of God and by His life within us; and the consecration meeting has suddenly brought out that thought, and it should do so more and more.

A word or two about the singing. It is a very lofty prayer, it is one of abandonment for the Lord, to pray, "Lord, wilt Thou crucify me if Thou canst not get me any nearer by any other means." I have noticed that my own people sing "Nearer, my God, to Thee," with a great deal of caution, and sometimes, since we have learned that thought through Christian Endeavor, we know that they are uttering a falsehood. They don't sing that first verse—they do not mean it. "By the Cross would I come near to Thee"—no, they dare not say it, nor do many of us, when we sing that beautiful hymn of Dr. Palmer's, written in his earlier manhood, "My faith looks up to Thee," mean what we say. We have not always meant that hymn when we prayed it, but we are learning from all these actual contacts with Christ, not alone to receive impressions from Him, but that we cannot worship unless we give expression, and that expression means new pledges, means deeper loyalty, means a more abiding faithfulness.

Just one more thought, and that is on the possibility of making the consecration meeting a means of coming close unto Christ Himself. One of our sculptors early in this century, I believe, determined to do the crowning work of his life in executing a statue of Christ, and he knew that the best success would be the judgment of some young girl. He worked upon it nearly a year, and, veiling it, called into his studio one morning, a little maiden who lived next door, and as he removed the cloth he asked her, "Who is this?" She looked at it carelessly, and turning away said, "Some great man," and the sculptor with great chagrin saw that he had failed. He determined that he would succeed, and at the end of seven years, after a great deal of study of the Gospel, after more communion with Jesus Christ, in his own heart, after seeing how the heart of Christ itself had existed within that human frame, he had by touches here, and new touches there changed that block of stone until, when he had called that maiden, now a young woman, in again, as he removed the cloth, she fell upon her knees and said, "That is my Master." That thought is the one that has come out. We have all noticed it in our Christian Endeavor work, in each different Endeavorer, in the spirit of each prayer-meeting, - another touch, a new thought from Christ, and we learn to express Christ by having Him within our own hearts and knowing that in all we do and say Christ's spirit indeed throbs within us.

"EVERY PRAYER-MEETING A PLACE FOR DECISION."

BY REV. J. F. BRANT.

This sentiment, coming, as it does, from headquarters, and suggested by our worthy president, is characteristic of the whole Christian Endeavor movement, as one the most apostolic and aggressive forms of Christian service of our times. The word "endeavor" the word "decision" the *en devoir* of the French. meaning "on duty," has had a tocsin ring throughout our land, and has given great popularity to the new movement. If we can now yoke with the word "endeavor" the word "decision" and send out from this Convention the watchword: " Every meeting a place for *decision*," we shall give to this new movement the swing of victory, and meet one of the deepest wants of the church.

This deepest want is not more intelligent and instructive ministers; not even more consecrated and devout workers. The field is well occupied with these already. Not more Christian sentiment. For by 250 years of faithful preaching of the Word, our land is filled to-day with the *sentiments* of Christianity but is wanting in that element of moral decision which acts promptly on principle, and for principle's sake alone. There is a defective balance in the assay office on Wall Street, New York, which illustrates this thought. It is as sensitive as quicksilver to any inequality in the weight of coin which may be rolled over its surface, but lacks decision, or promptness, in registering that inequality. This is the public conscience in and out of the church to-day It will be the mission of the Society of Christian Endeavor to train this sensitiveness of Christian feeling to reach up into the realm of will and purpose, where character is made, and achieve victories worthy of the Cross. The colossal failure of the church in general to exercise that peculiar fact which can lead a religiously moved soul to decide *now* for Christ, has created a wide-spread demand for evangelists, whose chief mission is to emphasize this *now* element of the gospel which we are discussing.

Take the picture of Mr. Moody seated on some manmoth platform, surrounded by the representative scholarship of his generation. What is the one central point of interest toward which those keen, observant ministers and Christian workers are looking? It is the peculiar tact and inspired strategy by which he is to lead long convinced and even convicted souls to decide *now* for Christ. What Mr. Moody and other successful evangelists and ministers are doing in an eminent degree, the church, through the Christian Endeavor Society inspired by this sentiment," Every meeting a place for decision ," may be doing throughout a much wider field. The average soul needs the cumulative impetus of an earnest Christian service to help it to its highest moral decisions. Left alone, the human soul vacillates, and native evil is amost sure to cast the deciding vote against it. Without the helpful influence of some such services, where moral decisions were planned for, urged, and expected, the most of us would be Jean Valgeans, who had heard "the soul's laughter at itself for its vacillation and indecision." If we would make apostolic draughts for Christ's kingdom, a net must be cast about the people, with finer meshes than that woven by an elegant sermon, and knotted with a graceful benediction.

"*Now* is the accepted time, *now* is the day of salvation." " Now, DECIDE NOW," is to be the thrilling appeal of the Society of Christian Endeavor, as well as of the God-inspired evangelist. The church, as never before, is ready to hear this from laymen's lips. All the forces of the church are to be called into the field, and a forward movement is demanded. During our late war there came a time when Gen. Sheridan wrote to Gen. Grant, " Things are in a shape to push." And then the time came when Gen. Grant wrote back to Sheridan, " Push things!" And the world knows the magnificent results of obedience to that famous order. Christian workers all over our land, as they have studied the field, the equipment of the church, the needs of the masses, and God's providence, have been saying, " The time has come to push things," and God is answering back through the Society of Christian Endeavor, " Push things!" With our glorious motto, " For Christ and the Church," and the sentiment, " Every meeting a place for decision," let us push for conquest.

OUR ASSOCIATE MEMBERS.—HOW SHALL WE REACH THEM?

BY REV. T. B. WILSON.

I am certain, Mr. President, that I have nothing to say on the topic, " Our Associate Members," worthy the six thousand ears of this assemblage, but if I understood my commission I am not expected to edify these six thousand ears, but, if possible, to make the three thousand tongues with which they correspond, anxious to make themselves heard in a debate upon the problem of our associate membership. I have used the word "problem" because neither associate membership in the Y. P. S. C. E., nor any other device, will accomplish the salvation of young people so rapidly as we would like to see it accomplished. " The greatest study of mankind is man," sings Pope; we take up the strain, and add, " The greatest study of the Christian man is the unsaved man." I have often been interested in turning over the leaves of an old Patent Office report, and judging what have been the hard problems of the world, as indicated by the number of patented attempts to solve them. And with regard to the mass of these problems on which patents are piling up by the hundred, year by year, such as coupling cars, furnishing us buttons which will give us no trouble of any kind, devices to shut off annoyances and nuisances, and devices to ease the drudgery of the household, the factory and farm, it may be taken for granted that only a part of the problem is soluble, and that the inventors are merely offering you your choice among partial solutions.

That all-absorbing problem for the Christian world is how to make Christians. To make them as rapidly as we would *like* to is an absolute problem, and *all* our most approved methods of Christian work are partial solutions. As to the methods of approaching it, some discoveries have been made. Chief among them is that we should begin with the youth. But, having begun with the youth, just how to proceed to obtain the best results, that is the ever-recurring problem At this hour we are to discuss *one* of the methods or devices recommended as more or less effective in Christianizing youth, viz , Associate Membership in Societies of Christian Endeavor. Is this the best method we may use, or shall we look for and work for another? Can we improve this one?

I suppose the first question we should ask ourselves with reference to the class of our youth, whom we are studying especially to reach, is, why have they not been reached already? The answers to these questions we know to be many and various. For one thing, we shall find that half our youth have the strangest and wildest ideas as to what Christianity is. It is a cyclone which passes over some people, and sets them marching for the rest of their days in a funeral procession. Or, it is a curious change that passes over a person, and, after it, he looks upon most sport as wrong ; would rather visit his grandmother's grave than go to the circus; and is willing to wear an awful millstone of piety around his neck forevermore. Not if he knows it, says one of these, shall any such thing fasten its clutch upon him. Or, again, take another case. This time he is one who had heard all his life, in his own home, that Christianity is hypocrisy. His infidel father has let pass no occasion for saying it, and his thoughtless and worldly mother has echoed it. How is he to be disabused of the idea? Or, again, his parents set him the example, in saying, "I make no professions." He is the third fellow in the parable who said, "I go not," and then didn't go. Or, again, his mother is a noble, praying, Christian woman, but his father is not only a scoffer, but has a moral weakness, and the son knows it. Thus the father stands squarely across the pathway in which the son ought to go. Or, yet again, both parents may be true and devoted Christians, and perhaps with the best of training, and perhaps with ill-judged training, the son is determined to go astray and be wild.

Let these few examples serve to point the remark we have made before, that, in reaching the shy, the prejudiced, the tempted young people, we have before us a problem which may not be finally and fully solved. And yet we have a feeling that our responsibility is *first* toward these shy, prejudiced, mistaken young people. who flutter around the edges of the kingdom, but who do not as yet harbor for an instant the thought of themselves coming into it. I say our first responsibility lies here, for many of these are our sons and daughters, our brothers and sisters. I used to be told when I was a small boy, and wanted to catch birds (as every small boy does, isn't it curious?), that if I could only put a little salt on their tails that was all that was necessary. I take it our associate membership is a device for landing a little of the salt of Christianity on the tails of some of these wild birds. It is, I suppose, a device for utilizing Christian young people as decoys for enticing their shy and prejudiced friends near enough to the kingdom to see what a different thing it is from what they had always supposed it was. I suppose it is a means of convincing the youth who has always waited outside the church door, to walk home with his girl, that nobody is going to hurt him, and that he will be a great deal more comfortable, if he does his waiting inside.

Coming now to the question assigned me somewhat more exactly, let us ask ourselves whether anything can be done to quicken the transit of our shy young people, who have ventured into associate, into full and active membership. And first of all, at this point let us try to appreciate the unspeakable importance of accomplishing this delicate, this slow, this special mission of Y. P. S. C. E., to-wit, bringing these front, these inmost files of the multitude who are attracted by the teachings of Christ, bringing these over into full, avowed, loving, working discipleship. So far as my own observation has gone, there are parts of the work that have attracted our attention, exercised us more, called out our helps and suggestions, and our prayers, beyond this feature of Associate Membership. But let us ask ourselves fairly, squarely, solemnly, at this hour, whether there is or ever can be *any* endeavor, whether spelled with a small or a capital E, to be compared for an instant with that which we may by any means bring to bear to assist one soul. With this glance at the supreme importance of the work with and for our Associate members, we are ready to inquire whether we may be able in any way to improve this priceless opportunity and discharge this intense responsibility. Our first impulse is perhaps to invoke first of all the aid of the Sociable, the lawn-fete, the oyster, the lemon, the dish of cream, the slice of cake, the charade, the button-hole bouquet. But while anything and everything which *can* be consecrated to the use of the kingdom should be, still, let us recall that the gospel once goes out of its way to mention the difference between eating and drinking in the Lord's presence and entering in by the straight gate. While therefore I would not discourage the oyster in his mission, nor melt down the influence of the ice-cream, nor dilute the efficacy of the lemonade, still, let us all recognize most properly the absolute subordination of all such agencies in the great work which God is giving us a rare chance to do. And now let me sacrifice this whole address,—let it all serve merely as forceps for seizing and lifting before all eyes the proposition that the means beyond all others of helping, reaching the Associate member, is for the Active member to show him a Christianity loved and lived. The means of reaching the Associate member is the *active* member. That which is blocking his pathway is to-day the *inactive* member. The Associate member has come near, and is for the moment looking to see just what we mean by all our exhortations and invitations. Now is the time to show him what kind of young people are saved young people, and what kind of endeavor is Christian Endeavor. It is said that Benjamin Franklin labored hard to convince the farmers of his day that plaster enriched the soil. All his philosophical arguments failed to convince them, so he took plaster and formed it into a sentence by the roadside. The wheat coming up through those letters was about twice as rank and green as the the other wheat, and the farmers could read for months, in letters of living green, *This has been plastered*.

I would then reach our Associate members with kept pledges; I would reach them by an exhibition of what kind of young people are Christian and consecrated young people; I would like to reach them by showing them just how God's great salvation is adapted to live, tempted, pleasure-loving youth, to make them stronger, nobler, heartier. I would reach them by means of young men who are strong, and have overcome the wicked one; I would reach them by showing them what are some of the *real* pleasures of life; I would reach them with youth who agree with the dictionary exactly as to what is meant by the word "necessity;" I would show them youth, who understand the expression "every meeting" to cover any and all meetings; I would reach them by making the "long pause" so short that two or three often sought to speak at once; I would catch them with the guile of earnestness, sincerity, Christian joy; and, once caught, I would make them fast with the "blest tie that binds in Christian love." Thus would I reach our Associate members.

JUNIOR SOCIETIES.

BY REV. W. F. MCMILLEN.

This hour is to be devoted to Junior Societies, by which I suppose is meant the work among the younger young people. Mr. Hill, in his address on the first afternoon of this Convention, practically made my address, only he made it to the older young people. I am to make it in behalf of the boys and girls of this great country, yea, and of the world. It is fitting that this convention devote a few moments of time to the consideration of the work of the Junior Societies. I do not, however, come to you with any marked experience as to the working of the Junior Societies, as such, because, as you know, this work is comparatively new and must needs grow more and more before we can offer anything like tabulated statistics or especially successful methods, but I regard it as a special privilege to speak this morning in behalf of the boys and girls of this great nation.

There are in the United States seven million youth between the ages of six and twenty-one outside of churches, Sunday Schools and Christian Endeavor Societies. This great and grand convention means more, in its possibilities, to this outlying mass of neglected children and youth than any yet held. The need of junior societies is obvious when we consider two or three facts.

1. The deficiency of religious training in so many of our American homes. To the home, belongs, primarily the duty of instructing the young in the knowledge of God and His Word. The family is a divine institution, an organic relation, which God has established for His own use, His own honor and glory. This sacred institution is the germ from which every other institution has grown in which men are organized for mutual assistance. The church and the school have their origin here. For centuries the only church God had in the world was the church in the family. God ordained the husband and father the religious instructor of his own household. This parental responsibility has not been abrogated. In these days when the duties of pastors and teachers to the children and youth are constantly reviewed, there is some danger of forgetting almost entirely the parents. The relation of the parent to the child is primary and paramount. No duty of one human being to another is more direct, positive, and intransferable than that of the parent to educate his children, both intellectually and religiously. This duty cannot be delegated. The most important part of the child's education must be given by the parents. The first few years of the child's are life entirely in the hands of the parents. The services they are asked to render are personal services. God will not dishonor His covenant with faithful parents. Covenant blessings are transmitted by law of descent. God is a jealous God, visiting the iniquity of the fathers upon the children to the third and fourth generation of them that hate him, and showing mercy unto the thousandth generation of them that love him and keep his commandments. The family then is not only a divine institution, from God and belonging to God, but if rightly employed it is the most effective agency for promoting youthful piety. Paul's address to Timothy teaches us that there is a possibility of a transmitted aptitude for faith. He speaks of "the unfeigned faith that is in thee; which dwelt first in thy grandmother Lois, and thy mother Eunice; and I am persuaded in thee also." The early and familiar intercourse which the parent has with his children gives him the most favorable opportunity for teaching and leading them into the ways of the Lord. The hold which he has upon their affections gives a charm and a weight to his instructions, which no one else can rightfully claim. It is to be deplored that this conception of the privilege and mission of the home has so largely faded from the minds of many parents. It is sadly true that multitudes of fathers and mothers take no interest in the religious training of their children. To meet this widespread deficiency of parental care the Junior Society, along with the other similar agencies, finds its pressing necessity.

2. Another reason for Junior Societies is shown when we consider

their relation to the Church. One of the greatest difficulties which I have had to contend with in organizing societies of Christian Endeavor has been to make, not only churches, but some pastors to see that a true Christian Endeavor is really an aid to the church; that it is not an institution outside of the church, but in the church and for the church, and will be the more successful as it is kept under the wing of the church. When I have succeeded in showing this I have had no difficulty in securing an organization. I believe in and especially advocate the Sunday School idea, but only as a department of the church. I have been asked a great many times, "if your boy could go but to the one service, would you send him to the preaching service, or to the Sunday School service," and sometimes the question has been as to the "Christian Endeavor service," and I say, "by all means, if my boy could go but to the one he should go to the preaching service." I do not believe that with all these popular movements that God is wheeling into line for the evangelization of the masses that we dare forget that He has ordained the church as the channel through which He has said He will bless the individual, the state, and the nation. Indeed he has gone so far as to say that "the gates of hell shall not prevail against her." To neglect this work of christian instruction is in effect to weaken every phase of church influence, and to increase the evil, already too much to be deplored, of thinly attended churches and declining congregations. If, therefore, we would keep up the attendance and increase that attendance we must, as the church is arousing to this work, vigorously take hold of the young, and keep hold of them by all the means in our power. We must earnestly desire to have them become trained and skilled workers, as well as liberal and influential members of the church. To do this we should teach them the possibilities of passing from a state of innocence to a state of grace so that they may never know a time when they were converted, when they did not pray; but, on the contrary, that they always prayed and loved the Lord Jesus Christ. The idea is to train them not so much for the church but in the service of the church and for Christ. We should receive children who give evidence of piety into the membership of the church. The atmosphere of the churches in this regard is greatly changing, so that not only an occasional, favored child in the community is received, but the number of such accessions is quite large and constantly increasing.

There are three lines in particular along which our youth need special training; worship, work and systematic giving. Above all other services the church service is best calculated to exalt worship. The sacred church walls, the ordained ministry, the precious gospel, the inspiring hymns, all conspire to make lasting impressions upon the child mind. Now as to the work of the church: I wanted to get up and clap both my hands when Mr. Hill said, "we see so many men and women in the churches to-day who are not practical christians. They are not ready to respond when you call upon them to pray or speak or do just a little work. Now I say that in all other lines of business every young man and lady is trained for a special vocation, and every business firm feels the need of this young blood. Shall the Church of Jesus Christ in this advanced and aggressive age of the world be without its trained workers? Shall we have a mass of men and women who cannot, who say they will not, pray and take hold of the practical work of the church? Not long ago an expert for the McCormick Self Binder said, "I was called to go a hundred miles recently to put my hand to just a little piece of machinery to set that binder in order." Now if the farmer had known just where to put his hand it would have saved all that long travel in a busy season. What we want in our church work is experts, men who know where to touch and whom to touch; persons who will make a business of their religion and a religion of their business. How are you going to get such workers if you do not commence with the boys and girls? We have young men in the various professions going to and from the churches, at least occasionally, who do not think to give a single penny of their substance during the entire year, to the support of the Gospel and the extension of the kingdom of Christ. I think it is essential that every boy and girl should be provided with an envelope just the same as the parents, and should contribute regularly every week to the Lord's treasury. This habit, once formed, will remain to bless the individual and the cause of Christ throughout one's entire life. We ought to be more in sympathy with the boys and girls. They should feel a hearty welcome in the various work of our churches. The older Christian Endeavor Societies should extend to the junior a hearty support. A little boy nine years old was the life of my young men's prayer meeting; a little girl about the same age wanted to be admitted to the Communion, and she was received into the church. It was but a little time until her father, nearly fifty years of age and hardened in sin, came and offered himself for membership in the church. I tell you that we are neglecting one of the greatest holds in church work when we neglect the work among the children.

3. Another reason why I believe in junior societies is that childhood is the formative period of life, the time for impression. The child-mind is most receptive and most responsive. No intelligent reformer has ever arisen, desiring to secure abiding results, who has not sought to secure his chief success in the young, in the generation that was to come after him. Another has said, "that when Cataline would overthrow the liberties of Rome he began by corrupting the young, especially the sons of the nobility. When Voltaire and his fellow-conspirators against the welfare of France sought to revolutionize that country, they commenced by corrupting the moral code of the nation, as taught to the young. When Moses would restore the lost image of God to fallen humanity, he received the moral law from heaven and then enjoined it in these words, "And these words which I command thee this day shall be upon thy heart, and thou shalt teach them diligently unto thy children, and thou shalt talk of them when thou sittest in thy house, and when thou walkest by the way, when thou liest down and when thou risest up." When the Saviour would test the love of the Apostles he said "Feed my lambs." When John Knox would place the Reforma-

tion in Scotland on the deepest and strongest foundation he placed a school-house by the side of every church, that the doctrines taught in the pulpit by the minister, might be imparted to every child of the church by the school-master. The same wisdom should be ours. The hope of our homes, of our churches and of our nation lies with the children. This work of training devolves very largely upon you young ladies assembled here in this convention. I appeal to you to-day; the married ladies, perhaps, and mothers, who like Hannah of old, have prayed for a son that you might give him to the Lord in blessed consecration for service.

As to who should belong to the junior societies, how to start them, their relation to the older society, the pledge they should make, I refer you to President Clark's little pamphlet on junior societies.

I will close by citing you a paragraph I have read since coming to this convention in one of the papers published in this city. It is stated there, that there are "WANTED: FIVE MILLION AMERICAN BOYS." Who wants them? the question is asked, and the answer is there printed. "The American saloons." Who else wants them? The church of Jesus Christ. Who shall have them? What shall be the answer?

The paper goes on to say that the answer will be deferred until the meeting of this great convention, and prays that God may give the young people here gathered, the wisdom and the grace to answer. I want to ask you from New York, and Massachusetts and Connecticut; from Florida and the South; from California and the great West; from Ohio and the middle states; what is your answer? How do you propose to answer this great question? Will you answer it, "The boys and girls of this great nation for Jesus Christ and His Church."

QUESTION BOX.

CONDUCTED BY REV. JAMES L. HILL.

"Is it wise for a Society to take Church members as associate members where they do not become active members on account of the inability to keep the prayer-meeting pledge?"

You had better appoint a meeting for special prayer for such church members as don't want to be active members. Let me say this: never make your associate list a black list. As a lady very well said once, in my hearing, "it makes a difference which way an associate member is faced. The associate list is just as legitimate a part of our active work as is the active list. Said a little miss on her way home with her sister—they were both talking—"what is the difference between an active member and an associate member?" "Why," said the one talking at the same time as the one asking the question, "why, the active members are those who are Christians, and the associate members are those who are just going to be".

What is the best means to raise money to meet current expenses?"

So that all will have a chance to know, I will tell you of a good way to raise money for the Society expenses; that is what we call the Envelope system. We have more than eighty persons who give systematically. We want our 197 members all to give, every soul, and if it were not for taking the time I would show you that if each one should give five cents a Sunday we should be in the same fix as the United States goverment; we would have to find out what we should do with our surplus.

"Ought Societies of Christian Endeavor to exclude the older members from membership or from its prayer-meetings?"

Yes and no. It is distinctly a young people's Society of Christian Endeavor. If they embarrass you in any way by their presence, and it cannot be a young people's meeting, they ought not to be present. In our own Society it makes no difference, as we do just the same for a thousand as for fifty. We are always glad of visitors. It is a Young People's Society of Christian Endeavor, the word is there and it is there to stay.

"Is the Prayer meeting pledge essential to a Society of Christian Endeavor?"

I would like to see the person who wrote that. There is no true Society of Christian Endeavor without it. Like the distinction between the animal kingdom and the human family, it is drawn at that point where you have ability to light a fire,—the animal cannot light a fire and a man can. Just so it is here. The distinction is drawn at the point of the prayer meeting pledge. If you have it you are a Society of Christian Endeavor, but if you do not have it you are not.

"Is it advisable to have the Lookout Committee composed of the Chairmen of other Committees?"

Why, no. What is the use of limiting yourselves to a few? All tendencies should be the other way, to bring in the members of your Society to the work of the Committees, and don't make up the Lookout Committee of the Chairmen of the other Committees. You don't need to do it.

"Is it best to retain a member of each committee more than six months"

Well, that depends upon the strength of your Society. We have such men in our own society, our President served us so well that we re-elected him. Finally they said, "this thing is going too far and we re-appoint these members with this understanding, that at the next election of officers no person who serves this society in any way shall be eligible, and any committee ought to know best what to do and go right on with it." That is the strength of the society, and it has not suffered in any particular. We distrust the idea.

"Which prayer meeting would you advise young people to attend when they say they can attend but one?"

The church prayer meeting every time. Do not have any tilt between the two. Some persons will sometimes say, "don't the attendance upon the young people's society interfere with the attendance upon the regular prayer meeting?" Why, no, they are not in competition in any way. A person might as well ask me if attendance upon the primary school did not interfere with a person being at the breakfast table. They are not in comparison; one of them is a training school, the other is a higher place. They are not competitors, they are not antagonistic in any way.

Here is—I would not say a chestnut; I would simply say a burr. "What is the age limit" — I won't read the rest of the question. I know what is coming.

I would simply say that there is no age limit. We always have that question asked. It does not depend upon age; it depends upon good health. If you have the dyspepsia or the jaundice you are too old at thirteen.

"What are the benefits to be derived from membership in the National organization?"

Well, I would like to see the person who wrote that. Why, that person has turned the whole thing round. The thing is the other way. Why, we are a missionary organization. We believe that it is more desirable to effect the christian work in our churches than to build up a specific work in Smithville, or in any other specific place. If you give $200 to some form of work you effect the work in one place. If you give money to us it may be that you will effect the work of God throughout the length and breadth of our land. It is of course desirable that we should have the opportunities of doing our work, but who will pay for it? We ask you to pay for it; we ask you to help pay for it. You come and ally yourselves with us to enable us to help to bear these expenses?

"In the case of a society not now a member of the National organization how shall we best convince its members of the benefits to be derived from membership?"

If I had time I would turn to the last of the gospel of Matthew. "Go ye into all the world and preach the gospel," and when you go into all the world identify yourself with the regular organization for doing the work.

"Should the roll call ever be dispensed with at the Consecration meeting?"

No. Our president has a very graceful and happy way of getting along with it. We have a very large society and sometimes it is necessary to hasten through. We meet fifteen minutes earlier at our experience meeting in order to give our membership an opportunity. Our President sits after the roll call, we will say here, and we pass right across the room taking the first seat, and then we begin at the next seat and so we go right through the house. What we want in an experience meeting is to designate the time at which the members shall participate in the meeting. You may have it either in the roll-call or by designating the time, but you will lose time unless you do something that will indicate to the person when it is time.

"How to conduct the Consecration meeting?"

Always have your book of membership with two columns of names on a page, one of them the active membership, the other the associate membership, with only one line between. Then I would have the person who is leading the consecration meeting begin to read, reading from the list, the first name which might be Annie S. Atwood. She would bow her head upon the rail of the chair in front and would respond "let us pray." The next name upon the list might be Harriet A. Green. She would bow her head upon the chair in front of her and say "let us pray," and so we would go through the entire list. Be very careful in reading to pass over the names deliberately and slow, always with falling inflection, and prayerfully and smoothly.

"What is the better time to hold the meetings, Sunday or week nights?"

It depends If you have a large Christian Endeavor, if you are doing lots of work, it is best to meet on week nights. If you have a smaller church and not so much business it is best to hold the meetings on Sunday night. Sometimes it is best to hold them before the other prayer-meeting.

"How many delegates are there in this Convention."

More than 4,000.

"What shall we do with those who have been active members and cannot attend the meetings?"

Make them do as well as they can. We used to have a hospital matron in our Society who used to sometimes send in this excuse: "detained by an amputation." When a person is detained by amputation I think he has a right to be absent. Sometimes there are persons who cannot usually be present. Never have them on the active list.

"What are the duties of the prayer meeting committee?"

Only one duty; have a good meeting.

"Do you favor uniform topics?"

Yes, because usually you get the best. Uniform topics will come just where uniform lessons are in the Sabbath school system.

"Would it be a wise thing to cut down the time taken for singing?"

Yes, yes, yes. Everybody knows what it means when you come to giving out pieces of music from the stand. Have all the impromptu singing that you can from the floor.

"What results can be pointed to in justification of the existence of the Young People's Society of Christian Endeavor?"

Think of the spirit of it; think of this great principle,—this is not the answer; this is just incidental. Now, the answer. Let me give it directly; let me give it in very few words in order that you may remember it: "What results can be pointed to in justification of the existence of the Young People's Society of Christian Endeavor?"

Just twenty-two thousand persons led to Christ in one year; that s all, and that is not one half of the answer. The great answer is this;

it has brought in not evangelists into the church, but an evangelistic movement among pastors that shall revolutionize their work. It brings every soul to a corner and makes him decide whether or not he is willing to be considered as endeavoring to lead a Christian life.

"Does not the meeting of the Young People's Society of Christian Endeavor lesson the attendance of young people at the regular prayer meeting of the church?"

No! The other night we had a little item of business in my own church, and I said it would be necessary for the Young People's Society of the Christian Endeavor, for the members present, to come and discuss the business at the end of the regular church prayer meeting, and it was done without any further introduction whatever, and do you believe that the most of the persons present came forward, and those who were remaining, not invited, felt very sorry they were not young, and felt very lonely in their situation.

"If I am present at each meeting and say a Scripture verse, does that fulfill the pledge?"

Only in the letter; not in the spirit. That matter in regard to that is simply for the use of beginners. It has reference to those persons that are new. It means to give every one a chance for participation.

"Is it advisable to start a Young People's Society of Christian Endeavor in a church where the only obstacle is the ungrounded prejudice on the part of the pastor?"

Now, I treat that with all candor and wisdom. My answer is this: if any of you young people have had better educations than your fellow-men it is not your place to correct their bad grammar. I know a man in this city who is of Irish decent, and his good old mother sits on the marble steps in front of his palace and smokes her pipe. He does not altogether like it, but, said he, "she is my mother, and there she can sit and smoke her short stem pipe." He may not believe in smoking, but it is not his place to correct his mother. It is not your place to do anything else than to be loyal to your pastor. It is your place, however, to pray for him; it is your place to come together in your company of praying christians and show your spirit, show your style, show him how desirable it would be to have those little knots of praying christians throughout the church.

"Is it best to attempt to carry on an Endeavor Society without the hearty sympathy and the co-operation of the pastor and the church?"

I want to say this; that all you young people that find yourselves in that situation, (and I am informed there are many), you have the most tender and most prayerful sympathy in your most delicate and embarrassing situation. There was a white cravated gentleman who sat next to me upon the platform yesterday when the different papers were being presented, and he would jump half way out of his seat when a sentiment was uttered, and say, "Did you hear that?" Why, it was something so dry and well worn that it seemed as if everybody must know it. If that thing could be understood in this city of Chicago this local prejudice would pass away. When those things were being offered I wondered at the nature of the man who would go over those well worn truths. We have gone everywhere at great personal sacrifice to try to make these things known, and yet they are not known, and here is a man evidently with prejudice in his heart saying to me that he has no use for these principles. We say that the desire of Christian Endeavor is of the church, is in the church, that it has no separate existence from the church, that it is to do the work of the church, that it is not to break down any denomination or religion, that it goes into the church and there to do the work of that church under the eye of the pastor, with the co-operation of the church Dear friends, you help us to let it be known.

"Should the pastor be the President, or Chairman Lookout Committee?"

No. The very idea is to aid the pastor. I never led a meeting in my life. I took care of the societies from about the beginning, but never led a meeting, never served on a committee, never expected to either.

"Is it best to have many or few committees?"

I should have just as many committees as there was work for. The more committees you have the better, if there is work for them all.

"Should a lessening of members and interest in the young people's meeting during the hot weather lead to a vacation?"

My rule is this; to advise the society never to have a poor meeting. If your meetings are poor, stop them; stop them quick. I want to say, however, that a few persons only present at a meeting does not necessarily mean a poor meeting.

"Should the young ladies as a rule lead in prayer?"

Why, yes, they are the best leaders we have.

"Should a large society with plenty of young men elect a lady President?"

I should elect the best president there was, even if it was Mrs. Cleveland.

"Is it right to drop members from the society without due notice?"

No occasion to drop any body from the society, as I said the other day; never drop anybody from the society, they drop themselves. Your rule provides for that. If they are not present at three consecutive meetings they are no longer of you. If they want to come back to you they come right back to the nominating committee. Our laws execute themselves.

"What authority, if any does the United Society have over young societies?"

None whatever.

"Is the Society of Christian Endeavor confined just to churches, or can they be organized in mission Sunday schools?"

Anywhere, but usually they are connected with a church and under the care of a pastor.

"Should the pledge for daily bible reading and prayer be included in the constitution?"

Not in the constitution. Put it in the by-laws if you have it.

Relation of the Society to the Church.

THE SOCIETY IN COUNTRY TOWNS.

BY REV. J. L. SEWALL.

In approaching the first division of the afternoon's topic, certain questions arise. Why specify the country town? why draw any line between the city church and its neighbors? Is there any ground for such discrimination? We answer, Yes. The mission of all Christian churches is indeed one, wherever in the world they exist; but locality has much to do with form and methods; environment determines type. Compare city and country churches at the point of present interest, the prayer-meeting. In starting for the social service, our Chicago friends step forth upon smooth sidewalks, and under the kindly guidance of street lamps pass the few blocks between them and their destination; or if a longer distance intervenes, the street car comes to their aid. Entering the church door, they find a room specially adapted to the purposes of the hour: good lights, comfortable, well-arranged seats,—in short, every material aid to a good prayer-meeting. Our country churches show a different picture. A scattered population; highways barely endurable at best, and for eight months in the year abounding in mud or snow drift; sidewalks, ditto; street crossings, purely imaginary; street lamps, not even imagined. The prayer-meeting room,—what is it? Perhaps a church auditorium, with its vast emptiness and dim irreligious light, or a low, unventilated basement vestry with a red-hot stove; or possibly a private dwelling house. Some of us appreciate these conditions without detailed description; our city friends can comprehend them only by experience.

Nor is the contrast simply in externals. Country isolation and city compactness represent traits of character. The solitary independence of the farmer's household discourages outside sociability; the close contact of the metropolis favors fraternal gatherings and educates toward free and fluent expression of thought. It is thus evident that the city or large village offers to our society, as an organized prayer-meeting, valuable facilities which are beyond the rural districts. It is therefore supposable that our organization might prosper in the one and fail in the other locality; and the fear of this has sometimes hindered the formation of societies in small places.

That this supposition is contrary to fact, let the reports of the morning and the words that shall follow mine bear witness. Remember that while the great majority of this audience are from large places, only one fourth the population of the United States is found in cities of over eight thousand souls; and it is safe to estimate that more than one fourth, say from fifteen to twenty millions, are living in scattered country homes, under conditions already pictured. We all believe and feel that these twenty millions need the Society of Christian Endeavor; let us see what it has done and what it can do for Christ and the Church in this distinct field.

Let me name certain particulars in which the typical country church is deficient when compared with its city neighbors. The mere mention of these points will suggest past and future triumphs of our society.

First, organization. We instinctively look to our larger places for examples of the church symmetrically equipped for work. The close scrutiny of ends and means, the assignment of the individual member to specific duty, the careful estimate of success or failure, in short, all that is covered by the phrase, "a well organized church," —these things are not usually conspicuous in a scattered community. Some do not wish organization; they regard the demand for it as dishonoring the Holy Spirit, and choose to follow the old ways into the shadow of increasing failure, rather than try new plans when old ones prove fruitless. Others would welcome helpful measures, but imagine this one available only for large bodies of believers. Still others address themselves to the task and soon find that organization implies organizers; and they look in vain for those men of affairs, whose consecrated talents so shine in some city churches. It must also be admitted and remembered that the task of reorganizing a feeble country church presents some unique problems, without parallel in larger places; a task which calls for as much energy, skill and persistence as any of the herculean labors which confront our city pastors. Some of you with a wider or different experience than mine may desire to modify the expression of these remarks; but I believe many here will agree with me in regarding lack of church organization a characteristic difficulty in rural districts.

Again, the average country church fails to find and hold the young people who belong to it. The lament of our feeble churches that their young people have vanished, is it not always well founded. Sometimes it means that the church ought to make a tour of discovery through every nook and corner of the parish, and search out young life of which it may be ignorant. Many have gone, but many are growing up in their places. True, this great west is laying its magic spell upon the best young life of our New England hill towns; the factory is robbing the plow, the counting room is proving more attractive than the dairy; but after all, it is easy to exaggerate the disappearance of young people from rural districts. The congregation and Sunday School may not see them; but it is still safe to infer that they are somewhere within town limits. The fashion which required every child, young or old, to appear in the family pew on a Sunday morning has passed into a desuetude which is by no means innocuous; but if you wish to count young faces, go to the village green during a base ball match, or to the public hall when there is a dance

In showing the existence of young people outside the cognizance of these churches, we have demonstrated what every wide observer has painfully seen, their feeble hold upon this young life. If we can discover the reasons for this, we may therein discern remedies. Some of the causes for this state of things are plain. Social gravitation attracts to the large congregation the young man who is rather repelled by the handful of worshippers. The wealthy church can furnish costly music and popular oratory, which is beyond the pocket book of the country parish.

A city church, stimulated by competition, makes special efforts to attract the young, where its country neighbor, frequently the sole possessor of the field, is heedless as to its self preservation, and passively yields to what it foolishly considers the inevitable. This is culpable inactivity. Social amusement is as essential food for the mental life of young people as is protein for their bodies; but how many churches are criminally indifferent to this truth! They practically say to youth with overflowing vitality, "Come to us for our preaching, but go to the devil for your fun!" and only the latter part of the exhortation is heeded. Young people are as sure to have social life as they are to eat; and where the church neglects its first and best chance to furnish this, Satan always gladly steps in and does the work for them. It would be unfair to imply that all city churches were fully doing, and all country churches wholly neglecting these duties; yet it is usually true, as regards social entertainment, that city youth are surfeited where their country cousins are starved; and I earnestly maintain that the general contrast here presented is a fair representation of the case.

I leave to others detailed illustration of how our society helps rural churches at these points of their distinctive weakness. Our success as a practicable organization, is in enlisting the youngest in work under wise leadership and constant responsibility;—to some chaotic churches this is a revelation of what might always have been, of what is constantly to be hereafter. The power of the society to discover young people ready for service or Christian association, gladly placing themselves in close contact with the church, and finding there a delightful centre for social, intellectual and spiritual life;—I am sure a great multitude of country pastors will join me in thankfulness for just these results, as they have come in greater or less degree. And I would earnestly insist that while the same results have gladdened city churches, we who have been aided in deeper need claim a peculiar right to emphasize our gratitude.

Permit me to use my remaining time in speaking of two features of society work, if such they can be called. Both are exceptional, one indeed existing only in the ideal; but both are closely connected with success among scattered populations. First, a Society of Endeavor formed by uniting workers from two or more churches, of different denominations. This is seemingly a radical departure from the greatly emphasized connection with some single church. The Model Constitution and the United Society's publications are silent concerning it. And yet in some places, it must be a union society or none. The young people who ought to affiliate in Christian work, who must do so if their unconverted associates are to be reached, are found behind different denominational fences, where too frequently the rails are stiff and high. There are not enough young workers obtainable in any one church to start the society with sufficient impetus to command respect and attract new members. In many such instances, the refusal of one church to unite with another would suggest an unfraternal spirit, arousing bad feeling and even opposition. Then again, in small country places, unlike the city, social intimacies run regardless of ecclesiastical walls; and he who would start a society of Endeavor cannot wisely disregard the social distribution of its expected membership. In Vermont, 15 per cent of our societies are nominally union, and others are virtually so. I recall one town, where these is no village, and only one church, Universalist; its pastor, a man of strong evangelical spirit, has organized an Endeavor Society in which Baptists, Methodists and Adventists unite cordially with his church members, and are doing a good work. In another instance, three small churches were starving to death where only one ought to live; the young people from the three organized a society, persevered amid discouragments, and to-day in that place Congregationalists, Baptists and Methodists unite under the pastorate of a Free Will Baptist minister. In such illustrations I read a cheering sign for the future of our over-churched country communities. Better acquaintance and closer sympathy is to bind together youthful Christians, making impossible the inheritance of sectarian feuds; and each church by reflex influence shall be built up in Christly power and spirit, side by side with others where our society existed independently from the start

One thing more. Scattered over our Vermont hillsides, far up in winding valleys, in the solitude of forest clearings, live one hundred thousand of our population, two miles or more from any church. Of this number, two thirds never attend any religious services and the remainder very rarely; though fully one half of that hundred thousand would attend if a church were within a walking distance. Here are thousands of youth who need our society, whom our society needs. Many are of the stock that has contributed so honorably to the business and professional circles of the whole nation, and has thus given to the Green Mountain State an influence greatly disproportionate to its size. Distance makes it impossible for these young people to become regular attendants in a society; and the post office, through which they might send communications to the meetings, is equally inaccessible. And what is true in our state is equally true in other parts of New England, is emphatically true in the newer parts of the west. Can the Society in country towns do anything for these thousands of needy souls? This is no trivial question; the pressure of tremendous facts is holding it to our notice; it waits, and will wait, for an answer. In its brief history our beloved organization, by God's blessing, has overcome apathy, distrust, conservative indifference. It has crossed the oceans, and thrives to-day in the oldest and newest countries of another continent. Has it the energy, the wisdom, the will to conquer the dreary spaces that separate our country homes? The Sunday School has its Home Department; can our trustees devise a parallel? Wise students of social science are turning to the family, as contrasted with the congregation, for the proper unit in evangelizing our rural districts; can the Society of Endeavor in any way adapt itself to such a movement?

I confess, Mr. President, that I should have hesitated to occupy precious moments of this convention, but for the desire to voice in this inspiring presence some of these perplexing questions that have burdened my heart during the past months. I feel that I may claim to be, in an humble way, the representative of uncounted youth in the smaller places and scattered homes of our land. Few of them can be at such meetings as this; yet none need more the help we are receiving. I speak in behalf of struggling—I will not call them feeble---in behalf of struggling societies, whose numbers range from a score downward. They have no special features to report for your instruction; but they have special claims upon your sympathy and help. I rejoice in the confidence that their claims are fully recognized in this convention and in the deliberations of our trustees; I rejoice in the anticipation that these claims will be, in coming days, fully and wisely met.

THE UNITED SOCIETY AN AID TO EVERY CHURCH.

BY REV. RALPH W. BROKAW.

"Running the gauntlet" is a phrase, used sometimes to express the painful experiences of severe criticism. It is the punishment a man has to bear for inventing anything new. In a progressive age, when new things in every department of life are so eagerly sought for and so cordially welcomed, this seems strange enough. Nevertheless, it is a fact. Every novel idea, worked out into practical shape for any person whatsoever, is game for the critics. Say they: "Here comes another victim. Keep quiet. Get your guns ready. Lie low Take aim. Fire!"

From this trying ordeal the Society of Christian Endeavor has not been spared. At first, among my brethren of the Presbyterian family especially it had to "run the gauntlet" of criticism on account of the experience, or monthly consecration meeting plan. Next, the blows were directed at us because we insist on that "dreadful pledge." For, with a Bible and a religion and an every-day business life full of covenants, there are some who stoutly affirm that no Christian ought to subject himself to the obligations of a pledge. And when the bubbles of these captious objectors had been successfully pierced, then came fault-finding with our Central organization. Said a certain loved and highly respected brother: "You say that you are a society made up of local societies belonging to each local church, and yet you are under the direction of a Board of Trustees. I don't want a society in my church run by a machine planted in Boston."

Thus, my friends, another gauntlet is thrown down. Well, what of it? Let it lie. Who wants to pick it up?. I do not. I confess frankly that I enjoy a fight as much as anybody, particularly if I am on the winning side. But I do not propose to enter the lists here, and now. The spirit of this convention is fatal to a polemic humor. Has it not been correctly said that the most effective way to crowd out error is to crowd *in* truth. Therefore, leaving the critics with their criticisms to shift for themselves; acting upon this principle, as a member of the Board of Trustees and hence as an insider, I desire to bring from the inside to the outside the exact truth about the operations of the United Society, and its agents in Boston and elsewhere.

Now of what does this working force consist? The united Societies, *i. e.* the legal corporation first of all elects a Board of Trustees. This Board is also the Executive Committee of the General Conference. Upon it devolves, subject of course to direction and approval, the entire responsibility for the management and furtherance of the interests of the Y. P. S. C. E.. It is *your* representative, clothed with *your* authority. It exists and stands for *you*. And in order to accomplish its mission, and thereby fulfil its obligations, it elects certain officers and employs certain assistants. These officers are the President, the General Secretary, the Clerk, and the Treasurer. The assistance is furnished by a competent stenographer and a lively errand boy. The office in Boston is made up of two commodious rooms, one of which is occupied by THE GOLDEN RULE COMPANY. I assure you they are a credit to our Society. And what do these persons thus housed do. It were better to ask what they do *not* do? With the exception of the stenographer and errand boy, they all speak, speak, speak; speak from Maine to California, and from the Lakes to the Gulf; speak night after night, at State local Conferences, at anniversaries and Sunday school assemblies, before minister's clubs and ecclesiastical meetings. Of course, many others scattered all over America, who believe in the value of this institution, do likewise; but very naturally the Trustees, and particularly the President and General Secretary, are oftenest called upon. And yet this address-giving function, if you leave out our General Secretary, is not the prime duty of the rest of us. The trustees are ministers and laymen with their own vocations to follow. As trustees, however, they are expected to be only directors. To do this, they meet once a month in Boston, and apply their highest wisdom to the task devolving upon them.

But need I go into details? Perhaps it were better that I should. That central office presents a lively scene every day. Every one in it is just as busy as he can be. Mr. Clark lets "no grass grow under his feet," which are like hinds' feet for swiftness in work. His well-known devotion to this Y. P. S. C. E. child, of which he is the mundane father, should be sufficient guarantee of his fidelity. He proves his faith by his abundant work ; day and night does he labor for the cause of Christ as represented in this organization.

Mr. Ward is our evangelist. In what State has his voice not been heard? Among the societies his name is as a household word. He has scattered with marvelous skill, patience, and success the seeds of Christian Endeavor over all our broad land. Deservedly popular, because unselfishly useful, your love for him is only equalled by your demand for him. Simply the mention of his name is the inspiration of enthusiasm and applause.

And then there is Mr. Shaw. He carrries the bag, but he is no Judas Iscariot. Ready to make any reasonable sacrifice, untiring in his zeal, and great in his energy, he stands at his post faithful and true. You may think, my friends, that I am indulging in flattery, but I am not. "Honor to whom honor is due," saith the Scripture. And when I remind you that Mr. Ward has been meeting appointments constantly since the first of October, from the Atlantic to the Pacific, besides writing much for THE GOLDEN RULE, and arranging for the great convention ; that Mr. Clark and Mr. Shaw receive and answer on an average from seventy-five to one hundred letters of inquiry a day, many of which require long, careful replies; that over 200,000 tracts of information regarding our work have been prepared and sent out since last July ; and all space allotted to us by THE GOLDEN RULE has been filled with thoughtful articles, not to speak of the printing done for local societies, the income of which is contributed to the United Society ; when I tell you this, who among you all will say that every complimentary word is not justified? Brethren, I speak that which I do know, and testify of that which I have seen."

But what *pay* do these men receive? Like salvation, the trustees "are without money and without price." Until recently they have even paid their own travelling expenses. And even now this account is balanced only for three meetings a year. As to the others, who give all their time and strength to this work, they are enjoying a "bonanza." Your money is not wasted. The strictest economy prevails in every department. And every dollar spent is made to tell an honest story of good done to somebody. So much then for these matters of detail. But do you now ask what is the good of all this? Why is this central organization and office necessary? I think I can answer these very pertinent questions satisfactorily.

Just across the Passaic River from the parsonage where I reside, the Jersey City water-works are located. Part of the pumping power there is developed in several immense Corliss engines. One of the engineers in charge, noticing a great waste of steam during part of the action of these giant machines, invented a little mechanical device by which the steam is automatically cut off at the precise time when this wasting would begin, and is let on again just when it is needed. So, day and night, year in and year out, his timely invention serves the double purpose of *saving* and *expending*. This, I take it, plainly illustrates the effect of the work and watch of your central office and board of trustees. They perform a dual function. They cut off and let on, save and expend the forces at their disposal. In other words they are the Conservators of Y. P. S. C. E. energy.

Conservation, you know, is preservation from waste or friction, the keeping intact of that which has been established. Just as the spokes hold the rim of a wheel in its proper relation to the hub, so does the central organization exert a powerful influence in keeping all the local societies together, within the rim of one confederation. It is a hub at the Hub. It is a hub geographically, too, now, because our work has gone east as well as west. How long do you suppose it would be, without this hub and the strong lines that radiate from it, before the Y. P. S. C. E. would be split up into the kindling wood of numerous small independencies, and this delightful unity, in which there is so much of our strength, be lost?

Not only is *esprit de corps*, so exceedingly useful for dignity, for attractiveness, for effectiveness, for loyalty, conserved by the United Society, but also unity of aim. We have constantly to be on the lookout against those intruders who want to grind their various kinds of axes on our grindstone. If we would permit, they would monopolize this machine. We, who have brought it into existence, developed and cared for it, would have to yield our right to make it accomplish our purposes, while others would run for their own benefit, and probably, soon run it into the ground. Moreover, the central office is a vigilant guard against the interjection of such ideas, wise and otherwise, as would eventually undermine the solid foundations upon which the Society of Christian Endeavor rests. It is not necessary that I should give to these, each and all, a local habitation and a name. Just a hint as to their existence and the nature thereof should be enough.

To my mind the conservative function of the United Society of Christian Endeavor alone justifies its being. But for it, such marvelous strides could not have been taken; but for it, such a splendid and unspeakably influential gathering as this could not be. The "conservation of energy" is not a whit more important to the well being of the physical universe than it is to the spiritual universe, or any of its parts. One of the remarkable features of our work is the enthusiasm it develops. This is one of the seals of God's approval stamped upon it. But were it not for wise conservation how this would be scattered and consumed upon itself! How it would beat the air to no purpose! Like a fine, untamed, muscular horse, running wild upon the prairies, it could accomplish nothing.

Without any display of false modesty in keeping quiet for fear of being charged with self-laudation, I tell you, my friends, the eternal power of this great society has succeeded in making what otherwise would be one of our greatest dangers, one of our greatest forces for good. For what is worse than zeal without knowledge, a veritable Jehu, driving furiously and foolishly? And this brings me to speak of the other of the two functions of the central office and board of trustees. I refer to its letting on of steam, its expending of energy, its aggressive utility. If this society is a good thing. ought not others to know it? No *man* and no *thing* liveth unto itself. And others constantly want to know of it. It has been so from the beginning. It will continue to be so for many years to come. This *duty* and this *desire* swing open before us a door into a broad territory. Together they say, "Go in and possess the land for Christ and His church." And who will go? What's everybody's business is nobody's business" is a proverb. Trusting the maintenance and the promulgation of great interests to indiscriminate, unregulated, irresponsible effort, is like attempting to put down a rebellion by guerrilla warfare. Aye, it is even worse. Thank God, your good sense has led you to decree more wisely. I am here to assure you that your wisdom has borne witness unto itself that it was heaven-sent. Your officers, representing you, from the tall watch-tower, constituted in their means of communication, in thousands of corresponding secretaries, in THE GOLDEN RULE and other channels, look out upon the whole field, take note of conditions, tendencies, needs; direct, advise and labor accordingly. Is not this as it should be? Does it in any way interfere with your local independence, or church connection? Whom will you ask to find out? Some pastor in whose church there is no society of Christian Endeavor, or one whose experience with such a society covers a number of years? Why, my friends, such *conservation* and *aggression* as I have tried to speak of, no more interfere with the plans and purposes of each individual church and society, than do the State or National Sunday school organizations interfere with individual churches and schools. On the contrary, both derive inestimable benefits from them.

A word more and I have finished. The application of this paper is, keep fire under and steam in your Corliss engine, support your central organization and its officers, be jealous of its reputation, stand by THE GOLDEN RULE. It is your own adopted organ. It is your authorized voice speaking good words to all the world of Christian Endeavor. Its help is incalcuable. You cannot do a better thing for *yourself* than to subscribe for it. Your society cannot do a better thing for *itself* than to secure copies of it each week for all your officers and heads of committees.

Oh, be loyal soldiers in this grand army of youth in the republic of God! Such was the energy and determination of the stout hearted Dutch burghers of Flanders, that within three weeks after the naval defeat off Zerick Zee, and the more important and complete victory of Phillip II, at Mous ed Puelle, where six thousand men were slain, they were enabled to advance against the King of Spain with a fresh army of sixty thousand men. Their noble patriotism and dauntless bravery so impressed Phillip that he resolved to abandon the contest and conclude a peace. With a fiercer, subtler, and more persistent enemy confronting us, there is need of similar courage and religious patriotism on our part. To defeat this foe to all that is beautiful and good and true among men, our ranks must remain unbroken. Together, in one grand confederation, thoroughly organized from centre to circumference, we must stand. Together march, together fight, and together gain the victory in utterly routing the enemy, and setting up everywhere the standard of the wonderful Counsellor, mighty God, everlasting Father, Prince of Peace.

HOW THE UNITED SOCIETY AIDS EVERY CHURCH.

BY W. H. PENNELL.

The subject assigned for discussion is important, for, if the United Society of Christian Endeavor does not help *every* church, it is so far short of accomplishing the object for which it was organized. The Christian Endeavor idea is *consecrated effort, organized for mutual assistance.* The Society of Christian Endeavor is the expression of that idea in living characters. Each member becomes a help to every other by the mutual assistance, made possible by the plan of the organization; the United Society is but the culmination of this idea. The lookout committee is an illustration of this. That supervision which would be offensive when performed by any unauthorized person, however consecrated that one might be, becomes only the kindly ministration of brotherly love when performed by the organized lookout committee The christian church was organized to publish the plan of salvation; our Saviour did not organize it for the passive reception of salvation. "Go, disciple, baptize, teach," was His command. The responsibility of publishing the plan of salvation rests with the church, the responsibility of accepting it is with individuals.

Nor were they to make disciples, and then leave them; they were to secure their complete, open, entire acceptance of Him by the rite of baptism, and *then* they were to *teach* them to observe all things, whatsoever He had commanded. And the work was to be His, for He was to be always present. It is apparent that all should have something to do. All were to "Go;" and, lest there should be confusion and loss of energy, organization was certainly implied. It was while they were all together and of one mind that they received the baptism of the Holy Ghost. The Christian church was organized to help forward God's plan of salvation. In order that this may be done with that celerity which the importance of the subject demands, it is necessary that all efforts should be organized for that end. New plans of work to meet changed conditions must be inaugurated. The methods may vary but the work remains the same, the end to be accomplished is the same. Whatever plan is found to be helpful in any department should be commended to others, so that it may be tried under *other* circumstances and under *other* conditions. If found thus successful, it should be made known as widely as possible.

A successful plan may, for want of development, become of no value. Hence the necessity of communicating plans of Christian work, that modifications or enlargements may be employed. It is very rarely that a plan can be brought out at once, and become a successful factor in Christian work. Criticism will strengthen all good methods. So, even adverse criticism may be necessary to develop Christian work. But criticism will be useless, unless the plan is understood, and the discreet publishing of tried and acceptable methods becomes the duty of the church Some schemes of Christian work are suited for a single church, others are susceptible of wider application. The Christian Endeavor idea seems to be fitted for the widest application. No church, no denomination, no section of this country, no foreign land, has tried the plan without evident benefit. All testimony of those who have tried the plan, conscientiously, is to the same effect. If, at any time, we find opposition or adverse criticism, we feel sure it is because the plan is not understood. One State superintendent found a pastor who could hardly find words to express his dissatisfaction with the Society of Christian Endeavor. Argument was of no use to him, for he would not hear argument. He *thought* that he knew the whole story. Being in a ministers' meeting afterward, where the work was thoroughly explained, this pastor became interested. He asked questions, he sought information, he went home and tried the experiment, and found it to be just what he wanted, just what it professed to be, a help to the church, and he has become an enthusiastic supporter of the idea. Without this information communicated by those who were acquainted with the idea, this pastor would never have tried the plan. This work of the State superintendent was under the direction of the United Society. This feature of the work has from the start been noticeable, that those who try the plan tell some one else of their success. "Frequent confession of Christ," says Mr. Clark, "is the peculiar feature of the society." No less peculiar is the loyal endorsement of its friends. It was not intended for silent work. It was especially fitted to help the church. It began its helpful work in 1881, in a church which I most thoroughly believe was fitted by its organization and condition for the planting and growth of such a society, and for that reason chosen of God for the great honor of being the pioneer in this experiment. Hundreds of churches were equally anxious to find something that would help them save souls, but in none of them perhaps, would the society have stood the test of time, but in this church it became an accomplished fact.

"Frequent confession of Christ" became a pleasing duty, telling others the story was also a duty; neither duty was neglected. It was watched by pastors of other churches it was talked about; I know it was made a constant subject of prayer. Rev. Mr. Mills, of Newburyport, Mass., was the second to adopt the plan; it helped his church. Rev. Mr. Dickinson tried the plan; it helped his church. A pastor of a Portland church said to some of his young men, "Why don't the young people come to church?" Perhaps they would," was the reply, "if you had what they have got at Williston." He tried it, and it helped that church to a revival, where there had been no addition to the church for years. It took a year and a half to induce five pastors to try the plan, but in a year from that time, fifty-six had reported that it had helped their churches; two hundred and fifty-three converts had come into the churches, as the results of the year's work.

A brief glance at the way in which this information had been spread abroad will help us to understand how the United Society helps every church. In the first place, the consecrated effort for mutual assistance impelled each one to do all he could to tell others the story; and the information obtained was passed on to others.

If the Christian Endeavor idea had been kept as close as some schemes of church work are, it would never have got beyond Portland, perhaps never beyond 1881. The story gains strength by telling, and the story was told as effectively as possible in many ways, and with only one object in view,—to help the churches.

Conferences were held, that those interested might meet together, and communicate by word of mouth the enthusiasm each felt. Reports of these conferences were published, and sent out as widely as possible under the imperfect organization of that time. Individual societies were very well organized for aggressive work, but beyond all that was done was by individuals, in the imperfect way that such work must be done, when busy men and women, with every-day duties pressing upon them, undertake to do extra work. The headquarter bills were paid by the executive committee from their own funds. These bills were largely for circulars and postage, to answer the repeated calls for information that came from all parts of our country, showing that the church was ready for some plan of better work for the Master. It became evident that some central organization must be provided to meet the demands which grew constantly more pressing.

An incorporation for this purpose was undertaken. Its object, to help every church, could only be indicated by uniting together those societies which helped individual churches, and so the Incorporated Society became the United Society of Christian Endeavor. It was not started with the idea that it would save itself, and so save labor to those who thus far tried to do what they could to further the ends of the Society of Christian Endeavor; but the rapid growth of interest necessitated increased labor, which could only be claimed from a paid agent. To raise funds for the increasing needs of the work was one of the objects of the United Society. The money so raised was to be spent in forwarding literature to all who asked for it. This helped the churches who were reached, as many testimonies proved. Each circular mailed seemed to make necessary several others. As no provision was made for assistance beyond selecting the general secretary, he found himself overworked. We can all judge, from what we know of Mr. Ward, how much work he really undertook before he asked for help.

Our earnest thanks are due to Mr. Ward for the zeal and energy and enthusiasm which he put into the work for the United Society in those early days.

It soon became necessary to provide other help to answer the ever increasing demands for information. Various ways were open to the society, but one way was adopted, which has proved to have been the right way. That was to procure a paper to be the medium of communication between the United Society and every local society in the land. THE GOLDEN RULE became our means of communication, first as an expedient, then as an experiment, then as a financial necessity to some of our trustees; now it is an absolute necessity to every society in the world, and by its aid the United Society is enabled to help every church.

The rule has always been to communicate all the information possible; that rule has now become THE GOLDEN RULE.

THE SOCIETY A TRAINING-SCHOOL FOR THE CHURCH.

BY REV. JAMES L. HILL.

It must be evident to all of you who are observers of the signs of the times that the generation which is now coming upon the field of action is destined to live in stirring times. During their day will probably be wrought out a more general and vital change in religious methods of work than in any one epoch since the beginning of the Christian era. It would be easy to show that during the past few years a general preparation has been in progress. The rays are beginning to focus, and the place where they seem bound to converge is not remote from where we now are. It is a great thing to live at such a time. The days are not without privilege, and certain it is they are not without peril. Questions that once were confined to a few extraordinary minds are now to be popularized. The voices of most men were lately but echoes of their chieftains, but now matters are to be so reversed that those who are leaders only voice the popular sentiment, and proclaim what in the hearts of the people has come to exist. You do not need now to change your position to come to a throne of influence. How the young men are coming to the front in these days in political life! It goes without saying that that party which commends itself most to young men and recruits itself from among them will hold the regnancy in our land. They always are a power at the political caucus, and it is there that our most important civil matters are shaped. This great age-trend is the more conspicuous when we come into the religious realm. With much solemnity it has just been resolved: "That the support of the religious life of the college is more and more devolving upon the students themselves, so that whereas, in former years, the students had looked chiefly to the faculty for stimulus and inspiration in religious matters, now there is a most earnest, spontaneous religious life in the body of the students." In the higher education of the past the bible has seldom been used as a text-book in our colleges and seminaries. The demand, strangely, is not now from our educators, but from the students themselves. Thirty men in one class at Yale, forty men at Amherst, are asking for an optional study of the English bible. Sixty colleges will thus next year include the English bible among their courses of study. At times there is little or no progress in the development of the religious life of the young, and now there is a sudden start, and the world moves on. It grows increasingly manifest that we are about to leave one of those periods when but very little progress can be observed, and enter rapidly upon an era where the method of work in our churches shall see very great change. The pastor of one of the most aggressive among the Western churches has said that all the work of his church was done by less than one hundred of its members, while the other five hundred simply use its benefits. Now it is with a change in this condition of affairs that we are in this convention chiefly concerned. And if workers are to be trained, as if in an industrial school, all experience conspires to teach that their training for their life work cannot be begun while they are too young. Ten per cent of each church, a trustworthy and powerful writer has just affirmed, is responsible for the atmosphere and temperature of the same. The church is what they make it, and the ninety per cent remainder use it as they find it.

Now, let it be remembered on the other hand, that the old Romans who conquered eighty-six foreign nations, had recognized the secret of success when they called their armies *exercitus*, bodies of drilled or exercised men. Exercise, practise, experience gained in one's own life of work ensure victory, overcome difficulty, and if their influence has any limits they never have been ascertained. It is to gain this use of one's powers, to secure the exercise of one's religious faculties, and that while he is young and in his most susceptible frame, that our Society is made a training-school to the church. The work is sometimes crude and the workers *jejune*, yet if we would have the expert and experienced Christian worker we must put the youth into service upon committees in our Society, which is the religious counterpart of our far-famed industrial schools. This is the divine law of education Even our God allows himself to be pictured, in a striking symbol, as engaged in this sort of education. Israel was spiritually in undeveloped childhood. See now in a figure, our God deal with immaturity. "As an eagle stirreth up her nest, fluttereth over her young, spreadeth abroad her wings, taketh them, beareth them on her wings, so the Lord alone did."

It requires patience, and yet eaglets must learn to fly by flying. After a good deal is done for the young as in the Sabbath school, there comes a time when in preparation for the work of the church they must do something in the training school which this society presents, for themselves. Religious training is in the committee work which our organization affords. In its initial stage it is with us however, patiently and hopefully carried forward. Some sincere souls contemptlate all evidences of immaturity with dismay. God bids us study his method of education and we, such are the encouragements in the work, are not unwilling students. If the young should be kept forever nested they would not reveal so much their immaturity; yet exercise is the only means of out-growing it. The mother-bird wisely accepts the fact that growth obeys a law that is beyond her control, and patiently adopts her conduct to it. This stage in development cannot be over leaped. It precedes the next, and is as necessary as any. It *must* be true that the immature are better fitted for the labor of the church by the earlier training which this society affords. And it must also be true that if the training school which this society presents were suspended another means precisely like it in form and proportions would have to be instantly adopted.

Multitudes are complaining, when suddenly called by the pastor to posts of particular responsibility in the church. "Oh really I must be excused; you see I never had the training that young Christian people now receive! Participation in public service comes hard to a man who is regenerated when he is old. To the young, taking them at the best period for development our society presents a school for the intellect. We learn by contact. The lessons of this life are not evolved from the idle brain of dreamers but are learned in the daily school of practical endeavor. A man first finds the power of a truth by being made to experience its action himself. Feeling its power he comes easily to expression. This art in our society meetings has repeated exercise. Thus beginning with the easiest of all truth our young people come by way of the training school into the highest employment of one's faculties—easy speech out of a full heart in the presence of those you desire to influence. Some eminent statesman like Senator Buckingham of Connecticut, and Governor Briggs firstlearned to meet audiences in little meetings for prayer and testimony.

The society furthermore presents an admirable training school in the matter of discipline. The great fact must not be overlooked that here all burdens and responsibilities and the so called iron-clad pledge are self-imposed. Said the Queen of song, "I must sing with the over plus of life. I would not for the world violate any one of the laws of health." Those laws were self-accepted for her well being. So are the obligations assumed by our hundreds of thousands of young people who are in training for the church. Behold of a sudden the ancient and well-nigh forgotten fable of Briareus has a divine realization. The daughter of Zion has now a hundred hands. When Heine the poet, in serious illness, was led by friends to the feet of the famous statue of Venus, which you remember is bereft of arms, he looked up in her face and murmured, "Oh my lady of Milo, help me!" and she seemed to answer, "I would do so, Heine but you see I have no arms." The daughter of Zion in many communities still is fair and statuesque. She pities and desires to help but she has no arms. Let the children of Zion organized into training schools everywhere consecrate to her beneficient service their thousands of willing hands.

FRESH FIELDS FOR YOUNG CHRISTIAN WORKERS.

BY REV. C. A. DICKINSON.

The impression has prevailed in years that have gone, that the Protestant Church is a kind of Saint's Rest; that it is for those who would like to ease their consciences while they are resting their bodies. The impression also has been and is prevalent that the Christian ministers have a very easy time of it. A lady once said to my wife, "I suppose your husband has a delightful time in the ministry! I often wonder what he can do to occupy his time. I suppose he does nothing but write two sermons a week and take care of the prayer meeting." I well remember coming to my old country home in Vermont after my first year's pastorate, pretty thoroughly exhausted by the cares and duties of a large parish; and some two or three days after my arrival, a church member of that place said to me, while shaking my hand, "Well, Charles, I suppose you have had a good year's rest and have now come home to do a little work on the farm." This illustrates the impression that the church is an impassive, inactive body, instead of an aggressive, active body; and this impression heretofore has been not a little increased and fostered by the week-day appearance of a great many of our Protestant churches, not only in the country but in the city.

While every other institution organized for beneficiary or profitable purposes has open doors, a cheery hospitality and moving wheels every day in the week, how often we find the church of God, which should be the centre and source of philanthrophic work, with a padlock upon its gates and darkness around its pulpit. This is a sad condition of things. About the only notice you will find on the average Protestant church, is that of the undertaker, which is certainly not at all suggestive of life and activity. Perhaps I am a little radical upon this subject, but I thoroughly believe that the church of God should keep open its doors every day of the week. I believe that it should be thoroughly manned, furnished with all requirements for every kind of Christian work. I believe that it should occupy such a position with reference to all aggressive work, that it would be impossible for any other organization, however worthy, to point to closed doors and folded hands, and ask, "What are you doing?"

The Christian should have for his motto, "For Christ and the Church," and he should believe that his most efficient service for Christ can be done only in and through the church. I believe that the divinely appointed mission of the Society of the Christian Endeavor has been, and is and will be, to bring about this happy state of things. It has been my good fortune to know a great deal about this child. Our seventh anniversary we are celebrating now. I have watched him ever since he was a handsome, bright child in the cradle, and I knew by the glint of his eye that he was destined to grow to a ripe manhood; and this baby has been a wonder, not only to Father Endeavor, but to all of his neighbors, ever since he jumped over the side of his cradle and went off by himself through the world. He has done more during this seven years to assist the spread of the Gospel than any other organization that has been founded during the past century. He has done more to bring together the grand idea of faith and works than any other organization. When Johnnie and Charlie got lost up in the garret, and were locked in up there, they both sat down on an old barrel and began to cry. After a little while, Charlie says to Johnnie, "What will we do?" Johnnie says, "I don't know, but I guess we better pray over it." Charlie says, "Johnnie, you go to praying, and I will go down to the door and kick;" and so between them they got the door open. It has always seemed to me that the Christian Endeavor Society seemed to combine the prayers and works of Johnnie and Charlie. It has been praying and it has been kicking; and it has succeeded, it seems to me, in opening a door through which the young men and the young women of this generation are passing into glorious opportunities.

Now permit me briefly to tell you what this agency has done for me as a pastor. I have had the good fortune to have it in the three churches of which I have been the pastor. Its characteristics, it seems to me are these: First, it is aggressive. It is an outlooker and it is an ingatherer. Secondly, it is thoroughly practical in all of its theories. It aims to bring the masses under the blessings of an active ministration. Thirdly, it is thoroughly evangelistic. It aims to divert and convert the young. In studying the work of this Society I have been exceedingly gratified. We have a church that is composed of several hundred members. It was proposed to do some active work last fall on the Christian Endeavor plan. We have a grand band of young men and young women who were ready for the work. The first thing we did was to canvas the city in a radius of half a mile. We found there about twenty thousand inhabitants, the majority of them attending no church whatever. The first thing we did in the way of reaching these people was to organize a series of three concerts and lectures, and we carefully distributed the tickets among a certain proportion of these unchurched people, and we found a large per cent. of the people who attended our entertainments were from this class. We did not attempt to evangelize them at once; our desire was first to get hold of them. To-day as a reward of our work we have a large proportion of our congregation made up of people who were formerly non-church-goers.

In the practical work of our Christian Endeavor Society we have introduced several departments, We have a department of intellectual culture; a library and reading room above, well stocked and furnished. In addition to this, we have instituted a course of lectures which have for their object the intellectual improvement of young men especially. Then believing that a sound mind in a sound body is a most desirable thing, we have established what we call a physical culture department which comprises a bicycle club, a lawn tennis club and an outing club, which has already had several very enjoyable trips in the country. We have also a hygienic department, with a course of lectures especially directed to the laws of health and the relations of life to the human body. We have also established an industrial department, which has classes in telegraphy, stenography, typewriting, wood-carving and other lines of practical business education. We have also an evangelistic department with special Bible training classes in which our young men and young women are educated in the study of the Scriptures and how to apply their knowledge to every-day life. We hope now, with the blessing of God upon our labors, to speedily hasten the evangelization of that part of the city where God has placed us.

You remember the story of Henry of Navarre. It was just before a battle. Riding in front of his troops he thus addressed them: "You are Frenchmen; yonder is the enemy; I am your king." Then pointing to a white plume that he had fixed in his helmet he said to them: "My children, look well to your ranks; if your standard falls, rally round this white plume; it shall lead you to victory." His soldiers fought like heroes, and the enemy was routed.

"A thousand spurs were struck
A thousand spears in rest,
A thousand knights were pressing close
Behind that snow-white crest"

We too have a leader, and thus we should follow Him. He is a leader who never suffers defeat. Like Henry of Navarre, He is always found in the front rank, and there we should strive to be.

"Am I a soldier of the cross,
A follower of the Lamb,
And shall I fear to own my Lord,
Or blush to speak His name?
Shall I be carried to the skies
On flowery beds of ease,
While others fought to win the prize,
And sailed through bloody seas?"

God forbid.

STATE UNIONS AND WHAT THEY MAY ACCOMPLISH.

BY J. W. HOWELL.

Why do we organize for State work? Mainly for the purpose of stimulating an interest in the Endeavor cause among our young people, and promoting their efficiency in Christian life and church work. Our unions are of very recent origin, and have a short history, but they have accomplished a vast amount of work. The United Society is responsible for their existence, as the various State superintendents, when elected, were empowered to call conventions of the Endeavor Societies in their respective States, and there perfect State organizations. Connecticut formed the first union in 1885, but today we have twenty States well organized, and doing effective work. Our unions are not separate and distinct organizations or bodies, but rather divisions of our grand army of Endeavor workers, with the United Society as our organizer, but with Jehovah as our leader.

These unions are instrumental in assisting and furthering the work of the United Society. They foster a spirit of unity among our young people, and help them to train themselves for effective Christian work. The methods of accomplishing these results are varied. The most powerful agency in the State work probably is the distribution of Endeavor literature, as it not only helps those who receive it, but the United Society which publishes it; and is about the only way of informing the majority of our people in regard to the aims of Christian Endeavor. We hope this literature will be scattered far and wide, until all hear the news, and that there may be many depositories through our land where this literature can be obtained. The number of letters written and received by the State officers show that they greatly relieve the work of the United Society in this direction.

These Unions are always instrumental in providing for State Conventions, which today are almost indispensable, as they enable our workers to become intimately acquainted, and to discuss practical questions, and the local needs of the work in each State, thereby supplementing the work of our national gatherings. This work alone is of sufficient importance to warrant their existence. Many of the numerous local unions, in every State, have been organized directly, or indirectly through the influence of our State Unions, and are indispensable in the State work, as they conduct the work in a particular town or district in the same manner that the State Union work is prosecuted through the entire State. The local societies thus united and working through their local unions strengthen each other, and in so doing aid the State Unions, which, in turn, aid the United Society. Thus the United Society does the planting, and our State and local unions do the watering, while God, working in and through all our work, has given the increase. One of the many evidences of the value of State Union work is the fact that our Endeavor Societies are the most fully developed where our unions have been in operation the longest, and there, also, shall we find the largest number of " local unions."

Our forms of organization vary somewhat, but so far as I have observed they are simple in plan, and in their operation economical. They always should be so, as there is no occasion or excuse for the payment of any salaries, office rent, etc., there being workers enough in every State ready to devote sufficient time without money remuneration to care for our State interests. Thus organized and operating on such a basis, no church or individual can justly accuse us of extravagance, and we must never afford opportunity for sucn criticism. This financial feature of our work is worthy of careful study. Our local societies should not be called upon to expend so much for State work, that they are unable to liberally sustain the general and broader work of our United Society. At our last National Convention held at Sarataga, many of our State Unions pledged large sums to the United Society. After the Convention adjourned most of this money had to be secured by the State Unions from the local societies. While this money was thus being raised it became necessary for the United Society to appeal direct to all the local societies for further contributions, many of whom were confused at being twice called upon for contributions for the United Society, in addition to calls for funds for State work. In order to avoid any such confusion, would it not be better for our *State Unions* at this Convention, and hereafter, to refrain from making any pledges or collecting any funds for the United Society work, requesting all of our local societies to make their contributions *direct* to the United Society? I would also suggest that all funds required for our State work be pledged at our State Conventions, so that our local societies will not be subjected to continued appeals for money. Now that we have so large a number of societies organized, and continually organizing in every State, let us bend our energies toward building up and strengthening our forces, rather than to be too anxious to swell the roll of societies. We want quality more than quantity, and this applies to every local society as well as to our State Unions. There is no danger of our numbers not increasing, but there is, perhaps, some danger of our societies failing to grow and develop as fast as they might. Here is where our State and local unions can and should be of great assistance in keeping our societies in a healthy spiritual condition. If we keep a high standard before our societies, and do what we can to help them live up to it, they will themselves be the means of organizing others. A strong and earnest society will be a powerful agency in extending the work, while a weak one that is Christian Endeavor only in name, will do much to injure our cause. Don't let us make the mistake of supposing that when our young people once become members of our societies, or when our societies are members of our unions, they need no further care, for it is then that our Union work is most required. The possibilities and opportunities in the work are countless, and the responsibilities are equally great, but God has put His divine seal upon all our work, and we can go forth in His name, laboring for Christ and the church, and know that God will bless our efforts even more abundantly in the future than He has in the past.

Relation of the Society to the Mission Work.

THE WORK IN FOREIGN LANDS.

BY REV. ARTHUR MITCHELL.

No one, I am sure, could look around upon this audience and have the privilege of speaking to such an assembly in behalf of any interest that lay upon his heart without a feeling of great thankfulness to the Lord for the privilege, and without thankfulness to the officers of the body for having invited him to such a pleasant duty, and it is, I assure you, with very great thankfulness that I come before you this afternoon to speak to you a few moments upon a subject which does indeed lie constantly upon my thoughts and upon my heart; and that is the relation of the young people of the church to the great subject of foreign missions.

If I were asked the question how the young people of the church can do most for the cause of foreign missions, I should answer, in the first place by assuring themselves that they have the mind of Christ respecting foreign missions; and if I were still asked what they might do more for the advancement of the cause of foreign missions I should reply, by doing all in their power to see that all around them also have the mind of Christ upon the subject of foreign missions. There never was a subject upon which it was more necessary that all our views and convictions should be founded on the rock of holy scripture and on the unmistakable revelations of the Lord Jesus Christ. This necessity exists especially with regard to the enterprise of foreign missions, from the fact that it is so vast that it staggers the faith of any assembly of christians who undertake to carry it on except as they know that they are going forward at the call of God. Not only is it so vast in its dimensions, but it faces such peculiar and well-nigh insurmountable obstacles that the courage and perseverance and enthusiasm of any body of christians who undertake it will be sure, very soon, to flag and fail unless they awake every morning of their lives, with this thought and this conviction born anew within their souls; it is the will of God, it is the voice of God that commands us on to this task of evangelizing the entire world of mankind. Not only is it necessary for the workers themselves, as I intimated to begin with, but it is of the greatest importance that the many of us who would further the interests of foreign missions amongst our own churches and at large through the land, shall endeavor to put all around us also in possession of the mind of Christ and of the words of holy scripture upon this subject.

It is somewhat astonishing how slow the heart of the church is and how much more slow the heart of the great christian communities which lie all around the church have been to accept the conviction that it is our duty to accept nothing less and attempt nothing less that the filling of this whole world with the knowledge of God, the idea of a worldwide religion and of a kingdom of God that should embrace all races and all nations of men; it is an idea which they have been astonishingly slow to adopt. Even the Jews seemed for long centuries to feel that they were exclusively the favorites of Heaven, and although Abraham, their father, based the whole system of Judaism itself upon that wide covenant, although the very corner stone of the whole faith of the Jews was the declaration of God to their great progenitor that in Him all the races of men, all the Nations of the earth should be blessed, yet nevertheless they considered that Abraham and Abraham's descendants were exclusively to receive the blessings and favor of Heaven. Even although their greatest psalmist, leading their devotion before the Most High with an outburst of expression of faith which sounds like a christian benediction, "Blessed be the name of the Lord, and let the whole world be filled with His glory," nevertheless the multitudes of Israel never followed the song of their divinely inspired singer, but still clung to their own faith that Israel, and Israel well-nigh alone, was to receive the blessings and the favor of the Most High. When their most conspicuous and illustrious King offered his prayer, the masses of Israel never followed him; they never considered the lessons of their prophets when they foretold the coming of Him whom the Gentiles should trust. They seem never to have understood the methods of those prophets who foretold the day when the whole earth should be filled with a knowledge of the Lord as the waters fill the sea, and therefore it was that when the Lord Himself, the living evangelist, the world's redeemer came in person to men, they were slow to see that he was to lay the foundation of a world-wide kingdom. And yet how ample is the mind of Christ respecting this, and it is before us in his own words. Turn to the Gospel and read the page that records the resurrection and on the very page where is written the marvelous story of the victory of the heart over death and of his rising from the grave, - upon that very page, as upon the very threshold of all the hopes and glories of the christian church, what do we there also read? That repentance and remission of sin were to be preached in His name among all nations beginning, not at Jerusalem, beginning from Jerusalem; Jerusalem the mere point of radius, the golden mile stone, the center from which the word should go forth to all the nations of mankind, and then before our Lord would bid His farewell to the disciples he must needs take them apart into Galilee and say to them,--"Go ye and teach all nations; baptise them in the name of the Father and of the Son and of the Holy Ghost. Lo, I am with you always, even to the end of the world." And still he lingered with them for those forty days before His final ascension to the skies, and at the very last, in the last recorded conversation that the Master holds with the followers, what is the burden of his speech to them? what is the lesson? It is this: "Ye are my witnesses both in Jerusalem and in Judea and in Samaria and in the uttermost parts of the earth."

Now, is it not marvelous that after such lessons so distinctly and so amply unfolded and sung in the devotion of Israel for successive centuries and reiterated in their ears, is it not marvelous that after all this the church should have seemed deaf to those words and blind to those lessons, so that after Pentecost and after the early gathering of the multitudes at Israel still there lingers the slowness of belief with reference to the conversion of the heathen, and Peter must receive that vision of the heathen to open his eyes at last and enable him in part to enlighten his fellow-countrymen respecting this neglected duty, and yet, after this, even, the task is but half attempted, the lesson seems only half learned.

Now, what is this that we see? Why, that Saviour on whose form we had thought that human eyes had rested for the last time until the final day,—that he may once more and in a manner of inconceivable emphasis in a great transaction which is the object lesson of the christian's transcendent power, that he should reiterate once more in the slow ears of his people his last and greatest lesson concerning their duty, there again with a brightness above the brightness of the noon-day sun he shines upon the eyes of men, and that voice whose last accent we thought had been heard by men on the slopes of Olivet, that voice is heard once more by human ears in this world of ours, and what are its words? What is its message? The Lord has risen from His Heavenly throne; He is addressing again the ears of listening men that he may commission and ordain the great missionary to the heathen world; that he may ordain and send forth that Apostle Paul who was to be the great leader of the christian church in coming centuries in her work of missions to the heathen world. Now, is there any subject upon which the mind of Christ is more ample and distinctly given us in His Word than this concerning our duty in missions to the heathen?

My brethren, write it upon your hearts as plain as the Ten Commandments that were written with God's own finger on Sinai. Just so plain and just so obligatory are those commandments of our Lord Jesus Christ which bids us go into all the world and give His Gospel to every creature. The church led on by Paul for a few years exhibited a spectacle of earnest and successful evangelism, but the merest tyro in the history of the church needs not to know how soon the church lost that early evangelistic zeal and how soon her interest was withdrawn from the distant nations of mankind, but thank God we are now living in a day when the signs of the times seem to be read aright by the church, as certainly never before for many christian centuries. And this is another of the points that I would urge upon the young people of the church that they should not only possess themselves of the mind of Christ respecting missions to the heathen as it is written in the New Testament, and as He spoke through the Holy Ghost to the Patriarchs of old, but I would also have them be able to discern the signs of the times in which we live.

In the first place we simply need to remind ourselves that there never was a time when the resources and the opportunities of the church for this work of foreign missions were as manifest and as ample as they are to-day.

Take for example our own America. What are her christian resources as bearing upon the evangelization of the heathen world? What are the resources of America in our day as bearing upon this work? Well, my friends, we can very soon dispose of that point. One needs only to remind himself that there are in this America with its sixty millions of people, about one evangelical preacher of the Gospel this Saturday afternoon for every seven hundred people, white and black, Jew and Gentile, old and young, native born and foreign—one evangelical minister preacher of the Gospel of Christ in America this afternoon for about every seven hundred of our population, and one needs not to be told that America is not dependent alone upon the ordained ministers for her evangelism. Call up the roll of your deacons in the Congregational and in the Baptish churches; call up the roll of the elders in our Presbyterian churches; you call men from the bench of the Supreme Court of the United States; you call men marked by thrift and leadership and intelligence, by Biblical knowledge and by the respect of their fellow-citizens, from almost every community where Presbyterian churches have been planted, and I take it it is true in respect to every evangelical church throughout America. Count up your christian colleges; count the pages of your christian literature ; count up your Young Men's Christian Associations, your marvelous societies of Christian Endeavor, and see what a splendid alliance, what a magnificent confederation of christian forces and power is here for the evangelization of this land.

Brethren, it a country with one evangelical minister for every seven hundred of her inhabitants, with a christian literature like the christian literature in America, with christian institutions like our christian colleges and academies and with these splendid helpers that are given us in the organized forces of the Young Men's Christian Association and the Young People's Society of Christian Endeavor—if those people are not ready, have not resources enough, so far as men are concerned, to now undertake with a gigantic generosity, the task of evangelizing the world—if any man will say that such a Nation with such resources in men, a nation sending people now to advance her plans and concentrate her forces upon the work of evangelizing the remote, the heathen nations of the world,—if any man shall speak against it—then we might as well turn our faces to the Lord and tell Him that the work that he has laid upon the church never can be done.

My friends, we have not only the resources in men; we have vast christian wealth. Why, I wrote a letter, without a thought of adverting to the fact here this afternoon, but for an entirely different purpose, —I wrote a letter from New York a few weeks ago to a gentleman of my acquaintance here at Chicago at the head of one of its best institutions, and I asked him what he estimated to be the wealth gathered, represented, in the Presbyterian congregations of Chicago. I was particularly interested in that. He kept the letter a few days and finally he wrote to me that he did not think there was less than fifty-five millions of money in the Presbyterian congregations of this city, and, he added, "I presume there are a good many in the city that would think I put it altogether too low." Then I wrote to the President of one of the largest banks in New York City, himself an elder in the church and qualified, perhaps, beyond any other man in the city to give correct information concerning such subjects. I asked him what he considered to be the wealth gathered in the Presbyterian churches of New York in its congregations, in the hands and possession of those who were either members of the church or habitual givers to its great benevolent and evangelistic enterprises. He wrote me in a few days five hundred millions of dollars, and then afterwards he sent me a letter saying that he found he had made a great mistake and it was necessary to add one hundred millions more to that sum.

Now, there is no need of spending any more time on that. I suppose you all believed it before I uttered a word. We need only have the men, and we have men to send forth of the kind that will offer themselves, with the consecration of God upon them, upon this new christian crusade. Thus we have all resources.

But how shall I speak to you of our opportunities? What shall I say of Japan? of China? What shall I say to you of Siam? What shall I say to you of this neighboring half continent of South America?

On that last point, since it is nearest home, I will allow myself a single word. Now, New York is very far from San Francisco, but we would think it very shameful indeed if there were a pestilence in New York if San Francisco should not send her help. We would think it very dastardly and mean if San Francisco should burn up if New York should not roll over the continent the generous gift of her citizens, but, my friends, do you know that there are cities on our continent, cities of fifty thousand souls, within eight days of New York harbor, where there is not one single minister of the gospel? Take the southern shore of South America; it is shamefully behind the times, so far as ministers are concerned. Look further into this; look at Venezuela and Ecquador and the rest of those States. There with a population of six millions they have only two ordained ministers of the gospel, for all those millions, and they are only within eight days sail of New York harbor. Why, it is a case of—what shall I say? A case of criminal embezzlement of Holy treasures of Heaven that we should have here in America seventy thousand evangelistic preachers of the Gospel, with all these other agents and agencies of which I have spoken a moment ago, and that within eight days steaming of our principal city that we should leave the entire population to live and grow old and go down to their graves without a message of the power of the evangelical truth of our Lord Jesus Christ.

Now, my friends, I see that the time is growing nigh when I mus sit down, though I have only just opened a vast subject, and if it were allowed me I could stand here four hours and speak to you of the great necessities for your taking hold of this work, of interesting your own selves and your comrades and young friends in this cause of foreign missions.

I want to tell you this one thing before I close, and that is that this work which is so ordered of Heaven is also endorsed of Heaven, and that there are no churches on earth that are growing so rapidly to-day as the churches gathered by your foreign missionaries in heathen lands. I want to tell you another thing, and that is if this work is done it must be done in a very large measure directly by the young men and young women of America.

A few hours before I came from New York there came into the misssion rooms a lady who wanted to be sent as a foreign missionary. I conversed with her. I knew much about her; I knew her intelligence; I knew her devotion; I knew that in many respects she was splendidly fitted to be a foreign missionary, but I had to say to her, "My friend, you are too old, you are too old; you never could master the language in which you propose to work." It is the young men and the young women who have the gift of tongues from God and who can learn with facility these alien tongues. It is they who must undertake the work of foreign missions, and something of the buoyancy, something of the courage which is born of youth, must color your manhood which is to go forth to evangelize the world.

I should like to know who they were that led the churches of America in the great enterprise of foreign missions. I should like to know who they were who formed the first charter and organized the first society for the propagation of the Gospel in heathen lands. Why, they were five young people in a Society of Christian Endeavor. They were five young people in a Society of Christian Endeavor, under a hay-stack in a thunder storm who went down and devoted themselves to God and asked Him to teach them how they might so live that their influence should be felt upon the other side of the globe before they should die. Aud when those young men went to the pastor of the church they were told it was not practical. "Why, my dear sir," said the President of Yale College to them, "your enterprise to me savors of the chimerical, there is something venturesome about your plan," and those five young men could not get the church of America at that date to raise enough money to send them to heathen shores, and one of them had to go across the ocean to help secure the funds.

Who was that man? That man was Judson. And there is no argument for the blessing of foreign missions, beyond the grand work at home, like that which suggests itself at the name of Judson.

I am a Presbyterian, but I know who the Baptists were a few years ago. Why, they were about seventy thousand strong here in America; they were scattered in country places very largely; the strength of the Baptist denomination of that day did not lie in the great cities. The Baptists at that time had not more than one college—they did have one college in America, but they did not have one single theological seminary. If there was a denomination that ought to hang together it was the Baptist; they could not afford to divide; they needed all their strength, but they did split, and I thank God for it. Judson put his bugle to his lips and called the Baptists of America to evangelize the heathen. Thirty-five or forty thousand of them said they would obey that call and they would undertake the work of foreign missions, and thirty-five thousand of them said they would not; they did not believe in it; they did not take much stock in foreign missions; there was altogether too much to be done here at home, and talked in the old-fashioned idea of New England, that there was a tincture of venture about the whole enterprise, and one leading editor of the Baptist denomination said, "I think it is my duty to crush this rising spirit," and another good Baptist brother was right after him and said to him, "Well, sir, if you think it is your duty to do that I want to say to you I think you will die without doing your duty."

That missionary half of the church went on from its forty thousand until to-day they number I think 532,000, the leading Baptist denomination of America, but those who did not believe in foreign missions had thirty-five thousand then and do not count over forty thousand now.

For the sake of your organization, for the sake of the heathen in the distance and for the sake of the church in which you were born and in which you are working now, do you become a firm believer in foreign missions, and do you make a red hot advocacy of missions to the whole heathen world.

THE WORK AMONG OUR EMIGRANT POPULATION.

BY REV. H. A. SCHAUFFLER.

I always dislike to sail under false colors, but I have been so inextricably mixed up once or twice with my brother that I want to tell you that I am not my brother. I have received the most cordial thanks for my inspiring articles in the "Sunday School Times," even from over in the old country. It reminds me of the old story of Ammi, who said, "Am I Ammi, or am I not Ammi, and if I am not Ammi, then who in the world am I?"

I am called a Bohemian. It is because I have been a foreign missionary for many years in the land of the Bohemians, and am now working in that part of the population of this country. A good many of my friends call me a Bohemian, though I am a born American. It is a very pleasant situation to me, that I am permitted to speak immediately after my dear friend and honored brother who has spoken of the foreign work, for it comes in most properly at this time.

God sees we have not been wide awake to this foreign work of which we have heard such eloquent and bnrning words this afternoon. God sees that we do not begin to understand the length and depth and height and extent of this great work of evangelizing the world, and so He is sending them to us, and they have been coming in upon us at such an alarming rate that we hardly know what to do. I reckoned up from the time of the census to last fall and we have been receiving at the rate of 525,000 emigrants every year, within a fraction, great armies of occupation; not Goths and Vandals indeed, but those who have come in to take possession of this land of ours. Just think for a moment what the extent of this foreign population is. In 1880 one-third, or more than one-third of the white population of our country was of foreign parentage, that is, those born abroad and who came to our shores from other shores, and their children of the first generation born here.

In 1880 we find that Massachusetts had within a fraction of a quarter of her whole population of foreign birth, and within a fraction of half of the population of Massachusetts of foreign parentage. We find that Boston had over 63 per cent. of its population of foreign parentage. When we come to this State in which we are now convened, we find that there are nearly 19 per cent. of foreign birth and 42 per cent. or over of foreign parentage, and then the most remarkable thing is how this population of foreign birth and foreign parentage is massed in our great cities. You can find no more striking example of it than in this city in which we are to-day. This city has, by careful computation, more than 91 90-100 per cent. of foreign parentage, those of foreign birth and their children.

In Wisconsin over 72 per cent. of the whole State is of foreign parentage, and I beg you to note—if I had a map here you would see that almost the whole of that foreign population is massed in the northern part of the country. In the South the question is, "What shall we do with the freed slaves?" In the North the question is, "What shall we do with the imigrant population?"

Now, I have not time this afternoon to go into the question of the influences that are at work amongst this foreign population and their children. I cannot speak of the noble men, men and women both, that come to our shores. We need only mention John Hall and William M. Taylor to show that we owe to foreign shores some of the noblest of those that are in the van-guard of all that is good, and let us also remember that one of the greatest dangers to our land to-day, and especially in the great cities, is the foreign element that comes to us without the gospel of Jesus Christ, with prejudices, with habits, with feelings deep in their hearts and in their very lives which are opposed to our free christian institutions, and unless we can in some way equal and assimilate that great mass of foreign population that comes sweeping in upon us in these great floods, we shall not stand as a Nation, a Christian Nation, very much longer, because our cities are to-day in the hands of foreigners; they are to-day controlling the politics of our great cities, and the longer we delay with the evangelization of this great mass that is coming in upon us, the worse will it be for our land.

Now, I want especially this afternoon to call the attention of this Young People's Society of Christian Endeavor, this United Society—God be praised that it is united, and that they have come together on a common platform—I want to call the attention of all you young people to the Y. P. S. C. E., in Cleveland. I stand before you as a representative of our Bohemian Y. P. S C. E., I believe the first of the kind in the land, and last Sunday evening they sent you their most cordial greetings, which I am more than glad to convey

What I wanted to say to you is that it is for the young people of our land to meet the young of the emigrant population, to meet those who are foreign born and come to us, and those of foreign parentage born here. We all need a helping hand, we all need the Gospel of Jesus Christ, and let me assure you that it is folly for us to think that the mere fact of their being here and attending our public schools is proof that they are going to become Christian citizens of this great empire. Far from that is the fact. Why, the simple fact is that as Bohemians tell me, that in this country they find it harder to bring up their children right, there is more sinning, there is more drinking and all that. A Bohemian once said to me, "Why, in the old country every man pays for his own drinks; here he has to stand treat all around."

Now, you ask me, how are we going to oppose the evil influences? We must bring a different influence amongst our foreign population, the great mass, the great majority, and those who manufacture and those who sell intoxicating liquors to foreigners.

Here is something which I received from this city of Chicago before that bomb exploded in the Haymarket Square. I was a subscriber, in order to see what was being published, to the Arbeiter Zeitung, a German paper published in this city, and in the course of time there came this wall calendar, sent to me to hang up on the wall of my home, to give my children instruction in Nihilism. Here you have, in the first place, a caricature of a Protestant and of a Catholic Priest; they are leaning on the money bag; and here you have French soldiers impaling Chinese babies, and in the middle, a lurid plain surrounded by darkness, you have Nihilistic principles inciting the populace to revolution and to blood-shed. And this picture is hung up in hundreds and thousands of German homes to teach the rising generation Nihilism.

In that terrible affair in Cincinnati some time ago the cry of "The

Jail!" was raised, not alone by the foreigner; it was raised by the young German-American element,—"On to the Jail!" and so we see how absolutely necessary it is that if we are to evangelize, if we are to equal this foreign population of our country, for us to reach this second generation.

That brother of mine in New York, to whom I alluded, and who has been engaged for many years in city missionary work amongst the foreign population, said, "All we can hope to do for the first generation, for the most part, is to send them to heaven, but after the second generation make missionaries of them."

That is what I want you to do. How are you to do it? Why, in the first place, love them. There is no use trying to do any christian work for anybody you do not love. How can we love such people? How can we love people that are not lovable? Just exactly as the Lord Jesus Christ loves you, no other wise.

Well, friends, if we have in us the spirit of the Master, if we have in us the spirit of Christian endeavor, then we shall love them; we shall love those who need to be loved, not those who do not need it so much as those who do need it. God sends these foreigners to our shores that we shall help them seek the Lord.

Our good friend,—and we have a right to say our good friend,—Mr. B. F. Jacobs, who is a good friend of every Sunday school worker told us some years ago a story, which I shall never forget. I think it was he that told us of a boy here in Chicago who went past half a dozen or a dozen Sunday schools to one particular Sunday school, and a lady asked him why he went by so many Sunday Schools to that special one, and he looked up at her, and he said, "Why, madam, they love a fellow there." That was the secret, that was what carried him by all the other Sunday schools, because "they loved a fellow there."

I heard something that interested me as I was going through Boston once. A man with his little boy stopped at an hotel over-night, and there was a burly colored porter down in the lobby of the hotel who paid some attention to the little boy, and his father told him to give that porter his hand, and so the little fellow went up—he was a little afraid at first, afraid his hand might be blackened by the contact, but he obeyed his father and gave his hand. The next morning the little boy walked right up without any fear of the old porter, and put his rosy lips up to kiss him. The old porter was perfectly transported with joy. "Bress the boy; God bress the boy; gee whittaker, he kiss me; God bress the boy."

That little boy might have done anything he wanted to with that old negro porter, and so when God puts His love into our hearts, then let our hearts go into the hearts of the poor, and the half of the battle is won just the moment that we feel that we do truly love them. The second point is, help them. Love without service is a poor thing.

What was the first Christian Endeavor Society? My very good friend, Dr. Mitchell, of course carries us back to the Berkshire Hills, but there is an older Christian Endeavor Society than that. What is it! Well, go back with me to the shores of Lake Gennesaret and to Galilee, and we see the Lord Jesus Christ with that band of twelve men, eleven faithful and one unfaithful, and then on the shores of the lake surrounded by that multitude of five thousand men His disciples are appalled and say, "Lord. send these multitudes away."

Well, some people are saying the same about the foreigners to day; "Send the Chinese back to China; send the Irish back to Ireland." That was not what the Master thought. He said to that little Christian Endeavor Society "give them something to eat," and then they brought all they had, though it was but five loaves and two fishes, but let us not forget that it was less the loaves and fishes than it was the disciples themselves who laid themselves at the feet of the Master; when the disciples carried that light supply of food, when the disciples offered themselves and all they had and laid it at the Master's feet, and His blessing was poured out upon it, it was sufficient for all those multitudes.

And just so it is with us. It all depends upon the question whether we are ready to bring all that we have and all that we are and lay it at the feet of the Master and say, "Lord, here I am; it is all I have." Friends, we are not afraid of the devil and all the powers of hell; we are not afraid of all foreign emigrants pouring in upon us, but what I am afraid of is that the church of Christ should not be faithful to her mission, should not say, "Though I am weak yet am I strong; I can do all things through Christ which strengtheneth me."

Now, I have an idea in reference to the way in which this work should be done. My friends, help them wherever you can. The Lord Jesus Christ did not tell the disciples to go first and teach them, but He told them to go with the loaves and fishes, and so we must do that way and so if you know a man that you know wants to read for himself, try to get him along and help him. You housekeepers—for I see some housekeepers here in this congregation—if you have got an Irish servant girl or a servant girl of any Nationality, try in every way to reach her with the Gospel. My wife once said to a christian lady very much interested in foreign missions, "My dear friend, do you do anything for the conversion of your servant girls?" Why, she had never thought of such a thing; she was devoted to the conversion of the Chinese and Japanese and Hindoos and Hottentots.

Allow me to relate an incident that will be familiar to some Chicago friends, if not to all of them, but it so aptly illustrates the point I want to make that I shall, at the risk of repeating to some, give it to you. Some years ago in the city of Springfield, Ohio, there lived a young German. He was a splendid looking young man, tall, over six feet three or four inches high; he was a beer-drinking and sceptical young man, like the other Germans with whom he associated. He worked in a factory. Next to him worked a christian young American and that young American had asked this young German to go to church with him. The young German did not care anything at all about church and if that young American had given up once he never would have seen the inside of a church possibly to this day, but that young American was one of those truly christian endeavorers; he would not give up the first time or the second time or the third or the sixth. He kept at him until he got that young man inside the church, and when he got him inside the church most providentially he got him into the pew of one of those ladies who do not draw aside their dress when a poor looking fellow comes in, and look disgusted. Instead of doing any such thing that lady took her card and gave him a most cordial invitation to a place in her pew every Sunday. That went to the young man's heart. The pastor of that young American was in front of this young German. He got him into his studio, and I must say with rare tact and with rare courage, for at the first interview with a man who was an infidel almost, if not quite, he knelt down and prayed with him.

Well, friends, let us believe in the power of prayer. That pastor knelt down with that young man and prayed for him, and that young man told me that he had a new sensation during that prayer, and he never felt in all of his life what he felt during the moment of that prayer, and the result was he was soon converted. He began working with Greek, and in a wonderfully short time he was able to enter the seminary at Oberlin, went through, and hardly had he graduated from there when the American Home Missionary Society was requested to appoint him as a missionary. I speak of the Reverend G. E. Holbrook. When it seemed laid upon him by God to go to Japan there was weeping amongst those to whom he had endeared himself, but to-day he is in Japan and learning that language. To-day there are young men in Chicago who are preparing themselves for this work.

I would like to tell you of a young man I saw in Detroit; he was a young Pole, a Catholic; thrown into connection with the Young Men's Christian Association, to-day a missionary for the 25,000 Poles of Detroit. I would like to show you a picture of ten young men who have been studying the last year in Oberlin; ten Bohemian young men who have been studying and preparing themselves for missionaries to their fellow-country-men. I would like to tell you of one that is preaching in Minnesota, preaching in four different cities. I would like to show you seven young ladies, six of them Bohemians and one American, in Cleveland. I would like to tell you the story of one one after another of those, but time forbids. (I believe it is as wrong to steal another man's time as it is to steal a watch.)

You have heard the address of the foreign secretary of the Presbyterian Board of this country. Dr. Washburne, the President of the Robert College, wrote to a friend in this country not long ago as follows: "The fate of the world is to be decided where you are Every one of your people should feel that he ought to care for nothing so much as for the Home Missionary work. "You are not half awake to it," this foreign missionary says to his brothers at home. It is enough to make a person weep if the Home Missionary Society should fail in this work by lack of means.

Dr. Parkhurst of New York says that when we are ready to have

God use us, he will make us magnificently successful. Therefore, let us look to God, dear brothers, for our help in the evangelization of this land and in the evangelization of all the lands, and God's blessing will be poured out upon us.

RAISING MONEY FOR MISSIONS.

BY S. L. MERSHON,

How to raise money for missions, that is the question. After what we have just heard by way of addresses, the answer is an easy one. Place Drs. Mitchell and Schauffler on your platform, and let them loose on your audience. While these brethren were speaking, I thought of the Irishman who came to this country and secured a job as hod-carrier and who wrote back to friends in the old country that he had found the "aisiest job in the world for sure. Faith, all he had to do was to carry the bricks to the top of the house, and the man up there did all the wark." These brethren have been bringing to us great blocks of information, piling them up, and piling them up, and all that you and I have to do is to properly arrange them in our memories, and use them for the building up of a mighty work to the glory of His great name.

In wandering through our great manufacturing institutions I have noticed that fire on the grate-bars, and water in the boiler, means steam in the cylinder. You cannot put fire on the grate-bars, and water in the boiler, without raising steam into the cylinder, and you will have steam in proportion to the quantity of the water, and the intensity of the fire. Pour into our churches missionary information, and apply thereto the fire of missionary enthusiasm, and you will have the uplifting and outpouring of the financial strength.

The church of God is becoming marvellously intelligent, devoutly consecrated, intensely diligent, and wisely discriminating. Eloquent specialists, from every department of Christian effort, are presenting their claims at the bar of Christian philanthropy; and if the cause of missions is to be successfully submitted, it must be in a way that will command the intelligence, devotion, and common sense of the Christian public. A clap-trap plan or a momentary impulse may be utilized in extorting a contribution for missions, from which a deadening reaction may follow. The Society of Christian Endeavor proposes to lay broader and deeper its foundations of Christian giving. To accomplish this, we must be systematic and must build from bed rock.

Appoint a missionary committee. This committee should be provided for in your constitution, and should be on an equality with your lookout and prayer-meeting committees. Make no sub or secondary committee of it, or you will receive half-hearted support and unimportant results. Its efficiency will be impaired by the very fact of your considering this committee of less importance. Let this committee realize its value, by your giving it the dignity to which it is entitled. Place squarely on its shoulders the entire responsibility of the missionary work of yuor society. Let it feel that the Master will look to it as ac. countable for your society's fulfilment of His last great commamd to go in to the world and preach the Gospel to every creature.

Have this committee composed largely of missionary enthusiasts. Make your perpetual motion brother or sister chairman of it.

Give this committee one meeting in each month for its exclusive control, as a missionary meeting — the second Sunday being most appropriate, because of the time for publication of the various missionary journals.

The programmes of these meetings should be attractive, varied in character. The country or field, under consideration, should be presented as an artist or literary club would develop it. Having aroused an interest in the field itself, press home the claims of Christ's kingdom. Show the romance of missions, the love that impels, and the courage that leads to martyrdom; the joys of redeemed souls, and the immortal glory of final victory. Have you an artist among your number? Seize his crayon for vivid illustrations. Is there a cornet, violin, or flute? Have it consecrated for one hour per month to ringing out the battle music of the redemptive hosts.

Interesting information vividly illustrated interspersed with inspiring music, must result in the development of a mighty missionary sentiment. Kindle a fire of this character each month, *varying the material used for fuel;* and you will generate forces that will respond to every reasonable appeal.

Prepare your programmes a month in advance. Devote thereto the executive energy that would make a high school entertainment a success; and put into your plan for a missionary rally, the heart throb and brain power that characterize a political rally. Let the only motive be the glory of His name, and the upbuilding of His kingdom.

Throw your forces, if possible, into personal contact with those who need help. The eye will transmit vividly a message to the heart that the ear would be slow in receiving. We draw our illustration from our Evanston brethren. We see them organizing a committee of investigation,—a committee of twenty. We behold them early on a Sabbath morn visiting the destitute districts of our great city. Two spending the day among seven Chinese Sunday-schools, two laden with flowers and loving messages, giving the day among the sick and suffering, including the invalids' prayer-meeting at the hospital; two among the waifs, and so by twos' scouring our city ;—and how our hearts did burn within us as He talked with us by the way.

The heart that was touched by the cry of distress from our city alley, is keenly alive to the moan of the mother as for weeks she lies burning before the fires of Siam, to keep the demon from snatching away her child. The eye that dropped the tear, that day, at the sufferer's cot in the Cook County hospital, will quickly see the need, as it is presented, from the far away lands to whose conquest we are pledged. As a result of that day's work, six hundred dollars will go this year from the treasury of that society to the Adelphi Mission of Chicago ; while, at the same time, that society stands sponsor for another mission in Evanston, and is doing largely for other foreign fields.

The heart says to the hand, Give, because the eye has seen, the ear has heard and the brain has thought. As to minor plans for collecting the funds, no general rule will apply. The plan that would be adapted to the metropolis, would be impracticable in the rural districts, the manufacturing town, or the mining village. This must be left to the good sense of the local committees.

Last—Best—Prayer. Last month the Anchorage Mission of our city, for fallen women, ran out of funds. The devout women in charge, who are not above the example of the pure and holy Redeemer, had put forth every effort in their power to raise money sufficient, and yet a bill of $35.00 that must be paid, stared them in the face. Falling on their knees they raised their prayer to the Saviour of Mary Magdalene. By the next morning's mail, from one of the most prominent ladies of our city, who was unconsious of their dire extremity, came a check for exactly $35.00 ; and thus every bill for June was paid. God's promises are fulfilled—one hundred cents to the dollar.

A short time ago, there came a swift messenger to the door of one of our city missions, begging that some one would hasten to an evil resort, to see a young dying girl. A young lady missionary went thither with flying feet, and pressed her way into a room, where on a bed lay the dying woman, being held by a sister in sin. From the sufferer's lips came this awful cry, "I am going to be lost! how dare I go alone! how dare you let me go alone!" and with this frightful cry, she passed over the line.

Her companion, turning to the angel of salvation standing at her side, said, "Oh, tell me of Jesus! tell me of Jesus!" Remember the picture. The world in sin crying to the world in redemption, Tell us of Jesus! Tell us of Jesus!

OUR LITERATURE.

BY REV. ERASTUS BLAKESLEE.

(Only an abstract can be given as no stenographic report was taken.)

Rev. Erastus Blakeslee spoke of the literature of the Society and especially of the GOLDEN RULE. He said that an organ is absolutely essential to the success of the Christian Endeavor movement ; that it is impossible for the societies to furnish the capital necessary to establish one, and that therefore Mr. Clark and a few others of those most deeply interested in this work had assumed the heavy financial responsibility of the GOLDEN RULE. It is due to them as well as to the cause so dear to us all, that we sustain them in this important enterprise. It is the only regular means of communication between the societies, and the only official way of reaching them with plans and information. Through it the father of these societies from his editorial rooms speaks weekly to their members everywhere, and keeps his guiding hand on all christian endeavor thought and progress. There is no other human agency so important as this to the right development of christian endeavor ideas and principles. Besides, as a Sunday School help, and as a general family newspaper it is one of the best. It richly deserves the united and hearty support of all Christian Endeavor workers. He closed by offering the following resolutions, which were unanimously adopted.

Resolved, That this Convention extend its hearty thanks to the Golden Rule for its exceedingly valuable service to the Christian Endeavor cause during the past two years.

Resolved, That we congratulate it on the high order of excellence it has attained, and gladly reaffirm our adoption of it as the official organ of the Christian Endeavor Societies.

Resolved, That we regard this paper of paramount importance as a means of disseminating information on Christian Endeavor matters, of cultivating a proper *esprit de corps* in Christian Endeavor Societies, and of enforcing and conserving the essential Christian Endeavor principles, and therefore that we express our earnest desire that it find its way into the hands of every Christian Endeavor worker in the land.

Resolved, That while thus emphasizing its Christian Endeavor character at this time we would not forget its still wider scope as a thoroughly good, undenominational religious paper, and would specially commend it for its helpfulness to the Sunday School, its devotion to the best forms of our common church life and work, and for its warm sympathy with all that aids in the Christian nurture of the family.

Addresses and Sermon.

ABSTRACT OF SERMON.

BY REV. J. W. BROOKS, D. D.

(As no stenographic copy of the sermon was taken, only a brief abstract can be given.)

The Young People's Society of Christian Endeavor in its marvelous growth and in the possibility of a vastly increased expansion seems like a sign of the promised outpouring of the Holy Spirit upon our sons and daughters, and a seal of the prophecy that both our young men and maidens shall unite in a universal anthem of praise that shall surely ascend to God. But if they would help this sign forward to a glorious fulfilment, if by their assistance they would have the seal receive the stamp of a splendid confirmation, it must be done through their holding fast to a few essential principles and fundamental truths that do not touch at all upon denominational lines, but are thoroughly biblical and evangelical. First, every member of the society must be affirmatively and fully persuaded that all scripture was given by inspiration of God. No portion of the Bible must be considered as unworthy of their attention and study and of moulding their character. The second great truth to which the society must hold fast was the divinity of Jesus Christ as the actual possesor of the incommunicable attributes of the eternal God. Next, the members of the society must hold fast to *the doctrine of atonement.* Finally, they must work in the power of the spirit; they must study their Bibles; they must be men and women of one book; not that he would have them despise other books, but that they should let all their reading turn on the Bible—the great book of God, the source and monitor of a Christian life. Let them thank God that 22,000 souls had been brought to Christ by the efforts of their society during the past year, but let them pray and make endeavor that 40,000 souls shall be brought to Christ next year. With earnest zeal in the service of Christ, with deathless love for the souls around them, let them stretch out their hands to those that are hungering, and guide them through God's grace.

AN ADDRESS.

BY B. F. JACOBS.

(It was expected that Mr. Jacobs would make one of the addresses of welcome, but being unavoidably detained at the opening he spoke as follows on his arrival.)

I don't dare to tell you how I got left, but I suppose you have been welcomed to Chicago and to the Churches, and to the Sunday Schools by the brethren who have spoken before me. It is refreshing to meet so many young people who have made up their minds that they don't know all there is to learn, and who have determined that they will endeavor to do something that no one else did before them.

When I was a boy, in an old log school house, we used to have a motto, taken from an old story book, that said, "What man has done, man can do," and if they had written it now they would have added, "So can a woman." I read a motto, however, a few months ago that made an impression upon my mind, in these few words: "Be all that it is in your power to be." Put that before you, then, add this motto that I also read that helped me: "Whatever we desire, that for one little moment we are," so that if we can walk from that desire to the possession of that thought, or to the attainment of what other men have desired and thought, we may grow exceedingly and do a great deal.

If I had had the time yesterday, I would have been glad to have spoken a word concerning the word of God. That is your text book and guide as well as ours in the Sunday School. I am delighted with the expression that has been given to the thoughts concerning the word of God here this morning, and you remember our interpretation of it, but the interpretation of the Spirit of God helps us to realize the position that has been brought to our attention. There is a wide difference, of course, in the minds who study the Word, and in the interpretation of that Word.

I heard a man tell of a little colored boy in Louisiana who had been converted, and holding his testament in his hand and speaking of his religious experience he said: "It's sweetr'n lasses" That was the best thing he knew; and that is what David said, when he said, "It is sweeter than honey." One of them lived in a honey country, and one of them lived in a "lasses country." Our interpretation of the Word will be in proportion to the circumstances in which we are placed; our interpretation of that Word will be measured by the opportunities that surround us, but be sure that the experience is one and the same to us all.

This is not the beginning of Christian Endeavor Societies. Seven years ago, I believe it was, I was in Portland. I met Mr. Clark when there was only one Christian Endeavor Society in the United States. I heard what he said about it, and I have been wonderfully pleased with its growth. But that is not the first. Christian Endeavor Societies have existed back almost to the beginning, and they have grown in this country, out of the enthusiasm and love of some warm heart that has been kindled from fire on high. Every great and commanding movement in history is the result of enthusiasm, but then, it does not live upon enthusiasm. A fire may be fanned by the wind, but it must be fed with fuel, so we must be built up, if we are to grow and accomplish anything. I believe in Christian consecration; I believe in youthful consecration; I believe in a healthy consecration, a consecration of development that is a great deal more accomplished than it was yesterday or is to day. The Christian has a right to expect that thirty, sixty and one hundred fold will be the progressive step of his own Christian experience.

Once you remember there was a great convention held in a valley, and the Hosts of God were trembling before one giant form of evil, and by a special train there was a delegate arrived just in time to take part in the discussion. He performed a very noble feat, he was indeed a chosen instrument for a chosen time. You remember with what enthusiasm they rallied around him; you remember the far-reaching influence of that effort that was put forth, and let us expect that even now and here are the young men and women that God will use just as he used David.

There was another mighty movement later on, when the delegation of Christian Endeavor Societies of Jerusalem started a branch in Babylon. You remember they had a pledge, first of all, "We will not preach and do that which is not right." Second. "We will not bow down." You remember the influence of that Endeavor Society. I pray God the influence of these meetings may be like the influence of that gathering, far-reaching, mighty in its effects, and I know you will realize in your own experience that God has provided better things for us than for David or Daniel. Let us be true to our great privileges and prove ourselves faithful endeavorers.

ADDRESS.

BY REV. J. H. BARROWS.

I am a new convert from the ranks of unbelief unto the faith which fires the ranks of Christian Endeavor. But I confess it takes time to bring a conservative Presbyterian like me up to that height of enthusiasm which marks this magnificent convention. When I heard the stirring addresses of yesterday, and read this morning the reports of President Clark and Secretary Ward; when I learned of the 2,000 young Christians at the 6.30 o'clock prayer meeting, a sight never seen in Chicago before, or even in Boston or St. Louis, when I grasped the hands of old friends whom I learned to love in Massachusetts (for I, too, once lived in Arcadia), I felt very much like the dog that I met last March in New Orleans. I went to the French Market one morning and saw a blind beggar. The blind beggar saw me. The blind beggar had a dog in whose mouth was a tin pail, a Jehoiada-box, into which the benevolent cast their offerings. I let a nickel from my hand rattle into the pail, whereupon it was the dog's duty to bow his thanks and hold out his paw for a shake. The blind beggar saw that the dog failed to perform this duty for me, and he cuffed him severely and said: "Dog not good enough for such kind people." I feel just like that dog before this consecrated host to-night. But I am endeavoring to be better.

It is my first duty to state, like a loyal Presbyterian, my confession of faith. I believe from six months observation of the splendid workings of a society of Christian Endeavor in my own church: 1. That the iron-clad pledge is the sheet-anchor of success and the essential element of continued prosperity. It is a great pleasure to go to a prayer meeting and find the people there. 2. I believe that the society changes what is many a pastor's chief burden and anxiety, the Christian training of the young, into his chiefest joy. I believe that it augments his knowledge and love of his young people, and their knowledge and love of him, beyond any other known means of securing such results 4. I believe that under its happy workings I can hear my young people grow in grace, as you can hear the corn grow on the Illinois prairies. 5. I believe that it solves, as Mr. Hill said to my people the other night, the question of amusement in the church. 6. I believe it is so sensible, so healthful in its workings, combining testimony, prayer and benevolent and social activity, and so completely identified with the church, and in no peril whatever of divorce from it, even in Chicago or Connecticut, that every pastor in the land should welcome it as the best means of promoting his church's prosperity. 7. I believe that the young people's societies of Christian Endeavor are capable of becoming a vast aid to home and foreign missions. 8. And finally, I believe that this movement which we represent, is so Christian, so catholic, so comprehensive and grand that it is worthy to have been born, and that its only misfortune is that it was not born in Chicago!

The wise Germans have a saying that whatever you would put into the next generation must first be put into the lives of young men under 25. And with that thought in mind, it is to me a great inspiration to address such a multitude of the young on the lofty themes of Christian patriotism. John Winthrop, founder of Boston, declared that out of the churches the civil state must be reared. Lord Beaconsfield maintained that Great Britain and America were strong because they have been true to the Hebrew idea of God's supremacy in the commonwealth. The Nation, said Mulford, can meet the forces with which it has to contend only as it realizes its origin and end in God. The friends of America in France have placed at the entrance of our chief harbor a colossal statue of Liberty, holding in her hand a torch, "Freedom Enlightening the World." Blessed be liberty! Her garments are sweet with the breath of the morning, and her feet with the blood of heroes, but if her torch is to enlighten the world it must be feed from the golden lamp of divine knowledge; it must be fanned by the pure flame of justice; it must glow like an angel's cheek in the holy light of faith in God. Before the convention which framed the National Constitution the sagacious Franklin, least inclined of all America's great men toward a Hebrew conception of life, said solemnly: "Except the Lord build a house they labor in vain who build it."

Scorning or forgetting these truths, we shall become as an oak tree whose leaf fadeth, and as a garden which hath no water; or, looking for grapes we shall find only wild grapes. We are citizens of the only nation that ever sprang from the purpose of making Christ its King. Mastering this thought we may understand the profounder meanings of great national events, and discover the origin as well as the secret and the strength of our continual nationality. Unexampled destinies have been announced for us, borne by strange, prophetic voices across the Atlantic sea. The faith of the fathers, bequeathed to us, the eighth generation of their children, was that a divine purpose and Providence lay back of our beginnings.

> "Lo I uncover the land
> Which I hid of old time in the West,
> As a sculptor uncovers his statue
> When he has wrought his best."

De Tocqueville declared that the Mississippi Valley is the most magnificent abode which the Almighty ever prepared for the habitation of man. This central vale, touching the Eastern and Western mountains, and holding the Nation into a geographical unity, this imperial domain through which descends the father of waters, draining the snows of a thousand peaks and fed by the currents springing from a thousand lakes, was discovered by the chivalrous vanguards of French and papal enterprise and exploration, and few events in our history are of equal importance with that long, fierce fight, which gave the supremacy of the infinite West, not to the Frenchman and the Jesuit, but to the Anglo-Saxon and the Protestant.

After the French and Indian wars came the struggle for independence, launching a new nation on the stormy sea of democratic liberty. At the close of this momentous conflict Christian men were moved to consider the spiritual needs of the ever widening and advancing lines of frontier settlement. The new nation for Christ! Such has been the purpose, deepening I believe, year after year, intensified by manifold and inner perils, renewed after the glorious revivals which followed the earnest efforts at evangelization in the West and Southwest, sublimed and strengthened by a perception of the position which America is fast assuming in Christian civilization, and which is being burned into the very souls of thousands of young Christian disciples in our land as they perceive the mighty and manifold perils which threaten to corrupt and destroy our nationality.

To any mind that broods largely over the coming ages of our National development I know of no more suggestive spectacle than a company of Christians, girded with the splendors of gentle, golden, and all-hopeful youth. I regard as of immense moment the convictions and purposes, the spirit and temper with which these Christian societies, East and West, North and South, engage in their splendid work. In the last few years America has unquestionably awakened to a new consciousness of herself, and it is noticeable that scholarly men have been inquiring into the origin of our majestic nationality. This awakening is contemporaneous with similar developments of Providence elsewhere. In European history the great fact of the century has been the resurrection of nationalities under parlimentary forms of government. In 1815 there were forty distinct sovereignties, with seven different names, in Germany alone. Thus divided, the national life of a great people had no development and little power. But the instinct of unity was not dead in these petty dukedoms and principalities, and to-day, thanks to the force of kindred speech and blood, not less than the genius of a Bismarck, the German Fatherland, one and indivisable, sits down under a constitutional government beneath the spiked helmet of her youthful Kaiser. So of Italy. Nature has marked out her boundaries. God meant her to be one. And in our own day eight separate sovereignties have yielded their individual lives to the greater life of the nation. This is the story of Mazzini and Count Cavour, of Garibaldi and Victor Immanuel—one flag from the Alps to the hoarse Sicilian shore, one national life where Venice dreams over by-gone grandeurs. looking out on her peaceful lagoons, and where Palermo nestles beneath her southern crags, one hohe beating in the gay Neapolitan boy and the sturdy Lombard shepherd, Florence saluting Rome,and Rome blessing all, as the long divided nation of Dante, Rienzi and Mcihael Angelo fulfils the spirations of her sages, and poets, and martyrs.

Thus Hungary, also, has come to the light. The free spirit of the Magyar has snapped the Austrain chain, and now clasps the Austrian hand in friendly alliance. The national life would not down after Kossuth had blown the trumpet of its resurrection. So, too, with the Greeks. Their classic soil has been redeemed from the blight of the Turk, and a vigorous national existence now centers in the city of Athens, once the intellectual treasure-house of mankind.

But what mean those rising states along the Danube, Bulgaria, Roumelia, and the rest, fragments of the broken Ottoman Empire? They mean that, beneath the brutal camp of the Turk there lived in those Christian peoples an invincible national consciousness which the scimiter could not destroy in four centuries of cruelty, and which the Toryism of England and the watchful jealousy of Europe were at last compelled to recognize.

In one of the cartoons in the Pantheon, in Paris, a French artist has portrayed the beginnings of Christianity undermining the pagan empire of Rome. In the upper zone of the vast picture you behold a scene of light and gorgeous, victorious pomp, a Cæsar entering the capital in triumph, with his splendid legions, his captured enemies, his golden and jeweled spoils, and his colossal elephants. But in the lower zone of the picture, in darkness just visible, you behold the early Christians praying in the catacombs, whose long galleries seem to be the sepulcher into which the Roman pageant and the Roman Empire above must soon fall. And thus also with the national spirit in the European states. Often it was forced to hide underground, over-topped and crushed by imperial power, but its resurrection came in the shaking of thrones, the rubbing out of old boundary lines on the map of the continent and the rehabilitation of Europe around the national idea. There is a God in history. He who made one blood all nations hath also determined the times before appointed and the bounds of their habitation, and by the nation as such he is carrying out His Divine will. Babylon, Persia, Greece and Rome appeared one after another in the prophetic vision, and each had its work to accomplish. By the nation called Israel God wrought out redemption for mankind. England, Germany, France, Russia have parts in the great world drama which no others can fill, and shall we hoodwink ourselves to our National life and destiny, we, about whom so many prophetic voices have gone forth from the wise and good of many lands?

We have just been exploding a few billions of fire-crackers to celebrate our Nation's birthday, and I understand that the New England delegates en route to this convention disturbed the peace of three commonwealths with their fiery and thunderous patriotism. But we need to go back of the Declaration of Independence to find the beginning of our life as a people. Nations are older and greater than the governments they ordain. In the colonial mind and heart, in the convictions, habits, aspirations, and purposes of the men who occupied this territory, from Falmouth to Savannah; men whose fathers had fled from the corruptions and tyrannies of the old world, and who had battled with the savage and soil, the winter, and the wilderness in the new; men whose psalms and prayers rose heavenward with the smoke of their cabins; men whose axes rung amid the pine trees of the North and the palmettos of the South, while their adventurous commerce spread its white arms over every sea—in the minds and hearts of these yeomen, sons of English Puritans and Scotch Covenanters, Hollanders, and Huguenots, Germans and Swedes, heirs of the great ages of Elizabeth and Cromwell, of Henry of Navarre and Gustavus Adolphus, and William the Silent, there existed, confused but potential, the sentiment of American nationality. Let no man imagine that the Nation sprang to life at Bunker Hill or Yorktown. Of older lineage and nobler parentage is the great Republic. Shall we, with grave historians like Bancroft, find her germinal form in the compact form made in the Mayflower? Shall we, with others, seek her origin in the pulpit of John Knox of Edinburgh or that of John Robinson at Leyden? Shall we, with the great German historians declare that John Calvin was the virtual founder of the United States of America? Were the roots of our nationality fastened, as many believe, in the soil of Marston Moor where Cromwell's Ironsides broke in pieces the royal army?

Or shall we go back of all these to the holy fields of the New Testament, which the sixteenth century opened again to mankind, and say that "free America was born of the Bible." Hence came many of the strongest impulses which colonized these shores; hence came the simpler forms of self-government in church and state which had followed our civilization in its Western march; hence came the observance of ths Lord's Day, the bulwark of our freedom, and hence the teaching of Biblical truth to the young, which Webster declared has done more to preserve our liberties than grave statesmen and armed soldiers; hence came our public schools and the long line of Christian colleges which stretch from the elms of Cambridge to the Pacific shore. From the Bible came, as Edward Everett declared, the better elements of our National institutions; it was an echo of Christian truth which Jefferson sounded in the great Declaration, and from the same source have sprung the moral reformations which have thus far withstood the wasting of corruption.

Our nationality is of heavenly birth Its fountain head is far up among the shining hills of God; and, remembering its origin, and recalling what precious interests and celestial truths it enshrines, I can not doubt its continuance. But it must meet the new perils as it met and conquered the old. It must occupy the new Territories with the same divine forces which shaped its primitive life by the Atlantic sea-board.

We are planting colonies in our new dominions far more heterogeneous and perilous than the old. Around the camp-fires of the Pilgrims gather the representatives of one or two nationalities; around the camp-fires of the California miners and in the streets of our great Western cities may be seen the representatives of a score of nationalities. I know of no grander field for the exercise of Christian faithfulness and heroism than is opened here to the young men and women of our own land. Carlyle once said that America had never done a grandly noble thing, but history does not present a record of more patient heroism or more self-sacrificing patriotism than is found in the unwritten lives of the humble missionaries and teachers of America. Through forests primeval, over plains and mountains, these modern pilgrims have gone forth, upbearing in their hands the Bible, and on the fourfold foundation of the Christian church, the Christian school, the Christian home, and the Christian Sabbath; they have helped to build this hugh fabric of our American life. And when we remember the vastness of the territory which is to become the battle-ground of humanity; when we think of the golden Northwest—the world's granary; the golden Southwest—the world's pasture-land; the golden far West—the world's treasure-house: when you remember that ours is the "largest continuous empire ever established by man;" that in the region west of the Mississippi you might place 351 States, like the grand historic Commonwealth of Massachusetts; when you remember that two of our Western Territories are capable of supporting 35,000,000 people, and when you think of the moral perils threatening these newer regions—the perils of drunken lawlessness, barbarism, Mormonism, communism and Romanism, and unbelief—it becomes apparent that we have here a field for a Christian heroism as shining and supreme as ever gilded the missionary annals of the Orient.

Men and women of the finest fibre have left the cultured East, and endured hardships and sickness, and the loss of those things which love would shower upon its own; laying down their lives amid the malarial swamps of Michigan, the forests of the Western Reserve, the prairies of Illinois, the flowery sods of Wisconsin and Nebraska, the vast plains of the Southwest, and amid the golden crags of the Sierras, which they have helped to coin with Jesus' holy name, and amid "the continuous wood where rolls the Oregon," making sacred with a new sacrement the-far-reaching fields of this America for whom the ages have travailed in birth.

I would that through all our societies there might be rekindled the holy fires of a Christian patriotism. From the midst of our numbers are to come the consecrated toilers who should proclaim the gospel throughout our land. From our ranks are to be trained up the large-hearted Christian workers and generous givers on whom the future evangelization of America shall depend. The next twenty years are to determine the coming century of our National life. It is a time for aggressive and combined action. A conservative and cautious policy in Western evangelization may have been well enough when emigration was slow, when the pioneers' wagons toiled heavily through the deep mud of the Illinois prairie, but all that is now changed; the locomotive has taken the place of the emigrant wagon; villages spring up as by the stroke of an enchanter's wand in golden-hearted valleys of the Wahsatch Mountains, capital is swifter than the flying buffalo, and "city lots are staked for sale above old Indian graves." To-day Salt Lake City and Santa Fe are linked to New York and Chicago by bands of iron. Capital rings the locomotive bell at the front door of Mormon and Mexican; their land is full of silver, their land is full of idols, and shall we lag far behind with the life-giving gospel? That Englishman told the truth who said that America is bounded on the west by the day of judgment. All our lives are bounded on the west by the day of judgment, and God will hold us responsible for the use we make of them. Did you ever hear of the Illinois Circle? There are few things that you haven't heard of! An Illinois farmer plants corn to feed swine to get money to buy land to plant more corn to feed more swine to get more money to buy more land to plant more corn to feed as many swine as possible, and woe be to us if our boasted civilization ends only in swine, in the fruits of a material civilization. I would that in the midst of our luxurious and easy going lives we might catch something of the spirit of that home missionary who once had a vacation and went to a boarding-house in Saratoga and thence wrote home to his wife that a certain fashionable woman's habiliments and adornments were equivalent to one meeting-house, seven cabinet organs, and forty-two Sunday school libraries!

What we most need is a new revival of faith and love and righteousness in our hearts and homes, our churches and schools. We need that Christianizing of our common life for which Mr. Hill spoke so eloquently yesterday afternoon. We need the vast extension of that healthful atmosphere which this society breathes forth continually.

When I think of the possibilities of missionary activity and consecrated giving locked up in these young people's societies, I am persuaded that Christian endeavor has come into the kingdom for such a time as this. We need not despair. What has been shall be. The divine life which has glowed through all the years of our history shall not fail us now.

It was my privilege, three years after the Franco-Prussian war, to be present at the trial of Marshal Bazaine in the little palace which Louis XIV had built for one of his favorites. Bazaine, as you remember, had shown irresolution at the siege of Metz, resulting in disaster to the cause of France, and when he thought to shield himself on the ground that he did not know what was the government of the country, or if indeed it had any government, the president of the military tribunal burst forth on the Marshal with the pathetic and passionate cry, "But France! but France!" The instincts of a nation's indestructible life found expression in that intense and thrilling utterance. France still lived, and to her every soldier and every citizen owed supreme and instant allegiance. Though her Emperor was a prisoner, and his Empire a ruin, though her army had been swept away by the Prussian artillery at Sedan, and a hostile ruler encamped his troops in the very heart of Paris, France, the nation was not dead. She extemporized her government, paid her indebtedness, and rose up purified and strengthened, to moral heights never reached before.

And so, though our horison be lurid with the camp-fires of evil; though the daughters of Zion seem to have gone into captivity to strange masters, and the inhabitants of Babylon are building their temples in the vales which have been dedicated to a pure gospel; though mammonism and barbarism and superstition have built ten thousand altars in our great cities, and the envious hosts of other lands shake their fists at the towers of Zion to-night amid these young soldiers of the cross, let the ringing cry go forth: "But Christ! but Christ!" He still lives, Christ the God-man who was delivered for us and raised again for our justification; Christ who has all power in heaven and earth. He still lives and holds in his hand the reins of universal government; and shall yet stand upon the earth, holding America as a resplendent diadem in his hands, while other crowns with many stars from many lands shall be laid at his feet, and the Nation, having wrought out the divine purpose, shall be no more, since the kingdoms of this world shall have become the kingdom of our Lord and of his Christ.

ADDRESS.

BY BISHOP FALLOWS OF THE REFORMED EPISCOPAL CHURCH, OF CHICAGO.

[Abstract.]

The trend of the age is toward unity. Nations are coming together. Our routes are coming together. The boys in blue and the boys in gray are coming together. Gettysburg, which once separated them, now unites them arm in arm, heart to heart, and with them a solid South and a solid North should rejoice together in one common country and one glorious flag. The churches are coming together. Dissevered Methodism is consolidating and federating. Presbyterians, who have been cleaving asunder are cleaving together. Other religious bodies are also feeling the unifying impulse. This society means union because it is a young people's society.

Young people are fond of union. God made them so. The foundation of all union begins with them—the union of hearts, the union of hands, the home union; and then the ties which bind. May these ties ever be many and blest. The Young Men's Christian Association has done more, I believe, than any other outward agency, up to the organization of this society, to bring the churches together.

But this last and this present society—what a grand presence it presents—is bearing the palm in securing union, because it is a society of young men and young women—young people. The better half of the young people is not left out. Mrs. General Logan told me she once visited one of the most charmingly situated of our Soldier's Homes. She met there a very old soldier, scarred and worn, hobbling about with great difficulty. One might justly have supposed that he was beyond any special regard for anybody but his own sex. But

> "You may break, you may shatter the vase if you will,
> But the scent of the roses will cling to it still."

She said to him: "This is a beautiful place; you must be very happy here."

"H'm," he replied, "well, yes, madam, it is a beautiful place, but how can a man be happy where there are no women?"

There is not only music, but union in the air, in this society. It is not good for man to be alone. Our county officials, the Mayor of our city, and the Governor of our State, just before your coming here—was it a mere coincidence?—appointed women for the first time on our Boards of Education. The women have come to stay, both in the Society of Christian Endeavor, and in our Boards of Education, because they rightfully belong there.

This society means union because it is a Society of Christian Endeavor. It does not ask: "Do you want to become a member of Baptist, or American Reformed Endeavor?" but of "Christian Endeavor."

There came once, as you remember, a man in New York to the naturalization office to be made a citizen. "What is your nationality?" he was asked. He said, "I don't know. I would like you to tell me. My father was an Englishman; my mother was Spanish; I was born at sea on a French vessel flying the Dutch flag I don't know, nor do I care particularly what I am, but I want to become an American citizen."

When all the family on the maternal side of our home gather together in the homestead of the beautiful Connecticut River, in dear New England—you know an old New Englander like myself can call New England "dear," when his dearest gives it a peculiar preciousness by being of New England lineage; at the head of the united household sits one of the most cultured, honored, and efficient bishops of the Protestant Episcopal Church. One son comes who represents the most advanced churchmanship on the continent, others represent the conservative phase, shaping down to the tone and color of the Reformed Episcopal Church. Others come from the pulpits and seats of learning of the Methodist Church, others from the ranks and pulpits of the Congregational Church, and still others from the membership of the Presbyterian Church. The young people have brought about this church union, and made possible in that household a whole evangelical alliance. And when they all read in the New Testament, what they repeat from their hearts, "Our Father, who art in Heaven." it is not, as Mr. Moody says, "through the red light of Methodism, or the violet light of Episcopalianism, or the blue light of Presbyterianism," but in the clear white light of Christianity—the Christianity of Him who taught this universal, uniting prayer.

And as above the flags of all the States represented here to-night waves forever the one flag of beauty and glory in its entirety and supremacy, so above all our church ensigns floats the one single and supreme banner of the cross. This society means union because it is a Society of Christian Endeavor. By personal consecration and devotion to Christ, and by an undying missionary zeal, its members are endeavoring to bring about the reign of the one King of kings, and Lord of lords, and their labor shall not be in vain in the Lord. Those two memorable pictures in the Dore gallery, once in London, tell the story. In one the thorn-crowned Saviour is leaving the Prætorium, going on the sorrowful way to the cross. In the other Jupiter is seen, with an affrighted countenance, looking at the Olympian crown broken at his feet. The gods of Egypt, Greece, and Rome are hurrying off in wild dismay. The gods of your ancestors and mine are fleeing in hottest haste, pursued by the helmed cherubim and the sworded seraphim, and high above them in the everlasting light of heaven, directing the embattled celestial hosts, is the once crucified Son of God.

> "The head that once was crowned with thorns,
>   Is crowned with glory now,
> A royal diadem adorns
>   The mighty victor's brow."

And He shall reign forever and ever. Hallelujah!

THE SYSTEMATIC STUDY OF THE BIBLE.

BY PROF. W. R. HARPER.

It is a plain and practical question which I am to discuss—a question of business. Plain, yet involving issues of a magnitude scarcely to be appreciated; practical, yet connected with principles as deep and wide-reaching as those of true life and Christian activity. You may call this question a superficial one, if you understand that everything which relates to externals is superficial. But it may much more fairly be called a fundamental question, because it deals with that which, so far as you and I are concerned, is highest, deepest and greatest.

What is the question? Shall the Society of Christian Endeavor undertake, as a part of its prescribed work, a systematic study of the Holy Scriptures? Let us analyze the question. It contains two factors.

Factor number one: The Bible, unique, exalted, God-given, dating back thousands of years, to-day as new, as fresh, as living, as if it were of yesterday, destined in the coming years to conquer all mankind, a book presenting history; and is there anywhere such a history? The world's greatest characters and events, not of time but of eternity; a book, or rather the book of prophecy, for where else, pray, will prophecy be found? And do you know, have you ever studied the depths and the secrets, the heights and the glories of prophecy? A book abounding in heaven-inspired hymns of praise and prayer; simple and pathetic, heart-reaching and soul-stirring; used in the past, and to be used through all time in expressing man's deepest, purest thoughts as he communes with God. A book, whose writers were of every age of life; of every condition in life (some mighty monarchs, others down-trodden captives); of every degree of education and refinement (Isaiah, a man of royal culture, of royal stamp; Amos, a poor ignorant herdsman, who spoke but faultily his native tongue), yet a book whose variety of authorship is lost sight of in the broader, higher authorship of the Holy Spirit. A book whose parts, it is true, owe their origin to occasions quite diverse, the Pentateuch connecting itself with the conquest of Palestine; the Books of Samuel with the establishment of the monarchy; the Books of Chronicles with the return from captivity; Isaiah fighting with the desperation akin to madness the alliance which his royal master would make with Assyria; Haggai and Zechariah encouraging and exhorting most earnestly to the building of the second temple; yet a book of which the diversity of occasion dwindles into small proportion in view of the great occasion of Israelitish history and Israelitish literature, the preparation of the world for the Messiah. A book, characterized by remarkable differences of spirit; here the ceremonial, there the spiritual; here the actual, there the ethical; here the threat and curse, there the promise and blessing. A book, however, in which all this is as nothing when we contemplate the all-controlling purpose, the spirit of love, and the spirit of justice which lies back and beneath. The book, out of which the prattling infant even finds that which delights and fascinates him; in which the man, fighting life's battles, care-burdened, mind-distracted, finds encouragement and relief; in which, too, the aged pilgrim, almost ready to pass over, reads, and with what satisfaction, of that heavenly rest beyond.

This book, the Bible, your book, my book, God's book—this book is factor number one.

Factor number two:—The Society of Christian Endeavor. Need I enlarge? You, whom I address; you, the society itself; you, its officers, and you, its members—what are you? What is the society? A society whose membership counts as many thousands as its organization counts weeks. A society whose constituency comes from the most intelligent and most highly cultured homes of our nation. A society organized to foster and develop a true Christian life; a live Christian life, not a dead one; a life of Christian activity. A society which, with God's blessing, is destined to turn upside down and inside out some of the antiquated notions which have hitherto not only ruled but ruined. A society to which the Christian world—at all events that part of it which is not asleep—looks in expectancy for results far greater even than those which have thus far been realized. A society in the churches and for the churches; yet more, for Christ and for the Bible.

Now bring together these separate factors, and consider the question. Shall this society study, *i. e.*, undertake, as a part of its prescribed work, the systematic study of this Bible? Do we understand the question? I wonder if I have made it clear. Shall you, my friend, weaken organized effort in the line of Bible study, or shall you make this a part of your work, and agree to go at it, and into it, and under it, with the same persevering spirit, the same determination, with God's help, to conquer, which characterizes your other work?

Shall, now, the Christian Endeavor, throughout the world, undertake, as a part of its prescribed work, a systematic study of the Bible?

I answer, Yes, and I believe that God in heaven hears my answer with approval. Nay, more. Could we, as in days of yore, apply direct to God by prophet, or by Urim and Thummim, the divine answer wonld itself be, Yes. Yes, because to-day, as never before, the Bible needs study; yes, because to-day, as never before, the Bible repays study; yes, because such study is necessary as the basis, the only basis, for the work which this organization has set out to accomplish; yes, because such study will but assist and enhacne the work of that noblest of modern institutions, the Sunday School. But suppose the sentiment of your society favors this proposition. It then remains to consider, and the consideration will be very brief, the method which should be followed, the particular kind of work which should be undertaken, the spirit should characterize it.

It is the great aim of the Bible student so to study the Bible as to himself, and himself the most sufficient worker possible in advancing master its contents, as to make it of the greatest possible value to cause of divine truth in this world. In working out this purpose it is necessary, first or all, that a student, or Christian worker, shall have a spiritual grasp of the Scriptures; he must have that familiarity with certain portions, that personal experience of certain truths, which will enable him to make practical use of the same in the hand-to-hand work of the street or the inquiry-room.

One's strength in Christian work is measured largely by one's ability to make this use of Scripture truth. This kind of work is, of all kinds, the most practical and the most essential. It is a work for which, in preparation, years of study and prayer, and often many seasons of affliction are needed. It is not to be obtained at once. It does not come with the memorizing of verses here and there, or with the repetition of a few selected exhortatory sentences. It is the highest of all possessions, the deepest of all knowledge. It will come in time to the child of God, but to him only, and only in time.

But is there not among some, and particularly among those who have done this work, and profited by it most, a feeling that it is not all that is wanted, that something additional is wanted? Are such satisfied with a kind of Bible work which, although from one point of view the deepest, is from another superficial? There is no contradiction here. What in one sense is deep, may in another sense be of the surface. It is, or aims to be, deep, spiritually; while, intellectually, it is confessedly and necessarily too often superficial.

For the uneducated, the undisciplined, this is sufficient. It is, indeed, the only kind of work such a one is capable of doing. But to one who thinks, questions will continually present themselves which he must have answered.

In meeting the sceptic, difficulties arise, and they will most certainly lead to doubt and scepticism, if they are not met, if the principles which explain them are not set forth. What kind of a pupil is he who does not ask, "Why is this? When was that?" and if one accustomed to ask these questions, and to have them answered, in reference to subjects outside the Bible, does not ask them in reference to the Bible, one of two things must be true: His interest in the Bible, like seed sown on stony ground, will be short-lived, for it has not taken root; or his conception of the Bible is so shallow, so imperfect, so erroneous, as to render his Christian life and ministrations of no permanent value. The Bible student, it may be repeated, if he is a student, will think; he will inquire; he will investigate; he will know all that is to be known so far as his circumstances will allow the acquisition of this knowledge.

And so appeal for a kind of Bible study which, in some respects, is different from that which hitherto has been generally in vogue. I do not make this appeal with any desire to see the other kind of study slighted. It is needed and must continue; but it is not all that is needed. This work, intended, we repeat, not to supersede, but to supplement and strengthen that now being done, may, for want of a bette term, be called intellectual work. The term critical would be more appropiate, but is liable to be misunderstood. Its detailed description must be brief. What is the plan? It would be an historical work, including a mastery, so far as possible, of the details of Bible history; a putting together of this and that event; an investigation of the great epochs; a study of the great characters; an inquiry into the causes of things, as they are represented in Scripture, and in their relations to each other.

It would be a literary work, including the study of the literary forms of various books; the question of their authorship and date; the circumstances under which they had their origin; the purpose they were intended to subserve; the people for whom they were originally written; their history It would be a work of interpretation, including an application of those great principles common to the interpretation of all writings; and in addition, the study of those special principles demanded by the unique character of the Bible; a going down beneath the surface, a searching after things deep and hidden; an investigation of prophecy; a study of the divine plan for the redemption of man, as it began and developed, and was finally accomplished in the life, work, and death of Christ. It is for work this kind, critical, to be sure, yet necessary to a conservation of the truth; intellectual, yet forming the basis of the deepest spiritual work, that I appeal.

But with what spirit shall this work be done? A bad work, with bad methods, but with good spirit, often succeeds. A work, good or bad, with bad methods, but with good spirit, generally sccceeds, while a good work, with good methods, but with the wrong spirit, generally fails This first thing is to satisfy ourselves that the work proposed is a good work. Next in importance is the spirit. Last of all comes the method. The spirit must be a reverent one. In this day of flippant and often blasphemous criticism, reverence is a thing to be cultivated. Perhaps, it is thought, this caution is not needed. Of those who have sufficient interest in the Bible, to study it, a reverential spirit would be expected. Bnt it must be confessed that in the kind of work which has been referred to, there is danger of losing, to some extent, that reverence for the Sacred Volume which the other kind of study increases. In the critical handling of the book a liberty is taken, a familiarity is gained, that seems, in the case of some, to destroy the feeling of respect and awe, which, from one point of view, ought to characterize the student's attitude toward the Holy Book. Now. so far as this study destroys that Bible-worship of which so many Christians are unconsciously guilty, it is well. There are those who treat the Bible as they would treat an idol. It is regarded by them with a snperstitious, sanctimonious feeling, as a kind of charm. This is a use for which the sacred book was never intended; and one great result to be accomplished by the kind of work here advocated is the removal of this unfounded and mischievous idea True reverence for divine truth, and proper regard for the instrument through which that truth has been revealed, are things quite different. These must be cultivated.

The spirit must be a historical spirit. It is the truth we seek; and this truth, when found, we should be ready to accept at whatever cost. It is a sore trial to have ideas, with which we have been familiar from our infancy, shown to be erroneous. It is most difficult to put aside the prejudices that years have hardened. Yet the former will take place, and the latter must take place, if the historical spirit is to have sway. This historical spirit is one slow of acquisition. To do what it requires seems, at first, like parting with one's dearest treasures. It cannot be acquired without a struggle. But why should not you be in the foremost in seeking it, the most careful in its application, and its stanchest defenders when it is assailed. The spirit must be an independent one. That student makes no real progress, who is satisfied with having learned what some one else has said concerning the meaning of a verse, or the scope of a passage; who always follows, who is always leaning upon another. Such a student crams; he does not digest. His work is done for the moment; not for all time. He examines only results; never the processes leading to the results. The fact is, he does not do honest work. And yet all the world knows that the knowledge which does not come by honest work does not stay; it may, indeed, be said never to have come. By what method should this work be done? Having considered the kind of work and the spirit of the work, it only remains for us briefly to take up the method. No two men will do the same thing best, in the same way. Each man must work largely by his own method. A method helpful to one man, or set of men, might be ruinous to another man, or set of men. Independence, not only of spirit, but as well of method—of any and every method—is a thing to be sought after. A constant effort should be made to keep out of the ruts. Yet, after all, there must be a plan of work. He who works without plan, and aimlessly, will find his results without form and void, chaotic. A poor method is better than no method; but in making a selection it is wise to use the best. Our method must be one which will be disciplinary in its influence: it must be one which will train the mind and keep it trained; for, if it does not help, it will injure the mind. Good habits of study, if already required, should be strengthened by it. Bad habits should be corrected. How many men expend the same amount of mental energy in the preparation of a Bible lesson, as in preparation for a school or college recitation? In the latter it is work; in the former, to often, at the best, half work. This is all wrong. Our method of work should be one which will demand the same rigid, unflinching effort required by the school or college tasks, the only difference being that in the former case the effort is to be a voluntary one, while in the latter it is compulsory.

It must be a definite method. It must be a method which will lead to definite results. When one has finished a course of study in any department, he will surely be disappointed and dissatisfied with the subject his teacher and himself, if he is not able to put his hands on certain definite results. Now the Bible is a small book. It consists of a definite number of separate books, each of which has its place in the canon for a certain purpose. It is, we all believe, an inexhaustible book; and yet the work of mastering this book is, in one sense, a very definite one. With a plan of study looking toward through work and definite results, the facts, the purpose, the teachings of book after book will come into our possession; one principle after another will become familiar; one period of history after another will gradually develop itself before us. But to accomplish this the method must itself be definite, and indicate definite work. It must be a logical method. If it teach a list of events without also teaching the relation of these events to each other, it will not answer. If it takes a verse here and a passage there, without considering that verse in the light of its context, it will not answer. If it attempt to exhaust the meaning of a verse without first a study of the character of which the verse is a part, or of a chapter without first the study of the book of which the chapter is a part, it will not answer. There must be consecution, connection, logical order. The method must be comprehensive as possible. Mastery of details is needed, yet also mastery of the subject as a whole. It is a mistake to suppose for a moment that Bible study consists in the study of isolated texts, or in the study of single chapters, or even in the study of entire books. A man might study verses all his life, and know comparitively little of the Bible. Besides, the man who studies only verses does one-sided, imperfect, narrow work. He who does not have in mind the entire book, and from this standpoint do his work, does not and cannot appreciate the full forces of a single verse contained in that book. The same thing holds good in a higher sphere. It is not sufficient merely to have gained comprehensive knowledge of a given book. Although we may know the contents, the analysis, the occasion, the purpose, the author, etc., of a book, there is still something to be ascertained. What? The place of that book in the Bible as a whole; its relation to other books; the relation of its contents to the contents of the whole Bible, to the entire plan of God for the salvation of man How comparatively contemptible, after all, is the study of mere verses. How much he loses who satisfies himself that, having done this, he has done all. We should be close, critical, accurate students of a verse: we should be searching, analytical, systematizing students of a book; we should also be broad, comprehensive, general students of the Bible. Let our method, therefore, whatever else it is, be a comprehensive one. And now just one word more. The feeling may not be unanimous, it is, nevertheless, rapidly growing, that work like that which I have indicated, work characterized by the spirit which I have described, work according to some such method as that which has been outlined, should be undertaken. You may ask, are those who have been considering this matter prepared to suggest a plan? I answer, yes, and I can only regret that the time at my disposal will not allow an expanded presentation of this plan. I may, however, say this much: A course of forty studies, arranged according to the ideas which I have tried to present, based on the Gospel of Mark, and taking up in detail the life and the work of the Christ, will be published in successive numbers of your official organ, THE GOLDEN RULE, beginning about September 1st. These studies have been specially prepared for you. While intended to lead those who take them up who do independent work, work for themselves, they will not be found too difficult, or too taxing. In order that you may see for yourselves just what it is proposed to do, printed pamphlets, containing the first study of this course, will be distributed among you here to-night. And may we not ask for this study, which will shortly be placed in your hands, a careful examination, not here in the midst of the hurry and heat of this great convention, but at home, where, in quiet, you may decide whether or not it is something which will help you. My friends, God has placed upon you, in this matter, a great and fearful responsibility. Will you be equal to it? Will you not consent, here and now, to do what the times demand of you, and what God, your leader, clearly and unmistakably calls you to do?

ADDRESS.

BY MISS FRANCES E. WILLARD.

Dear younger brothers and sisters of the grand army of Christian Endeavor, only second to me, if indeed second, in the affection I bear you, to my own White Ribboners of the W. C. T. U. Standing now before you, I can but think of the first recollection that has come to me along the years concerning my Christian Endeavor. Go back in your thought as I do in mine, to the very first remembrance of a time when the blessedness of Christianity came to be something to you, no matter how dim, no matter how shadowy, no matter how little organized it was. With me it was a Sunday morning in Oberlin, Ohio, and mother had gone to church and left the little ones with father. We were a very democratic household in the enjoyment of our privileges and the performance of our duties, and so it was that father and mother took turns about in going to church. On this Sunday morning he got down his hymn book and took me upon his knee and said: "My little daughter, I'm going to teach you a hymn. You won't know much about it now, but some day you will understand it." And so, to please my father, I said over after him, "A charge to keep I have, a God to glorify." That has always been to me a hymn filled with meaning, and often when I come forward to speak to an assembly, I wonder what my father thinks to see me—he was a conservative Vermonter, with a good deal of granite and the iron of his native State in the make-up of his character—I often wonder what he thinks to see his daughter go about talking to anybody who would listen? I'm afraid he would shake his head wisely; but I can't but think that in the high heavenly place he knows about it, and says: "It was I who taught her that verse, 'Oh, may it all my powers engage to do my Master's will.'" I can but think of the first time I tried to stand up and speak in prayer-meeting. Go back in your thought to when first you did that thing. Reared a Methodist, it yet was so hard for me that my heart beat like a trip-hammer, but a voice sweet and holy said to me, " My child, he that confesseth me before men, him will I confess before my Father and the holy angels," and I wanted to be of that company, and so I confessed. Sweet and sacred those early memories to you and me. The first time, too, when the kind Christian people asked me to read an essay for the Sunday school, when I rose in the school—I was then a student at Evanston—the paper trembled in my hand as I tried to tell a little something about foreign missions, and my mouth so dry and hard, I so scared; and now not a bit scared by all these people. Not a bit—just thinking that it's like reaching out my hands, knowing that a thousand hands would clasp them. Some people say it isn't womanly. But the age is kind—so kind—and it's so homelike here, and a woman may go anywhere that it's homelike; that's the touchstone. An age of force wouldn't have been appropriate to woman's presence and woman's voice. She can come forth after the clouds have broken and the sunshine of Christ's righteousness has made the world so kind—woman can come forth like the singing bird after the sunshine. I'm so glad of the many women here; not less than that our brothers are here; vastly gladder that both are here than I would be if either were here alone.

Our honored scholar from Yale brought out to you his pet idea, so grand, so vast, so blessed—just what he wanted to say was what you cared for most. Just what you want to hear from me is just what I care most to talk about, and I feel a little like carrying coals to Newcastle—for I don't doubt every one of you is a friend of temperance. Of course, in the temperance spelling book you begin with the a, b, c, of total abstinence. And then we pass to the polysyllables, and come to prohibition, and I am sure you are all its friends—you must all be friends of the home, and the home is a shorn lamb to which no wind is tempered. America is a wonder country for protection; they tell us we have the tariff. It is a hard thing to find out what it means. To use the words of Lord Dundreary, " No fellow can find out where it is." It is said to be for the protection of industry. We have patent laws to protect patents, subsidies to protect railroads, charters to protect companies, but, I, as a woman, come here to say that the home is the place we have forgotten to protect. A nation is judged by the wisdom and care with which it protects its choicest treasures, and the choicest treasures of a nation are its homes. If it succeeds there it succeeds truly. If it fails there then it fails indeed.

Upon this basis then, deep as the human heart, changeless as a mother's love and holy as a father's faith, we ground our doctrines of prohibition against the dram shop, and protection for the home. We believe these are parts of one tremendous whole. We believe this is the living issue before the people of this country. It is Banquo's ghost. It will not down at any one's invitation. I have a faith dear to me, sacred as a prayer, a faith that on next Friday night I shall speak out clearly here when Clinton B. Fiske comes to talk about it. But tonight I do not wish to bring that thought before you, but only wish to teach sovereign citizenship. We have carried our petition to many a Legislature, and we have found grave legislators rolling that petition into balls to put into the waste-basket. We have seen them toss from one to another those balls. We have seen honorable men, dressed in a little brief authority, do this. We have now taken our case from them. We are taking it to the court of last and highest resort—the supreme court of the Nation—the ballot-box. We women are unrepresented save by you; we ask you to represent us women. If you don't represent us then we are surely those you left behind you.

If you do not represent us, then you vote down the sermon on the Mount on election day. We ask you to remember that it is the women who have given the costliest heritages to fortune. We ask the manhood of the Nation to remember the sorrowful hearts of women, and to come forth to the stern arbitrament of election day, and let the broken hearts of women become the strength of manhood. Let the appeal of the defenceless become the vote of the defenders. God bless you as you bless us in this great decesion. I have this other thought that not alone stands in our spelling book, and that is that in the evolution ot the great movements of this great age there is none so great, none so central, as that of which this assembly is a magnificent object lesson. When I was in Florence twenty years ago the famous sculptor Hart said to me, " I am working out my idea of American womanhood." He said, 'I go over to the gallery. I study the Venus de Milo(no, it was the Venus of Medici.) I see the small head, I see the beautiful shape, I see the small eyes, and I say that would do for Europe, but it will not do for the American Republic.

For that Republic there must be a woman with broader brow, an ample figure, a more motherly heart in her breast. To work out that idea I dedicate my life. And now his life's work is perfected, and it has been brought to this country and placed on a pedestal at Lexington —a perfect woman, made to comfort and console, and yet a spirit pure and bright, with something of the angel like. She is the woman of the future, a woman to be wrought out by such teaching as the Endeavor Societies are endeavoring to give in their most Christian work. Ithank God that issue has come and is being won ; that the evolution has been wonderfully rapid in these days. I thank God that woman is ceasing to be dependent upon man, and is now becoming his counsel. I am glad that we are invading masculine solitude, and that there can now be friendship between man and woman everywhere. It rejoices my heart to see how grandly manhood is moving on and upward to the heights of true conquest, and is learning a chivalry that the world knew not of before. In the home world man votes against the saloon and the woman wears the blue ribbon.

We know that the chief corner-stone of the State is the home : that the world exists for the sake of its homes. I am interested, then, not only in the temperance movement, but in this great and blessed movement for social purity and the White Cross. I ask you, too, to take it into your thoughts, your heart, and your prayers, as I believe you have done already, and will do more and more. It is in the home that you and I and all of us are sheltered. In its tenderness and beauty we rest. In it lies the form of every holy thought. The husband and wife, the father and mother, the son and daughter make it up. It is the center of the love of all human kind. It has had the love of every heart since the world began, and will have to its close. And holy marriage makes it so. Protect it, then, and make it sacred."

THE CONDITION OF SPIRITUAL POWER.

BY REV. ARTHUR LITTLE, D. D.

This is the last hour of the feast. It is, therefore, an impressive hour. Here, through a series of days, a great company of Christian workers, gathered from all parts of this broad land, you have been sitting together in heavenly places in Christ Jesus. You have been exchanging salutations, enjoying sweet fellowships, discoursing upon great themes, forgetting denominational differences, surrendering to high enthusiasms, stirring up each others pure minds by way of remembrance, and seeking to refurnish and equip yourselves for the work.

You have been getting more distinctly before your minds the precise object of your organization, and raising the question of how its ends may be most fully subserved. You have decided that it is not an ultimate end in itself, but only a means to an end. You have been upon the heights. But here you can no longer tarry. The summons is to service, to holy and earnest endeavor for Christ and His cause.

What is to follow? The question now comes as to the utilization of this occasion. How can it be turned to best account?

Statement, argument, fact, appeal, to these you have listened, until you have room for no more. You do not need to be reminded that there is always more or less peril in allowing the feelings to be played upon, the emotions excited, the will persuaded, the judgment convinced, unless appropriate action follow. There should be a wise expenditure of the force that has been generated, or else a disastrous reaction is almost sure to come.

What, then, shall be carried away from this convention? Have I obtained anything that will help me in my own Christian life as a Christian worker? And let it here be emphasized that we shall be able to help others only as our own spiritual life is robust, vigorous, vital. The element of personality is the great element in the problem. We have come here to be empowered, to be clothed with spiritual strength.

Let me call your attention, briefly, to some of the conditions of spiritual power.

Negative conditions.—Comprehensively speaking, there is only one reason for lack of spiritual power in you or me, one reason for anything less than the fulness of God in your soul and mind, and that is sin. Hence, the first step is to search out and remove every form or remnant of sin. Of the grosser forms of sin, the professing Christian is presumed not to be guilty. Sin is very subtle and insidious in its workings. It has methods and resorts which we little suspect. Its hiding-places are innumerable. "Cleanse thou me from secret faults." "Search me, O God, and know my heart; try me, and know my thoughts, and see if there be any wicked way in me, and lead me in the way everlasting." Brethren, we need such views of sin as come with clear visions of God. We need a glimpse into our hearts, as seen under the white light of the burning throne; as brought face to face with the perfect law of God. We need a careful inspection of our motives. We need that sorrowing after a godly sort that is described in Corinthians. "What carefulness it wrought in you, yea, what clearing of yourselves, yea, what indignation, what vehement desire, yea, what zeal, yea, what revenge." What a clarifying, energizing, intensifying of the passions and emotions, as the result of their godly sorrow. Break up your fallow ground. "Every branch in me that beareth not fruit, He taketh away, and every branch that beareth fruit, He purgeth it, that it may bring forth more fruit" "Put off concerning the former conversation the old man, and put on the new man." "Let us lay aside every weight, and the sin that doth so easily beset us." Brethren, is not the church of God weighted down, water-logged with a great multitude of weights that impede its progress? Entangling alliances have been formed. We must get rid of the weights, all entanglements, all compromises with evil, all questionable habits and doubtful practices.

Positive conditions. 1.—Faith. We need a revival of faith. There is so much doubt, uncertainty about things that seem to be simple and fundamental. Unbelief is always weakness We expect it outside the church, but not inside. Nothing is possible without faith. Not many mighty works because of their unbelief. Men who have no convictions achieve nothing. "I have believed, and, therefore, have I spoken."

2 Faith is a condition of power, because it gives God and His word their appropriate place in the order of things. And there can be no power until there is a proper adjustment of the forces involved. Reason, science. philosophy, decline to do this. They either rob Him of His personality, or dethrone Him, or subordinate Him to His own laws, or declare Him to be unknowable, and put His book in the same low level with other books. It is only a reverent faith that exalts God, puts Him on the throne, and sinful man in the dust, Jesus Christ, as the gracious mediator between the two, and makes the Bible the blessed proclamation of the terms of pardon.

3. The binding power of faith.—Faith is a condition of spiritual

power, because it brings man into right relations to God, the source of power, and holds him there. It answers to the belting in the factory. It connects the machinery with the great wheel of power, and then holds the unwrought material in proper relation to the machinery. It binds the finite with the infinite. It helps a man to hitch his chariot to a star. It couples vacillating weakness with everlasting strength. It makes man the channel through which God pours blessings.

4. Faith is a condition of spiritual strength, because it, and it only, adequately interprets the problem of probation. The world has no conception of the problem God is solving in behalf of a fallen race, in the person of His Son, Jesus Christ, through the agency of the Holy Spirit. It does not detect the drift of history. It is busy asking, What shall we eat and drink and wear? Faith, discloses the appalling need, the terrible emergency. Faith has an adequate remedy to offer.

5. Faith conditions power, because it lays hold of the only transcendent motives. All other motives are petty, compared with those that rise before the believing soul. It commands motives from three realms—earth, heaven, hell. It keeps forever echoing the startling question, "What shall it profit a man if he shall gain the whole world and lose his own soul." To the eye of faith come majestic and awful epiphanies of the resurrection, of Jehovah enthroned, of the impending judgement, of heaven and hell, of a race separated on the ground of character.

6. Faith conditions spiritual power by harmonizing the paradoxes of the gospel. "When I am weak, then am I strong." "He that saveth his life shall lose it." Is not faith the fountain head of spiritual power? "According to your faith be it unto you."

Time will fail me to speak of prayer and hopefulness and courage as sources of power. I must venture, however, to mention one other source, inclusive of all others, the presence and indwelling of the Holy Spirit. "But ye shall receive power, after that the Holy Ghost is come upon you." His presence in human hearts is like the presence of the sun in the midst of an arctic winter, like the coming of spring with its affluent life.

I believe that we can have the Holy Spirit with enduring power, on these conditions; If we want Him more than anything else He must have the first place, the right of priority. Do we want Him more than pleasure, riches, honor, position, ease, success? If we show this want by preparing for Him. When a guest has been invited to our home we make preparations for his coming. The guest chamber is put in order, and we are exceedingly careful to make sure of his welcome. A willingless on our part to co-operate with Him in His work. Fulfil these conditions. With the swiftness of light, with the certainty of God, with the power conferred by a risen Christ, will he come, and will not tarry. O that we might hear the Master saying to our longing hearts this hour, " Receive ye the Holy Ghost !" That to Him we might be anointed for a higher service.

The glorious result. When Garibaldi was raising soldiers among the Piedmontese, they asked him what he had to give. His answer was: "Long marches, weariness, sickness, wounds, death—and victory." Whereupon the youths tossed their caps in air, and rallied to the standard of the liberator of Italy. A similar call, only with higher motives, comes to the youth of our land, from the great Captain of our salvation, to rally round the standard of the cross, and march to the world's conquest. Let us, to-night, renew our allegiance to our great Leader, and follow cheerfully where he leads the way.

ADDRESS.

BY REV. NEHEMIAH BOYNTON.

My dear friends: A religious warfare has never been waged more hotly than that to-day between the forces of General Surmise and of General Certainty. The hoarse cry is forever heard in the hostile camp, "Prove it! prove it!" and the rejoinder ever comes from the camp of faith, "Perceive it! perceive it!" In fact, General Surmise has offered unconditional surrender upon the simple condition that General Certainty will demonstrate his faith, and General Certainty does not accept the proposition, because he knows that he cannot, in any real sense of the word, demonstrate his faith; you and I know that General Certainty is right because of the fact that the deepest experience of our lives and the most blessed knowledge which comes to us is too deep for demonstration. We can discern it; we cannot demonstrate it; we cannot prove it; we can perceive it.

Two people, for example, are gazing upon Niagara, and one sees in those thundering waters the beauty and the power of God. The other sees there nothing but magnificent water power for a saw mill. By no process of demonstration could you make the man who sees only the water power there see the beauty. There is an eye in his soul which has been closed, and which cannot be opened by any power of logic.

We have been listening to this beautiful song about the Jesus who can save a sinner like me, and I doubt not in the soul of every one of us there has been a response of sympathy as we have discerned the beauty therein, but in this city to-night there are thousands who, having no ears to hear, should they express the thought of their minds, would couch it in language like this: "Stop that noise," and you could not by any process of demonstration make them see the beauty there is in that song. They must discern it with another eye; they must perceive it with another faculty. You and I, dear friends, have another eye than that which holds the pupil; we have another ear than that which holds the tympanum; we have, thank God, another intelligence than that which clothes our information for use within the confines of the syllogism. We have, every one of us, in our souls a latticed window which looks out toward God, and our lives take their coloring and their significance from the fact, whether that window is opened or whether that window is closed.

If you will take pains to notice the lives of those who on the one hand demand what they call proof for their spiritual inspirations, and of those on the other who take what they call perception for their spiritual uplifting—if you will follow those two sets of lives until the mellow light of the evening sun begins to hem them in, and the darkness begins to limit their horizon, you will see a gulf between the one kind and the other, broad as the earth and high as the heaven.

It is related, for example, of Victor Hugo, that when the hoar-frost of age had touched his brow he sent to his publishers one day a picture which he wished to have inserted in his famous work, " The Toilers of the Sea," and upon the back of the picture he wrote these simple words : " Upon this paste-board I have sketched my destiny and my life ; a steamboat tossing upon the angry waves of the uncontrolled ocean, the rudder gone, no one to man the ship, with only a bit of smoke, which men call glory, left, which a moment's summer wind may deprive me of."

Another, in the sunset day of his life, has given to us his life experience and his life hope. He has not written it upon pasteboard, but in the flowing measure of sacred song. Listen as in the twilight of his years he sings beautifully, wonderfully and tenderly.

> We may not climb the heavenly steeps
> To bring the Lord Christ down;
> In vain we search the lowest deeps,
> For Him no depths can drown.
>
> But warm, sweet, tender, even yet,
> A present help is He;
> And faith has yet its Olivet,
> And love its Galilee.

The Frenchman, you will observe, was depressed beneath the thought of the emptiness of life; the Quaker was inspired by the thought of its fullness. The Frenchman could see beyond him nothing but the dim forms of the shades of darkness, but the path before and around the Quaker was filled with the living angels of God. Now, let us for a moment, bring the Frenchman and the Quaker to this platform, and the Frenchman in his despair shall say to the Quaker, " Whence came that glowing faith of yours which supports your soul in these twilight days?" and the poet, catching the words which have fallen in song from our lips this evening, shall answer :

> At the cross, at the cross,
> Where I first saw the light,
> And the burden of my sin rolled away;
> It was there by faith I received my sight,
> And now I am happy all the day."

Happy in the sense of a present God; happy in the thought of a protecting Christ, real, present, manifested. But do you know, friends, that I sometimes think that we forget and lose sight of this thought of the manifestation of God in the other awe-inspiring thought of His majesty. I sometimes fancy that we lose the thought of a present God as we embrace the other thought of a far away God. We are forever confessing, with a faith implicit, that no man has seen God at any time. We forget the only begotten of the Father who hath declared Him. We ask ourselves who, by searching, can find out God? We forget those other blessed words, "I will come in and sup with Him and He with me." We have given to the devil a privilege which practically we have denied the Deity. And so it has come about that this God of ours, this longing and yearning and sacrificing God of ours is, to many, a being dwelling in some far away Olympus, clad in garments of fire and dwelling with the clouds round about Him. If our faith permits us to hope that He is a being who can be touched with the feeling of our infirmities, still there are many of us who never dare to hope that He really and truly touches us.

But is it not time, dear friends, is it not time that you and I lay aside the swaddling clothes in which tradition and logic have bound us, and that we accept, and accept heartily, the simple testimony of our faith that God is here, not there; that we can see Him, that we can look upon Him, that we can embrace Him really, actually, truly.

How many things our eyes have seen during these last few days! Some of us have stood before that great rolling, thundering cataract at Niagara, and have wondered at the prodigality of nature. We have gazed upon that suspension bridge which sits so gracefully over the falls, and we have marvelled at the ingenuity of man. We have seen for the first time a city surrounded by rolling prairies, with their grasses and their flowers of green, of blue, of yellow, of white. Your beautiful city, friends, has been our delectation, as we have walked along your avenues and your boulevards, as we have ridden upon your cable cars and through your tunnels and along your parks; as we have looked out upon that beautiful lake, as we have experienced your generous-hearted and open-handed hospitality: all these things that have come to us filled us every one, not alone with amusement, but with gratitude and with keen delight.

But friends, what is the gladdest vision which has come to any one of us in these beautiful days here in Chicago, the thing for which more than anything else we raise our thanksgiving to God; it is this, that the same God we *have* seen before we do see, we are seeing now; the same God whose face was our joy and whose smile was our sunlight in our far-away homes by the shores of the billowy Atlantic or on the banks of the rolling Oregon. That is the thing which gives us largest joy, which gives us truest hope; that God, our God, is here, and that we can see Him, that we do see Him, that we must see Him whenever we go under the guidance of faith to look for Him. He is not far away over there; He lives in us. He does not send to us the white-winged messengers of His from the throne of grace. He comes: oh, blessed truth, He comes himself!

There is a spirit in man, and when that spirit goes out to seek the great Spirit of God then there surely comes a time, and that right speedily when the heart rises to meet with heart. God is here! Oh,

> "Speak to Him, then, for He hears,
> And spirit with spirit can meet;
> Closer is He than breathing,
> And nearer than hands and feet."

But I want to remind you, dear friends, of the condition on which you and I shall catch this blessed present vision of God, which I am sure is possible for every one. We turn to the scripture and read that "The pure in heart see God." Purity of heart, then, is the medium through which you and I look out upon this vision beatific. It is the effect always of divine ambitions; it is the offspring ever of a Heaven-born excellence. Are we not, says one, like clay in the hands of the potter? Yes, but we are also soldiers upon life's battlefield. Let the potter look out for the clay: He will not make any mistake; look without to your own armor; it must be burnished and made bright, not by any oil and sand-paper process, but by continual use in the battle of life. Write, dear friends, over the opening years of your life, this one truth: that no son or daughter of mankind was ever to the manor born so far as purity of heart is concerned; they come to it gradually only by day-by-day struggles, only by hour-by-hour contests, but it is always after the contest that there comes the crown.

You remember the story of the Monk who had seen around his hermitage for many years a great lion, of whom he was terribly afraid, and one day the lion got a thorn in his foot and the Monk went and took it out, and in his gratitude for the kindly deed the lion ever after was the servant of the Monk. He followed him to the house of prayer, and home again. Wherever he went, whatever he did, his lion friend was there, and at the end he came to support him, to assist him.

I tell you, my dear friends, the great virtues of our lives when we get a thorn in then become the vices of our lives, and when you and I for the sake of Jesus Christ pull out the thorn, then that which was yesterday a vice becomes a virtue to-day, that which was weakness then is strength now, that which was impurity there is purity here, and there is no other way by which you and I can come to purity of heart, through the grace of Jesus Christ, our Lord, than by these daily, hourly momentary struggles.

You remember that the Moslem always leads his cohorts to war shouting this battle cry; "Fight! Fight! Paradise! Paradise!" We can change the battle cry and adapt it for ourselves as the necessity of our lives: "Fight! Fight! Purity! Purity!" For purity of heart is the medium through which, in Christ's name, you and I shall see God.

You remember that beautiful story of Margaret Wilson in the seventeenth century, that blooming young girl, who, for her faith, was condemned to be drowned in the river, and just as they had put her into the river, the Priest, laying one hand upon her head asked her, before he let her go into the deep, if she would recant her faith; you remember the simple words which she flung back to him, "Let me go: let me go, I am Christ's."

And so as you and I learn every day to say to these temptations which would throttle us, "Let me go; let me go; I am Christ's," in the blessed assurance that whatever else might happen we shall fall as she fell, into the loving arms of our God; then shall we find ourselves every day and every hour as servants of Jesus Christ, growing, increasing in the knowledge of our Lord and Saviour. Then shall we find that purity of heart gradully dawning upon us as we become pure, ever more pure through it, and through which alone you and I can be received to God.

And here, dear friends, and this is my final thought, herein is the true blessedness of life. We have been playing in our thought around that beatitude; let us bring it now to our full vision. It is Jesus Christ who says, "blessed are the pure in heart for they shall see God." Here is the true blessedness of life. Do you ask me still further, what is blessedness? I reply to you it is not leisure, in which we coax and indulge ourselves. What is blessedness? It is not labor alone, which brings weariness to our tired bodies and weakness to our strength. It is not luxury, that effeminate thing which is so liable to unman us all and lead us away from God to whom it ought to guide us. Blessedness is two-fold. It is loyalty that owns allegiance to the King whose crown has never been taken from His brow, and whose scepter has never been snatched from His hand, and it is liberty, which, in the strength of love, goes out into the world to lead others to the lamb of God; it taketh away the sins of the worldly ones who hitherto have not yielded to His claim or acknowledged His love.

"Give me," said Archimedes, "Give me a place where I may stand and I will move the world." He could not find a place, he could not move the world, but he who is blest of God can stand upon his loyalty firm as upon the Rock of Ages, and with His lever he can pry up the sinful lives of men until he shall bring them, for Christ's sake, in some faint resemblance to the true christian life.

Do you say that the man who has this blessedness of life has not many other things? Well, what has he not? He is a man who can laugh at the storm cloud, because he has heard one whom he has seen saying unto him, "Lo, I am with you always, even unto the end of the world." He is a man who can face the great sorrows of life,—whatever else he may have, whatever else he may not have, if he has this blessedness which is made up of two-fold kind, of loyalty on the one hand, and of liberty on the other, he has all because he has Christ.

I have read this beautiful legend, that a Priest had two boys to help him at the hour of mass, and it was their duty before breakfast to go and light the altar candles, to say the mass, to tinkle the bell, sing the sanctus, and then to put out the lights after mass and retire into the chapel for their morning prayer. One day they came and said, "Father, who is the strange boy who breakfasts with us every day?" "I know not, my sons," exclaimed the father. "From whence comes he?" "He comes straight from the altar," they said. "And is there any way by which I should know him," said the father. "Aye," responded the elder boy; "he wears a white robe; his hands are pierced, and whenever he takes bread the blood trickles down upon it until it blushes like the rose." "Oh, my boys!" said the father, "It is the child Jesus who breakfasts with you, and when he comes again say you to him these words; 'Oh, Jesus, thou who hast often breakfasted with us, grant that we may one day, and the good Father, may sup with thee,'" and the Saviour smiled and said, verily, it shall be so. Upon Ascension Day you shall thus sup with me." And when the day dawned the boys went in from breakfast to the chapel, for they were to sup with Christ. They saw the Priest and visited him as usual, they sung the Sanctus, they rung the bell, they chanted the hymn, they knelt in prayer, and, after the Pax Nobiscum had been said, they fell asleep and then woke up, the boys and the father, to find themselves around the marriage supper of the Lamb.

The legend, to be sure, is not true, but it has a truth in it, and the truth which makes the legend true is this, that you and I may be so blessed in our purity of heart that we too can really, really see God; that we too can really feel His presence and be more certain that He is by our side than we are, that these friends are there who are sitting so lovingly about us.

Oh, beloved friends, as you come to-night to consecrate yourselves anew to God, be sure that through the influence of His spirit you see the Christ to whom you are consecrating yourselves. Ask Him for the Heavenly spirit and you shall sup with him; ask Him for the living water and He shall give it to you and quench your thirst; ask Him to abide with you and He will not fail to do the thing you ask. Thus you get yourselves into a relation of personal sympathy and friendship with God. Thus you come to assure yourselves in your faith that God is your God here and now; that His holy spirit revealing Him unto you enables you to see those things which are invisible, and to love with a tender love Him, who, not having seen, you love.

Do this: be pure in heart, for the sake of Jesus Christ, by battling with temptation every day and every hour, and you, you shall see God, and when you see God your life will be a song that is perennial and your eternal home paradise.

Blessed, blessed are the pure in heart for they shall, aye, they do see God.

N. B.—Our acknowledgements are due, and cheerfully made to the Publishers of the Chicago "Inter-Ocean" for the use of their reports of portions of the foregoing addresses.

LIST OF SOCIETIES.

NOTE.

The following statistics, coming as they do from so many different sources are of necessity somewhat incomplete. Although great care has been taken to avoid duplicating, yet it may be possible that this has occurred in a few instances, from the fact that some churches are known by more than one local name. It will be a great convenience and add to the value of future Reports if any inaccuracies and errors are reported as soon as noticed, to G. M. WARD, Secretary, Box 1,235, Boston, Mass.

LIST OF SOCIETIES.

If the name of the Secretary is not given the name of the Pastor is inserted when reported.

ALABAMA.

CITY.	CHURCH.	Act. Memb.	Asso. Memb.	Ch. Memb.	United with C.	Secretary and Address
Marion............	Congregational......	....	....	....	....	Rev. L. T. Harris.
Florence...........	Methodist...........	80	103	80	....	
Florence...........	Baptist.............	....	....	....	....	G. A. Viel.
Graham	Methodist..........	90	13	23	6	C. B. Curtis.
Selma.............		....	....	....	....	
Shelby............	Evangelical Union..	25	12	17	3	Ed. T. Witherby.
Talladega.........	Congregational.....	47	94	130	15	L. E. Aldridge, Car Tal. College.

ARIZONA.

Prescott...........	1st Congregational...	....	....	....	....	Walter G. Scott.
Phoenix...........	Presbyterian	....	....	....	....	Abbie Gilbert.
Tucson	Congregational......	49	16	10	....	Minnie Meeker, Ott St.

ARKANSAS.

Rogers............	Congregational	....	....	....	....	J. B. Agard.

BRITISH PROVINCES.

Antigonish, N. S.	St. James' Presb.....	29	9	....	....	W. H. McDonald, Jr., Church St.
Belwood, Ont....	Congregational.......	....	....	....	....	Rev. J. C. Wright.
Bridgewater, N.S.	Methodist	30	22	28	9	Mrs. Brownrigg.
Bridgewater, N.S.	Baptist..............	....	....	....	....	P. W. Harding.
Caledonia Cor. NS	Methodist Episcopal.	15	8	13	....	Rev. R. S. Stevens.
Canso.............	Baptist..............	52	10	54	3	F. G. Creed.
Charlottetown ...						
P. E. I.........	Zion Presbyterian...	45	9	45	....	Miss Mary Laird.
Coaticook, Queb.	Methodist Episcopal.	....	....	....	....	Rev. C. Flanders.
Coaticook, Que.	Baptist	16	6	12	....	Flora N. Nevers.
Dartmouth, N. S.						
Dwindell, P. Q...						
Elmira, Ont......						Mima Reid.
Glenelg Queb....	Presbyterian.........	....	....	....	....	
Great Village,N.S.						
Guelph, Ont......	Baptist..............	....	....	....	....	Rev. Mr. Weir.
Guelph, Ont......	Congregational......	35	10	35	1	Jessie McRoberts, 83 Glasgow St
Halifax, N. S.....	Ft. Massey Presb....	35	11	33	3	John S. Smith, 24 Bland St.
Halifax, N. S.....	St. Johns Presb......	22	15	30	....	Rev. H. H, Macpherson.
Halifax, N. S.....	1st Baptist...........	....	....	....	....	J. Burgoyne, 58 Granville St.
Halifax, N. S.....	Chalmers Presb......	....	....	....	....	Rev. John McMillan.
Hamilton, Ber'da	Wesley M. E.........	36	16	36	11	Miss Tola L. Smith.
Hamilton, Ont...	Central Presbyterian	32	24	30	10	Louise Furnival, 25 Pearl St.
Hespeler, Ont....	Presbyterian.........	....	....	....	....	
High Bank, Murray Harb., P.E.I		....	....	....	....	T. G. Hayter.
Kirkwall, Ont....	Presbyterian.........	43	18	36	29	Samuel Carruthers.
Lindsay, Ont.....	Baptist...............	39	....	33	22	E. S. Jackson, Melbourne St.
Lindsay, Ont.....		....	....	....	....	E. W. Anderson, Box 333.
London, Ont.....	St. Paul's Cath., Epis.	34	16	30	13	Lizzie Kirkpatrick, 387 Colborne
" "	King St. M. E........	....	....	....	....	Rev. Mr. Holmes. [St.
" "	King St. Presb.......	....	....	....	....	Rev. Mr. Rogers.
" "	Talbot St. Baptist....	....	....	....	....	Rev. Mr. Porter.
" "	Adelaide St. Baptist.	....	....	....	....	Rev. Mr. Johnson.

LIST OF SOCIETIES.

BRITISH PROVINCES.—(Continued.)

CITY.	CHURCH.	Act. Memb.	Asso. Memb.	Ch. Memb.	United with C.	Secretary and Address.
London, Ont......	Pall Mall M. E.......	30	25	15	8	
Maitland.........	Presbyterian.........	25	....	24	....	Wm. M. D. Douglass.
Melbourne........	Congregational......	....	....	....	....	Rev. G. F. Brown.
Milltown.........	Congregational......	....	....	....	....	Rev. W. R. Cross.
Mont'l, Cameron	Presbyterian........	....	....	....	....	G. F. Goddard.
Murray Harbor, Napanee, Ont.....	Eastern M. E........	16	....	16	....	Mabel Agelsworth.
North Sydney, C.B						
Oshawa, Ont.....	Ladies' College Un...	40	13	....	....	Abbie B. Howland.
Oxford...........						
Port au Pique....						
Port Hastings....						
River Charlo, N.B	Charlo Presbyterian.	21	30	20	14	Minnie Murray.
Sherbrooke Queb.						Rev H. E. Barnes.
Sherbrooke, Que	Presbyterian.........	....	....	....	....	Tena Fraser.
Shubernacadie...	Presbyterian.........	13	7	13	....	Ellen Kirkpatrick.
So. P. E. I. Can.	Methodist...........	....	....	....	....	D. D. Hugh.
St. Andrews, Que	Union...............	....	....	....	....	Lillie A. MacMartin.
St. Johns, N B....	Germain St. Bapitst.	21	8	16	5	Rev. G. A. Gates.
St. Johns, N. F...	Congregational......	....	....	....	....	Martha C. Whitten, 210 Gower St.
St. Johns, N. B...	Presbyterian........	....	....	....	....	Rev. F. F. Fotheringham, Mt. Stewiacke. [Pleasant.
Toronto, Ont.....	Congregational......	39	27	35	9	Nellie F. Arms, 27 Bellevue Pl.
" "	Zion.................	24	3	16	1	A. F. Wickson, 402 Church St.
" "	Hazelton Ave. Cong.	....	....	....	....	Rev. Geo. Robertson.
Toronto, Can.....	St. Clarens Ave. Meth.	....	....	....	....	Rev. W. W. Andrews 59 Jameson Avenue.
West Bay.........						
West River, Antigonish, N. S.....						D. H. Williams.
Yarmouth, N. S..	Tabernacle Congreg.	20	1	18	....	Robt. E. Perry, P. O. Box 375.
Yamouth, N. S....	Presbyterian........	....	....	....	....	Rev. A. Rogers.
Yarmouth,........	St. John's Presb.....	....	....	....	....	Maggie D. Jack.

CALIFORNIA.

CITY.	CHURCH.	Act. Memb.	Asso. Memb.	Ch. Memb.	United with C.	Secretary and Address.
Auburn..........	Congregational......	....	....	....	....	Rev. Mr. Cooke.
Alimatos.........	Union...............	....	....	....	....	
Alameda.........	First Congregational	....	....	....	34	
Alameda.........	First Presbyterian...	30	14	....	12	Rev. E. J. Garetti.
Antioch..........	Congregational......	28	4	6	1	Annie F. McKellips.
Berkeley.........	First Congregational	37	....	33	....	Mrs. Alice G. Howard.
Berkeley.........	Congregational......	....	....	....	....	
Berkeley.........	First Presbyterian...	17	1	15	6	Alice H. Byxbee.
Berkeley.........	First Methodist......	....	....	....	....	Rev. Mr. Carroll.
Bethany.........		18	11			
Clayton..........	Congregational......	20	....	20	20	Mrs. George Duncan.
Campbell........		....	....	....	....	Mrs. R. D. Shaw.
Eureka..........	Congregational......	....	....	....	....	Rev. W. H. McDougall.
East Oakland....	Presbyterian........	....	....	....	....	
East Oakland....	Presbyterian........	59	6	50	10	Chas. E. Connell, 13th. Avenue.
East Oakland....	Baptist.............	....	....	....	....	Julia A. Wilson, 582 E. 12th St.
Fresno City......	First Presbyterian...	14	5	17	9	Helen L. Hurd.
Fresno City......	First Congregational	....	....	....	....	Rev. Mr. Chaddock.
Fresno City......	Second North Meth.	....	....	....	....	Rev. Mr. Judy.
Fresno City......	South Methodist.....	....	....	....	....	Rev. Mr. Hyden.
Fresno City......	Methodist	....	....	....	....	Elmer L. Craig.
Fresno Ci y......	Congregational......	....	....	....	....	
Fresno City......	Presbyterian........	....	....	....	....	M. H. Heitzig.
Haywards........	Methodist Episcopal.	15	10	15	8	H. D. Rice, 56 Bluxome St. San
Haywards........	Eden Congregational	....	....	....	....	Rev. W. W. Madge [Francisco.
Jackson..........		....	....	....	....	George W. Brown.

LIST OF SOCIETIES.

CALIFORNIA.—(Continued.)

CITY.	CHURCH.	Act. Memb.	Asso. Memb.	Ch. Memb.	United with C.	Secretary and Address.
Los Angeles	Main St. Methodist.	35	10	37	10	Miss I. L. Spencer, 30 East Pine
Los Angeles	First Presbyterian	65	....	65	....	Lewis S. Bell, 138 W. 1st. St. [St.
Los Angeles	Morris Vineyard	....	....	....	....	Rev. Mr. Stevens.
Los Angeles	First Cong. [Pres.	75	15	75	33	Emma Grant, 6 Clay St.
Los Angeles	Third Presbyterian	35	5	32	5	Ally Peine, 15 Martin St.
Los Angeles	Vernon Cong.	....	....	....	....	Nellie Cheesman, Box 184.
Los Angeles	Boyle Hgts. Pres.	10	3	11	2	Miss Ella Harrington.
Livermore	Methodist Episcopal.	..	....	....	....	Rev. Mr. Phelps.
Livermore		6	6	5	....	Hazzie Graham.
Lodi	Congregational	....	....	....	....	Jennie Perkins.
Luzonia	Union.	21	....	7	2	K. H. Candee.
Martinez	Park Congregational	74	....	55	10	Mamie McClellan.
Oakland	First Presbyterian	15	13	14	....	Miss F. H. Miller, 1277 Webster
Oakland	Golden Gate Cong.	25	8	25	....	Miss M. M. Graff, 1087 32d St. [St·
Oakland	Plymouth Ave. Cong.	38	28	19	....	H. W. Mooar, 444 Edwards St.
Oakland	Second Cong.	31	24	31	7	A. Crandall, 1678 Lincoln St.
Oakland	Second Presbyterian.	170	50	130	23	H. H. Chamberlain 1652 7th St.
Oakland	First Congregational.	....	....	....	....	Grace C. Richardson.
Oakland	Berkeley Cong.	62	24	....	....	
Oakland	First Baptist.	21	2	....	....	Chas. F. Baker, Box 256.
Oakland	Market St. Cong.	....	....	....	....	Hattie E. Benton, 684 25th St.
Oakland	San Pablo Baptist.	52	8	37	8	
Pasadena	Congregational	....	....	....	....	Grace Thomas, Lock Box 194.
Pasadena	Friends	....	....	....	....	Ella M. Hadley, Box 554.
Pasadena	Christian	18	10	13	5	Rev. F. W. Pattee.
Petaluma	Pilgrim Cong.	....	....	....	....	Kate Denman.
Pomona	Baptist.	....	....	....	....	Walter A. Lewis.
Pomona	Congregational	....	....	....	....	Eva Rolph, Box 374.
Pomona	Presbyterian	..	.	2	....	Mrs. I. F. Tobey.
Rocklin	Congregational	5	8	2	....	
Santa Cruz	Methodist Episcopal.	....	....	....	....	Miss Mattie Dunlap.
Santa Cruz	Congregational	....	....	....	....	Miss Fannie Taylor.
Santa Rosa	Baptist.	27	7	....	....	
Santa Rosa	Presbyterian	40	6	....	....	D. D. Baxter.
Santa Anna	Baptist.	45	44	45	3	Rev. J. B. Banker.
San Juan	First Congregational	23	7	16	....	Mamie Kemp.
San Diego	First Congregational	60	9	....	....	Hattie Brooks, Cor. 12th & A St.
San Diego	First Presbyterian	50	6	50	....	George Fleming, Box 79.
San Diego	First Baptist.	37	11	....	....	Rev. Mr. Harper.
San Diego	Central Christian	19	9	....	....	Fannie Thompson.
San Diego	South Methodist E.	12	1	....	....	
San Diego	Keneer Chap. M. E.	....	....	....	....	Rev. E. T. Hodges.
San Diego	Unitarian	....	....	....	....	Rev. Mr. Daniel.
Sacremento	Congregational	48	14	40	23	Mrs. G. M. Merrill, 158 N· St.
Sacremento	First Baptist.	20	8	16	....	Kate Y. Rudolph.
Sacremento	14th. St. Pres.	8	7	....	....	Jennie McCaslin, 1328 O. St.
Sacremento	Cal. Baptist.	....	....	6	....	
San Francisco	Fourth Cong.	36	....	20	3	Lila M. Lang, 1714 Mason St.
" "	Bush St. M. E.	22	3	24	2	E. A. Guoin, 2203 Webster St.
" "	Third Cong.	140	....	....	....	Wm. A. McQuilly, 107 Mason St.
" "	Plymouth Cong.	42	3	40	15	J. D. McKee, 26 12th. St.
" "	Calvary Pres.	51	....	....	....	Sophie A. Coney.
" "	Grace M. E.	82	21	....	....	Miss N. I. Moore 446 16th St.
" "	First Congregational	150	....	....	....	
" "	First Presbyterian	80	4	85	....	W. M. Fairchild.
" "	Centenary M. E.	..	....	....	....	
" "	Larkin St. Pres.	18	....	16	2	Ernest Knoderer, 1108 Powell St.
" "	First Free Baptist	19	4	18	1	Lillie L. Fales, 923 Sutter St.
" "	Glen St. Cong.	17	43	33	10	
" "	St. John's Pres	15	10	....	....	
" "	Mariner's	17	....	11	1	Ed. I. Brigden 1108 Powell St.
" "	First Methodist	94	61	....	....	John Potter.
" "	Central Pres.	27	4	27	5	E. N. Jones.
" "	Central M. E.	88	46	....	....	
" "	Howard Street M. E.	....	....	....	....	
" "	Trinity M. E.	21	4	....	....	Will T. Plevin, 922 16th St..
" "	Third Baptist.	9	11	....	....	

LIST OF SOCIETIES.

CALIFORNIA.—(*Continued.*)

CITY.	CHURCH.	Act. Memb.	Asso. Memb.	Ch. Memb.	United with C.	Secretary and Address.
San Francisco....	Second United Pres..	16	22			
" "	Westminster Pres....	17		15	4	A. M. McCarty, 10 Market Sq.
" "	Howard Street Pres..					
San Bernadino...	First Congregational	25	29	27	9	Arthur Stoughton.
Santa Barbara...	Congregational					Alice R. Huse.
San Jose	Congregational					Maud Yule, 307 South 5th St.
San Jose	Methodist					
Sonoma	Congregational					Mrs. F. J. Dunn.
Sonora	Congregational	14	1	7	3	
Suisan						Martha Green.
Sierra Madre...	Congregational					J. C. Dixson.
Vermontdale.....	Church of Christ Cong	23	1	20	9	N. Cushman Box 184 Los An-
Westminster.....	Union	8	6	9		Miss Stella F. Mack. [geles.

COLORADO.

Brighton	First Presbyterian...	51	7	39		Jessie S. Wilson.
Boulder	Congregational					Miss Grace Deitrich.
Boulder	First Presbyterian...	33		26	2	Mrs. A. S. Langtry.
Colorado Springs	First Presbyterian...	33		31		W. W. Williamson, Box 72.
Colorado Springs	Congregational					Frank O. Wilson, No· Weber St.
Colorado Springs	First Methodist					Rev. O. C. Peck.
Colorado Springs	First Baptist					Rev. R. Montague.
Colorado Springs	Presbyterian					
Cheyenne	Congregational					Rev. A. W. Williams.
Cheyenne	Presbyterian					Rev. R. E. Field.
Cheyenne	Methodist Episcopal					Rev. Mr. Rader
Canon City	First Presbyterian...					E. S. Robinson.
Denver	Wheat Ridge M. E....	24		24	20	John Tobias, Box 2981. [St.
"	West Denver Baptist	17	13	17	14	Ella E. Dudley, 1049 So. 11th [St.
"	First Congregational	43	23	43	3	E. B. Mitchell, 2156 Wilton [St.
"	Calvary Baptist	19	8	19	5	Miss A. Goodnow, 1839 Lafayette
"	Broadway Baptist	19	1	17		Miss J. Hilton, 132 South Lincoln
"	Junior Society					[Ave.
"	Second Cong.	44		20		Miss B. Simmons, 2732 California
"	Mission Schools					[St.
"	Congregational	37	21	31	10	Rev. R. T. Cross.
"	German Methodist...	14	5	12		Miss E. Reitze, 801 E.18th & Clark-
"	Curtis St. Methodist	15	1	13	9	J. W. Collins, 1619 Cal. St. [son
"	Park Ave. Cong.					Rev. Mr. Brodhead. [Sts.
"	Highlands Boule-.........varde Cong.	15	5	12	10	R. C. Lunbeck, 2246 Larimer St.
"	St. James M. E.					B. L. Olds, 1223, 17th St.
"	Zion (Colored) Bap.	46	2	70		Miss S. Riley, 2019 Larimer St.
"	California St. Meth...					J. R. Henderson, 1736 Cal. St.
"	United Presbyterian.					Rev. J. D. Romkin.
"	Westminster Pres....					Rev. Mr. Lewis.
"	English Lutheran....					Rev. P. A. Heilman.
Fort Collins	First Methodist	12	3	12	9	Attie Keon.
Georgetown	First Presbyterian...					W. B. Galway, Box 358.
Greeley	Park Congregational	33	20	20		Rev. George Michael.
Highland Lake...	Church of Christ Congregational	17	6	15	5	M. L. Mead, M. D.
Idaho Springs....	Presbyterian	14	2	4	4	Miss Vinnie Pierce.
Idaho Springs....	Methodist					Rev. George Oliver.
Longmont	Presbyterian					
Longmont	Congregational					Rev. H. E. Thayer.
Leadville	Church of Christ					Harry Oviatt.
Leadville	First Presbyterian...					Rev. Mr. Armstrong.
Manitou Springs.	Congregational	31	20	25	2	Mrs. T. C. Green.
Otis	First Congregational	37	17	39	3	J. P. Edwards.
Pueblo	First Presbyterian...	18		18		L. C. McClung, 423 West 11th St.
Pueblo	Main St. Methodist..					H. S. Foster, 216 West 9th St.
Pueblo	First Baptist					Rev. Mr. Murphy.

COLORADO.—(Continued.)

CITY.	CHURCH.	Act. Memb.	Asso. Memb.	Ch. Memb.	United with C.	Secretary and Address.
Pueblo	Christian					Rev. J. C. Hay.
Pueblo	Congregational					Rev. Mr. Wright.
Silver Cliff						L. W. Baldwin.
West Denver	Congregational					Grace Sylvester.

CONNECTICUT.

CITY.	CHURCH.	Act. Memb.	Asso. Memb.	Ch. Memb.	United with C.	Secretary and Address.
Ansonia	First Congregational	24	28	24	3	Mrs. E. P. Gager.
Ansonia	Baptist	38	12	38	3	J. L. Crocker, 236 Main Street.
Bantam	Baptist					
"	Congregational					
Barkhamstead	Congregational					Rev. J. B. Clark.
Berlin	Second Cong	43	13	36		Hattie A. Roys.
Bethel	Congregational	62	2	61		Lizzie M. Barber, Centre St.
Bethlehem	Congregational					Clinton H. Bird.
Bill Hill						Mrs. C. P. Bell.
Birmingham	Congregational	26	22	26		Nellie C. Beard.
"	Methodist					Rev. Mr. Lightbourne.
Bloomfield	Congregational	22	6	17	2	Mrs. E. T. Atwood.
Bozrah	Congregational					Rev. George A. Miller.
Bridgeport	First Congregational	35	30	37	9	A. B. Naramore, 437 Fairchild.
"	First Presbyterian	58	29	63	9	R. M. Keys, Box 1729. [Ave.
"	South Second Cong.	115	18	110		Geo. J. Brown, Box 1969.
"	Park Street Cong.	46	60	80		L. H. Baker, W. & W. M'f'g. Co.
"	Olivet Cong	26	27	20		Jessie L. Hall, Beach Ave.
"	West End Cong					L. A. Norton.
Branford	First Congregational	26	13	29	1	M. M. Robbins, 37 East Main St.
Bridgewater	Congregational	17	2	12		Fannie M. Treat.
Bristol	Baptist	50	30	60	9	Millie C. Gowdy, 16 Elm St.
"	Congregational	52	67	88	20	J. T. Chidsey.
"	Methodist					J. G. Goodwin.
Brooklyn						Lewis C. Lawton.
Broad Brook	Congregational					E. C. Blodgett.
Canton Centre	Congregational	18	12	26		Hattie Humphrey.
Centre Brook						Rev. Mr. Griggs.
Chester	Congregational	44	29	49	8	C. H. Moss, P. O. Box 4.
Cheshire	First Congregational	50	20	47	8	Hattie E. Beach.
"	Methodist					
Clinton	First Congregational	40	4	35		Lena E. Kelsey, Box 210.
Cobalt	Congregational					Nellie Selding.
Collinsville	Congregational	59	32	60		Frank H. Thayer.
Colchester	Baptist	14	6	13	2	Mrs. William Wagner, Main St.
"	Congregational	24	6	22	2	Mrs. A. R. Bigelow, W. Chester.
Cornwall	West Second Cong.	24	4	21	3	J. Cochrane, West Cornwall.
"	Congregational	28	2	18	13	Rev. O. G. MacIntire.
Cromwell	Congregational					Rev. Mr. Marshall.
Danbury	Second Baptist	60	10	61		T. W. Gillett, 30 Foster St.
Danbury	First Congregational	91	25	91		J. A. Maxwell, D. D.
Darien	Congregational	29	16	27	4	Rev. S. J. Austin.
Danielsonville	Congregational					Joel Witter.
"	Congregational					
Dayville						
Derby	First Congregational	31	3	22	9	Wm. S. Browne, 40 Derby Ave.
"	Second Cong					Dr. Bullock.
"	Baptist					Rev. Mr. McKinney.
"	Methodist					Rev. W. C. Blakeman
East Hartford	First Congregational	77	27	66	7	Jennie M. Williams.
" "	Senet Congregational	38	8	34	5	Miss M. Bidwell, Hockanum.
East Windsor	First Congregational	46	4	38	2	Lucy M. Bartlett.
East Canaan	Congregational	20	30	17		Lena J. Roberts.
East Berlin						
Ellington	Congregational	39	25	42	8	H. H. McKnight.
East Haven	First Congregational	72	17	56	7	Mrs. C. S. Dowe.
Enfield	First Congregational	76	19	65	15	Homer W. Patten

LIST OF SOCIETIES

CONNECTICUT.—(*Continued.*)

CITY.	CHURCH.	Act. Memb.	Asso. Memb.	Ch. Memb.	United with C.	Secretary and Address.
Easton	Baptist					Rev. A. Gregory.
Ekonk	Congregational	9	7	7	7	Rachel Frink, Sterling.
East Haddon	First Congregational	29	4	25	16	Eugene W. Chaffee, Moodus.
East Hampton	South Cong.	26	11	29		Caddie V. Sears.
Essex						
Fairfield	Congregational					
Fair Haven	Second Cong.	62	81	67	5	J. E. C. Lancraft, So. Quinnipiac
"	First Congregational	82	48	85	15	M. Edith Groot, 43 Houston [St.
Forestville	Methodist Episcopal.	33	10	35	18	W. A. Richard. [St.
Franklin	Congregational					W. C. Smith.
Georgetown	Congregational	12	6	12		Mrs. Mary Davis, P. O. Box 7.
Glasgo	Bethel M. E.	8	4	8		Eliza H. Young.
Glastonbury	Congregational	42	20	39		S. H. Williams.
Glenbrook	First Congregational					Rev. Saml. Scoville.
Greenfield Hill	Congregational	11	13	11		Martha C. Meeker.
Greenwich	First Congregational	10	12	9		Miss Fannie A. Ferris, Sound
"	First Presbyterian			21		S. A. Brush. [Beach.
Griswold	First Congregational	25	5	21		Edward A. Geer.
Griswold	Bethel Methodist	7	5	8		Eliza H. Young, Glasgo.
Griswold, Pach'g.			4			
Groton	Congregational					Rev. A. J. McLeod.
Guilford	Third Cong.	44	23	57		Belle C. Lee.
"	First Congregational	35	3	34		Rev. Mr. Vittum.
Haddam	Congregational					Rev. Mr. Lewis.
Hadlyme	Congregational					Maria Selden.
Hamden	Methodist Episcopal.					Rev. N. Hubbell.
Hampton	Congregational	21	23	20		Mrs. Fannie M. Robberts.
Hanover	Congregational					Maggie E. Allen. [St.
Hartford	Pearl St. Cong.	88	9	68		Maggie L. Brainard, 135 Wash.
"	New Britain Ave. Un-	26	6	23		Edw. L. Gage, 8 Ellsworth St.
"	First Cong. [ion.					S. S. Hotchkiss.
"	South Cong.	30	14	30	3	H. C. Hayden, Lock Box 425.
"	Union Mission	24	16	20	3	Mrs. E. J. Pratt, 30 Wash. St.
"	Fourth Cong.	45	70			Rev. Graham Taylor.
"	Baptist.					Horace B. Austin.
"	Windsor Ave. Cong.	41	4	36		F. M. Dawson, 122 Clark St.
"	North M. E.					
Hebron	First Congregational	24	2	24	1	Minnie Sumner.
Higganum	Congregational					Estella E. Clark.
Hockanum	Congregational	44	11	38		Rev. F. R. Waite.
Huntington	First Congregational	18	2	13		Miss Ella Wooster.
Jewett City	Congregational	12	9	9		Rena E. Sweet.
Jordan						
Kensington	Congregational	25	25	23	6	Henry C. Cowles.
"	New Britain South					A. J. Benedict.
Kent	Congregational	25	1	15		Mrs. E. S. Porter.
Lakeville						
Lebanon	First Congregational	23	14	23		Louise W. Robinson.
Litchfield	Congregational					A. D. Palmer, M. D.
Long Ridge						
Madison	First Congregational	36	5	36		Mary E. Coe, Wall St.
Manchester	Centre Cong.	49	17	38		Annie I. House, So. Manchester.
"	Second Cong.				5	Rev. C. H. Barber.
Mansfield Centre	So. Manchester Cong.	35	23			Stella E. Johnson.
Meriden	Broad St. Baptist	71	22	71		Nettie A. Ives, 391 Broad St. [St.
"	First M. E.	92	45	110	19	Miss Ida B. Goodrich, 525 Broad
"	Methodist Episcopal	27	35	34	20	W. H. Stannis, Jr., 69 Col'bia St.
"	Centre Cong.	45	42	46	11	Miss Flora E. Buckley, 72 Curtis
"	First Congregational	106	90	108	2	Mrs. T. H. Pinks, 26 Linsley Ave.
"	Main St. Bapist	55	15	56	17	Ella F. Buston, 31 Crown St. [St.
"	Trinity M. E.	17	9	18		W. H. Stannis, Jr., 69 Columbia
Middletown	Mission Chapel	16	14			Thos. M. Hodgdon. [St.
"	Cong. [Union					Rev. Mr. Hazen.
"	Bethany Chapel	17	15	8		Rev. G. H. Cummings.

CONNECTICUT.—(Continued)

CITY.	CHURCH.	Act. Memb.	Asso. Memb.	Ch. Memb.	United with C.	Secretary and Address.
Middletown	So. Cong. [Cong.	64	88	83	....	Geo. S. Deming, Box 588.
Middlebury	Congregational	33	17	20	....	Rev. Mr. Murphy.
Middlefield	Congregational	35	4	34	....	Lucina C. Miller.
Milford	Methodist Episcopal.	22	9	22	....	Albert L. House.
"	First Congregational	95	30	91	....	M. Ellen Clark.
Monroe	Congregational	22	12	21	....	Miss Hattie L. Curtiss.
Montville	Congregational	....	....	....	....	Rev. Charles Cutting.
Morris	Congregational	34	11	30	10	Flora M. Randolph.
Mt. Carmel	Congregational	52	9	48	5	Laura L. Dickerman.
Mystic Bridge	Congregational	16	8	17	....	Martha W. Dean.
Naugatuck	Union	82	49	73	6	C. H. Booth.
New Britain	Congregational	46	9	54	2	Edith A. De Wolfe, 72 Elm st.
" "	First Baptist	64	15	67	12	S. Elizabeth Barks, Burritt st.
" "	So. Congregational	130	20	120	4	Miss S. P. Rogers, 37 Prospect st.
" "	Methodist	....	....	....	....	Rev. J. Pullman.
" "	First Congregational	49	1	49	....	Fannie Norris, 4 Winter street.
New Canaan	Congregational	....	....	....	....	Rev. F. Hopkins.
" "	Methodist	38	3	38	3	M. S. Raymond.
Newington	Congregational	48	23	48	4	George E. Churchill. [street.
New Haven	George St., Third M.	51	....	51	....	Miss M. E. Benkler, 108 Hill [st.
" "	Davenport Cong	100	10	85	10	Miss S. F. Landfear, 125 St. John
" "	Taylor Cong	37	26	23	3	Hettie E. Cooper, 729 Dixwell av.
" "	Grand Ave., Baptist.	53	39	60	3	Lillian Preston, 92 Woolsey st.
" "	United Church, Cong.	84	44	84	6	Edw. T. Murray, 49 Elm street,
" "	Emmanuel Baptist	54	12	54	14	C. C. Alexander, 87 Star street.
" "	Humphrey St., Cong.	90	25	75	....	A. H. Hayes, 75 Humphrey st.
" "	Dwight Pl., Cong.	105	6	56	....	G. Y. McDermott, 1346 Chapel st.
" "	College St., Cong.	75	11	75	....	W. W. McLane.
" "	Ch. of Redeemer Con.	46	31	58	....	Ed. L. Chapman, 520 Chapel st.
" "	Dixwell Ave., M. E.	....	....	....	....	Rev. Albert P. Miller.
" "	Colored Cong.	....	....	....	....	
" "	Calvary Baptist	21	....	21	....	G. H. Bean.
" "	Howard Ave., M. E.	....	....	....	....	
New Hartford	North Cong.	25	30	20	....	W. C. Woodruff.
New London	Second Cong.	....	....	....	....	Rev. J. G. Johnson. [ington st.
" "	First Baptist	47	7	47	3	Mrs. Jennie Saunders, 65 Hunt-
" "	First Ch. of Christ	37	8	33	11	Fanny L. Bristol, 109 State st.
Niantic	Baptist [Cong.	23	8	20	....	Rev. J. Naylor.
"	Congregational	18	30	13	5	Fannie C. Raymond.
New Milford	First Cong.	48	12	44	....	Miss Bertha Beecher.
New Preston	First Cong.	13	13	13	....	Lizzie M. Whittlesey.
Norfolk	Congregational	24	8	....	15	J. D. Bassett.
Northfield	Congregational	20	....	17	....	Minnie G. Morse.
North Brantford	Congregational	....	....	....	....	Edward Cole.
North Canaan	Congregational	15	13	18	....	Richard Bebee.
North Haven	Congregational	47	10	36	2	John H. Todd.
North Manchester	Second Cong.	83	44	70	....	Miss Mary Williams, Buckland.
Norwich Town	First Cong.	80	7	66	8	Helen M. Lathrop, No. Wash. st.
Norwalk	First Cong.	55	27	69	14	Mrs. Emily L. Ely, P. O. Box 446.
"	First Baptist	40	9	40	4	Mrs. V. R. Torrey, 19 Berkley pl.
Norwich	Second Cong.	51	8	50	8	Lillian B. Hawes, 49 Union st.
Orange	Congregational	27	24	28	7	E. L. Clark, Jr.
Plainfield	First Cong.	11	18	10	....	Sarah E. Frances.
Plainville	Congregational	69	8	55	....	Helen M. Pierce, Whiting st.
Plantville	Baptist	14	9	5	....	Jennie E. Winchell.
Plantville	Congregational	64	29	56	3	Eugenia J. Wilcox.
Plymouth	First Cong.	46	28	41	....	H. E. Stoughton.
Preston City	Congregational	....	....	....	....	Rev. R. H. Gidman.
Pomfret	First Cong.	15	12	14	....	C. M. Grosvenor.
Portland	First Cong.	22	22	21	....	Miss Jennie P. Payne, Cobalt.
Poquonock	Congregational	....	....	....	....	Rev. Mr. Pettifone.
Prospect	Congregational	50	17	47	....	Mrs. Wm. H. Phipps.
Putnam	Second Cong.	47	3	46	2	Annie C. Carpenter.
"	Congregational	50	....	50	....	Jennie Carpenter.
Ridgefield	Congregational	....	....	....	....	Arthur W. Northrup.
Riverton	Congregational	....	....	....	....	Mrs. L. C. Hart.

X. LIST OF SOCIETIES

CONNECTICUT—(Continued.)

CITY.	CHURCH.	Act Memb.	Asso. Memb.	Memb. Ch.	United with C.	Secretary and Address.
Rockville.........	Methodist............					Rev. Orange Scott.
"	First Cong............	45	15	40	....	T. C. Hoffman.
"	Second Cong..........	52	5	50	....	Luther H. Fuller, P. O. Box 282.
Rocky Hill........	Congregational	15	29	20	2	Mrs. W. F. Griswold.
Salem.............	Union	24	25		....	L. C. Minor.
Salisbury.........	Congregational......					Rev. J. C. Goddard.
Saybrook.........	Congregational.......	41	11	33	6	
Shelton...........	Methodist............					E. Jennie Chadeayne.
"	Baptist...............					Albert H. Bray.
Sherman..........	Congregational.......	10	16		....	Annie Giddings.
Scotland						
Simsbury.........	Congregational.......	30	....	24	....	Robert Clark.
Sound Beach, .Groton		10	13	10	....	Miss Hannah Ferris, Riverside.
Southington......	Baptist...............					Mrs. V. M. Laity.
Southington......	Congregational					Rev. Mr. Stevens.
South Killingly..	Union	26	....	20	11	W. S. Beard.
South Meriden...	Methodist Episcopal.	15	14	17	4	Etta M. Sweet, P. O. Box 81.
South Norwalk ..	Congregational.......					Mrs. W. L. Porter.
South " ..	Baptist	57	7	57	....	Miss Angeline Scott.
South Windham..	No. Church Union...					
South Windsor...	Congregational.......	19	27	18	4	G. A. Collins, Wapping.
Stratford.........	Methodist Episcopal.	15	1	14	....	William Enerle.
"	Congregational	50	28	51	4	Henry C. Evans.
Stafford Springs.	Congregational					Rev. J. P. Hawley.
Stamford	First Cong............	19	4	17	1	Minona M. Pierce, Warren st.
"	First Presbyterian...	62	42	66	....	Miss J. B. Weed, 17 Prospect st.
"	Baptist	47	1	47	....	Alice L. Snelling, 20 Division st.
"						Warren Morse.
"	Presbyterian.........	42	35	47	....	Edward P. Fuller, 57 Atlantic st.
Stony Creek......	Congregational.......	26	11	24	1	Miss Alice A. Maynard, Box 68.
Suffield	First Cong............	32	7	28	....	Clara E. Crane.
"						Willis E. Russell.
"	Second Cong..........					Clara E. Crane.
Taftville.........	Congregational.......					G. W. Kellogg, Box 33.
Talcotville.......	Congregational.......	47	24	29	....	Mrs. C. D. Talcott.
Terryville	Congregational	58	46	51	....	Hattie C. Allen.
Thomaston	First Cong............	40	22	35	5	George H. Stoughton.
Thompson.........	Union	35	12		....	Annie Dunning.
Thompsonville ..	United Presbyterian.	14	18	27	....	Belle Alcorn.
" ..	First Presbyterian...	60	49	47	....	Miss L. A. Burnett, Box 308.
Torringford	First Cong............					
"	Second Cong..........	28	2	22	....	Nellie P. Griswold.
Torrington	Third Cong...........	47	43	79	....	Frank M. Travis.
Unionville........	First Ch. Christ, Cong	44	34	34	6	Frank S. Brewer.
Vernon Center ...	Congregational.......	28	1	23	....	Evelyn R. Clark.
Wallingford......	First Cong............	73	36	50	3	F. E. Olmsted.
"	First Baptist.........	41	20	39	3	R. W. Morris, 28 So. Main street.
Wallens Hill.....	Br. 1st Cong. Winsted					
Wauregan........	Congregational.......	10	21	9	....	Mrs. F. S. Downer.
Warren...........	First Cong............	26	4	24	5	C. W. Humphrey.
Waterbury........	Second Cong..........	37	9	35	....	Ernest Welton, 70 So. Elm st.
"	First Baptist.........					W. J. Stanley.
Waterford........	Baptist...............					Laura Fancher.
Watertown.......	Congregational.......	49	14	46	12	Abbie L. Sperry.
Wapping..........	Second Cong..........	22	28	18	....	G. A. Collins.
"	Methodist............					
Washington......	Congregational.......					Rev. H. B. Turner.
Westchester.....						Mr. W. P. Adams.
Westerly.........	Congregational.......					Rev. G. L. Clark.
"	First Ch. of Christ....					
West Hartford....	First Cong............	45	7	32	4	E. S. Hamilton.
West Haven......	First Cong............	118	10	57	3	F. W. Mar, 138 First avenue.
" "	Methodist Episcopal.					Albert C. Coe.
" "	Howard Ave. Cong...	93	25	87	9	Eli Manchester, Jr., Box 1199.
West Winsted....	Second Cong..........	109	8	55	14	E. W. Jones, 385 Lake street

CONNECTICUT.—(Continued.)

CITY.	CHURCH.	Act. Memb.	Asso. Memb.	Ch. Memb.	United with C.	Secretary and Address.
West Winsted	Methodist	....	....	....	....	
West Suffield	Congregational	....	....	....	....	
West Torrington	First Cong	....	....	....	....	Edward L. Butler.
Westport	Congregational	30	15	27	....	Mrs J. E. Tuttle.
Wethersfield	Congregational	51	7	46	1	Miss Nellie E. Griswold, Box 26.
Whitneyville	Congregational	38	30	32	....	Rev. C. A. Dinsmore.
Willimantic	Baptist	60	....	60	....	Fred Rogers, 120 Main street.
Windham	Congregational	37	3	21	7	Mrs. H. C. Lathrop.
Windsor	Methodist	23	6	14	2	Mrs. E. S. Talbot, Maple ave.
"	First Cong	37	18	36	5	Alice E Morgan.
Winsted	FirstCong	124	8	....	....	J. S. Bingham, 47 Main street.
"	Second Cong	....	....	....	....	Rev. H. H. Kelsey.
"	Methodist	72	53	84	5	Luman C. Colt.
Woodbury	South Cong	55	3	29	....	Helen A. Shore.
Woodbridge	Congregational	23	18	23	....	Leroy C Beecher, Box 53.
Wolcott	Second Church	....	....	....	....	Rev. F. E. Woodworth.
Woodstock	Congregational	34	16	34	6	Nellie D. Chandler.

DAKOTA.

CITY.	CHURCH.	Act. Memb.	Asso. Memb.	Ch. Memb.	United with C.	Secretary and Address.
Aberdeen	First Presbyterian	25	20	25	....	F. D. Thompson.
Ashton	Congregational	20	8	10	1	Nellie House.
Appleton	Methodist	....	....	....	....	Rev. William Selleck.
Bismarck		....	....	....	....	Byron Millard.
Brookings	Union	70	25	65	20	D. V. Kilpatrick.
"	Agricultural College	41	14	45	10	A. A. Humphrey.
Canova	Congregational	28	2	20	15	H. A. Lincoln.
Centerville	Baptist	....	....	....	....	H. F. Ward.
Chamberlain	Congregational	....	....	....	....	Rev. W. B. Hubbard.
Columbia	Congregational	....	....	....	....	
Cummings	Congregational	14	8	15	7	Fannie B. Jewett.
Dakota	Presbyterian	....	....	....	....	
Deadwood	Congregational	15	27	5	2	Rev. William H. Buss.
De Sueet		....	....	....	....	F. H. Huntley.
Devil's Lake	Westminster Pres	14	7	16	8	B. E. Cole.
Eden	Congregational	....	....	....	....	Marion Cable.
Fargo	Plymouth Cong	....	....	....	....	Ella Miller.
Faulkton	Congregational	....	....	....	....	Ettie B. Mason.
Frankfort	Congregational	....	....	....	....	
Gary	Methodist Episcopal	24	11	12	....	H. A. Sturgis, Jr., Box 4.
Grand Forks	Presbyterian	....	....	....	....	Rev. H. D. Mendenhall.
Henry	Union	21	2	21	8	Miss M. A. Johnston.
Huron	Congregational	....	....	....	....	
Ipswich	Congregational	25	3	20	....	F. J. Pool.
Lake Henry	Congregational	25	....	6	....	Mary Dunlap.
Millbank	Congregational	17	12	18	12	Maud L. Randall, Box 356.
Miller	Methodist	....	....	....	....	Rev. I. C. Phifer.
Mitchell	Congregational	....	....	....	....	
"	Baptist	....	....	....	....	Mrs. Carrie Winegar.
Parker	Baptist	....	....	....	....	
Rapid City	Congregational	....	....	....	....	Rev. J. W. Davis.
Redfield	First Cong	45	24	24	....	F L. Ransom.
Bee Hights	Congregational	....	....	....	....	Rev. J. G. Campbell.
Roscoe	Congregational	....	....	....	....	Fred J. Poole.
Sioux Falls	First Presbyterian	17	7	18	3	Will S. Dewey.
Tower City		....	....	....	....	
Valley Springs	Union	18	20	29	5	Carrie E. Riley.
Vermillion		....	....	....	....	A. T. Lyman.
Watertown	Congregational	13	12	....	....	Ada Daniels.
Woonsocket	Presbyterian	....	....	....	....	Mrs. Geo. H. Baker.
Yankton	Congregational	....	....	....	....	Nettie E. Miner.

LIST OF SOCIETIES

DELAWARE.

CITY.	CHURCH.	Act. Memb.	Asso. Memb.	Ch. Memb.	United with C.	Secretary and Address.
Dover	First Baptist	23	5	22		Louise H. Hope, 104 Gov. Ave.
Marshallton	Methodist					
Middletown	Methodist					
Valley Springs	Union					Miss Minnie Percival.
Wilmington	Second Baptist	35	15	40		Miss S. A. Wells, 608 W. 6th st.
"	Asbury Methodist					Rev. Mr. Bryan.
"	Baptist					M. S. Bratten, 808 W. 4th street.
"	Brandywine Meth					Rev. C. A. Grice.
"	Central Presbyterian					Dr. Howard Nixon, 906 King st.
"	Delaware Am. Bap.					Dr. Boothe.
"	First Presbyterian					H. D. Lindsay, 1216 Wash. st.
"	Grace Memorial Meth					Rev. Jacob Todd, D. D.
"	Mount Salem Meth					Rev. W. E. Avery.
"	Newport Methodist					
"	Olivet Presbyterian					Rev. Mr. Newbury.
"	Scott Methodist					Rev. V. S. Collins.
"						
"	Stanton Methodist					
"	St. Paul Methodist	60	3			Miss Mary Morrow, King st. [st'
"	Union Centenary	61		61		Hannah P. Denison, 201 Monroe.
"	West Presbyterian					Rev. A. N. Keigwin, 209 Wash. st.

DISTRICT OF COLUMBIA.

Georgetown	Presbyterian					George F. Auld.
Rock Hill	Baptist	12		12		
Washington	Unity Presbyterian	40	10	40	4	P. C Warman, 1520 Kingman st.
"	Fifth Cong	12	5	9	4	L. J. Robinson, 1012 H st., N. E.
"	Tenth Street Pres					
"	Ch. of the Covenant					
"	First Presbyterian					Miss Arlson, 514 3rd street.
"	Presbyterian					H. B. F. MacFarland.
"	Western Pres	43	22	43	8	Irene M. Toomb, 1019-22 St.
"	Foundry Methodist					J. E. Pugh, Y. M. C. A. bld.
"	Lincoln Mem. Cong.					Janie Tavern. [N. W.
"	Wellesley Chapel					Wm. R. Woodward, 517-6th st.,

FLORIDA.

Citra	Baptist					Rev. S. V. Marsh.
Daytona	Congregational					Miss Grace D. Bingham.
Gainesville	First Presbyterian	89	29	53		Effice Earl Williams.
Jacksonville	Congregational					Rev. H. B. Mead.
Lake Helen						
La Pute						
Longwood	Union	34	1	33	19	
"	Congregational	30	2	27	11	Charles W, La Rue, 2 Bay street.
New Carlisle						
Ocala	South M. E	34	21	53	4	S. S. Burlingame, Box 319-
"	Presbyterian	37	17	42	6	Charles C. Sinclair, Box 393.
"	First Baptist					J. N. Strobahr.
Orange City						
Orlando	Presbyterian					Miss Mamie McLeod.
Tampa	First Congregational					N. H. Comime, Box 67.
"	Methodist Episcopal					Rev. C. E. Pelot,
"	Baptist					Carrie Taylor,
Valparaiso						
Winter Park	Congregational	47	9	40	3	Mrs. E. N. Coan.

GEORGIA.

CITY.	CHURCH.	Act. Memb.	Asso. Memb.	Ch. Memb.	United with C.	Secretary and Address.
Augusta	Hosanna Baptist					Rev. Geo. Barnes, 1246 Market st.
Barnesville	Sardis Baptist	66	24	66	13	James Gardner.
Cartersville	Baptist					Wm. H. Cooper.
Macon	First Baptist					L. T. Stallings, 115 Wash. ave.
Millner						[Circle.
New Bethel	Baptist					Rev. I. Abercrombie, Social
Rome	Second Methodist	15		15		Lillie Huffaker.
Savannah	Independent Pres					Rev. W. T. Price, Pulaski House.
Social Circle	Liberty Hill Baptist	46	24	30	21	Rev. J. A. Henderson.
Woodstock	Baptist	15	3	15		W. H. Deems.

IDAHO TERRITORY.

CITY.	CHURCH.	Act. Memb.	Asso. Memb.	Ch. Memb.	United with C.	Secretary and Address.
Lewiston	First Presbyterian	15	2	2		Mr. Clyde Parker.

INDIAN TERRITORY.

CITY.	CHURCH.	Act. Memb.	Asso. Memb.	Ch. Memb.	United with C.	Secretary and Address.
Muscogee	Baptist					

ILLINOIS.

CITY.	CHURCH.	Act. Memb.	Asso. Memb.	Ch. Memb.	United with C.	Secretary and Address.
Abington	Congregational	33	22	33		May Pindy.
Albion	Cumberland Pres	33	22	33		Anna B. Stewart.
Aledo	Presbyterian	56	19	3	7	George L. Rodgers.
Alton	Presbyterian	33	3	33		Mary J. McClure.
" (Upper)	Baptist					Omega Irwing.
"	Congregational					
"	Shurtleff College					
Amboy	First Cong	44	13	40	5	Flora M. Farwell.
Arlington H'ights	Presbyterian					George Fleming.
Aurora	First Cong	32	5	31	9	Mrs. E. M. Tucker, 214 N. 4th st.
"	New England Cong	28	2	27	4	Anna Frazier, 175 So. Lake st.
"	First Baptist					Rev. D. D. Odell. [st.
"	First Pres	40	2	40		Thomas B. Swan, Binney & Fox
Bartlett	Congregational	39	9	27	8	W. M. Shaw.
Batavia	Congregational	39	12	46	25	C. S. Leeper.
Beardston	First Cong					Abbie Winden.
Belvidere	South Baptist					Ida Bassett.
Belleville	Presbyterian	21	16	21	2	Cora L. Affleck.
Bement	First Presbyterian	26				Gertrude Ragan.
"	Presbyterian	18		17	6	Ella Camp.
Bethany		20	5			Mr. L. D. Putney. [ferson st.
Bloomington	Second Presbyterian	95	22	94	17	Miss Jessie C. Finch, 510 W. Jef-
"	First Presbyterian	23	16	25	4	Effie B. Best, 305 E. Market st.
"	First Baptist	22	1	22		A. E. Aldrich.
"	First Cong	49	6	52		F. H. McIntosh, Durley Block.
Blue Island	Congregational	17	4	13	2	M. Jennie Kibbe.
" "	Bethany					
" "	Lutheran					
Browns	Congregational					J. G. Curtis.
Buda	Congregational	21	9	20		Mabel F. Prutsman.
Burlington						Miss Clara Porter.
Bunker Hill	Congregational	52	21	43	2	Emma R. Ross.
Byron	First Congregational	37	8	34		Elsie C. Knowlton.
Cambridge	First Cong	25		20		Minnie Jones.
Camp Point						Lily Ligget.

LIST OF SOCIETIES

ILLINOIS.—(Continued.)

CITY.	CHURCH.	Act. Memb.	Asso. Memb.	Ch. Memb.	United with C.	Secretary and Address.
Canton	First Cong	39	7	38		Minnie L. Coleman.
Cairo	Presbyterian	30	25	11		May Richards.
Carbondale	Presbyterian					Rev. Mr. Stoltz.
Carmi						J. W. Van Clere.
"	Christian					Minnie Draper.
Carrolton	Presbyterian					Mary Ellis.
"	Baptist	20	6			Fred H. Kelly.
Carpentersville						William Orbly.
Cedarville						J. H. Dillingham.
Centralia	Presbyterian	40	51	33	5	Miss Eunice Cogswell.
"	First Cong					F. R. Green.
"	First Baptist					Rev. B. Foskett.
"	First Presbyterian					Miss E. Cogswell.
"	Methodist Episcopal					Rev. J. K. Wallar. [ave.
Champaign	Congregational	24	6	22	3	Frank Balcom, 511 University
Cerro Gordo						
Charleston	Presbyterian					Helen Weiss.
Chebanse	Congregational	14	11	14	1	Miss Fannie Schrader.
"	Methodist					[ave.
Chicago	Campbell Pk, Pres	24		24		Dr. F. H. Booth, 402 So. Oakley
"	Mosely Mission					W. C. Bentley, 73 25th street.
"	Tabernacle Cong					Miss M. Edwards, 38 N. Cent'l av.
"	Union Park Cong	63	1	64	3	Emma C. Caswell, 637 Wash. Bdc.
"	Moody's Church	22	3	18	2	Jennie K. Eckstrom, 1754 Fred-
"	Western Ave. Cong					Rev. Mr. Brooks. [erick st. [st.
"	Warren Ave. Cong	19	35		17	Frances B. Patterson, 656 Walnut
"	Belden Ave. Pres	30	32	45	15	Otto C. Bruhlman, 206 Racine st.
"	Westside Pres					[ave.
"	West'n Av. Ch. Christ					Rev. Mr. Allen, 303 Claremont
"	St. John's R. E.					P. F. Chase, 3730 Johnson place.
"	Leavitt Street Cong.	47	5			L D. Taylor, 154 Irving place.
"	Second Baptist					Rev. W. M. Lawrence.
"	St. Paul's R'f'md Epis.	35	4	37		Bishop Fallows.
"	Sheffield Ave. M. E.					Rev. Mr. Harkness.
"	Central Park Cong					Miss A. C. Beach, 145 Avers ave.
"	California Ave. Cong.	17	5			Rev Mr. Lloyd. [ave.
"	Chicago Ave. Society					Mrs. F. N. Penoyer, 342 La Salle
"	N. E. Congregational					Emily M. Higbee, 333 E. Ohio st.
"	Grace Cong	38	7	20	5	Maud McNeal, Maplewood.
"	Grace M. E.					
"	So. Park Cong					Anna H. Peck, 5850 Wash ave.
"	Immanuel Baptist					[street.
"	Armour Mission					John L. Cassell, 449 35th [ave.
"	Fifth Presbyterian	106	50			Rev. W. G. Woodbridge, 3657 Ind.
"	Bethany Cong					Carrie E. Kewan, 492 W. Superior.
"	Jefferson Park Pres					W. J. Sinclair, 330A, So Morgan st
"	Chicago Ave. Pres					Jennie Ecstrom, 1754 Fredk. st.
"	Westminster Pres					Miss C. Powell, 215 So Morgan st
"	Fullerton Ave. Pres					C. A. Nourse, 17 Wisconsin st.
"	Lincoln Park Cong					
"	Campbell Park					D. E. Postle, 452 Oakley ave.
"	Eighth Pres.					Wm. Frances, 1129 Adams st.
"	Sedwick St. Mission					Mr. Richardson, Law Institute.
"	Hyde Park Cong					[Langley ave.
"	South Cong					Miss A. L. Astwenchart, 3725
"	Beldin Ave. Pres					O. B. Bruhlman, 206 Racine ave.
"	North Cong					C. D. Eckstrom, 6024 Mich. ave.
Clarendon Hills	Presbyterian					Mattie Lemmon.
Clinton	Presbyterian	34	10	40	10	Mrs. Wesley Kelly.
"	Methodist Episcopal	27	20	25		Carrie Morlan.
"	Baptist					Rev. P. Reynolds.
Coakville	Presbyterian					
Cobden	Pres. & Bap. Union	32	6	38		L. M. Linnell.
"	Congregational					Rev. O. G. Graner.
Cooksville	Presbyterian	35		33		J. C. Wilson, Jr.
Colehour	Evang. Asso					H. S. Belkne.
Colehour						Samuel Better.

ILLINOIS.—(Continued.)

CITY.	CHURCH.	Act. Memb.	Asso. Memb.	Ch. Memb.	United with C.	Secretary and Address
Concord	Joy Prarie Cong					Rev. H. Tupper.
Cutler	United Presbyterian					
Danville	Presbyterian					
"	South Cong	18	21	14	11	L. H. Crawford.
Dansville	First M. E.					Prof. Coleman.
Decatur	Church of God	20		12		A. C. Smith.
"	Christian	62	11	62	4	J. E. Patterson, 304 W. Macon st.
"	First Pres.	50	17	40	5	E. A. West, T. H, & P, R. R, Co.
"	First M. E	65	3			W. C. Loughborn.
"	Stapp's Chapel	80	7	85		Belle M. Steele, 651 W. Prairie
"	United Brethren	25		12		Miss Zoa Gilbert. [st.
"	First Baptist	56	9	56	15	J. N. Martin, Jr., Box 133.
"	Union					W. L. Shellaberger.
Deering	Methodist Episcopal					Rev. J. D. Leek.
De Kalb	Methodist	20	18	25		Lou M. Allen.
Des Plaines						Bert Allen.
Dixon	Methodist Episcopal	59	1	59	18	Callie B. Morgan.
"	Baptist					J. F. Howard.
"	Lutheran					Milton Missman.
Dover	Congregational	33	1	28	1	Emma Harford.
Downer's Grove	Congregational	25	9			Miss Cora Blodgett.
Dundee	Baptist	52	14	50		Bertha Mann.
"	Congregational					
Dwight	Congregational	31	2	26		F. E. Donaldson.
Earlville	First Congregational	22	23	16	4	Frank Wiley.
Elgin	First Congregational	67	10	44	8	H. F. Derr, 170 No. College st.
"	First Baptist	80	1	80	4	Harry D. Barnes, 21 Hill st.
"	Bent St. Chapel Bap.					
"	Methodist Episcopal					Rev. Mr. Clendenning.
Elmdale						S. B. Wood.
Emington	Congregational	8		7	1	Edith Gilbert.
Englewood	North Cong	54	7	38	15	A. T. Poulson, Atlantic st.
"	First Congregational	30	6	26		C. M. Lyman, 6623 Perry ave.
"	Baptist					
"	Presbyterian					E. M. Smalley.
Erving	Baptist					P. C. Allen.
Evanston	First Congregational	54	8	52		Miss M. F. Kedzie, 430 Ridge
"	Baptist					Rev. Mr. Clatworthy. [ave.
"	Presbyterian	45	14	50		Rev. Dr. Noyes.
Evansville	Grace Presbyterian	30		30	5	W. J. Lewis.
"	Cumberland Pres.					
Farmington	Congregational					Rev. Chas. E. Marsh.
Fairmount						Leah France.
Fairfield	First Presbyterian	25		20	10	J. S. Davis.
Flora	Presbyterian					Isaac Smith.
Forest	Congregational					R. E. Hellus.
Fountain Green	Union					H. A. Preston.
Freeport	First Presbyterian					Ella Nun.
Golconda	Presbyterian					Rev. N. C. Galleaitt.
Galesburg	Presbyterian	60	10	50		Winoona Hoover, 418 W. Cedar
"	Ch. of Christ 1st. Cong					May Arnold. [st.
"	Second Cong					Rev. A. R. Thain.
"	First Congregational					Rev. J. W. Bradshaw,
Galva	Congregational	34	6	34	5	Mrs. Eva Ray Dickinson.
Geneva Junction	Congregational					Rev. W. H. Harbaugh.
Gibson City	First Presbyterian	33	9	23	6	Anna Le Fevre
" "	Methodist Episcopal					Frank Foxworthy.
" "						J. N. Steele.
Granville	Congregational					D. Wellesley Wise.
Grayville	Cumberland Pres.	59	20	61	39	Ollie Clarke.
Geneseo	First M. E.					
"	First Congregational					Rev. A. Bushnell.
Hamilton	Oakwood Cong.					J. W. Pierce.
Hamlet						Isaac D. Whittemore.
Hanover	First Presbyterian					Effie Wilson.
Hermosa	Congregational					Chas. B. Starbaird.

LIST OF SOCIETIES

ILLINOIS.—(Continued.)

CITY.	CHURCH.	Act. Memb.	Asso. Memb.	Ch. Memb.	United with C.	Secretary and Address.
Heyworth	Presbyterian	....	....	....	....	Rev. Mr. Black.
Highland Park	Union	55	15	25	....	Clarence M. Downs, Box 75.
Highland	First Congregational	14	1	13	4	Miss Grida S. Rietman.
Hinsdale	Congregational	46	33	44	6	G. E. Troeger.
"	Congregational	....	....	....	....	Lizzie Bowles.
Hillsboro	Methodist Episcopal	....	....	....	....	Florence Howard.
Hopewell	Wesleyan Meth	20	4	20	....	Mrs. O. C. Bedford, New Windsor.
Hyde Park	First Presbyterian	61	33	66	4	Julia S. Huggins.
" "	First Baptist	....	....	....	....	Arthur W. Cates.
Illiani	Warrensburg Cong	....	....	....	....	Kate Bachelder, Harristown.
Irving Park	Union	....	....	....	....	Charles Hayward.
Jacksonville	Congregational	44	2	42	....	Alfred E. Day, Kosciusko st.
"	Westminster Pres	59	1	59	....	S. W. Morton.
"	Grace Methodist	....	....	....	....	Rev. W. V. McElroy.
"	Christian	....	....	....	....	Clarence L. DePew.
Janesville	United Brethren	....	....	....	....	Rev. Mr. Rider.
Joliet	First Baptist	68	17	73	18	Kate White, 209 No. Broadway.
"	First Pres	....	....	....	....	Rev. W. M. Hindman.
"	Central Pres	....	....	....	....	Hattie L. Adams.
Kankakee	First Pres	50	....	....	25	Clarence E. Holt.
"	Hospital for Insane	....	....	....	....	Annie Burnett, M. D.
Kansas	Presbyterian	....	....	....	....	Claude Shaver.
Keithsburg		....	....	....	....	Abbie Van Denburg.
Kenwood	Hyde Pk. Evang	25	32	....	....	Katherine Strong.
Kewanee		....	....	....	....	Grace E. Lewis.
"	Congregational	47	1	39	17	Charity R. Palmer, Box 503.
"	Presbyterian	31	2	31	6	Chas. R. Clapp, M. D.
"	First Baptist	....	....	....	5	Rev. J. H. Delano.
Knoxville	Presbyterian	....	....	....	....	Dora Thompkins.
Lacon	Union	24	12	22	5	George A. Bangs.
"	Baptist	....	....	....	....	G. P. Bangs.
La Grange	Congregational	....	....	....	....	Pearl Morey.
"	Methodist	....	....	....	....	E. W. Currier.
"	Baptist	....	....	....	....	
Lake View	Ch. of the Redeemer	29	....	20	5	Anna J. Nicholaus Wright.
" "		....	....	....	12	E. A. Hunsinger, 542 La Salle ave
" "	Evanston Ave. Cong	....	....	....	....	Emma Ruhbaum, 244 Evanston ave.
Lebanon	Presbyterian	....	....	....	....	Isaac Smith.
Lincoln	Presbyterian	....	....	....	....	Rev. A. Michals.
Litchfield	Presbyterian	10	2	12	2	Cora Loughmiller.
"	Methodist Episcopal	....	....	....	....	Rev. W. L. Thompson.
"	Baptist	....	....	....	....	Rev. M. Buckley.
"	Christian	25	5	25	....	Mrs. B. F. Adams.
"	Lutheran	....	....	....	....	Dr. D. H. Snowden.
Lockport	Presbyterian	....	....	....	....	Rev. Mr. Hoke.
Lockport	Congregational	....	....	....	....	Hiram Warton.
Lyonville	Congregational	....	....	....	....	
Macomb	Presbyterian	28	....	28	....	Lucy A. Wheat.
Macon	Presbyterian	82	....	33	27	Mamie Chamberlain.
Marion		....	....	....	....	H. H. Hazeltine.
Mason City	Presbyterian	68	10	68	18	Laura Ironmonger.
"	Baptist	....	....	....	....	J. S. Hutchinson.
Mattoon	Cumb. Presbyterian	....	....	....	....	Rev. E. N. Johnson.
Maywood	Congregational	....	....	....	....	Rev. John Ellis.
McLean	Congregational	15	....	15	....	Rev. J. Brenton.
Mechanicsburg	Methodist Episcopal	27	2	28	1	Mrs. C. A. Sparrow.
"	Christian	....	....	....	....	Rev. David Wetzel.
Mendon	First Cong	13	4	11	....	Harriet E. Peet.
Millburn	Congregational	23	18	16	....	Julia H. Pantall.
Monmouth	First Pres	64	5	62	....	Inez McClung.
Monticello	Presbyterian	....	....	....	....	
Morequa		....	....	....	....	
Morgan Park	First Cong	14	8	12	5	R. S. Hale, P. O. Box 63.
"	Congregational	....	....	....	....	Rev. M. E. Baldwin.
Morris	Baptist	30	2	30	....	Della Woodbury.
Mt. Carrol	Church of God	....	8	....	7	Ida Ely.
" "	Lutheran	....	....	....	....	Silas H. Hine, Box 554.

OF CHRISTIAN ENDEAVOR.

ILLINOIS.—(*Continued.*)

CITY.	CHURCH.	Act. Memb.	Asso. Memb.	Ch. Memb.	United with C.	Secretary and Address.
Mt. Forest	Congregational					
Milko Grove						
Mt. Pulaski	First Meth.	12	12	12	4	Jennie J. Schraeder, Chebanse. Lyman Hershey.
Murphysboro	First Pres.	10	9	15		Mrs. F. M. Alexander.
Neponset	Congregational					Rev. Mr. Smith.
Newman	Cumb. Pres.					Grace Bulsley.
New Windsor	Wesleyan Methodist					
"	"					
Normal	First Cong.	25		25		
"	Presbyterian					Rev. John Kerr.
"	Baptist					Rev. Mr. Rhodes. [Salle st. Chi'go
Norwood Park	Am. Reformed	26	24	22	4	F. B. Cleveland, Room 26, 114 La
Norwalk	First Cong.	10		10		Anna P. Knight.
Odell	Congregational					Rev. J. V. Smith.
Ontario	Congregational					Jennie Clark.
Ornville	Union					Mabel Merriam.
Oregon	Presbyterian	31	30	23		Clara A. Leslie.
"	First Pres.					Clara A. Leslie.
"	Lutheran	?				
Oswego	Union	30	18	19	1	Mamie S. Smith.
Ottawa	First Baptist	90	5	89	15	Beckie Yentzer, W. Main st.
"	Congregational					Rev. Warren F. Day.
Pana	First Pres.	40	21	38	8	Lida Lawrence.
Park Ridge	Congregational	13	16	12	4	Arthur P. Bourns.
Paxton	Congregational					W. D. Hasbrouck.
Pecatonica	Congregational					Rev. Mr. Ward.
Peoria	Grace Pres.	19	17	29	6	Mrs. C. C. Lines.
"	Calvary Pres.	33	1	30	4	Prudie Slater, 621 Howett st.
"	First Presbyterian					Emma Coleman. [st.
"	Second Pres.					Madge M. Thompson, 407 Perry
"	Christian					Lorena Simenson, Main st.
"	Bethany Mis., Bap.	20	7	16		L. D. Putney, 1100 Perry st.
"	First Baptist					Stella Patterson.
"	First Cong.	59	11	59	17	J. D. Kinney, Box 404.
Petersburg	Presbyterian					Eva Knowles.
Peru	Union	22	6	11		Lydia Hackman.
Phoenix	Cumb. Pres.	23	19	1		
Plano						
Pontiac	Methodist Episcopal	28	4	29	1	Cora E. Reed.
Polo	Independent Pres.					Emma R. Pierson.
Princeville	Presbyterian	39	5	39	8	C. J. Cheesman.
"	Stark Cong.					
Princeton	Congregational					M. Elizabeth Reed, 407 Perry st.
Providence	Congregational					Rev. Mr. Clark.
Port Byron	Congregational	26	20	16	1	Mrs. A. W. Grant.
Pullman	Presbyterian					Maggie MacDonald.
Riverside	First Pres.	25				John T. Snodgrass. [man st.
Rockford	First Baptist	32	7	32	2	Lillian R. Chapman, 208 Hors-
"	First Cong.	69	1	64	17	Hattie L. Herrick, 404 So. 5th st.
"	Second Cong.	68	11	63		Emma A. Leach, 701 No. Court st
"	State St. Baptist	44		42	2	Ida L. Allen, 504 No. 3rd st.
"	First Pres.					Dr. Sutherland.
Rockton	Congregational					Rev. F. A. Miller.
Roodhouse	Congregational	10		10		Stacy G. Clarkluff.
Rock Island						Jennie T. Thompson.
Rossville	Presbyterian	31		3		Lulu McCoughey.
Rosamond	Congregational					
Rushville	First Pres.	43	6	40	9	E. S. Griffith.
Salem	Cumberland Pres.	43	24	51		Miss Ida Spencer.
"	" "					J. P. Sproules.
Sandwich						Beecher Greenfield, Box 577.
Seward	Congregational					Rev. Wm. Cooley, Pecatonica.
Shelborne	Congregational					Rev. W. C. Miller.
Sheffield	Congregational	39	3	28	18	Maggie A. Hanson.
Shelbyville	Presbyterian					Rev. Mr. Frazier.
Sparta	Congregational	10	2	10		J. M. Nickles.
South Chicago	First Evangelical	21	5	17		Herman Behuke, Lock Box 83.

LIST OF SOCIETIES

ILLINOIS.—(Continued.)

CITY.	CHURCH.	Act. Memb.	Asso. Memb.	Ch. Memb.	United with C.	Secretary and Address.
Savannah	United Pres					James Daley.
South Chicago	First Pres	36		30		Ada M. Winsby.
" "	First Cong					Flora Arnold.
" Park	Congregational					Anna H. Peck, 5850 Wash. ave.
South Danville						S. H. Crawford, Danville.
Springfield	First Meth	60	10	60		Miss Stratton, Bettie Stuat Ins.
"	First Congregational	40	12	31	5	Mary L. Johnson.
"	First Pres	47	7	50		Mary E. Brooks, 927 So. 8th st.
"	Second Pres	39	6	43		Dr. Johnson.
"	Second Meth					Rev. R. J. Hobbs.
"	Third Pres					Emma Post.
"	First Baptist					
Stark						
Staunton	Presbyterian					Rev. Mr. Townsend.
St. Charles	Congregational					Anna Eddy.
Sterling	First Congregational	25	20	26	83	Chas. T. Russell, 702 Second ave.
"	Christian	23	28	23		Marion V. Cassell.
Streator	Congregational	18	10			Annie Haefer, No. Monroe st.
Sublette						Leon A. Wood
Sugar Creek	Cumb. Pres					Frank Allen, Chatham.
Tallula						M. Olive Blunt.
Tamaroa	Presbyterian	24	13	23	7	Louise Woods.
"	Methodist					Rev. B. F. Smith.
Taylorville	First Pres	15		15	4	Lillian I. Horner.
Tonica						Fannie Shumway.
Toulon	Congregational	40		40		Addie M. Smith.
Towanda	Union	28	7	27		W. L. Rayburn.
Upper Alton	Presbyterian	34	12	25	21	Cassie M. Brown.
Villa Ridge	Congregational					Rev. John Gibson.
Virden						J. R. Moore.
Urbana	Presbyterian	16	14	13		Minnie A. Kyle.
Warren						Rev. Alba F. Hall.
Warrensburg	Methodist					Rev. Gilmore Cunningham.
Waukegan	First Cong	60		35		Carrie F. Knights.
"	Baptist	51		35		Herbert Griffin.
"	Methodist Episcopal					
"	Presbyterian					
Wash. Heights	Lutheran					Rev. F. H. Patzer.
" "	Bethany Union	36	21	30	12	Alice S. Barnard.
Waverly	First Cong	16	7	19	1	Ida M. Sackett.
Wayne	Congregational	7	8	9		Hattie Sayer.
"	Congregational					Mr. B. F. Ellis.
Wenona	Presbyterian					Rev. E. N. Lord.
Western Springs	Friends and Cong	40	4	40		Miss Gertrude Hill.
" "	Lyonsville Cong	10		10		A. Strout.
West Hallock	Day Baptist	20		13		Belle Butts.
" "	Congregational					Rev. S. Burdick.
Wheaton	First Cong	11	6	10	5	Frank L. De Wolf, Box 446.
"	First Baptist	20		10		Eva. M. Lanelon.
Wilmette	Congregational					Rev. Mr. Beardsly.
Winnetka	Congregational	25		15	3	Mr. Frank Fant.
Woodlawn	First Pres	33	30			S. F. Hawthorne.
Woodhull	Presbyterian					Rev. A. E. Chase.
Wyanet	Union	16	18	13		Winnie Schureman.
Yates City	Presbyterian	75	5	75	3	Emma McKeighan.
" "	Congregational					

INDIANA.

Bloomington	Walnut Pres					John Ehni.
Cannelton	Methodist Episcopal	20		19	10	Fred Wagner.
Carlisle Hill						[ave.
Crawfordville	Center Presbyterian	40	26			Rev. E. B. Thanson, W. Wabash
Connersville	Methodist Episcopal					S. W. Dove.
"	Presbyterian					Rev. T. H. Hench.

OF CHRISTIAN ENDEAVOR.   xix.

INDIANA.—(*Continued.*)

CITY.	CHURCH.	Act. Memb.	Asso. Memb.	Ch. Memb.	United with C.	Secretary and Address.
Covington	Methodist					Rev. Wm. F. Switzer.
Delphi	Presbyterian	50	16	46	6	W. L. Seawright.
Elkhart						Rev. Geo. B. Safford.
Evansville	Grace Presbyterian	35	3	35		W. J. Lewis, 7 Main street.
"	Walnut St. Pres	49	6	49		H. J. Plafflin, 416 Third avenue.
"	Cumberland Pres	72	18	80	15	Carrie Hacker, 1313 E. F'kl'n st.
"	Trinity Methodist					Rev. Mr. Woods.
"	Methodist Episcopal					Rev. Mr. Reid.
"	Christian					Rev. Neil McLeod.
Fort Wayne	Congregational	28	7	28	1	Etta Potter, 9 West street.
" "	Second Presbyterian					Rev. J. M. Fretton.
Franklin	Christian Church	40		40	40	Rev. C. S. Scott.
Goshen	Presbyterian					Mrs. H. D. Van Nuys.
Granger	Presbyterian					Rev. George W. Healy.
Greenfield	Presbyterian					Rev. D. R. Love.
Indianapolis	Mayflower Cong	45	3	43	12	H. L. Whitehead, 357 N. East st.
"	Seventh Pres					Bettie M. Wishard, 89 Huron st.
"	Second Presbyterian	50	30	60		Clara A. Shover, 451 N. Del. st.[st,
"	Presbyterian					Belle Behymer, 235 Bellefontaine
"	First Presbyterian					H. C. Sickles.
"	Fourth Presbyterian					Rev. G. L. McNutt.
"	Fifth Presbyterian	29	9	32		Miss M. L. Hitchcock.
"	Sixth Presbyterian					Rev. Charles Evans.
"	Memorial Pres					Rev. H. A. Edson, D. D.
"	Eleventh Pres					Rev. Mr. Dickey.
"	Twelfth Pres					Rev. W. A. Hendrickson.
"	E. Washington					Rev. E. P. Whallen.
"	First Baptist					Rev. Reuben Jeffrey, D. D.
"	Central Christian					Rev. E. J. Garetz.
"	Hall Place M. E.					Rev. M. L. Hyde.
"	Tabernacle Pres					Edna McGillard.
Irvington	Methodist Episcopal	14	6	14		Nellie Krumrine.
(M. E. Connersville)						
Jonesville	Methodist Episcopal	40		40		Will B. Wright.
Kendallville	Disciple					
La Grange	First Presbyterian	19	11	19		Ella M. Barrows,
La Porte	Presbyterian	65	14	54	9	Rev. John F. Kendall.
" "	Congregational					W. F. Miller.
" "	First Baptist					Carrie F. Page.
Liberty	Presbyterian					Rev. Geo. A. McIntosh.
Lima	Union	25	9	28		Miss Katharine R. Williams.
Madison	Vine St. Baptist	26		26	9	Lizzie Green, 509 N. Broadway.
"						S. A. Moffett, 112 E. Main St.
Michigan City	First Presbyterian	35	11	30	12	J. M. Throckmorton, Cor. Wash.
" "	Congregational	42	20	29	7	F. W. Miller. [& 9th. sts.
Mishawaka	Presbyterian	29	2	29	1	C. A. Loring.
"	Baptist	16	12	16	6	Allie Eggleston, 308 W. Joseph
Mt. Vernon	First Presbyterian	21	15	21	5	Bessie H. London. [St.
New Carlisle	Christian	26	14	27	2	Ralph W. Harris.
" "	Methodist Episcopal					Flora A. Biddell.
Niles	Baptist					Miss Ida A. Hunter.
Orland	Congregational	14	20	14		Sarah A. Benedict.
Princeton	Presbyterian					Rev. William Ward.
Richmond	Presbyterian	55	10	50	5	Mrs. Cora Lane, Main St.
"	English Lutheran					Rev. J. W. Kapp.
Rising Sun	Presbyterian	22				Rev. H. F. Olmstead.
Rushville	Presbyterian					Rev. W. H. Sands. [ette st.
South Bend	First Baptist	70	10	70	20	Miss A. L. French, 233 N. Lafay-
" "	First Presbyterian	64	12	64	20	Miss A. H. Stanfield, 124 S. Wil-
" "	First Christian					F. A. Marsh. [liam st.
" "	Second Pres	23	18	23	6	B. R. Thomas, 811 E. Wash. st.
" "	First M. E.					Miss Lizzie Rush.
Sparta						
Streetsboro						
Terre Haute	United Brethren	21	20	15	13	Mrs. M. Borden, 1659 Poplar st.
" "	Central Pres					S. E. M. Caulter.
Valparaiso	First Presbyterian	67	30	55	20	Sadie J. Pierce. P. O. Box 183.
Versailles						

LIST OF SOCIETIES

INDIANA.—(Continued.)

CITY.	CHURCH.	Act. Memb.	Asso. Memb.	Memb. Ch.	United with C.	Secretary and Address.
Warsaw	First Presbyterian	43	23	13	2	Walter Chipman, 109 Ft. Wayne
"	First Baptist					Rev. J. H. Winans, [st.
"	Methodist Episcopal					Rev. Mr. Lynch.
"	United Brethren					Rev. J. Simons.
Wayne	Second Pres.					Rev. J. M. Fretton.
Winamac	Methodist					Allie Harris.
Wolcottville	Baptist					

IOWA.

CITY.	CHURCH.	Act. Memb.	Asso. Memb.	Memb. Ch.	United with C.	Secretary and Address.
Ackley	First Presbyterian	32	9	23		Maud S. Beach.
Algonia	Congregational	26		26	4	Rev. W. Bennard.
Ames						Rev. E. C. Moulton.
Anamosa	Baptist	70	12			Miss Nora Peet.
Andrew						
Anita	Congregational					Rev. E. P. Childs.
Arthur	Union	24	17	24		Rev. Charles Wyatt.
Avoca	Congregational					E. E. Geischime.
Atlantic	Congregational	68		41	24	Grace Green.
Baxter	Congregational	25		25		Miss Jennie Williamson.
Bedford	Baptist	10	3	10	1	Rev. J. H. Scott.
"	First Presbyterian	22	6	18		Lizzie Graff.
"	Methodist Episcopal					Rev. Mr. McDade.
Belle Plaine	Congregational	19	3	15	6	A. C. Huston.
Bellevue	Congregational	22	9	23	4	Nettie Hughey, cor. 3d & Jeffer-
"	United Pres.					Rev. Mr. McArthur. [son sts,
"	Congregational					Nettie Hughey.
Big Rock						F. Mary Parsons.
Boone						C. S. Clapp.
Bradford	Union					Prof. L. A. Stout.
Brooklyn	Presbyterian					Miss Anna Caldwood. [ary st.
Burlington	Walnut St. Baptist	41	6	41	23	Miss H. Babcock, 1215 So. Bound-
"	United Presbyterian	35	5			F. J. Tallant, 706 Locust st.
"	First Baptist	22		22	4	Hattie Lane, 210 So. Augusta st.
"	First M. E.					Rev. C. H. Stocking, D. D.
"	South Hill M. E.					Rev. W. N. Hall.
"	Congregational					Rev. Wm. Salter, D. D.
"	First Presbyterian					Rev. J. C. McClintock, D. D.
Cedar Falls	First Presbyterian	39	19	25	5	Etta O. Chase, cor. Wash. & 6th.
" "	Congregational	19	15	18		Maggie Bixby. [Sts.
" "	First Baptist	10				Miss Lucy Plummer.
Charles City	First Baptist	17	15	17	10	W. N. Carter.
" "	Congregational	46	8	34		Miss Lucy Mitchell.
" "	First M. E.	16	12	23		Orra Allison.
Chester City	Methodist					Miss Fannie Sherman.
Cherokee	Presbyterian	19	42	17	3	Mary Russell.
"	Congregational					Rev. W. A. Evans.
Cincinnati	First Congregational					
Clarksville	Presbyterian	9	10	10	2	H. Graham.
"	Union					Emma Cave.
Clarence						May Conroe.
Clay	Congregational	18		17	3	Miss Bessie L. Little.
Clarion	Union	13	5	14		Alice Gibbs.
Clinton	Methodist	42	18			B. F. Robinson, 624 Camanch
"	Congregational					Rev. Mr. Denney. [ave.
"	Presbyterian					Rev. Mr. Burrell.
Corning	Congregational					Warren Aukeny.
Creston	Baptist	25	5			L. C. Teed.
Cresco	Congregational	20	25	30		Rev. Mr. McConnell.
"	Methodist Episcopal					Rev. J. Tull.
Danville	Denmark Union					Rev. Fred Blackington.
"	Methodist					W. R. Stryker.

OF CHRISTIAN ENDEAVOR. xxi.

IOWA.—(*Continued.*)

CITY.	CHURCH.	Act. Memb.	Asso. Memb.	Ch. Memb.	United with C.	Secretary and Address.
Decorah	First Congregational					Emma Beard.
Denmark	Congregational					Mary C. Ingalls.
Des Moines	Central Christian	38	10	37	11	Ettie Elliott, 1135 7th St.
" "	Presbyterian	39	8	36	3	M. B. Sturgis, 1012 Court ave.
" "	Presbyterian	91	25	91	8	Clara C. Matthews, 945 Third st.
" "	Westminster Pres	23		22		
" "	No. Park Cong					Rev. Mr. St. John.
" "	Plymouth Cong					Annie B. Merrill.
" "	Friends					Rev. Mr. Pennington.
" "	Trinity Evangelical					Rev. E. F. Mell.
" "	Pilgrim Cong					Rev. Mr. Kinzer.
" "	Calvary					Ella Reinking, 1308 E. Sycamore
" "	Evangelical	30	3	30	5	Flora Wirwost. [st.
" "	E, side Baptist	34	7	3		F. N. McGlothlen, 1206 Buchanan
" "	Central Pres					B. A. Lockwood, High st. [st.
" "	Methodist					
De Witt	Congregational	30	14	26	1	Miss Ida Blodgett, Dodge st.
Dysart	Presbyterian	30	7	27	9	Hattie Rowe.
Dysart						Miss A. Hollabaugh
Dubuque	First Congregational	43	17	46	19	Hattie E. Greenhow, 864 Bluff st.
"	Presbyterian					
"	Second Pres	24		24		Lizzie Coy, 60 Broad st.
Earlville	Congregational	25	24	28	4	L. W. Winslow.
"	Junior Cong	10	28			
E. Des Moines		50	11	49	4	Winard Sturges, 524 E. Walnut
Eddyville	Congregational					Miss Lucy Fais.
Eldora	First Congregational					Emma Beard.
Eldon	Congregational					Mary Howell.
Emerson	Presbyterian	12		12		Cyrus D. McLaughlin.
Fairfield	Congregational	22	13	19		Miss Helen Rose.
"	Methodist Episcopal	40	10	37		Emma Gilbert.
"	Baptist					
Fayette	Congregational	18	7	10		Rev. A. S. Huston.
Fort Dodge	Presbyterian					Rev. E. B. Newcomb.
Fort Madison	First M. E.	23	11	21	2	Miss Laura Eitman.
Garden Grove	Presbyterian	20	8	21		Mrs. A. W. Stearns.
Genoa Bluffs	Congregational	13	6	13	5	George R. Howard.
Gilmore City	Presbyterian					
Gilman	Congregational					Rev. A. S. Houston.
"	Union Society	10	6	10		Annie Marerling.
"	C. Junior Society	20	50	10	5	
Golden	Congregational					S. V. Haigh.
Granger						Annie Marerling.
Green Mountain	Congregational	10		10		Pearl Somers.
Greene						Rev. Mr. Greene.
Grinnell	Congregational	110	1	75		Hattie F. Jaines.
Grundy Centre	First Presbyterian	22	24	25	5	
Harlan	Congregational	19	2	14		Rev. J. W. Geiger.
Hopkinton						Mary R. Johnson.
Hubbard						
Hull	Congregational	22	6	17	1	Bertha Ayerbright.
Independence	First Presbyterian	35	48	33		Mamie Markham.
Iowa City	Congregational	50	17	50	2	Laura Clarke, 516 So. Gilbert st.
" "	Baptist	18		18	1	Kate C. Wickham, 809 Page st.
" "	Presbyterian					
Janesville						Emma Hand.
Johnson	Presbyterian					George W. Douglass.
Kellogg	Congregational	17	11	20		Miss Lala Gorton, Bolton st.
Kelly	Congregational	16	4	13		Geo. Ball.
Keokuk	United Presbyterian	38	5			George Stucker.
Kingsley						
Knoxville	Baptist					O. R. McKay.
"						A. C. Hart.
"	Presbyterian	30	10	30	2	Nettie R. Davis.
Le Clair	Presbyterian					Lulu Chapman.
Le Mars	Congregational	43	20	38	5	Olin H. Round.
Lewis	Congregational					May Rishel.

LIST OF SOCIETIES

IOWA.—(Continued.)

CITY.	CHURCH.	Act. Memb.	Asso. Memb.	Ch. Memb.	United with C.	Secretary and Address.
Logan	Congregational					
Logan	Presbyterian	13	9	13		Hattie L. Caldwell.
Lost Nation						
Lucas	Union	39	22	38	33	Effie Main, Box 257.
Lynville						
Magnolia	Congregational	17	1	17		Rebecca Raymond.
"	Presbyterian					
Manchester	First Congregational	28	20	20		Laura E. Dunham.
Marion	Congregational	40	20	35		T. J. Davis.
"	Baptist					Rev. N. D. Mason.
"	Presbyterian					Harry F. Echternacht, 311 East [State st.
Marshalltown	Presbyterian	22	4	19	11	
"	Congregational					Rev. W. R. Scannett.
"						Mrs. Byrant.
Maquoketa	Congregational	36	20	36	11	Libbie Smith.
Marble Rock						
Mason City	First Congregational	35	7	35		Mrs. George Knowlton.
" "	Methodist	66	11	64		Mamie Keon.
" "	Baptist					
McGregor	First Congregational	31	20	13		Mr. Arthur Hatch.
Mediapolis		22		11		Bell N. Hall, Box 93.
Middletown	Presbyterian	7	2	5	2	J. J. MacMakin.
Miles	Congregational	8	7	9	4	Alice D. Reimer.
Mitchell	Congregational	26	20	26	42	Archie Prime.
Monona	Congregational	35	20	15		Nettie Parker.
Monticello	Congregational	49	18	40		Chas. Clyde Hunt.
Monticello	First Presbyterian	12	14	12		Ada Gibson.
Morning Sun	Presbyterian	13	12	22		John F. Cochrane.
" "	First U. P.					
" "	First M. E.					
Mt. Pleasant	Congregational	27	3	27		Miss Ida Comer.
Muscatine	First Presbyterian	40		40	7	Ida Fath, 519 East 7th street.
"	First M. E.					Rev. W. G. Wilson.
"	First Baptist					Rev. S. E. Wilcox.
Nashua	First Cong.	33	30	31	17	Miss Mary V. Noble, Lock Box [79.
Newburg	Union	14	5	14		A. B. Heltzel.
New Hampton	Congregational					Rev. R. H. Gurley.
Newton	First Cong.	43	18	48	23	Ella V. Hough.
"	Juvenile Cong.	23	23	23		Ella V. Hough.
New Providence	Union	12	1	12	1	Flora Moore.
North Des Moines	Congregational	17	10	15	7	Emma Smith.
North English	Methodist Episcopal					Rev. Mr. Smith.
Oelwein	Free Baptist					Harry Netcott.
Ogden	Congregational					Mrs. C. B. Sylvester.
Osage	Congregational	27	6	26		Belle Sweeney
Oskaloosa	First Baptist	17	10	15	2	Mrs. H. H. Clouse, 209 So. 3d st.
"	Congregational					Rev. Mr. Keyes.
"	Baptist					Mittie Nelson.
Osceola	N. W. Presbyterian	24	3	24	4	Bertha Dunlap.
Ottumwa	Second Cong.	24	3	24	4	Leroy S. Hand, 388 Davis street.
"	First Presbyterian	33	3	33	6	Mattie E. Harlan, 228 E. Main st.
"	First Baptist					Rev. H. Williams.
"	Second Pres.					Rev. J. E. McElroy.
Oxford	Presbyterian					Rev. George F. Leclure.
Prairie du Chien	Congregational					Rev. A. Audridge.
Plymouth						
Pope City	Junior Society	95				Miss Lulie LaBelle.
" "	First Cong.	20	8			Miss Hattie Martz.
Postville	First Cong.	31	8	21		Mrs. Matie Welzel.
Preston	Union	9	5			Miss Emily F. DeReimer.
Quasqueton	Congregational					Rev. J. H. Orvis.
Riceville	Union	50	5	43		Ray R. St. John.
Rockford	Congregational	20	10	12		
Rockwell						
Rolfe	Presbyterian					Rev. H. Duty.
Sabula	Congregational	6	3	8		Jessie H. Long.
Salem	Congregational	14		14		Mrs. Anna Withrow.

IOWA.—(Continued.)

CITY.	CHURCH.	Act. Memb.	Asso. Memb.	Ch. Memb.	United with C.	Secretary and Address.
Sand Spring	Union	43	....	40	....	Anna M. Anderson.
Shenandoah	Congregational	....	....	....	30	Miss Lottie Valentine.
"	First Baptist	....	....	....	....	Rev. L. J. Shoemaker.
Sidney	Presbyterian	....	....	....	....	Rev. Mr. Hughes.
Sioux City	First Presbyterian	48	....	44	....	John A. Smith, 1209 14th st.
" "	First Congregational	....	....	....	8	Rev. Mr. Darling.
" "	First Baptist	....	....	....	....	Rev. Dr. Ricarton.
Sioux Rapids	First Congregational	26	2	15	3	Florence Sickles.
Spencer	Congregational	....	....	....	....	
State Centre	First Presbyterian	....	....	....	....	L. Sibley.
Stewart	Congregational	45	....	25	....	Annie Twombley.
Steamboat Rock		....	....	....	....	M. A. Taylor.
Storm Lake	Methodist Episcopal	....	....	....	....	B. M. Smith.
Strawberry Point						
Tabor	Union	50	10	....	....	Maggie Lawrence.
"	Congregational	42	3	29	....	Alice C. Piper.
"	Junior	23	17	14	3	Luella E. Jones.
Tipton	Congregational	17	15	21	....	Lulu Garbur.
Toledo		....	....	....	....	Rev. Mr. Blodgett.
Traer		....	....	....	....	
Vancleve	Congregational	26	8	15	....	E. Yocom.
Victor	Presbyterian	....	....	....	....	Rev. Mr. Stewart.
"	Union	24	3	26	....	Maggie Lewis.
Villisca		....	....	....	6	
Wancoma	First Congregational	54	24	43	....	L. J. Smith.
Washburn	Union	....	....	....	2	Mrs. Simon Clasey.
Waterloo	Congregational	30	1	....	....	
"	Presbyterian	15	4	16	4	L. C. Newcomb.
Washington	Methodist Episcopal	....	....	....	....	Frank Wilson.
Webster City	Congregational	44	2	38	....	Carrie B. Hillock.
" "	Baptist	21	6	21	26	Cora Call Whittlesey.
Williamsburgh	Union	25	55	27	....	Will M. Beck.
Winthrop	Congregational	20	31	13	5	Rosa Pierce.
Wittenberg	Congregational	....	....	....	....	Rev. J. J. Mitchell.
Winterset	Presbyterian	....	....	....	....	Jennie Cass.
Wyoming	Presbyterian	....	....	....	....	Will B. Hallett.

KANSAS.

CITY.	CHURCH.	Act. Memb.	Asso. Memb.	Ch. Memb.	United with C.	Secretary and Address.
Abilene	Trinity Luth.	12	4	12	....	F. M. Porch.
"	Methodist Episcopal	....	....	....	....	
Alma	Congregational	....	....	....	....	Rev. W. C. Wheeler
"		....	....	....	....	
Anthony	First Pres.	22	2	22	....	Miss A. E. Bullock.
"	Congregational	42	13	46	5	Columbia Farrar.
"	Methodist Episcopal	....	....	....	....	Rev. Mr. Buckner.
"	Baptist	....	....	....	....	Rev. Mr. Edwards.
Annelly	Methodist Episcopal	30	5	30	10	Annie Anderson.
Argentine	Congregational	24	14	31	....	D. Brickett.
Arkansas City	First Baptist	60	....	....	....	Walter Smith.
Armourdale	Presbyterian	....	....	....	....	Rev. Mr. Gillett.
Atchison	English Evan	24	1	24	....	W. C. Miller.
"	Congregational	22	1	11	1	Kate Harriman, 1021 Mound st.
"	Congregational	22	5	....	....	C. F. Smith.
Auburn		....	....	....	....	Will Case.
Auburn	Union	....	....	....	....	Rev. J. W. Talliot.
Bloomington		....	....	....	....	
Blue Mound	Congregational	....	....	....	....	
Burlington	Congregational	15	15	15	....	Clara Porter.
"	Christian	32	13	32	....	Miss Ora Ernman.
"	First Presbyterian	16	9	16	....	Almeda Andrews, Niagara st.
"	Methodist Episcopal	....	....	....	4	Rev. J. B. Ford.
Burton	Presbyterian	....	....	....	....	Miss Bertha A. Young.

LIST OF SOCIETIES

KANSAS.—(Continued.)

CITY.	CHURCH.	Act. Memb.	Asso. Memb.	Ch. Memb.	United with C.	Secretary and Address.
Cawker City						Rev. T. A. Humphreys.
Capioma	First Cong	23	21	5		Rev. Vernon Robinson.
Centralia	Congregational					Charles Andrews.
Chapman	Congregational	23	2	15		Forest J. Poor.
Cherokee	Union					
Cherryvale						Rev. Mr. Lowe.
Clay Centre	First Cong	17	7	17	15	C. L. Parker, Box 453.
" "	First Baptist					Rev. S. W. Phelps.
" "	Methodist Episcopal					Rev. Mr. Collins.
" "	Presbyterian					Rev. John Park.
Clements						Rev. Mr. Martin.
Clyde	Presbyterian	14		14		Miss Lillie Laughlin.
Cottonwood Falls						L. S. Hackett.
Detroit	Congregational	11	17			L. E. Steigelman.
Dover	Congregational	24	20			Ardelle Aldrich.
Dunlap	Union	18	14	14	6	Minnie E. Thomas.
El Dorado	First Baptist					Dora Green.
" "	Baptist					Adela M. Bacon.
Ellsworth	Presbyterian					
Elmdale	Union	20		18		S. B. Wood.
"				11	8	[st.
Emporia	First Cong	70	11	30		Mrs. Edwin Fowler, 831 Neosho
"	Second Cong				10	John C. Jones.
"	Union					Albert E. Ayers.
Enterprise	Congregational					Rev. J. F. Smith.
Fairview Village	Baptist	36	11			Nellie Evans.
" "	Congregational	65	8	55		Mrs. L. J. Belts.
Florence	Presbyterian	19	4	18	4	Kittie L. Mastin.
Fort Scott					14	Rev. Wm. J. Gray.
Garden City						Rev. S. Wood.
Garnett	Presbyterian	37		29		Mrs. Blanche Osborne.
"	Un. Presbyterian					
Gaylord	Congregational					
Geneseo	Presbyterian	11	15	11	1	F. H. Holme.
Girard						C. A. Giles.
Great Bend	Congregational	13	4	17		H. B. Torrey.
Greensburg						Mrs. H. F. Drydale.
Harlan	U. B.	20	5	16		Miss Ora Herman.
"	Gould College Chapel	90	5	15		P. M. Herrick.
Hays City	Trinity Lutheran					Mrs. E. E. Jones.
Hiawatha	Congregational	43	17		6	Miss Electa Babbitt.
Hillsdale	Cumberland Pres	26	1	26	15	Jennie Lewellyn.
Holton	Presbyterian					
Junction City	Presbyterian					Mr. Graves.
" "	Congregational					Florence P. Hastings. [st.
Kansas City	First Congregational	2	10	20	5	Mrs. W. E. Barnhart, 623 Orville
" "	First Presbyterian	37	10	37		Geo. M. L. Miller, 1802 4th st.
" "	First Baptist	30	3		4	O. R. Taylor, Station A.
" "	Clyde Junior					
Lawrence	First Presbyterian					A. E. Saxey.
"	First Baptist					
"	Plymouth Cong	30	10	26	1	Cora L. Kimball.
"	Congregational	25	15	20	18	Geo. Loit.
Leavenworth	Baptist					Rev. Mr. Anderson.
"	Christian					Rev. Mr. Swaney. [Stove Co.
"	Methodist Episcopal	31				M. M. Strader, Great Western
"	Presbyterian	62	3		7	S. O. Putnam, 101 5th avenue.
"	First Congregational	26	13	20		Minnie N Lewis, 528 Walnut st.
Lincoln	Disciple of Christ					T. J. G. King.
Logan	Union	7	9	6		E. I. King.
Louisburg	Union	12		12		Mrs. Julia Hermigh.
Louisville	Congregational					
Luctor	Reformed Dutch					D. Schotten.
Lyons	Presbyterian					D. H. Holmes.
Manhattan	First Cong	45	4	34	8	Bessie Perry.
"	Baptist					

KANSAS.—(*Continued.*)

CITY.	CHURCH.	Act. Memb.	Asso. Memb.	Ch. Memb.	United with C.	Secretary and Address.
Manhattan	Presbyterian					Rev. D. C. Milner.
McPherson	Baptist					Belle Fink.
"	Christian					
Michaelville						Edwin Hamilton.
Mound City	First Congregational	11	4	11		Mrs. O. E. Lake.
Morantown	Presbyterian					Minnie E. Jordan.
New Lancaster						A. C. Carpenter.
Newton	Presbyterian					H. E. Mills.
"	Congregational					Rev. Pearse Pinch.
No. Cedar	No. Presbyterian	30	8	23	5	J. S. Colbin.
Nortonville		29	4	31	1	G. M. Cottrell.
"	United Pres.					Rev. W. L. Garges.
No. Lawrence	Pilgrim Cong.	44	36	27		
No. Topeka	Presbyterian			35		Ella Shute, 1166 Quincy St.
Olathe	Congregational					Rev. A. W. Bishop
Ottawa	First Congregational	29	14	21	5	Mollie J. Marcell, 115 W. 5th St.
"	Pilgrim Cong.					
Paola	Congregational	37	10	33	6	Nettie Brayman.
"	Baptist	18	3	19	3	Lora Oldham.
"	Methodist					Rev. J. A. Price.
"	First Pres.					Etta Hills.
Partridge	Union	15		15	9	Mrs. A. E. Edgeworth.
Peabody	Union					Nina Bush.
Pleasanton	First Pres	20	19	20	4	Lora Oldham.
Pomona						
Reno						George Conrad.
Diciples						
Riverton						Emma E. Hoover.
Russell	United Breth.					Mrs. J. W. Kraft, 333 No. 10th st.
Salina	St. John Eng. Luth.	23	3	23	4	Chas. Husband.
"	First Presbyterian	29	6	26		Annie M. Anderson.
Sand Springs	Union					Lena J. Monney.
Sabetha	Congregational					Mrs. Cooper.
Sedalia						Dr. E. S. Johnson.
Seneca	Congregational					
Sterling	Congregational					Rev. W. R. Scott.
"	Presbyterian					Chas. Hill.
Stockton	Acad.	50	20	15		Annie Kingsley.
St. Johns	United Breth.					
Solomon City	Methodist Episcopal.					
Topeka	First Presbyterian	71	6	72		C. W. Douglass, 735 Kansas ave.
"	First Methodist					Bessie Boughton.
"	First Cong.	35	2	33		Ed. G. Smith, 627 Van Buren
"	First Baptist					Rev. S. R. Peters.
"	Lutheran	46	1	40		Viola Clandy, Box 137.
"	N. B					Q. M. Mcgraw.
"	Third Pres.					
"	Second Baptist	86		6		Mary Ashton
"	Methodist					Rev. Peter Johnson.
"	Christian					H. C. Lewis, 1626 Taylor st.
Tonganoxie	First Congregational	19	15	18	1	A. H. Sloan.
Valley Falls	Congregational	36				Rev. Mr. Bradley.
Wabaunsee						Mamie Thompson.
Wakefield	Union					Elsie Richardson.
Waverly	First Pres.	33	9	31		
Westmoreland	First Congregational					Warren Anthony.
White City	Congregational	8		8	1	Jay Baxter.
Wichita	Plymouth Cong.	30	3	32	1	F. A. Reed, Lock Box 69.
"	Lewis Academy					J. M. Naylor.
"						Rev. H. W. Mines, Box 182.[ave.
"	First Presbyterian	51	4	53		Annie E. Schanck, 440 River View
"						George B. Peets, 437 Campbell ave
Wyandotte	Congregational					E. M. Smith.

LIST OF SOCIETIES

KENTUCKY.

CITY.	CHURCH.	Act. Memb.	Asso. Memb.	Ch. Memb.	United with C.	Secretary and Address
Hopkinsville	First Pres.	27	1	28	....	Charles Boute.
Louisville	College St. Pres.	23	....	23	....	I. D. Hitchcock, 314 E. Grey st.
"	....	....	....	....	....	Miss M. T. Huber, 623 E. Br'dw'y.
"	Fourth Presbyterian	40	15	40	31	Virgie Milburn, 1024 E. Wash. st.
"	Congregational	....	....	....	....	Rev. S. S. Waltz.
"	First English Luth.	20	15	....	....	H. B. Prensu, 511 E. Chestnut st.
"	Warren Mem. Pres.	16	....	14	....	Robert Huline, 410 W. Main st.
"	11th & Walnut Street	....	....	....	....	Rev. J. R. Collier.

LOUISIANA.

Crowley		....	....	....	....	Minnie A. Williams.
Delhi	True Vine Baptist	15	15	20	3	H. R. Flynn.
Winnsborough		....	....	....	....	A. Turner.

MAINE.

Auburn	High St. Cong.	62	11	40	....	Miss Frances Little, Main st.
"	Sixth St. Cong.	27	9	22	....	Annie C. Haskell, 99 So. Main st
"	Pine St. Free Bap.	....	....	....	....	Rev. W. J. Trout.
"	Court St. Baptist.	....	....	....	....	Rev. Mr. Whittemore.
"	Court St. Free Bap.	30	4	25	....	Rev. T. H. Stacy.
Augusta	Baptist	....	....	....	....	
"	So. Paris Cong.	....	....	....	....	Grace B. Randolph.
Bangor	First Baptist.	41	42	46	5	Miss E. M. Robinson, 179 French
"	First M. E.	....	....	....	....	Rev. George D. Lindsey. [st.
"	Union St. M. E.	....	....	....	....	Rev. Mr. Rogers.
"	Hammond St. Cong.	....	....	....	....	Rev. H. L. Griffin.
Bath	Winter St. Cong.	66	14	60	1	C. C. Low.
"	Central Cong.	20	23	8	....	Rev. A. F. Dunnels, 889 Middle
Bethel	Second Cong.	26	2	17	1	Clara F. Twitchell. [st.
Biddeford	Calvary Baptist.	25	5	17	2	Maud Quimby, 45 Summer st.
"	F W Baptist.	....	....	....	....	Belle Smith.
Bingham	Congregational	11	12	9	14	E. A. Baker.
Blue Hill	First Baptist.	23	8	17	....	Miss Linnie A. Perkins.
" "	First Cong.	17	3	15	5	Miss Ida A. Bunker.
Brewer	Methodist Episcopal.	32	47	19	8	Mertie M. Moore,
"	Congregational	....	....	....	....	Grace E. Washburn.
Brewerville	....	....	....	....	....	Lettie S. Doak.
Bucksport	Elm St. Cong.	50	65	32	7	W. H. Gardner.
Buxton	Union	....	....	....	....	Rev. E. S. Palmer.
Calais	First Cong.	37	57	31	6	Kate G. Vose.
Cape Elizabeth	First Cong.	25	10	20	....	Rev. B. P. Snow, Willard.
Caribou	Baptist.	....	....	....	....	
Castine	First Cong.	113	68	25	6	Luetta Robinson.
Cornish [tre.	Hillside Cong	32	3	7	....	Marion Sanborn.
Cumberland Cen-	Centre Cong.	26	....	22	....	Carrie F. Wilson.
Cumberland Mills	Warren Cong.	86	....	56	3	L. E. Cordwell, 69 Main st.
Deer Isle	First Congregational	10	20	10	....	Kate R. Pickering.
Deering	Free Church	....	....	....	....	E. H. Goddard.
East Hiram	Union	....	....	....	....	Mrs. E. P. Eastman.
Ellsworth Falls	Congregational	25	25	18	....	Henry W. Conley.
" "	Methodist.	....	....	....	....	Hiram Bartlett.
Falmouth	First Congregational	20	8	23	....	Edgar B. Leighton.
Farmington	Union	30	5	30	....	Carrie W. Titcomb.
Freeport	First Congregational	....	....	....	....	B. M. Dennison.
"	Baptist.	....	....	....	....	Rev. J. B. Wilson.
Fryeburg	Congregational	....	....	....	....	
Gilead	....	....	....	....	....	

MAINE.—(Continued.)

CITY.	CHURCH.	Act. Memb.	Asso. Memb.	Ch. Memb.	United with C.	Secretary and Address.
Green's Landing.	Union	40	20	14	....	Mrs. L. C. Haskell.
Gorham	Congregational	59	67	43	8	Mary E. Alden.
"	First Parish	....	....	....	....	
Gray	Union	44	8	35	....	Annie L. Bean.
Harrison						Flora D. Bray.
Hiram	Union	20	....	20	16	Mrs. J. Pierce.
Harrington		....	....	....	....	
Holden	Congregational	18	14	13	4	Mary S. Wiswell.
Island Falls		....	....	....	....	Alice Sewall.
Kennebunk	Union Cong	36	11	27	....	Hattie E. Tripp.
Kent's Hill	Wes. Sem. &Fem. Col.	61	24	61	....	Sara M. Maxon.
Lebanon	First Congregational	21	10	16	2	Miss H.L.Shapleigh,W.Lebanon
"	F. W. Baptist	14	....	7	4	E. P. Wentworth.
Lewiston	Pine St. Cong	45	....	44	25	Lillian G. Burnham,17Walnut st
"	Bates St. Baptist	....	....	....	....	Rev. Mr. Tilley.
"	Pine St. Free Baptist.	60	6	24	6	Josie Witham, 278 Bates st.
"	Main St. F. Baptist	....	....	....	....	
Lincoln	Union	27	7	20	6	Grace E. H. Ballantyne.
"	Congregational					
Lisbon Falls.	Baptist					W. D. Plummer.
Livermore Mills.	Union					
Machias	Centre St. Cong	51	1	44	....	Miss M. O. Longfellow.
Madison	Congregational					Frank Dinsmore.
Mechanic Falls	Congregational	41	5	35	....	Nettie P. Grant.
Milford	First Cong	18	12	27	4	G. W. Toser.
Morrill's Corner.						
New Gloucester.						Sophie Stevens.
North Bridgton.	(Bridgton Acad.) Un.	40	30	25	....	N. Grace Bray.
North Yarmouth.	Congregational	16	4	15	....	Flora D. Bray.
Norway	Congregational	42	9	32	....	Nellie Buswell.
Oakland	Baptist					Mrs. Edwin Foster.
"	Methodist Episcopal					Jeanette Benjamin
Orland	Union	54	6	22	....	Mary Paige.
Oldtown	Baptist	30	8	14	....	H. H. Bryant,
"	Congregational					Rev. G. W. Christie.
"	Methodist					
Oxford	Second Cong	10	40	9	5	Mrs. Mary A. Ellis.
Passadumkeag	Baptist					
Parsonfield	F. W. Baptist	24	4	14	....	Frankie A. Hilton, S.Parsonfield
Peak's Island	Methodist Episcopal	27	6	13	2	Artette F. Parsons.
Pembroke						
Portland	Williston Cong	129	29	96	11	M. Alice Metcalf. [son st.
"	Abysinnian Cong	24	14	19	....	Mrs. R. E. Eastman, 54 Ander-
"	Second Cong	74	15	68	....	Miss H. M. Leach, 497 Cumberl'd
"	Congress St. Meth	74	10	42	6	A. W. Puddington, 461 Congress
"	West Cong	23	21	16	....	Ollie W. True, 1033 Congress st.
"	High St. Cong					Rev. W. H. Fenn.
"	State St. Cong					Rev. F. D. Bailey. [st.
"	St.Lawrence St .Cong	66	33	67	....	Alex. Merrick, 20 St. Lawrence
"	Chestnut St. M. E					Rev. W. F. Whittaker.
"	First Baptist					Rev. A. K. P. Small.
"	Free St. Baptist	51	16	48	....	Rev. A. T. Dunn.
"	Plymouth Free Bap					O. P. Wish, Argus Office.
Princeton	Congregational					Mr. G. Peabody.
Saco	Cutts Av. Free Bap.	43	7	38	....	Miss Carrie Emery, Temple st.
"	Main St. Baptist	18	2	18	....	Miss B. H. Winslow, 15 Thorn-
"	School St. M. E	28	3	26	....	Rev. A. W. Pottle. [ton Ave.
"	Calvin Baptist					Rev. G. B. Titus.
Sandy Point	Congregational					
Saccarappa	Second Cong	10	29	9	....	W. E. J. Haskell.
Searsport	First Congregational					Mary N. McClure.
Sedgwick	First Baptist	32	13	21	....	Susie E. Cole, Box 33.
Sebec						
South Berwick	First Congregational	22	2	17	....	Ella W. Ricker.
South Freeport	Congregational	22	18	13	....	Fannie A. Dunham.
South Bridgeton.	Congregational					Rev. E. P. Eastman.

LIST OF SOCIETIES

MAINE.—(*Continued.*)

CITY.	CHURCH.	Act. Memb.	Asso. Memb.	Ch. Memb.	United with C.	Secretary and Address.
South Paris......	Congregational	30	10	25	10	M. A. Plummer.
" "		40				Laura E. Clifford.
Strong...........	Methodist...........	18	9	18	....	Hattie Hartwell.
Upper Gloucester	Bald Hill Church....	15	3			Hattie True.
Waldoboro........	First Congregational	26	2	20	8	Mrs. Belle B. Gardner.
Warren..........	Congregational......					Rev. E. M. Cousins.
Waterville........	Pleasant St. M. E	64	29	48	5	Sara A. Copp.
"	Baptist..............					Rev. Mr. Owen.
West Falmouth ..	Free Baptist	17	2	12	....	Geo. F. Griffin.
" Sumner						Jeanette Wilson.
" Brookville..						
" Lebanon....	Free Baptist.........					Edith E. Hayes.
Wells	Second Cong.........					Chas. F. Littlefield.
West Minot.......	Congregational......					
Wilton	Congregational......	11	....	7	....	Vesta E. Fuller.
Winthrop	Union					Helen A. Loring.
Wiscasset	Congregational	10	25	11	7	F. C. Coffin.
Woodfords	Congregational......	81	17	72	5	H. A. Rackleff, 22 Lincoln st.
"	Clark Mem. M. E					Rev. R. Sanderson.
Yarmouthville...						Rev. L. Reynolds.

MARYLAND.

CITY.	CHURCH.	Act. Memb.	Asso. Memb.	Ch. Memb.	United with C.	Secretary and Address.
Annapolis	First Pres...........	30	11	27	....	Emma Abbott, 33 Gloucester st.
Baltimore........	Light St. Pres					Luther Martin, 623 Hanover st.
"	First Congregational	55				Rev. W. F. Slocum, Linden ave.
"	Second Pres.........					Frank Culver, [extension.]
"	Hugh St. Bap........					No. Broadway.]
"	Presbyterian........					Sallie E. Reff, 723 No. Fulton Av.
"	Presbyterian........					H. H. Rogers, 625 Carrollton Av.
"	Baptist.............					Dora Kirby, 821 Aisquith st.
"	Brown Mem. Bap ...					
"	Faith Pres					
"	Fulton Ave.........					
"	12th Pres...........					Maggie Graham, 1020 Eutaw st.
"						Rev. S. R. Hogg, 1123 Mulberry.
Hampden.........	Baptist.............					Rev. F. B. LeBaron.
Olney............	Emery Ch					
Woodbury........	Hampden Pres......	34	20	34	....	N. L. Eichilberger.

MASSACHUSETTS.

CITY.	CHURCH.	Act. Memb.	Asso. Memb.	Ch. Memb.	United with C.	Secretary and Address.
Acton	Congregational	15	20	15	....	Horace F. Tuttle. [Plain P.O.
Acushnet	Methodist Episcopal					Hannah L. Gammon, Long
Adamsdale.......	Cushman Un. Ch					Miss M. E. Lewis, Adamsdale,
Agawam..........						C. A. Hastings. [S.Attleboro.
"	Baptist.............	16	5	15	3	Miss B. I. Bodurtha, Box 25.
Alford...........	Congregational					Rev. Mr. Alvord.
Allston..........	Congregational	17	35	16	5	Edw. W. Appleton.
Amesbury........	Union Evang. Cong..	39	24	28	....	Mrs. Philip Bartlett, Box 469.
"	Main St. Cong.......	56	30	31	....	Clarence Schilling.
"	Baptist.............					Annie L, Bailey.
Amebury	Market St.Calvin Bap	25	10	20	2	Marion Clark.
Amherst.........	Congregational	44	8	43	....	F. W. Harrington, No. Amherst.
"	Second Cong........	30	18	30	....	Ella L. Peirce, Box 316.
"	First Congregational					Rev. Mr. Dickerman.
"	East Ch					
"	Methodist Episcopal					
Andover.........	West Cong..........	84	9	84	22	Emma L. Ward,97 No.Broadway,
"	Old South Cong.....					Rev. J. J. Blair. [Lawrence, Ms.

OF CHRISTIAN ENDEAVOR. xxix

MASSACHUSETTS.—(*Continued.*)

CITY.	CHURCH.	Act. Memb.	Asso. Memb.	Ch. Memb.	United with C.	Secretary and Address.
Andover	Free Christian Cong.	43	9	38	....	John W. Bell.
Arlington	Pleasant St. Cong.	58	28	43	8	Lizzie J. Merrifield.
Artichoke	First Cong.	40	20	37	14	Mrs. E. H. Winship.
Ashby	Congregational	40	8	35	8	Harlow R. Foster.
Ashburnham	First Cong.	25	10	15	....	Rev. C. H. Page.
Ashfield	Congregational	21	47	3	....	Gertrude E. Howes.
Ashland	First Congregational	25	11	22	1	Miss Ida E. Metcalf.
Attleboro Falls	Central Cong.	20	....	20	....	Rev. Walter Taylor.
Athol Centre	Congregational	74	4	46	10	Lottie L. Crosman.
Atlantic	Congregational	7	13	5	....	Justin Emery.
Auburndale	Congregational	60	6	50	6	J. P. B. Fiske.
Ayer	First Baptist	21	3	20	20	Geo. C. Prescott, Box 117.
Baldwinsville	....	....	....	....	....	Mrs. H. E. Robertson.
"	Congregational	....	....	....	....	Allina V. Fisher.
"	Baptist	....	....	....	....	
Ballardvale	Congregational	28	12	17	8	Mrs. S. E. Haynes, High St.
Barre	Baptist	....	....	....	....	
Barre		....	....	25	25	J. F. Gaylord.
Becket	Union	27	....	16	....	Emma J. Prenlin.
Bedford	Ch. of Christ Cong.	68	25	64	1	Kate E. Goodwin.
Berlin	Congregational	18	14	10	....	Isabelle C. Shattuck.
Bernardston	Union	30	14	16	....	Mrs. H. L. Crowell.
Beverly	Wash. St. Cong.	51	12	51	....	
Billerica	Congregational	26	9	21	1	Carrie E. Baker.
Blackington	Union	24	18	....	....	Lewis Evans.
Bolton	Friends	....	....	....	....	
Bondville		....	....	....	....	C. B. Collis. [Mattapan.
Boston	Congregational	26	18	23	1	Mrs. W. G. Swan, 1099 Wash. st.
"	Clarendon St. Bap.	140	7	140	15	C. S. Green, 145 W. Newton st.
"	Berkeley St. Cong.	108	14	70	....	J. A. Clark, 17 Woodbine street.
"	Shawmut Branch Chapel Cong.	42	15	25	4	Miss J. A. Hobbs, 40 Clarendon st
"	Shawmut Cong.	96	19	96	10	F. S. Allen, 94 Worcester st.
"	First Free Baptist	65	4	59	....	Miss C. A. Perkins, 48 Rutland st.
"	Tyler St. Old Col.Cha.	....	....	....	....	Annette J. Heazle.
"	Ebenezer Bap.	....	....	....	....	L. D. Spellman.
"	N. E. Conservatory of Music, (Men)	62	22	62	....	O. E. Mills.
"	N. E. Conservatory of Music, (Ladies)	100	....	83	....	
"	No. End Mission Un.	....	....	....	....	Miss F. Augusta Burnett.
"	1st Mariner's Ch.Bap.	55	6	56	....	C. S. McFarland, 59 Kingston st.
"	Church of Christ	34	....	34	....	J. H. Clark, 17 Woodbine st.
"	So. End Tabernacle	....	....	....	....	Jennie Marquis, Hotel Warwick.
"	Park St. Ch. Cong.	124	11	88	....	A. H. Colby, 14 Sudbury st.
"	Reformed Episcopal	....	....	....	....	H. M. Price, 197 W. Springfield.
" (East)	Saratoga St. M. E.	89	64	98	10	Miss S.F.Robinson, 72 Lexington
" "	Central Sq. Baptist	16	13	....	....	Lizzie I. Bishop, 88 Putnam st.
" "	Maverick Cong.	....	....	....	....	Rev. Elijah Horr, D. D.
" "	Presbyterian	....	....	....	....	Rev. J. L. Scott. [Boston.
" (South)	Fourth St. Baptist	39	24	33	11	Miss M. W. Hood, 135 O. st. So.
" "	Ch. of our Father	16	9	6	1	Carrie F. Elliott, G. st.
" "	Phillips Cong	153	41	112	5	Mary J. Brown, 39 Gates st.
" "	Fourth Pres.	39	31	41	11	Anna C. Cox, 406 E. 7th st.
Boylston	First Congregational	45	12	37	10	Miss A. S. Whitcomb, Box 388, [Worcester.
"		....	....	....	....	
Boxford	First Congregational	34	8	19	....	Miss A. L. Cleveland.
Boxboro	Congregational	....	....	....	....	Jennie L. Brown, West Acton.
Bradford	Congregational	102	....	32	....	W. Eugene Ellis.
Brewster	Baptist	18	7	16	....	James E. Kendall.
Bridgewater	Central Sq. Cong.	140	32	125	2	Miss Mabel H. Wilber.
Brighton	Congregational	....	....	....	....	J. I. Bennett.
Brimfield	First Congregational	35	2	30	8	Minnie J. Corbin.
Brookline	Harvard Cong.	54	83	75	11	Alice May Libby, Centre st.
Brockton		....	....	....	....	
Buckland	Shepard Cong.	18	6	16	....	Rev. A. C. Hodges.

LIST OF SOCIETIES

MASSACHUSETTS.—(*Continued.*)

CITY.	CHURCH.	Act. Memb.	Asso. Memb.	Memb. Ch.	United with C.	Secretary and Address.
Cambridge	Shepard Mem. Cong.					Rev. Alex McKenzie, D. D., 12
"	Harvard St. M. E.					Rev. C. S. Rogers. [Garden st.
"	No. Ave. Bap.	75	12	67		Rev. Wm. S. Apsey, 11 Cogswell
"	Old Cam. Bap.					Rev. F. Johnson, 855 Main. [av.
"	First Congregational	155	3	97		G.H.Taylor,493rd st, E Camb'dge
Cambridgeport	Wood Mem. Cong.	45	33	32		Clara A. Peterson, 46 Cherry st.
"	Pilgrim Cong.	58	10	56	1	J. Wm. Sparrow, 62 Auburn st.
"	Prospect St. Cong.	68	22	58	8	Irving W. Cotton,308 Harvard st.
"	First Baptist					Rev Mr. McWhinnie.
"	Charles River Bap.	45	33	43		R. Edget, 344 Pearl street.
"	North Ave. Cong.					E. F. Forbes,18 Beach st. N. Cam.
"	Grace M. E.					Rev. N. B. Fish, 10 Fairmount st.
"	Broadway Bap.					
Charlemont	Union	20	22	17	1	Alice Eldridge.
Charlestown	Winthrop Cong.	119	25	96	39	L. M. Primer, 31 Baldwin st.
"	First Baptist	57	11			Florence I. Morse, 11 Concord st.
"	Trinity M. E.	95	17	97		Miss B. Mailman, 27 Mystic st,
"	Bunker Hill Bap.	46		43		Florence A.Byam, 75 Baldwin st.
"	Young Ladies Soc'y.. St. John's Epis.					
"	Harvard Hill Cong.					Mr. Brooks.
"	First Congregational	58	12	55		G. A. Lincoln, 63 Bunker Hill st.
"	Monument Sq. M. E.	27	8	25	1	Miss M. A. Nichols, 17 Polk st.
Chelsea	First Congregational	72	30	70	11	Margie N. Diman, 131 Walnut st.
"	Bellingham M. E.					Rev. D. H. Ela, D. D.
"	High School:					Miss A. Louise Hutchins.
"	Third Cong.	43	19	40	11	Garafilia Taylor, 2 Franklin st.
Chester	Second Cong.	14	9	9		Estelle Kelly.
"	Methodist					
Chesterfield	Congregational	18	15	16		T. E. Smith, West Chesterfield.
Chicopee	First Congregational	7	6	7		W. J. Baker.
"	Third Cong.	30	23	24	2	Mary L. Blackmer, 263 School st.
" Falls	Congregational					Austin O. Grout.
"	Methodist Episcopal	17	10	21		Florence Fay 77 East st.
Clarendon Hills	Congregational					Rev- A. H. Johnson.
Clinton	Baptist					Rev. H. K. Pervear.
"	Congregational	52	28	42	6	Jennie B. Bourne,54 Chestnut st.
Cohasset	Second Cong.	20	21	15		M. Louise Cutler.
Coleraine	Union	10	35	9		Ella Donelson.
Concord	Trinity Cong.	46	37		2	G. H. Hopkins.
Conway	Congregational					W. A. Thomas.
"	Union	28	9	57	1	Mrs. E. D. Stearns.
Cotuit	Presbyterian					Arthur Hopkins.
"	Union	23	9	15	7	Mrs. Sylvester R. Crocker.
Cummington	Congregational	33	16	4		D. E. Lyman.
Curtisville	Congregational					Rev. T. A. Hazen,
Dalton	Congregational	65	45	65		Nellie J. Booth.
Danvers	Maple St. Cong.	104	52	84	7	Bertha F. Perkins, Box 456.
" Centre	Congregational	29	12	25		C. A. Keife.
Danversport	First Baptist	28	30	25	5	Marion C. Whipple, Box 49.
Dedham	First Congregational	30	33	22		Miss A. P. Channell, Box 256
"	Allin Congregational	34	21	31		A. W. Bigelow.
Deerfield	Congregational	26	7	20	9	Julia Chapin.
Dorchester	Pilgrim Cong.	58	25	58	20	Josie A. Jones, Lincoln st. [st.
"	Second Cong	51	31	47	9	Winifred V.Blanchard, Harvard
"	Village Church					Mrs. W. G. Swan, 1099 Wash st.
Douglas	Congregational	13	8	13	2	Rev. James Wells. [Mattapan.
Dover	Second Cong.	29	10	24	3	Roselle L. Holt.
Dunstable	Congregational	21	14	12		Jas. E. Kendall, No. 1 Forest st.
East Dedham	Baptist	13	6	13		Etta F. Howell, Walnut Hill.
" Dennis						Jas. E. Kendall.
" Douglas	Second Cong					Anna F. Hunt, Main St.
" Harwich	Methodist Episcopal					
" Longmeadow	Congregational	12	6	11	2	Mary R. McIntosh.
" Medway						Miss Lillie Marshall.
" Middleboro	Central Cong					Mary Q. Mays.

MASSACHUSETTS.—(Continued.)

CITY.	CHURCH.	Act. Memb.	Asso. Memb.	Ch. Memb.	United with C.	Secretary and Address.
East Orleans						Mary Q. Mays.
" Pepperell		70				Charles R. Andrews. [ham.
" Rochester		12	3			Evelyn C. Hathaway, W. Ware-
" Saugus	Methodist Episcopal	33	10	31	14	Clara C. Farnham, 23 Chesn't st.
" Weymouth	Congregational	25	8	23	10	Addie M. Canterbury.
Easthampton	Payson Cong.	76	17	70		Susie E. Winslow, 11 Park st.
Edgartown	Union	40	12	31	6	Lucretia S. Norton.
Enfield	Congregational	38	29	30	16	Miss L. E. Fairbanks.
Essex	Congregational	37	42	37		Sidney L. Burnham.
Everett	First Cong.	53	17	38	7	N. W. Frye, Jr., Chelsea st.
Fall River	Central Cong.	56	36	74	16	Chas. H. Wells, 28 Ridge st.
" "	Pearl St. Pres					Rev. Mr. Martin.
" "	First Christian Bap.					Rev. Mr. Merritt.
Falmouth	Congregational					Annie B. Tubbs.
Farmerville						
Feeding Hills	Union	16	20	15	3	Marietta H. Freeland. [st.
Fitchburg	Baptist	66	9	60	15	Addie E. Sandborn, 28 Kimball
"	Rollstone Cong.	124	30	124	19	Janet Y. Wright, 20 Linden st.
"	Calvanistic Cong.	51	15			Geo. Upton, 27 Mechanic st.
"	Methodist Episcopal					
Florence	Congregational	55	23	56	3	Harriet R. Cobb.
Foxboro	First Baptist	36	12			Charles L. Winn, Box 78.
"	Congregational	28	8	18		Addie M. Boyden.
Franklin	First Cong	73	25	63	3	Elsie M. Smith.
"	Baptist					E. R. Dennett.
"	Union					Nettie A. Wadsworth.
Freetown	Friends (Advent)	30		22	10	Elton D. Boyce.
Framingham	Plymouth Cong.	69	17	61	5	Miss Katherine M. Esty.
Gardner	First Cong.	62	30	50	13	Miss Helen R. Heywood.
Georgetown	Memorial Cong	38	15	33		Lewis H. Giles.
"	Baptist					Rev. A. J. Hopkins.
Glendale	Union	21	2	14	2	Jennie W. Hunter.
Gloucester	Evangelical Cong.	51	34	44	1	Mary Brooks.
"	Methodist Episcopal					Rev. T. C. Martin
Goshen	Congregational					
Grafton	West Cong.	15	11	13	3	Nellie F. Fay, Box 44.
Granby	Congregational	50	4	47		Mrs. Abbie W. T. Fiske.
Granville	Congregational	12	7	11		E. M. Dickinson.
"	Baptist					
Greenwich	First Cong.	31	9	25	2	Mrs. S. G. Crowell.
Greenfield	Congregational	50	20			
"						
Greenville						Deborah Norris.
Groton	Union Cong	64	15	48	12	Miss Alice D. Shumway.
"	Baptist					F. C. Whitney.
Groveland	First Cong.	35	15	29	4	Miss Hattie C. Pike, Main st.
Gt. Barrington	Congregational	28	8	32		Edward S. Hulbert.
Hadley	First Cong.	56	17	42	3	C. B. Newton.
Harvard	Congregational	25	18	19	4	Fannie H. Bradley.
Hatfield	Congregational					Rev. R. M. Woods.
"	South Cong.	64	4	56		Miss Emma J. Morton.
Haverhill	Centre Cong.	90	74	77	8	Flora L. Cluff, 12 Orchard st.
"	North Cong.	103	102	77	20	Charles M. Kimball, Box 33.
"	South Cong.	28	11	25	1	Mildred L. Burgess, 131 High st.
"	Winter St. Free Bap.	65	25	50	4	Rev. Mr. Cate.
"	So. Christian					W. D. Stearns, 25 Essex st.
"	West Cong.	42	2	39		Edna Hazeltine.
Haydenville	Congregational	40	1	34		N. Ray Smith.
"						W. M. Pennington.
Hinsdale	Congregational	73	32	72	7	Mr. T. A. Frissell.
Highlandville	Methodist	53	37	11		John W. Martin, Hillside ave.
Hingham Centre	Congregational	35	12	35		Rev. E. A. Robinson.
Holden	Congregational	16	21	14	4	Fred L. Moore, Box 92.
Holyoke	Second Cong.	73		60	21	Geo. S. Nisbett, 222 Pine st.
"	First Congregational	18	34	17	5	F. S. Whitney, 8 Taylor st.
"	Second Baptist	79	9	69		Thos. W. Spencers, 220 Pine st.
"	First Baptist					Rev. E. M. Bartlett.

xxxii.   LIST OF SOCIETIES

MASSACHUSETTS.—(*Continued.*)

CITY.	CHURCH.	Act. Memb.	Asso. Memb.	Ch. Memb.	United with C.	Secretary and Address.
Holyoke	Methodist					Rev. G. C. Osgood.
"	German Luth					Rev. F. B. Haule.
Holbrook	Winthrop Cong	54	7	53		Alice G. Leach, Box 172.
Holliston	Congregational	56	3	45		W. B. Whiting, Washington st.
Hopkinton	Methodist Episcopal	20	12	19		Miss Louie Hall.
Housatonic	Congregational	43	39	32	5	Florence Barnes.
Hubbardston	Congregational	17	3	17	2	Alice E. Underwood.
Hudson	Methodist Episcopal	27	3	21	4	Mabelle A. Wood.
"	Baptist	26	6	18	4	Myra B. Gott, Main street.
Hull	Methodist Episcopal	10	1	5		Grace W. Knight.
Huntington	Union	51	26	42	4	Nettie A. Wells.
Hyde Park	Congregational	43	18	39		C. E. Hathaway, Box 622.
Indian Orchard	Union					Rev. Mr. Morrow.
Ipswich	South Cong	33	31	23	6	Helen A. Marshall, Box 123.
"	First Ch	38	22			Lucy F. Cogswell.
"	Second Ch	21	6	16		Will F. Durgin, Box 439. [ave.
Jamaica Plain	Boylston Cong	19	9	19	5	Jennie M. Jackson, 43 Sheridan
"	Central Cong	75	16			Miss Effie Davis, Chestnut ave.
Jeffersonville	Chapel Union	31	22	32	11	Susie L. Austin.
Kingston	Union	24	11	18	2	Miss Lilian Bailey, Box 68.
Lanesboro	Union	23	16	12	5	Miss Hattie M. Nourse.
Lancaster	Congregational	22	12	7	1	Grace F. Closson.
"	Baptist					Rev. Mr. Morey.
Lanesville	Congregational	23	21	7		Grace Glidden.
"	Junior Society					
Lawrence	First F. Bap					Dottie A. Ames, Milton street.
"	Congregational					
Lee	First Cong	89	56	81	11	Bennett T. Gale, Box 454.
"	Methodist Episcopal	26	8	21	1	Rena M. Hurd, 23 East Park st.
"	Baptist					Rev. J. D. Pope.
Leicester	Congregational	59		30		Miss H. L. Holman.
Lenox	Congregational	14	5	13	2	Mrs. Charles S. Ross.
Leverett	Congregational	25	13	19		Charles H. Beaman.
Lexington	First Baptist	27	3	21	3	Geo M. Huckins, Box 135.
"	Congregational	30	15	23		Lillian Wing, Hancock ave.
Lincoln	Congregational	22		18		M. C. Flint.
Littleton	Congregational	32		25	6	Grace P. Conant.
"	Baptist					R. G. Johnson.
"	Unitarian					Rev. W. I. Nichols.
Longmeadow	First Cong	32	8	28	2	Annie E. Emerson.
Long Plain	Methodist Episcopal.	9	9	9	5	Miss Hannah L. Gammons.
Lowell	John St. Cong	48	16	46	11	A. K. Whitcomb, 8 Smith ave.
"	High St. Cong	68	40	60	3	Mattie S. Whittemore.
"	Highland Cong	68	7	55	16	Esther E. Davis, 40 Grove st.
"	Kirk St. Cong	91	17	73	7	Bertha Gardner, 68 French st.
"	First Cong	125	52			E. B. Colby. [good st.
"	Eliot Cong	78	127	70		Miss L. A. Wallingford, 40 Os-
"	Pawtucket Cong	47	19	42		Lilla Ward, 10 Varnum ave.
"	Fifth St. Baptist	48	21	47		I. Watts Whitman 69 Bridge st.
"	Primitive Meth					Rev. G. Jeffries.
"	Worthen St. Baptist.					Rev. W. S. Ayres.
"	Mt. Zion					Mary Turner, 78 Howard st.
"	French Prot	19	22	24		Miss H. Caron, 410 Merrimac st.
"	Highland Junior					Rev. S. W. Adriance.
"	Mt. Vernon F. Bap					Edwin Stiles, 15 Merrimac Corp.
Ludlow	Ch. of Christ, Union.	22	19	18		Mrs. Edward Day. [Ingalls st.
Lynn	Christian	55	14	29	2	Carrie I. Thrasher, 12 [Hill ave.
"	North Cong	63	19	39	7	Annie F. Attwill, 61 Beacon
"	Central Cong	80	30	75	3	Addie R. Phillips, 42 Stephens st.
"	Chestnut St. Cong	41	41	30	3	Geo. E. Sargent, 36 Parrott st.
"	East Baptist	70	33	70	10	S. M. Thompson, 10 Violet st.
"	First Baptist	30	2	34		Grace E. Hilton, 8 Church St. pl.
"	South St. Meth					Sadie Bailey, 88 Neptune st.
"	Society of Friends	23	1	20		Alice B. Paige.
"	No. Church Junior					
Magnolia	Union Cong	12	23	11		Lydia E. Smith, 110 Magnolia ave
Malden	First Cong	78	25	62	15	Carrie E. Norris, 146 Clifton st.

MASSACHUSETTS.—(*Continued.*)

CITY.	CHURCH.	Act. Memb.	Asso. Memb.	Ch. Memb.	United with C.	Secretary and Address.
Malden(Belmont)	Union	19	6	11	....	Miss Edith Smith, 349 Ferry st.
"	First Baptist	30	....	28	....	Mary A. Benton, Box 1524.
Manchester	Congregational	41	25	33	11	Annie L. Rust.
Manomet	Second Cong	26	20	19	4	Lydia A. P. Sampson, Box 22.
Mansfield	Congregational	....	....	....	....	Rev. J. Ide.
Maplewood	First Baptist	38	6	28	6	Catharine Chester, 169 Webster [st.
"	Congregational	....	....	....	....	[st.
Marblehead	First Baptist	50	16	46	13	Miss Georgie Eastlandt, Front
"	Old North Cong.	59	28	51	7	Miss Mary R. Stoddard.
Marion	Congregational	21	11	17	....	H. L Crane.
"	Congregational	27	22	18	....	Mary H. Hathaway. [st.
Marlborough	Union Cong	66	6	57	....	Florence A. Howe, 130 E. Main
Marshfield	First Cong.	11	2	11	2	Grace P. Hatch
Mattapoisett	Congregational	47	20	33	8	Cora S. W. Boody.
Medford	Mystic Cong	130	9	91	13	Miss Lillie A. Wilcox.
"	Baptist	60	15	....	....	Mr. W. H. Breed, West Medford.
"	Methodist Episcopal	40	25	37	....	Addie S. Harryott.
Medfield		....	....	....	....	Edith S. Crane.
Medway	Congregational	42	9	31	....	Frank P. Plummer.
Melrose	First Baptist	90	30	90	....	Alice B Tolman.
"	Congregational	....	....	....	....	Miss A M. Chapin.
" Highlands	Congregational	37	8	38	13	Lennie A. White.
Methuen	Lawrence St. Cong.	....	....	....	....	Rev. Mr. Wolcott.
"	First Cong.	45	9	27	5	Mary E. Sargent, 2 Tremont st.
"	Trinity Cong	....	....	....	....	J. L. R. Trask.
Merrimac	First Cong	78	42	50	26	Frank E. Pease.
"	First Baptist	59	14	52	4	Lulu A. Cate, Box 610.
Middleboro	Central Cong.	28	38	....	....	Wm. T. Tilson.
"	First Cong.	32	3	31	....	Irene L. Soule, Eddyville.
Middlefield	Union	29	8	28	....	S A. Rockwood.
Middleton	Congregational	37	26	29	....	Lillian P. Fletcher.
Millbury	Second Cong	35	3	33	5	Miss F. E. Putnam.
Millis	Congregational	20	4	18	12	E. F. Richardson.
Milton	Congregational	26	5	19	2	Ida M. Sears
Mittineague		....	....	....	....	
"	Congregational	36	27	45	....	A. N. Forsythe, Front street.
"	Methodist Episcopal	....	....	....	....	
"	Park St. Cong.	....	....	....	....	Lyman E. Smith.
Monson	First Cong.	49	3	33	....	Lilia D. Whitney, Main street.
"	Methodist	....	....	....	....	Charles A. Bradway.
Monterey	Congregational	43	17	38	4	Hattie M. Townsend.
Montague	First Cong.	....	....	....	....	Flora E. Kendall.
Nantucket	North Cong.	17	33	11	....	Madeleine Fish.
Natick	First Baptist	83	9	73	21	H. E. McLain.
"	Congregational	75	25	75	....	H. M. Wilson, Box 433.
Needham	Congregational	50	34	41	7	Frances A. Carpenter.
New Boston	Congregational	....	....	....	....	C. K. Shepard.
Needham	Baptist	....	....	....	....	Rev. S. Burton.
Newbury	First Cong.	26	23	20	8	Annie A. Humphreys.
"		....	....	....	....	
Newburyport	Belleville Cong	78	42	64	24	Elizabeth H. Cheever, 3 Howard
"	Old South Pres.	....	....	....	....	Rev. C. C. Wallace.
"	Oldtown Cong.	....	....	....	....	Rev. F. P. Sanborn. [st.
"	North Cong.	56	15	42	16	Fred L Townsend, 19 Boardman
"	Prospect St. Cong.	48	6	....	....	Chas. A. Bliss, 10 Allen st.
"	Green St. Baptist	54	35	51	....	Cora B. Lougee.
"	First Presbyterian	79	16	28	1	Abbie P. Noyes, 72 Lime street.
New Bedford	Presbyterian	....	....	....	....	Rev. Howell Buchanan.
"	Pleasant St. M. E	....	....	....	....	Rev. M. S. Kaufman.
"	North Cong.	28	5	28	....	Elmer E. Fuller, 10 Grape st.
New Salem	Congregational	15	18	12	2	Mrs. A. R. Plummer. [st.
Newton Centre	First Cong.	47	12	44	4	Miss Alice G. Holmes, Warren
"	Eliot Cong.	....	....	....	....	Emilie F. Emerson, Richardson
" Highl'ds.	Congregational	64	17	42	8	Anna S. Thompson. [st.
" Up. Falls	Union	20	40	15	....	Mamie J. Scott, High street.
Newtonville	Central Cong.	34	11	28	5	Miss E. P. Hale, Box 426
Newtonville	Methodist	....	....	....	....	Rev. Geo. S. Butters.

LIST OF SOCIETIES

MASSACHUSETTS.—(Continued.)

CITY.	CHURCH.	Act. Memb.	Asso. Memb.	Ch. Memb.	United with C.	Secretary and Address.
Nonantum	Congregational	30	8	26	....	Rev. J. S. Evans.
Norfolk	Union Cong	35	20	35	5	M. E. Rockwood.
Northampton	(Edwards) Cong	38	18	28	3	Miss L. C. Dyer, 225 Elm street.
Northboro	Congregational	32	2	28	....	Minnie L. West.
Northbridge	Rockdale Cong	24	31	27	....	Jennie I. Pierce, Northbridge.
" Centre	Congregational	17	4	13	....	Rev. J. H. Childs.
Northfield						
Norwood	First Cong	45	14	38	2	Miss Fannie P. Gay.
No. Adams	Methodist Episcopal	....	....	27	....	Clinton Larabee.
" Amherst	North Cong	45	22	4.	....	F. W. Harrington.
" Attleboro	Baptist	16	1	15	....	C. H. Wheeler.
" Brookfield	Union Cong	19	2	....	....	Laura Miller.
" "						Ida C. Gleason.
" Carver						
" Chelmsford						
" Grafton	Baptist					Rev. S. Burton.
" Hadley						
" Leominster	Ch. of Christ, Cong.	15	27	13	....	Mrs. M. L. Merriam, Nashua.
" Middleboro	Congregational	14	15	14	....	Percy W. Keith.
" Reading	Congregat.onal					
" Rochester	Union Cong	18	2	15	5	Geo. R. Randall.
" Weymouth	Pilgrim Cong.					Lena Battles.
" Wilbraham	Grace Union	34	18	35	10	H. W. Cutler.
" Woburn	Congregational	20	3	20	4	Albert Blake.
Orange	First Cong	35	14	35	2	Mrs. G. F. Metcalf, Box 517.
Orleans	Congregational	14	13	14	2	Miss Mary I. Mayo, E. Orleans.
Palmer	Methodist	15	19	12	....	Clara Collis.
"	Second Cong	86	12	52	....	Rev. H. W. Pope.
Peabody	West Cong	18	12	15	3	Frank K. McIntire. [Peabody.
"	Rockville Cong	15	9	11	....	Miss E.J.Williams,County st, So.
"	So. Cong	47	12	35	....	Annie I Thorndike, 117 Main st.
Pepperell						
Phillipston						Rev. Samuel B. Andrews.
Pittsfield	First Baptist	83	10	83	14	Alvah Wilson, 165 North st.
"	South St. Cong					Rev. I. C. Smart. [st.
"	Baptist	51	2	11	....	Martha D. Holyoke, 25 Summer
Plainfield	Congregational	20	7	11	....	Miss C. L. White, 4 Central st.
Plymouth	Pilgrim Cong	79	12	71	....	Jennie L. Hubbard.
Plympton	Congregational	18	7	17	....	Mrs. D. P. Holmes.
Quincy Centre						
" Point	Congregational	27	24	27	....	John Federhen, 86 Tremont st.
Randolph	First Cong	40	11	27	12	W. H. Leavitt.
Reading	Congregational	71	63	60	5	Miss Annie B. Parker.
"	First Baptist	40	50	51	....	Chas. H. Norris, Box 788.
Revere	First Cong	21	7	17	4	Nathan C. Hamblin.
Rochester	Congregational	18	9	12	....	Mrs. Geo. B. Haskell. [ham.
"	Congregational	13	8	6	....	Evelyn C. Hathaway, W. Ware-
Rockdale Mills		42	47	28	....	Jeanette E. Platt.
Rockland	First Cong	36	3	29	....	Julia D. Lane, 39 Market st.
"	Baptist	15	5	15	....	Grace E. French, Box 65.
"	Methodist Episcopal					Mrs. F. D. Lantz, Box 36.
Rockport	First Cong	33	33	22	4	Lizzie B. Jewett.
Rockville	Congregational	6	5	5	....	Mrs. J. Bucklin.
Roslindale	Baptist	35	5	35	....	Mrs. C. A. Dunham, Poplar st.
"	Methodist					W. C. West. [ville st.
Roxbury	Walnut Ave. Cong.	62	41	62	2	Fannie E. Merriam, 40 Green-
"	Eliot Cong	66	29	66	6	Miss L. M. Marston, 68 Zeigler st
"	Immanuel Cong	96	50	87	14	Miss Ida. E. Kittredge, 92 Mt.
"	Warren St Meth					Rev. Mr. Thorndike. [Pleas. ave
"	Highland Cong					Rev. W. C. Campbell.
Salem	Tabernacle Cong	75	29	59	13	Susan E. Choate, 25 Norman st.
"	South Cong	53	45	53	7	Lillie R. Atwood, 136 Federal st.
"	Central Baptist	44	5	41	1	J. C. Pulsifer, 65 1 2 Essex st.
"	Calvary Baptist					
"	Crombie St. Cong.	28	15	27	....	Miss M. F. Stout, 22 Linden st.
Salisbury						
Sandwich	Congregational					Della R. Baker.

MASSACHUSETTS.—(*Continued.*)

CITY.	CHURCH.	Act. Memb.	Asso. Memb.	Ch. Memb.	United with C.	Secretary and Address.
Saugus Centre	Congregational	27	13	23		Anna F. Newhall.
Saundersville	Congregational	37	5	27	7	Annie Killen
Saxonville	Edwards Cong.	32	12	21		Rev. M. A. Stevens.
Sharon	Congregational	33	29	15		A. E. Billings. [Box 473.
Sheffield	Congregational	43	18	41	4	Miss M. Sheldon Gt. Barrington
Shelburne	Congregational	25	20	30	2	Mrs. Austin L. Peck.
Shelburne Falls	Congregational	48		42		J. H. Hoffman.
" "	Baptist					A. M. Crane.
Sherborn	Congregational					Rev. Mr. Dowse.
Shirley	First Baptist	14	4	9		Walter E. Griffin, Box 157.
Shrewsbury	Congregational	15	3			Rev. Frank Allen.
"	Methodist					
Somerset	First Congregational	19		11		
Somerville	First M. E.					Hattie C. Tallman, 50 Cedar st.
"	Prospect Hill Cong.	62	32	57	2	C. W. Silsbee, 49 Springfield st.
"	Perkins St. Baptist	106	7	109	1	Nettie E. Littlefield, 95 Pearl st.
"	Franklin St. Cong.	53	38	39	8	Louise E. Pratt, 20 Lincoln st.
"	Winter Hill Cong.	27	28	25	3	Miss Emma S. Keyes, 154 Central
"	Winter Hill Baptist	21	10	19	6	Albert Hallett, 194 Pearl st. [st.
"	Broadway Cong.	29	30	36	9	C. W. Coleman, 34 Marshall st.
"	Union Square Bap.					Rev. Mr. Scott.
"	Spring Hill Baptist	45	7	38		Rev. Mr. Cunningham.
"	Day St. Cong.	85	15	85		S. A. Collinson, Newbury st
"	Elm St. Baptist					Rev Mr. Wyman.
"	First Baptist					I. M. Story, 24 School st.
" (West)	Park Ave. M. E	30	10	23		A. J. Dowling, Box 576, Medford.
South Amherst	Congregational					
" "		17	15	17		Miss M. L. Dana.
Southampton	Union	20	17	24		Etta F. Ranger, No 4 Maple st.
Southboro	Congregational					I. W. Horn.
"	Pilgrim Cong.	31	21	24	1	Mary C. Adams.
South Braintree	Congregational	16	16	9	2	Ida E. Smith, P. O. Box 111.
" Brookfield						
" Byfield	Congregational	17	12	20	7	Miss Carrie J. Horsch.
" Danvers						
" Dennis	Congregational	30	21	19	2	Nellie H. Underwood.
" Deerfield	Congregational	26	15	11		
" Easton						C. E. Abbott.
" Egremont	Congregational	30	25	25		Lizzie Wilcox.
So. Framingham	Congregational	58	11	56		Blanche M. Amsden. [st.
South Franklin	Union Cong	10	18	10		Miss N. A. Wadsworth, 5 Spring
" Hadley	Mt. Holyoke Sem					
So. Hadley Falls	Congregational	45	14	28	2	Grace W. Skinner.
So. " "	Methodist Episcopal					Lena S. Ellis.
South Harwich	Methodist					
" Natick	John Eliot Cong.	29	12	26		Ada M. Caswell, Box 16.
" Peabody	Rockville Cong.	19	4	17	3	Eleanor I. Williams, County st.
" Sudbury	Congregational	16	13	15		Waldo L. Stone.
" Weymouth	First Congregational	51	42	56		Helen M. Rockwood.
Southville	Congregational	21	12	9		A. B. Taylor, Box 58.
Spencer	Congregational	70	33	57	16	Miss Jeanette Prince.
"	Methodist Episcopal	35	20	18	5	Miss Julia L. Munroe.
"	Baptist					G. E. Hamburg.
Springfield	North Ch. Cong.	65	38	72	7	Ralph P. Alden, 2d Nat'l Bank.
"	Olivet Cong	47	3	36	12	G. E. Buchanan, 129 Sherman st
"	Florence St. Meth.	26	2	23	3	Minnie H. King, 452 Central st.
"	1st Ch. of Christ, Cong	69	16	69	6	Horace Sanderson, 77 Walnut st.
"	First Baptist	57	11	57	12	Jennie Bowman, 41 Mulberry st
"	State St. Meth.	58	28	54	9	Miss Bidwell, No 11 School st.
"	State St. Baptist	67	18	67	20	H. M. McGregory, 36 Tremont st
"	Hope Cong					Lizzie Wheeler, 28 Sherman st.
"	Memorial Union	37	36	41		C. R. Gale.
"	Third Baptist	38	4			C. W. A. Fisher, 111 Quincy st.
"	South Cong	38	4			Grace W. Oliver.
"	Carew St. Baptist					Rev. Mr. Waterbury.
Springfield	Highland Baptist					Rev. Mr. Goodspeed.
"	Grace M. E.					Rev. Mr. Heath.

MASSACHUSETTS.—(*Continued.*)

CITY.	CHURCH.	Act. Memb.	Asso. Memb.	Ch. Memb.	United with C.	Secretary and Address.
Springfield.......	Trinity M. E............					Delia M. Morse.
"	Brightwood Union ..					Rev. F. M. Sprague.
"	....					
Sterling...........						
Stockbridge......	First Congregational	33	5	27	13	Agnes N. Canning.
Stoneham.........	Congregational......	80	45	57	25	Mrs. D. A. Newton.
Sudbury...........						
Sunderland........	Congregational.......	40	3	37	....	Chas. E. Hubbard.
Swampscott.......	Congregational.......	29	11	29	....	Carrie Millett.
Taunton...........	Winslow Cong.......	52	....	33	2	Lila B. Williams, 5 Bow st.
"	Whittenton Cong....	31	71	25	....	
"	Union Cong..........	31	71	25	....	Lewis Luther.
"	Westville Cong.......	2	18	2	2	Lewis Luther, Box 8 Walker P.O.
Tewksbury........	Congregational......					Maud Foristall.
Three Rivers.....						
Townsend.........	Congregational......					C. F. Wallace.
"	Methodist Episcopal.					Rev. Mr. Howard.
Upton.............	First Congregational	60	26	48	13	Alfred T. Wood, West Upton.
Wakefield........	First Congregational	56	57	47	10	Nettie E. Skinner.
Walpole..........	Congregational	56	36	35	17	Miss Helen R. Stanley.
Waltham..........	Trinitarian Cong....	97	20	97	11	Annie C. Skeele, 16 Maple st.
Wareham..........	Union	20	1	18	....	Hattie E. Smith.
Ware..............	Union	25	7	....	....	
Warren............	First Congregational	33	7	....	....	May W. Powers.
Watertown........	Phillips Cong........	56	17	50	....	J. M. Johnson.
Waverly...........	First Congregational	....	....	....	....	Jennie M. Blake, Box 47 Belmont
Wayland..........	Congregational......	18	17	14	....	Miss Susie M. Ward, 34 Summer.
Webster..........	First Congregational	56	46	42	8	Florence Holman.
Wellesley.........	Congregational......	52	25	32	....	W. F. Stearns.
Wellesley Hills...	Congregational......					G. Clinton Fuller.
Wellfleet.........						D. M. Clark.
West Acton	Baptist................	36	14	36	....	Miss Fannie E. Wetherbee.
Westborough	Evangelical Cong....	107	8	84	29	Edith L. Howard.
"	Methodist Episcopal.					Montague Hunt, 50 South st.
"	Baptist................	50	....	....	....	Rev. G. F. Babbitt.
"	First Meth............	65	....	....	....	Rev. A. W. Tirrell.
West Dennis	Methodist............					Rev. Mr. Morse.
Westfield	Baptist................					John J. Hanchett.
"	Central Baptist......	45	....	44	....	Henry O. Brigham, P. O. Box 1229
"	First Cong............					
"	Second Cong.........	97	40	97	....	Mrs. J. T. Case, 14 South st.
"	State Normal School.	45	40	40	....	F. M. Russell, Normal Hall.
Westford.........	Union Cong..........	23	9	25	....	Quincey W. Day.
Westhampton....	Congregational......	60	15	58	4	Mrs. F. C. Montague.
West Medford...	Congregational......	28	5	27	....	Rev. Mr. Hood.
West Medway...	Baptist................					Rev. Geo. Nichols.
"	Congregational......	36	26	38	12	Miss Mary L. Rogers.
Westminster.....	Congregational......	42	4	35	....	Geo. S. Greene.
West Newbury..	Second Cong.........	51	97	32	....	Rev. Mr. Slade.
" Newton.....	Newell Cong..........	42	26	45	....	Mrs. C. G. Phillips.
Weston...........						
Westport.........	Saugatuck Cong.....	30	15	37	....	Mrs. J. E. Tucker.
West Roxbury...	Congregational......	36	4	30	....	Rev. C. A. Beckwith. [st.
" Somerville..	Baptist................	49	12	42	....	Herbert L. Henderson, 3 Wallace
" Springfie'd.	Park St. Cong........	30	3	25	2	Nellie R. Davidson.
" "	Methodist Episcopal.					Rev. G. A. Vilts.
" Stockbridge	Congregational......	23	25	19	....	Libbie Edwards.
" Tisbury....	First Cong............	14	....	12	....	Jerry B. Mayhew.
" Townsend..	First Baptist.........	16	7	13	....	Lottie Tower, Box 24.
Westville.........						
"	Congregational......	2	25	13	....	Frank E. Kavanagh.
West Wareham..	Pierceville Cong.....					Rev. Mr. Andrews.
Whately..........	Congregational......	40	....	32	5	Charles Waite.
Whitinsville	Evan. Cong..........					Rev. John R. Thurston.
Williamsburg....	First Congregational	17	14	17	....	Henry W. Hill.
Williamstown...	Congregational......	15	3	45	....	Eleanor R. Duncan.
Wilmington	Congregational......	35	18	31	4	Agnes C. Eames.

MASSACHUSETTS.—(Continued.)

CITY.	CHURCH.	Act. Memb.	Asso. Memb.	Ch. Memb.	United with C	Secretary and Address
Winchendon	North Cong.	61	27	48	2	Hattie M. Wyman, Box 406.
"	Methodist Episcopal.					Mrs. Leslie Woodcock.
"						Rev. Mr. Lorford.
Winchester	Congregational	111	31	105	37	Miss M. A. Elliott, Chestnut st.
Woburn	Congregational	105	18	99	1	Clara M. Fox, 25 Kilby st.
Wollaston	Congregational	19	11	19		W. J. Thompson, Arlington st.
Worcester	Salem St. Cong.	80		79	6	C. S. Shaw, 19 Benefit st.
"	Park Cong.	34	16	25	6	Annie B. Parker, 4 Tufts st.
"	Pilgrim Cong.	31	5	25		Etta H. Wilcox, 14 Kilby st.
"	Ch. of Covenant Cong					Rev. A. Bryant.
"						[Co.
"	Old South Cong.	40		40		Chas. D. Nye, Putman, Davis &
"	Dewey St. Baptist					Rev. D. H. Stoddard.
"	First Baptist.					Miss M. J. Walker.
"	Grace Meth.					Rev. A. Galbraith.
"	Main St. Baptist	49		49	8	Anna B. Collier, 2 Wachusett st.
"	Summer St. Cong.	53		45	16	Mary E. Sleeper. 8 Linwood pl.
"	Union Cong	88		88		Emma S. Cutting, 32 Newbury st.
"	Central Cong.					Rev. Dr. Merriman.
Worthington	Congregational					Miss N. S. Heacock.
Yarmouth	Congregational	39	6	26		Carrie A. Gorman.

MICHIGAN.

CITY.	CHURCH.	Act. Memb.	Asso. Memb.	Ch. Memb.	United with C	Secretary and Address
Adison	Congregational					
Alamo	Congregational	7	3	7		Mabel Bigelow.
"						Stella A. Barber.
Albion	German Evang. Luth.	96		0	6	John A. C. Fritz, No. 8 Oak st.
Allegan	First Cong.	16	17	16	4	Lizzie Hudson.
"	Baptist					Rev. E. A. Gay.
Almont	Congregational					
"	Presbyterian					Jennet Roman.
Ann Arbor		60		55		Rev. W. H. Ryder.
Augusta	Congregational					
Bancroft						Abbie E. Phillips.
Bangor	Union	30	10	30		A. B. Chase. [sion st.
Battle Creek	First Pres.	34	12	34		Miss Florence Cook, 128 N. Divi-
Bay City	Fremont Ave. Bap.	27	5	27	1	Walter H. Braddock.
" "	First Cong.	34	14	12	3	Miss A. Venty, 2946 Water st.
" "	First Baptist.					Walter H. Braddock.
" "	First Presbyterian					Henry B. Smith.
" "	Mission Pres.					Rev. B. E. Howard.
Bear Lake	Union.	16		16		Alice Crook.
Benton Harbor	First Baptist.	60	20	59		Addie L. Ruggles.
" "	First Cong.	35	18	33		Miss Maud Eastman.
" "	Methodist Episcopal.					
Big Rapids	Congregational					
" "	Westminster Pres.					Rev. Henry Johnston.
Bridgman	Olivet Cong.	43	25	30	20	Rev. J. J. Bunnell.
Calumet	Congregational	39	40	60	9	Maria Fliege.
"						
Carson City	Congregational					Rev. W. H. Spentlebury.
Cass City	Presbyterian	13	5	13		Lizzie Reid.
Charlotte	First Cong.	90	23			Helen L. Cole.
"	Baptist					Rev. D. Baldwin.
Charlevoix						Ina Gage.
Chase	Undenom.					Alice Bachant.
Cheboygan	Congregational	22	10	22		Clara S. Burdick.

LIST OF SOCIETIES

MICHIGAN.—(Continued.)

CITY.	CHURCH.	Act. Memb.	Asso. Memb.	Ch. Memb.	United with C.	Secretary and Address.
Church's Corners						
Clare	Congregational	22				Edna S. Elden.
Clayton	Union		6	17	5	E, T. Swift.
Clifford	Baptist					
Clinton	Congregational	21	6	20	3	Mary L. Fitzgerald, Box 186.
"	First Baptist	19	8	16	15	Minnie L. Hess.
Clio	Congregational	8	4	8		Lena Griswold.
Coldwater	First Presbyterian					Rev. H. B. Collier.
Corunna	Presbyterian	12		11		A. D. McIntire.
Crystal Falls	Presbyterian					Rev. Mr. Dogelt.
Davison	Free Will Baptist	39	5	30	17	Jennie A. Foot.
Detroit	Thompson Cong	48	8	40	18	Rev. Norman Plass.
"	Trumbull Ave. Pres.	53	36	57	9	J. D. Ryan, 132 Laurel st.
"	First Congregational	36	9	37		Rufus N. Crosman, 360 E. Cong. st.
"	Calvary Pres					W. A. Torney, 162 Mabury, Grand
"	Memorial Pres					Rev. D. M. Cooper. [ave.
"	Woodward Av. Cong.					
"	First Pres					Rev. W. A. Barr.
"	Central Cong					Rev. T. F. Dickie.
"	Ft. Wayne Cong					Rev. T. M. Robinson.
"	Unity					Rev. C. E. Hulburt.
"	Reformed Epis					Rev. H. T. Wrigman.
"	Warren Ave	26	3	26		Clara B. Kelso, 538 Crawford st.
"	North Baptist					Rev. Mr. Manning.
"	Harper Ave. Cong.					
"	Mt. Hope Mission					Allan Brown.
						W. Mitchell, 740 8th st.
Dexter	Congregational	28	10	28	20	David T. Wilcox.
Douglas	Congregational	22	15	21		Miss Ada Gerber.
Durand	Baptist	25		20		Kittie Jones.
Eaton Rapids	Congregational	18		15		Lillian Walker.
East Saginaw	Wash. Ave. Pres.	18	11	13		C. B. Richardson, 432 Grant st.
"						Della E. Francis, 2311 Wash. ave
Edmore	First Congregational	20	14	13		Willard J. Wright.
Edwardsburg	Presbyterian	26	1	23	3	William I. Wallace.
Elk	Presbyterian					Rev. M. A. Lyttel.
Escanaba	First Presbyterian	21	16	9	7	Marion V. Selden.
Essexville	First Cong					
Evart	First Presbyterian	7	4	6		Lena Turner.
Filer City	Congregational	5	4	6		Miss Nellie O. Hoffman.
Flint	First Presbyterian	25	8	25		Miss Bessie Hicock.
Freeport	Congregational					Rev. D. L. Eaton.
Fruitport	Congregational	13	6	3		Mrs. J. E. Jones.
Galesburg	First Cong					
Grand Haven	Congregational	20	20	14		Mary Lewis.
" "	Presbyterian					Rev. J. H. Sammis.
Grand Rapids	Plainfield Ave. M. E.	27	4	27	1	Lizzie Rhines, 313 Plainfield ave
" "	First Presbyterian	34		29	7	Elsie D. Kellogg, 185 Third ave.
" "	Wealthy Ave. Bap.					Rev. Benj. T. Sargent.
" "	Ames M. E.					Rev. Mr. Crozier.
" "	Second Cong					Rev. H. A. McIntire.
Greenville						
Hancock	Congregational					
Hickory Corners	Baptist					
Hillsdale	Methodist Episcopal					
Howell	First Presbyterian	24	15	21		Mr. Wm. Fish.
Hubbardston	Congregational	24	25	24	3	Miss Jessie Miles.
"						J. G. Redner.
Hudson	Congregational					Rev. G. S. Bradley.
Imlay City	First Cong	18	12	19	4	Minnie Stranahan.
Ionia	Presbyterian					
Ishpenning	First Presbyterian					LeRoy Christian.
Ithaca	Congregational					Rev. A. H. Norris.
Jackson	F. W. Baptist	26	2	22	1	Lizzie Feather, 217 W. Wesley st.
Jackson	First Cong	64	4			Miss Mattie C. Walcott.
"	First Presbyterian					Rev. C. S. Armstrong.
Jonesville	Union	27	19	20	12	Nellie Loomis, Box 247.

MICHIGAN.—(Continued.)

CITY.	CHURCH.	Act. Memb.	Asso. Memb.	Ch. Memb.	United with C.	Secretary and Address.
Kalamazoo	North Pres	25	6	25	6	Miss S. W. Valentine, 412 Harri-
"	First Presbyterian	38	2	33	....	Genevieve R. Vail, 835 S. [son st.
"	First Cong	65	3	60	10	Helen U. Cowlbeck, 831 [Park st.
"	Mt. Holyoke Sem	....	....	....	....	[Lovell st.
Kingston	Baptist	....	....	....	....	
Lainsburg	Congregational	....	....	....	....	
Lake Linden	Congregational	22	30	22	....	J. M. Savage.
La Peer	Presbyterian	....	....	....	....	Rev. Charles N. Frost.
Leslie	First Cong	....	....	....	....	Rev. Fred M. Coddington.
Lexington	Congregational	16	....	16	....	Agnes Anderson.
Litchfield	Union	74	32	58	....	Agnes Gilberth.
Ludington	Congregational	....	....	....	....	Rev. I. W. McKerver.
MacBride	Union	14	8	12	....	E. J. Quackenbush.
Manistee	Maple St. Baptist	29	7	28	15	Alf. E. Poulson.
"	First Methodist	31	15	27	5	Mattie V. Conklin, 412 Third st.
"	Oak St. Cong	48	3	37	....	Stella A. Barber.
Manton		....	....	....	....	Mrs. Irene Bumps.
Marlette	Presbyterian	20	6	11	4	J. K. Osgerby.
Marquette	First Presbyterian	61	41	45	3	W. D. Smith, 222 Front st.
Mattawan		....	....	....	....	
Memphis	Congregational	23	28	23	....	Savilla J. Thompson.
Menominee	First Pres	30	33	15	....	Fred Sherman.
Midland	Presbyterian	17	10	17	....	W. A. Huych.
Middleville	Congregational	12	....	10	....	Ethelwyn Whalley.
Milan	Baptist	....	....	....	....	Elsie Dexter.
Minden City	Congregational	....	....	....	....	Rev. Mr. Warren.
Mt. Pleasant		....	....	....	....	Nellie Loomis.
Muskegon	Congregational	71	44	55	14	Miss Lulu Rice, 18 Jefferson st.
"	Baptist	22	24	25	....	M. F. Dewar, 117 Munroe ave.
New Haven		....	....	....	....	Rev. P. Schermerhorn.
Niles	First Pres	36	11	32	12	Esther R. Clapp, St. Joseph ave.
"	First Baptist	....	....	....	....	Rev. Mr. Davis.
No. Adams		....	....	....	....	
No. Branch	Baptist	....	....	....	....	
Northport	Congregational	....	....	....	....	Rev. C. D. Bannisters.
Omena	Congregational	17	11	14	5	Mrs. Lavina McLean.
Onekama	Congregational	12	16	12	....	Clara P. Smith.
Otsego	Congregational	....	....	....	....	Rev. J. R. Chaplin.
Owosso	Congregational	....	....	....	....	
Overisel	Holland Ch	....	....	....	....	Rev. P. Lepeltak.
Paw Paw	Disciple	28	....	28	....	Mamie L. Rowland.
Penn		....	....	....	....	J. M. Anderson.
Perry	Congregational	35	1	36	....	Leila Calkins.
Pinckney	Congregational	....	....	....	....	Mamie Sigler.
Pittsfield		9	8	7	....	M. W. Williams.
Port Huron	First Cong	56	22	36	....	Maude Bodewig, 719 White st.
Prairieville	Methodist Episcopal	....	....	....	....	Rev. O. H. Perry.
Reading (North)	F. W. Baptist	29	2	23	3	Minerva H. Vaughn.
"	Union	57	21	46	2	I. E. Ewing, Box 455.
Reed City		....	....	....	4	
Richland	Presbyterian	29	17	26	....	W. C. Bissell.
Romeo	Congregational	50	....	28	....	Helen Giddings.
Salem	Congregational	....	....	....	....	Irene Mills.
Saline	Presbyterian	38	....	19	....	Minnie R. Jones, Box 374.
Sangatuck	First Congregational	25	12	22	15	Mrs. L. A. Phelps.
Sheridan	Congregational	25	....	22	....	Emma Hunt.
So. Bay City	Baptist	21	20	....	....	W H. Braddock, Portsmouth.
So. Bay City	Pres. Mission	....	....	....	....	
So. Haven	Congregational	31	10	28	....	Florence E. Ramsdell.
Springbrook	Methodist Episcopal	....	....	....	....	Rev. Mr. Kitzmiller.
Stanton	Congregational	....	....	....	....	Rev. W. C. Burns.
St. Ignace		....	....	....	....	
St. Johns	Congregational	32	3	21	....	H. H. Fitzgerald.
St. Joseph	First Congregational	23	7	26	....	Rev. Jno. B. Hicknor.
Sturgis		....	....	....	....	A. D. Hayes.
Three Oaks	Baptist	11	5	16	....	Coral Pason.

LIST OF SOCIETIES

MICHIGAN.—(Continued.)

CITY.	CHURCH.	Act. Memb.	Asso. Memb.	Ch. Memb.	United with C.	Secretary and Address.
Traverse City	Congregational	32	28			Flora Campbell.
Utica	First Congregational	11	14	9	3	Emma Wilson.
Vermontville	Union	40	4	40		Ettie Denning.
Vernon	Congregational					
Vicksburg	Congregational					
Webster	Congregational	46		43	8	Mrs. S. G. Scadin.
Watervliet	Congregational					[st.
Ypsilanti	Congregational	62	4	58		Lutie M. Dinsmore. 60 N. Huron

MINNESOTA.

CITY.	CHURCH.	Act. Memb.	Asso. Memb.	Ch. Memb.	United with C.	Secretary and Address.
Alexandria	Nonsectarian	24	25	24		E. A. Hinds.
"	Methodist Episcopal					Rev. S. D. Kemerer.
Albert Lea	Presbyterian	35	21	38	10	DeWitt C. Armstrong.
Appleton	Congregational					
Austin	First Baptist	10	7	9	3	Charles Gibbons.
Blue Earth City	Presbyterian	10	8	12		Rev. L. H. Mitchell.
Brainerd	First Congregational					Rev. J. A. Rowell.
"	First Baptist	24	3	20	6	Miss A. M. Annis, Cor. Main and
Canby						M. E. Danielson. [8th sts.
Cannon Falls	Congregational					James M. Smith.
Chatfield	Presbyterian					Milton Trow, M. D.
Clearwater	Congregational	25		22		Mrs. F. A. Ranney.
Crookston	Congregational					Rev. W. H. Medlar.
"	Baptist	47	23	47		Nettie I. Brown.
"	Presbyterian					Rev. O. H. Elmer.
Dover	Methodist	9	3	9		Laura A. Tyler.
Duluth	Pilgrim Cong.	52	23	26		Helen L. Olmstead.[Michigan st
"	Second Pres					Miss B. S. Robertson, 1010 W.
"	First Pres					Edward M. Noyes.
"	Imanuel Baptist					
Excelsior	Congregational	30	11	24		Ella Stratton.
Faribault	Congregational	37	11	30	4	Stella G. Stanford, 516 N. 3d. st.
Fairmont	First Congregational	24	4	19	1	David S. Wade.
Farmington	Presbyterian	12	14	14		Lizzie E. Withrow.
Fergus Falls						Rev. Frank L. Sullivan.
Glencoe	Congregational	17	7	15	2	Stephen Raymond.
Glyndon	Independent	11	10	12	5	C. W. Bird.
Hamilton	Congregational					Nellie M. Grant.
Hastings	First Presbyterian	42		38		Addie H. Meeks.
Helena						
Howard Lake	Christian					Effie Horn.
Hutchinson	Congregational	21	7	16		Louise Butler.
Lake City	Congregational	19	16	19		William Selover.
" "	Baptist					Rev. F. L. Fiske.
LeRoy	First Baptist					Anna W. Kasson.
Litchfield	First Presbyterian	11	15	11		Wm. R. Burns.
Mankato	Centenary M. E.	30	12	31	3	J. H. Door, 422 E. Cherry St.
Mazeppa						
Mentor	Congregational					
Minneapolis	Plymouth Cong.	122	4	119	2	Jessie Carimore, 40 10th st, North
"	Westminster Pres	111	16	111		Nellie M. Miller, 1800 1st Ave. S.
"	Central Baptist	96	15	96	12	Miss Zilla Stout, 611 Frankl'n av
"	Highland Park Pres.	40	3	43		Belle M. Palmer. [st. S. E.
"	Olivet Baptist	42	5	40	8	T. H. Soares, cor. 15th av. & 7th
"	Franklin Ave. Pres.	68	19	41	8	HattieE.Thompson, 2123 23d ave.
"	Bethlehem Pres	30	6	10	5	Mary W.Saddall,2728 Stevens av.
"	Hennepin Ave. M. E.	70	82	70	25	Mora Huntoon, 719 1st ave. S.
"	First Baptist					Rev. N. T. Chase.
"	Free Baptist					Miss M. E. Cook, 114 W. 15th st.
"	Central Baptist					

MINNESOTA.—(Continued.)

CITY.	CHURCH.	Act. Memb.	Asso. Memb.	Ch. Memb.	United with C.	Secretary and Address.
Minneapolis	Presbyterian					Addie Redfield, 17 East 26th st.
"	Andrew Pres.					Dr. Stryker.
"	Union Park Cong.					Rev. Mr. Jones.
"	Emanuel Baptist					D. D. McLauren.
"	Bl'omington Av. Pres.					Rev. J. M. Patterson.
"	" M. E.					Evelyn Foster, 3202 Cedar ave.
"	Swedish Baptist					Rev. F. Peterson.
"	Lyndale Cong.					Rev. A. Hadden Norris.
"	Merriam Park Cong.					Rev. J. Macy.
"	St. Anthony Pk. Cong.					Rev. J. H. Chandler.
"	Fifth Pres					Rev. J. W. Donaldson.
"	Second Cong					
"	Friend's Church.					
"	Forest Heights M. E.					
"	Como. Ave. Cong					Mrs. J. T. Elwell.
"	Pilgrim Cong.					
"	Open Door Cong					Alice Webber.
"	Riverside Pres.					Eva McIntyre.
"	Calvary Baptist.					
"	Baptist.					Miss J. Bradbury, 719 University [ave.
Morris	First Congregational					D. F. Wheaton.
Morristown	Union	35	1	34	1	Erwin Temple.
"		14	1			E. E. Jackson.
Northfield	Congregational					
Owatonna	Baptist	53	3	53		Maud McIlvain.
"	First Congregational					Rev. J. N. Brown.
Paynesville	Union	21	2	19	2	L. M. Bennett.
Plainview	Union	18		18		W. A. Robinson.
Preston	Presbyterian	17	5	16	1	Effie M. Hayes.
Redwood Falls	Methodist Episcopal.	44	26	34	8	Helen Hitchcock.
Red Wing	Presbyterian	70	16	57	15	Nellie L. Sherman, 828 4th st.
Rochester	First Cong.	30	24	2		Alice Younglove.
"	First Pres	38	6	39	1	Ruth Gove, 304 W. Trumbro st.
Rush City	Presbyterian	16	9	10		Mrs. S. E. Gibson,
Rushford	Union	17	7	18		Christie B. McLeod.
Rushmore						J. M. Irvin.
Sauk Centre	First Congregational	66	6	60		W. W. Harmon.
" Rapids	Congregational					Rev. P. J. Smith.
Spring Valley	Congregational					Maggie Gordon.
St. Cloud	Congregational					Dr. W. T. Stone.
St. Paul	Woodland Pk. Bap.	52	1	53	7	Florence Perry, 752 Laurel ave.
" "	First Methodist.					Rev. F. O. Holmare.
" "	Atlantic Cong.	14	3	12		C. L. Colton, 700 East 3rd st.
" "	Plymouth Cong.					Miss Alice Warner.
" "	House of Hope Pres.	42	12	49		Mary C. Houghtaling.
" "	Ninth Pres.	15	4	15		
" "	Goodrich Ave. Pres.	12	6	18		J. Staples.
" "	Westminster Pres.					
" "	First Pres.					J. Jewett.
" "	Pacific Cong.					G. C. Brett.
" "	St. Anthony Pk. Cong					Rev. J. H. Chandler.
" "	Olivet Cong.					Mr. E. D. Parker.
" "	East Presbyterian.					Rev. Mr. Dyzart.
" "	Brainerd Cong.					J. W. Mattrass.
" Peter	Presbyterian	10	21	21		Jennie Kennedy.
Taylor's Falls	Union	5	5	5		Mrs. Mary Folsom.
Tracy	First Pres.	17	4	9	9	Edward W. Hughes.
Wabasha	Congregational	28	16	15		Flora Oliver.
Waseca	Baptist	45		42		C. S. Chaney.
Waterville	Baptist.					
"	Congregational					E. R. Holbrook.
Westminster	Free Baptist.					
"	Hennepin Ave. M. E.					
"	First Pres					
"	Central Baptist					
White Bear	Presbyterian	14	4	10		Carrie M. Gundlach.

MINNESOTA.—(Continued.)

CITY.	CHURCH.	Act. Memb.	Asso. Memb.	Ch. Memb.	United with C.	Secretary and Address.
Winona	Presbyterian	35	8	15	....	Rev. Robt. J. Thompson
"	First Congregational	....	....	....	....	
Winnebago		....	....	....	....	W. W. Fleming.
Yarmouth		....	....	....	....	
Zumbrota	First Congregational	30	7	30	....	Emma Carpenter, Box 52.

MISSOURI.

CITY.	CHURCH.	Act. Memb.	Asso. Memb.	Ch. Memb.	United with C.	Secretary and Address.
Atchison	Methodist Episcopal	....	....	....	....	
Amity	Congregational	....	....	....	....	Rev. J. P. Field.
Aurora	Congregational	....	....	....	....	E. S. Meredith.
Cameron	Congregational	15	3	15	....	Bertha L. Ensign.
Carthage	First Baptist	....	....	....	....	Carrie Jenks, 408 W. Vine st.
"	Congregational	23	11	23	....	Grace Howenstein.
"	Presbyterian	....	....	....	....	Rev. W. S. Knight.
Conway		....	....	....	....	Albert H. Richardson.
Eldon	Methodist Episcopal	13	1	8	....	Mrs. M. S. Parker, Box 21.
Fayette	First Baptist	....	....	....	....	Rev. Manly J. Blosser.
Glenwood	Methodist Episcopal	12	10	20	....	C. B. D. Austin.
Hamilton	Congregational	....	....	....	....	Rev. Mr. Mathews.
Hannibal	First Pres	23	4	24	3	E. S. Dunning, 201 S. 9th st.
"	Fifth St. Baptist	16	2	18	....	E. G. Cary, cor. 9th & Lyon sts.
"	Congregational	....	....	....	....	Rev. A. B. Allen.
"	Park M. E.	....	....	....	....	Minnie Shoklin, 105 7th st.
Hopkins	Union	46	10	34	....	W. L. Robb.
Independence	First Baptist	84	2	34	13	Nellie Rider, 103 No. Main st.
Jameson		....	....	....	....	Mrs. Maud Coe.
Joplin	Congregational	48	40	14	....	Craig P. Johnson.
Kansas City	Fifth Pres	48	16	47	18	S. I. Chalfant, 1314 Brooklyn ave.
" "	Clyde Cong	57	9	49	....	A. L. Cross, cor. 9th & B'dway.
" "	Olive St. Baptist	32	5	29	....	Miss Ella M. Gardner.
" "	Memorial	....	....	....	....	Rev. J. C. Taylor.
" "	Olivet Cong	....	....	....	....	Mrs. L. S. Austin, 2223 Vine st.
" "	Christian Union	....	....	....	....	
" "	Clyde Junior	....	....	....	....	
" "	First Baptist	....	....	....	....	Ella M. Garman, 621 E. 13th st.
" "	Hill Mem. Pres	....	....	....	....	
Kidder	Congregational	22	9	19	....	Maggie M. Whitelaw.
"	Central M. E.	15	....	....	....	Rev. J. M. Bowers.
"	Kidder Institute Un.	54	36	25	....	Beatrice Starner, Box 37.
Kirwood	Baptist	....	....	....	....	
Kirkville	Presbyterian	....	....	....	....	Rosa Patterson.
LaGrange	First Pres	16	25	16	8	B. P. Thomas.
Lebanon	Congregational	....	....	....	....	Miss Winnifred Searl.
Oregon		....	....	....	....	Pearle Bennett.
Pierce City	First Cong	20	....	19	....	Geo. S. Ricker.
Potosi		....	....	....	....	
Sedalia	First Cong	69	15	60	....	H. L. Berry, 609 W. Broadway.
"	Broadway Pres	....	....	....	....	Rev. John Herron.
"	Cumberland Pres	....	....	....	....	Rev. A. H. Stevens.
"	Christian	....	....	....	....	Rev. M. M. Davis.
"	First Baptist	....	....	....	....	Rev. J. B. Fuller.
Springfield	Congregational	....	....	....	....	Emma Hardie, No. Springfield.
"	First Baptist	23	1	23	....	Ethel Benedict, 460 Cherry st.
"	Presbyterian	....	....	....	....	Rev. B. G. Putnam.
"	Mission Baptist	30	1	30	....	Lizzie Trenary, 507 New st.
"	St Paul's M. E.	....	....	....	....	C. W. Scribner.
"	South M. E.	....	....	....	....	Robert Allen.
St. Charles	Madison St. Pres	20	....	20	....	Miss A. Martin.
" "	Union	....	....	....	....	
" "	Linderwood College	....	....	....	....	
" Joseph	Presbyterian	26	10	27	....	Harvey J. Mann, 2103 No. Main [st.

OF CHRISTIAN ENDEAVOR. xliii.

MISSOURI.—(Continued.)

CITY.	CHURCH.	Act. Memb.	Asso. Memb.	Ch. Memb.	United with C.	Secretary and Address.
St. Joseph	(Chris.) Dis. of Christ	36	3	40	....	Geo. L. Peters
" "	Fifth St. M. E.	66	20	....	....	Miss Mollie Johnson, cor. 13th
" "	First Baptist.	....	....	....	....	Rev. Mr. Lawless [& Felix sts.
" "	Cumberland Pres.	26	10	19	4	Lolla Brock, 115 So. 16th st.
" "	No. Pres. Chapel	....	....	....	....	H. J. Mann, 2008 N. 3rd st. [st.
" "	Methodist Episcopal.	....	....	....	....	Miss Nellie Donnelly, 212 N. 11th
" "	Congregational	....	....	....	....	A. P. Wolcott.
" "	South Pres	....	....	....	....	Rev. Dr. Bullard.
" "	Savannah Ave. M. E.	....	....	....	....	Rev. J. J. Lace.
" "	French M. E.	....	....	....	....	
" Louis	North Pres	94	31	71	24	Mary A. Israel,, 2113 N. 13th st.
" "	(St.Mark's)Eng. Luth	50	7	52	5	Miss L. M.Rickart, 3120 Sheriden
" "	Second Baptist	104	11	114	4	John F. Davies, Pub. Libr. [ave.
" "	LafayettePk.Jr.Pres	81	3	64	19	S. L. Biggars, 2803 Russell ave.
" "	Pilgrim Cong.	69	22	83	8	Mamie L. Richards, 1337 Garri-
" "	Lafayette Pk. M. E.	....	....	....	....	Rev. Mr- Werlein. [son ave.
" "	Fourth Christian.	23	5	23	3	L. E. Gettys, 1417 Penrose ave.
" "	Glasgow Ave. Pres,.	....	....	....	....	Rev. A. N. Thompson.
" "	Central Pres	....	....	....	....	Eugene Williamson, 2815 Mor-
" "	Compton Ave. Pres.	....	....	....	....	Dr. Brooks. [gan st.
" "	Compton Hill Cong.	....	....	....	....	Edward Meyer.
" "	Mt. Calvary Epis.	20	7	....	....	Archie T. Haskins, 3010 Geyer av
" "	Westminster Pres	18	....	18	1	F. P. Harris Jr., 2852 So. 13th st.
" "	Soulard Market Mission, Pres.	....	....	....	....	
" "	Aubert Pl. Mis. Cong.	24	4	10	....	Mrs. S. P. Merriam,1216 Bayard
" "	First Presbyterian	....	....	....	....	ave.
" "	Second Presbyterian	34	7	31	....	Miss Carrie Roth.
" "	Union Presbyterian.	....	....	....	....	
" "	Central Christian.	....	....	....	....	
" "	Mound St. Christian.	....	....	....	....	
" "	Tabernacle Baptist.	....	....	....	....	
" "	Union Cong	....	....	....	....	
" "	Carrondelet Bap	....	....	....	....	
" "	Church of the Advent, Episcopal.	....	....	....	....	A. S. Bradley, 2006 Division st.
" "	Church of the Redeemer, Cong.	....	....	....	....	
" "	Mem. Tabernable.	....	....	....	....	Rev. J. B. Brandt,1120 N.18th [st
" "	Centenary M. E.	....	....	....	....	Rev. J. Matthews, 7601 Chestnut
" "	Third Cong.	36	8	36	....	Ida Roeder, 6901 Plateau ave.
" "	First Cong. Mission.	15	7	8	....	Mrs. S. P. Merriam, 624 Wash. av
" "	Lucas Av. Cumb. Pres	33	....	31	....	Rev. W. H. Black, 4361 Laclede av
Sturgeon	Baptist	....	9	35	....	Kathalne T. Moody.
Webster Grove	Congregational	35	9	35	....	Kathalne T. Moody.
" "	Presbyterian.	27	26	31	....	Mary E. Holton, Box. 22.
Windsor	Congregational	22	10	30	....	Anna Pomeroy.

MISSISSIPPI.

CITY.	CHURCH.	Act. Memb.	Asso. Memb.	Ch. Memb.	United with C.	Secretary and Address.
Columbus	Baptist	30	4	32	....	Sam. Kline Jr.
"		....	....	....	....	S. W. Baker.
Meridian	Presbyterian	....	....	....	....	Ernest T. George.
Starkville	Pine Grove Baptist.	19	13	32	....	W. A. Colcolough.

MONTANA.

CITY.	CHURCH.	Act. Memb.	Asso. Memb.	Ch. Memb.	United with C.	Secretary and Address.
Billings	Congregational	12	....	9	....	Miss Hattie E. Vaughan.
Helena	Congregational	10	....	10	2	Thos. E. Goodwin.
"		....	....	....	....	T. D. Kelsey.
"	Presbyterian	....	....	....	....	Rev. T. V. Moore.

xliv.   LIST OF SOCIETIES

NEBRASKA.

CITY.	CHURCH.	Act. Memb.	Asso. Memb.	Ch. Memb.	United with C.	Secretary and Address.
Ainsworth.......						
Arborville.......	Congregational.......					Rev. J. E. Storm.
Ashland.........	Congregational.......					Miss M. Chamberlain.
Aurora..........	Union................					Fred Herman.
Beatrice.........	First Pres............	50	10	47	6	Harriet V. Erving, 323 Court st.
"	First Congregational	25	5	23		Lillie Molouy.
"	First Baptist.........					Rev. S. B. Randall.
"	First Christian.......					Rev. R. H. Ingram.
Bellevien College						Rev. Dr. Housha.
Blair............	First Presbyterian...		1	12		Nellie Fairchild.
Central City.....	Presbyterian.........	11	1	12		Mary V. Lee.
Chadron.........	Congregational.......	13	9	13		Mary E. McDill, Box 345.
Clay Centre.....	Congregational.......					Lizzle Moulton.
Columbus........						Mr. Hitchcock.
Crete............	Congregational.......	66	7	33		Miss Florence Jones.
"	Doane College........					A. V. Hanse.
David City......	First Cong...........	6	18	5		Maggie M. Miller.
Fairfield........	Congregational.......					
Fairmount.......						
Falls City.......						
Fremont.........	First Presbyterian...	25	13	25		Miss Emma Treat.
Friend...........	Congregational.......	7	12	7		Robert Hoxsey.
"						Sidney Strong.
Genoa...........						Mrs. N. C. Bosworth.
Grand Island....	Congregational.......					
Greenwood......	Congregational.......	12	6	10		Miss L. A. Foster.
Hartington......	Baptist...............	20	5	17		
Hastings.........	Congregational.......	25	3	21	6	Mabelle Miles, West Third st.
"	Baptist...............					Henry J. McLaughlin.
Kearney.........	First Presbyterian...	32		32	20	J. P. Hooley.
Lincoln..........	First Presbyterian...	45	15	44		Chas. Hanna, 514 So. 16th st.
"	First Congregational	32	4	30		W. A. Sellick, 1127 O. st.
"	Methodist............	85	11	96		E. R. Welles, cor. P. & 10th sts.
"	Plymouth 2nd Cong.	28	7			W. B. Crombie, 842 So. 12th st.
"	Trinity M. E.........					Cora Gilbert, 1507 A. st.
Madison.........	Presbyterian.........	13	4	11	7	Miss Nellie Davis.
Milford..........	Congregational.......					W. S. Dillenbrick.
Minden..........	Presbyterian.........	24	7	27	10	Wilson Dunlevy.
Nebraska City...	Congregational.......	129	1	80		Rev. Allen Clark.
Neligh...........	Yates College........					Rev. W. L. Holt.
Norfolk..........	Congregational.......					Rev J. I. Parker.
Oakdale.........						P. T. Buckley.
Ogalalla.........	First Cong...........	17	2	17	3	George Conn.
Omaha..........	First Presbyterian...	58	1	58	14	Miss Ella Allen, 310 N. 22d st.
"	Seward St. M. E......	64	15	64		C. R. Wilson, care Freight Aud.
"	Second Pres..........					Wm. R. Henderson. [U. P. Ry.
"	Christian.............					
"	Hillside Cong........					Rev. H. C. Crane.
"	First Cong...........	58	2	56		Rev. A. F. Sherril.
"	Plymouth Cong.......					Rev. A. B. Penniman.
"	Park Place Cong.....					Rev. M. L. Holt.
"	So. West Pres........					Rev. D. R. Kerr.
"	First Baptist.........					Lewis Riley.
"	Calvary Baptist......					Rev. A. W. Clark.
"	North Pres...........					
"	Beth. Eden Baptist...					Rev. W. L. House.
"	Immanuel Baptist....					Rev. T. W. Foster.
"	First Christian.......					Rev. C Newman.
"	First Presbyterian...					Ella N. Allen, 310 N. 22d st.
"	Second Pres..........					
"	Third Cong...........					
"	St. Mary Ave. Cong..					Nellie Hall, 606 So. 25th st.
"	Park Place Cong.....					
"	Hillside Cong........					
"	Calvary Baptist......					
"	Tenth St. M. E.......					F. W. Young.

OF CHRISTIAN ENDEAVOR.   xlv.

NEBRASKA.—(Continued.)

CITY.	CHURCH.	Act. Memb.	Asso. Memb.	Ch. Memb.	United with C.	Secretary and Address.
Palmyra	Baptist	12	10	9	5	Rev. E. D. Burwick.
Pawnee City	First Presbyterian	43			6	R. W. Story,
Ploversville						
Red Cloud	Congregational	17	7	15	6	Harry L. Markell.
Schuyler	Union	27	14	27	15	E. H. Phelps, B. & M. Station.
St. Paul	Presbyterian					Rev. Fred. Johnson.
Strang						
Stromsburg	Presbyterian					Rev. E. C. Haskell.
Waverly	Congregational	15	10	15	3	Florence J. Post.
Wayne						F. P. Balser.
Weeping Water	Baptist					Beth Norton.
York	First Congregational	40	14	38	13	Miss Genevra Grippen.
"	Baptist	14	9	14	1	Sadie I. Granger, cor. Burlington
"	Methodist Episcopal					Rev. Duke Slavens. [ave. & 1st st

NEW HAMPSHIRE.

Amherst	Congregational	23	11	18		Emma Fuller.
Antrim	Congregational					Rev. W. R. Cochrane.
"	Baptist	32				Rev. G. W. Riggles.
Barrington	Congregational	10	3			Rev. F. E. Holden.
Bennington	Congregational					George A. Gray.
Berlin Mills	Ch. of Christ, Cong.	38	18	22	3	Q. A. Bridges.
Brentwood	Congregational	11	4	5		Mabel B. Taylor.
Candia	Congregational	16	4	15		George W. Bean.
Charlestown	Congregational					Rev. G. H. French.
Claremont	Methodist Episcopal	15	4	12		Mary A. Babcock.
Concord	First Congregational	59	28	51	8	Lizzie A Brickett, 175 N. Main st.
"	West Cong	25	16	23	2	Miss Lydia R. Farnum.
"	South Cong	56	21	52	9	Mrs. G U. Johnson, 39 N. Main st
"	Pleasant St. Baptist	43	6	43		Rev. James K. Ewer.
Contocook	Methodist Episcopal					
Derry	First Cong	29	13	25	5	Cora B. Goodwin.
Derry Depot	Baptist	31	2	32	12	Frederick S. Pillsbury.
Dover						
Durham	Congregational	15	14	9		Miss C. E. Buzzell.
East Barrington	Congregational	17	13	12		Anna M. Buzzell.
" Jaffrey	Congregational	28	6	31	3	Kate B. Runells.
" Lempster						Hester J. Porter,
" Rochester	Methodist Episcopal	17		10		M. A. Hayes.
Enfield	Union	9	15	8	2	Minnie D. Cummings.
Epping	Congregational	41	17	33	12	Clara A. Lane.
Exeter	Second Cong	30	15	29	13	Miss Gertrude Nason, 16 High st
"	First Cong	38	20	33	15	Miss Frances Perry.
"	Baptist	22	8			Grace Frenyear.
Francestown	Congregational	23	15	24		Miss J. Y. Bixby, Box 116.
Franconia	Union	23	23	21		Frederick E. York.
Franklin	Christian Baptist	52	18	35		Grace G. Woodward, Box 127.
"	Calvanistic Baptist					Rev. Mr. Davis.
"	Free Will Baptist					Rev. Mr. Adams.
"	Methodist Episcopal					
"	Congregational	36	22	31	2	Elsie Y. Closson.
" Falls	First Baptist	28	3	26		Sadie J. Dearborn.
Farmington	Union	30	8			Miss Sadie Cook.
Gilsum	Congregational	43		9	3	Gertrude M. Fleming, Main st.
Great Falls	First Cong	20	16	19	7	Marion F. Thurston. Box 419.
" "	F. W. Baptist					George F. Hill.
Greenfield	Congregational					Rev. G. W. Ruland.
Goffstown	Congregational	15	21	9		Miss Belle M. Hoyt.
Guildhall	Congregational					
Humptstead	Congregational	27	15	27	3	M. Etta Tabor.
Hampton	Congregational					Rev. Mr. Ross.

xlvi.   LIST OF SOCIETIES

NEW HAMPSHIRE.—(Continued.)

CITY.	CHURCH.	Act. Memb.	Asso. Memb.	Ch. Memb.	United with C.	Secretary and Address
Hanover	Union	61	43	38	....	Miriam E. Demond.
Hancock	First Congregational	22	3	20	....	Miss M. L. Knight.
Henniker	Congregational	....	....	....	....	Rev. F. L. Allen.
Hillsboro Bridge	Congregational	14	5	....	....	Rev. R. J. Mooney.
Hinsdale	Union	52	14	42	9	Cora A. Wellman.
Hollis	Evangelical Cong	21	14	17	6	Miss E P. Flagg.
Hopkinton	First Baptist	27	5	22	....	H. H. Straw.
Jaffrey	First Congregational	32	6	25	3	Mary E. Phelps.
" Centre						
Keene	Baptist	31	....	31	....	Myra N. Perkins, 57 Union st.
"	Second Cong	79	....	61	....	H. C. Aldrich.
"	First Congregational	....	....	....	....	Rev. Mr. Harrington.
Laconia	Congregational	45	27	25	6	Grace A. Vaughan, 175 Main st.
Lancaster	Congregational	30	9	34	1	Frank Spooner.
Littleton	Congregational	....	....	....	....	F. G. Chutter.
Manchester	First Baptist	31	1	31	4	Mrs. C. E. Fellows, 314 Pine st.
"	Franklin St. 2nd Cong	63	26	44	4	Carrie R. Everett, 936 Elm st.
"	First Congregational	92	8	89	30	Clara N. Brown, 166 Concord st.
"	Junior Society	52	....	....	....	
"	So. Main St. Cong	....	....	....	....	Rev. E. C. Crane.
Mason	Congregational	21	30	21	....	Eva M. Hodgman.
Meredith Village	Union	21	14	17	....	Lizzie C. Caverly.
Milford	First Cong	60	14	57	....	C. S. Emerson.
"	First Baptist	39	2	37	....	Rev. A. E. Woodsum.
Milton	Congregational	....	....	....	....	Alice M. Ricker.
Mt. Vernon	Congregational	30	6	20	....	Jennie W. Beal.
Nashua	First Congregational	48	24	51	1	Josie Stevens, 35 Bowers st.
"	Pilgrim Cong	91	26	78	....	Rev. G. W. Grover. sq.
"	First Baptist	....	....	....	....	Arthur W. Hopkins, 3 Jackson
Newmarket	Congregational	....	....	....	....	Rev. I. C. White.
Newport	Congregational	30	16	....	....	Emma F. Gilman.
North Hampton	Congregational	24	2	24	....	George W. More.
Northwood C'ntre	Congregational	27	9	20	....	Mamie F. Brown.
" Ridge	Baptist	34	11	30	....	Emma B. Hill.
Nottingham						
Pembroke	Congregational	....	....	....	....	Annie M. Sargent.
Penacook	Congregational	29	4	26	2	M. Elizabeth Putnam.
Peterboro	Union Evan. Cong	20	4	16	1	May Knight.
"	Methodist Episcopal	....	....	....	....	
Piermont	Union	42	6	30	....	Katella Jones.
Pittsfield	Congregational	28	7	25	8	Anna M. Sargent, Box 82.
Plymouth	Congregational	18	19	14	....	Lela G. Weeks.
"	Congregational	....	....	....	....	Luther T. Jackman, 4 Pleasant st
Portsmouth	North Cong	32	36	29	....	Annie E. Fletcher.
"	Baptist	....	....	....	....	Rev. W. H. Alden.
Rindge	First Cong	24	13	18	3	Idella E. Gibson, Meadowview
Rochester	Congregational	....	....	....	....	Mrs. E. N. Thorn. [Farm.
Rye	Congregational	31	9	30	....	Frederick D. Parsons.
Salem	Congregational	....	....	....	....	John F. Hall.
Stratham		....	....	....	....	James D. Littlefield.
Suncook	Baptist	28	9	4	....	Theodore A. Howe.
Sullivan	First Congregational	9	2	9	....	Estella A. Marston.
Warner	Union	13	11	11	....	Mrs. C. H. Jones.
West Concord		....	....	....	....	Rev. C. F. Roper.
" "	West Cong	20	5	17	....	Lydia R. Farnum.
" Lebanon	Congregational	44	44	42	....	Rev. Mr. Havens.
Wilton	Second Cong	25	4	25	....	Emma C. Crane.
Winchendon		....	....	....	....	
Winchester	First Congregational	40	14	31	....	Miss Julia T. Bliss.

NEW JERSEY.

CITY.	CHURCH.	Act. Memb.	Asso. Memb.	Ch. Memb.	United with C.	Secretary and Address
Allentown	Baptist	....	....	....	....	Rev. H. Tratt.
Asbury	Presbyterian	....	....	....	....	Samuel L. Stout.
Atlantic Highl'ds	Baptist	30	4	30	1	Ada Leonard, Leonardville.

OF CHRISTIAN ENDEAVOR.   xlvii

NEW JERSEY.—(*Continued.*)

CITY.	CHURCH.	Act. Memb.	Asso. Memb.	Ch. Memb.	United with C.	Secretary and Address.
Basking Ridge...	Presbyterian.........	39	....	37	....	Julia P. Roberts, Bernardville.
Belleville.........	Reformed Dutch.....	38	19	38	13	Annette Van Vorst.
Bergen	Reformed.............	....	....	....	....	
Beverly............	Presbyterian.........	50	9	49	....	Eleanor S. Ker, Pine street.
Blackwood	Presbyterian.........	30	25	35	....	Alice R. Bateman, Spring Mills.
"	....	....	....	....	7	Rev. F. R. Brace.
Boonton...........	Reformed.............	13	18	13	....	Flora C. Woodruff.
"	Presbyterian.........	68	....	67	....	Rev. Thomas Carter.
Bordentown.......	....	....	....	....	....	H. B. Ayers.
Bound Brook.....	Presbyterian.........	32	8	32	....	Miss Clara Goltra.
" "	Methodist Episcopal	....	....	....	4	Rev. Mr. Gaston.
" "	Congregational	35	....	....	....	Rev. W. W. Jordan.
Brick Church....	....	....	....	....	....	Rev. H. B. MacCauley.
Bridgeton	Commerce St. Meth..	47	6	47	....	John B. Price, 25 Coral avenue.
"	" Bap...	....	....	....	....	Rev. T. Y. Cass.
"	Pearl St. Baptist.....	....	....	....	....	Rev W. R. McNeal.
"	Central Methodist...	55	8	55	....	Reuben C. Hunt, 41 Elmer st.
"	First Presbyterian ..	....	....	....	....	
"	M. E. Reformed......	....	....	....	....	W. D. Stultz, 288 Land street.
"	First Baptist..........	....	....	....	....	John F. Watson.
Cadlwell...........	Presbyterian.........	78	3	78	10	George F. King, Box 196.
"	Baptist...............	....	....	....	....	Rev. J. Marshall.
Camden	First Presbyterian...	56	13	64	10	Alice C. Hall, 834 North 2nd st.
"	Methodist Episcopal	22	2	22	....	J. Haddom.
" Linden ..	Baptist	....	....	....	....	Gilbert Landis, 827 Penn st
Canton	Baptist...............	....	....	....	....	Rev. J. J. Davies.
Cape May City ...	Cape Island Pres.....	15	1	15	....	Hannah H. Smith, 92 Wash. st.
Chambersburg....	Presbyterian.........	....	....	....	....	Frances S. Karr.
Chester	First Congregational	39	21	37	5	Amelia Dawson
"	Presbyterian.........	....	....	....	....	Rev. Mr. Brewster.
Clayton	....	....	....	....	....	George H. Chew.
Colt's Neck.......	Reformed	14	7	14	....	Sadie W. Statesir.
Cramer's Hill	First Baptist.........	21	3	21	4	Dollie Morris.
Danville...........	Presbyterian.........	....	....	....	....	Rev. Mr. Bryant.
Dayton............	Presbyterian.........	....	....	....	....	
Delaware	Presbyterian.........	15	11	15	....	Miss Emma E. Bodine.
Dover.............	Presbyterian.........	80	43	80	2	Miss Mary B. Condict.
"	Union.................	....	....	....	....	George E. Jenkins.
Dunnellen........	Presbyterian	....	....	....	....	Rev. Mr. Sellinger.
Elizabeth.........	Presbyterian.........	28	3	11	....	Albert Thorn, 314 Centre street.
"	Third Presbyterian..	77	9	78	2	George S. Leary, 1155 Wash st.
"	First Baptist.........	25	40	25	....	A. H. Kent, 318 Fulton street.
"	Presbyterian Chap,..	....	....	....	....	Rev. Mr. Kerr.
"	First Congregational	....	....	....	....	Rev. J. G. Evans.
"	East Baptist..........	36	15	36	....	Rev. J. Madison Hare.
Flanders..........	Presbyterian.........	18	1	18	18	T. Naughright, Jr.
Flemington.......	Presbyterian.........	51	5	51	....	Harry C. Cathers.
Franklin..........	Congregational	....	....	....	....	
"	Dutch Reformed.....	....	....	....	....	Lillian M. Post, Oakland.
Freehold..........	Second Reformed....	30	6	30	....	Rev. Isaac P. Brokaw.
Goshen............	Immanuel Baptist...	....	....	....	....	Meannie Springer. [st.
Greenville........	Reformed	40	3	40	16	Miss E. J. French, 999 Garfield
Hackettstown....	First Presbyterian...	110	....	110	3	Nora Stephens.
"	Second Reformed...	108	....	62	....	Miss Conrie McRae, Main st.
Haddonfield......	Baptist...............	67	6	66	19	Lillie Underown.
"	Presbyterian.........	....	....	....	....	Rev. J. E. Werner.
Hightstown	Church of Christ, Bap	104	22	83	6	Frank Jemisou, So. Main st.
"	Presbyterian.........	27	15	27	....	A. S. Voerhees, Main st.
"	Baptist...............	90	25	90	....	Hattie Dalrymple.
Holendel..........	Baptist...............	32	4	32	....	H. H. Ely.
Jacobstown	Baptist...............	17	....	17	....	Fannie B. Ernley.
Jamesburg........	Presbyterian.........	114	50	117	3	Frank B. Everitt.
Jersey City	Summit Ave. Baptist	85	34	91	23	Helen Bridgart, 11 Magnolia ave.
" "	Bergen Baptist	45	16	10	3	Edgar F. Corfield, 13 Madison ave.
" "	So. Bergen Reformed	20	9	19	....	Chas J. Golden, 618 Bramhall ave.
" "	First Presbyterian...	45	5	....	8	D. W. Hull, 534 Bergen ave.

LIST OF SOCIETIES

NEW JERSEY.—(Continued.)

CITY.	CHURCH.	Act. Memb.	Asso. Memb.	Ch. Memb.	United with C.	Secretary and Address.
Jersey City	Claremont Pres.					Parker McIlhiney, 621 Grand st.
" "	Greenville Reformed					Rev. Mr. Bruce. [vonia ave.
" "	Tabernacle Baptist					Mary E. Chamberlain, 284 Pa-
" "	Waverly Cong.	30	15		30	Avonia A. Benson.
" "	Tabernacle Cong.	160	52	150		Rev. John L. Scudder.
" " Heights	Westminster Pres	39	37	39	3	G. C. Harman, 272 Baldwin ave.
Lakewood	Presbyterian					
Leesburgh	Methodist Episcopal.	43		43	22	Anna V. Carlisle.
Little Falls	Reformed Dutch	26	11	26	5	Abbie L. Mitchell, Paterson.
Long Branch						William Maxsen.
Manalapan	Presbyterian					
Marlboro	Reformed	36	13	36		D. DuBois Scott.
"	Baptist					Jennie E. Layton.
Matteawan	Presbyterian					
Mechanicsville	Methodist Episcopal.					
Metuchen	Presbyterian	27	10	25	3	Mrs. Edward C. Rowland.
"	Dutch Reformed	35	5	28		Edith C. Mundy.
Milford	First Presbyterian	23		23	7	Miss E. G. Patterson, Box 26.
Middlebush	Reformed Dutch	25	12	25	5	Esther D. W. Le Fevre.
"						Arthur B. Tolten.
Millstone	Reformed Dutch	19	25	23	4	Ella F. Smith, Weston.
Millville						L. M. Merrill.
Montclair	Baptist	22	7	22		C. M. Slade, Box 465, N. Y. City.
"	Presbyterian					Arthur L. Wolfe
"	Congregational					E. N. Benham.
Moorstown	Baptist					
Morristown	Baptist					Rev. Mr. Parker.
Newark	Sixth Presbyterian	29		25		Kizzie W. Ely, 128 Prospect st.
"	South Baptist	44	19	61	16	F. W. Callaway, 96 Thomas st.
"	Sherman Ave. Bap.	33		33		Alice B. Peirson. [st.
"	Roseville Pres.	43	1	43		Miss Lizzie Schenck 27 So. 11th
"	Emanuel Refd. Epis.	39	2	39	3	Miss M. L. Keons, 21 Halsey st.
"	Belleville Ave. Cong.	47	3	47		Rev. Mr. Nutting. [st.
"	First Baptist					William G. March, 167 Walnut
"	High St. Pres.					Belle Grover, 97 Court street.
"	South Baptist					T. E. Vassar, 29 Walnut street.
New Brunswick	George's Road Bap	17	5	15	3	H. B. McNair. [ave.
" "	First Reformed	52	3	52	8	Miss S. H. Wilson, 31 Cadwise
" "	First Baptist					H. B. McNair.
" "	Runsen Ave. Baptist.					Rev. W. V. McDuffie.
" "	St. James M. E.					Rev. J. J. Reed.
Newton						A. D. Everitt.
"	First Presbyterian	96	13	96		Edward E. Bouns.
Oakland						
Ocean Beach	Presbyterian	13	7	10		Robert P. Miller. [place.
Orange Valley	Congregational	38	8	44	10	Caldwell Morrison, 15 Randolph
Oxford	Second Presbyterian	39	1	38	10	J. A. Henry.
Passaic	First Reformed	22	8	23		Francis A. Van Nostrand.
"	First Presbyterian	54	27	54	4	Mrs. O. S. Freeman, 82 Wash. pl.
Paterson	Baptist	15		15		Miss May Perry, 226 Division st.
"	First Reformed	24	5	23	2	Miss L. W. Benjamin, 54 N.West
"	First Presbyterian	40	35			Mary E. Crane, 81 Ward st. [st.
"	Auburn St. Cong	28	25	29		Rev. C. L. Merriam.
"	Cross St. M. E.					Rev. P. G. Blight.
"	Westminster Pres.					Rev. D. W. Hutchinson.
"	First Baptist					Gertrude J. Seeman.
"	Congregational					F. S. Wiggin, cor. Auburn & Van
"						F. A. Beekman. [Houlten sts.
"	Union Ave. Baptist.					Emma J. Steele.
"						A. W. Hand, 285 Broadway.
Perth Amboy	Simpson M. E.	18	7	18	1	Geo. W. Parisen, cor. Smith &
" "	Baptist	30	21	28	1	Miss Alice Martin. [High sts.
" "	First Presbyterian	37	32	37	7	Miss F. E. Kent.
" "	Baptist					Alice Martin.
Phillipsburg	Westminster Pres	17	4	17	1	Miss Emily A. Seebelspurger.
"	First Presbyterian					

NEW JERSEY.—(*Continued.*)

CITY.	CHURCH.	Act. Memb.	Asso. Memb.	Ch. Memb.	United with C.	Secretary and Address.
Pluckamin	Presbyterian	36	13	36	6	John C. Holden.
Plainfield	Trinity Reformed	94	21	85	16	Miss Ella C. Benedict, Box 1362.
"	First Presbyterian	38	2	35	5	Flora R. Petrie, 49 East 6th st.
"	Congregational					M. C. Van Ansdale.
Port Elizabeth						
Port Norris						Rev. E. R. Smith, D. D.
Preakness	Reformed					Richard Bensen.
Red Bank	Presbyterian					Rev. Mr. Harbaugh.
Roadstown	Baptist					Frank O. Fithian.
Salem	Memorial Baptist	51	10	52	15	Fannie S. Newkirk, 18 Walnut st.
" City	First Baptist	36	32	63	16	Eva M. Ayars.
"	First Presbyterian	38	7	38	10	Sarah M. N. Dunn, 32 Walnut st.
Somerville	Second Rfmd. Dutch.					
South Amboy	First Baptist	10	6	10	2	Kate D. Emmons.
" "	Presbyterian	19	6	19		George V. Bogart.
" "	First Baptist	9	5	7		Kate D. Emmons.
" "	Methodist Episcopal					
" River	Baptist					
South Seaville	Calvary Baptist	23	3	20		Lizzie Voss.
Springfield	Presbyterian	31	11	31	1	William Graves, Box 35.
Stelton	Piscataway Baptist					Rev. J. W. Searles, D. D.
Succasunn	Methodist Episcopal	14	2	14	4	Bertha L. Thomas.
"	Presbyterian					Rev. Dr. Stoddard.
Trenton	Clinton Ave. Baptist	49	26	49		Lizzie Brown, 45 Lincoln ave.
"	Bethany Pres.	61	8	58	28	Frances S. Karr, 308 Hudson st.
"	Prospect St Pres	20	23	25		Miss Amy Slade, 435 Bellevue av.
"	First Baptist					Rev. Mr. Lucas.
"	Calvary Baptist					Rev. Mr. Foote.
"	Second Presbyterian					Rev. Mr. Woolverton.
"	Fifth Presbyterian					
Upper Montclair						F. L. Van Gilson.
Verona	Methodist Episcopal	28	13	32	7	Elmer E. Brooks.
Vineland	First Baptist	37	14	30	8	Sadie B. Davies, 212 7th street.
"	First Presbyterian	79	45			Maurice Gay, 720 Almond st.
"	First Methodist					George W. Lamb.
Warren	Mission					
West Concord	Congregational					Hannah E. Smith, 92 Wash. st.
" Millstown	Reformed Dutch					Rev. Dr. E. T. Convin.
Westmont	Baptist					
White House	Rockaway Dutch Refd	26	14	26	3	Miss Ella T. E. Schomp.
Woodbridge	Methodist Episcopal	22	6	22	9	Mary E. Wyhe, Box 96.
"	Presbyterian	20	12	25	6	Josie Harriot.
"	Congregational	24			7	Mary E. Fink, Box 185.
Woodbury	Baptist	27	3		24	Albert E. Simmons.

NEW MEXICO.

Socorro	First Presbyterian	8	6	8		Frank A. Leonard.

NEW YORK.

Adams	Presbyterian	52	6	48	8	Nettie L. Dodge.
Adams Basin						Ada Marshall.
Adams Centre	First Day Baptist	50	1	46	34	Mary E. Fuller.
" "	Presbyterian					Mary E. Fuller.
" "	Seventh Day Baptist					Rev. Mr. Prentice.
" "	First					
" Village	Baptist	26	10	28	7	Emma S. Brown.
Addison	Methodist Episcopal					Minnie Davis.
"	First Baptist					Charles Manning.
Afton	Union					Mrs. Marcus Brown.
Alfred Centre	Seventh Day Baptist					

LIST OF SOCIETIES

NEW YORK.—(Continued.)

CITY.	CHURCH.	Act. Memb.	Asso. Memb.	Ch. Memb.	United with C.	Secretary and Address.
Albany	First Christian	32	0	32	10	Lena Davis, 304 Hudson ave.
"	First Baptist	25	12	37	1	M. C. St. John, 22 Myrtle ave.
"	First Congregational	29	24	37	5	C. H. Moore, 341 Hudson ave.
"	Clinton Ave. Cong.	46	16	52	35	Mary Rea, 42 Knox st.
"	Trinity M. E.					Rev. Mr. Farrar.
"	First Reformed					Rev. W. Chapman.
"	Third Reformed					Rev. Mr. Tracy.
"	St. Luke's M. E.					Gertrude Rieman.
"	All Soul's Univ.					Jennie Williamson.
"	First Methodist					Dr. J. P. Southworth.
Albion	First Baptist	115	17		8	Lottie E. Chester.
"	Presbyterian					Margaret R. Cain. [Albany.
Altamont	St. John's Lutheran	25	15			Eugene Crounce, 76 Dove st.,
Amsterdam	First Presbyterian	46	11	41	8	Alice D. Shuler, 10 Shuler st.
"	Methodist					Clara Van Brocklin, 11 Forbes st.
"	Second Presbyterian	16		6		
"	First Baptist					Delos Lewis.
Andes	United Presbyterian					W. C. Oliver.
Antwerp	Congregational	53	40	22	4	Mabel Bentley.
"	Methodist Episcopal					Mrs. Cora Graves.
Arcade	Baptist	45	18	44	4	Ellen Wilson, W. Main st.
"	Methodist Episcopal	12	15	9		Emma Odell.
"	Congregational					
Argyle	United Presbyterian	33	11	33	3	Katherine T. Packard.
Arkport	Presbyterian	40	23	36	3	Mary Hurlbut.
Athens	Reformed	46	15	38	15	Lydia C. Downing.
"	Baptist					Rev. Mr. Cornell.
Attica	Presbyterian					Mrs. E. P. Norton.
Aquabogue	Presbyterian					
"	Congregational					Nellie W. Young (Jamesport, L. I.).
Auburn	Disciples	29	17	38	16	Hattie E. Armstrong, 96 No.Division
"	Calvary Presbyterian	34	4	34	7	Ella Stevens, Morr's st. [st.
"	Second Baptist	19	14	19		Fannie E. Hickok.
"	Central Pres.	53	41	79	4	Alice H. Stoppard, 165 E. Genesee st.
"	First Baptist	38	20	51	4	Mary A. Payne, Box 51.
"	First Universalist	58				D. J. Crowley, 31 Barber st.
"	First Presbyterian					Mary Bates.
"	Second Presbyterian					Nellie J. Moore, 47 Mechanics st.
"	Westminster Pres.					Winifred Thornton, 100 Cornell st.
"	First Methodist Ep.					A. E. Bradt, 39 Franklin st.
"	Trinity M. E.					Mrs. Arthur Copeland.
Augusta	Presbyterian					G. H. Norton.
Aurora	Presbyterian					Rev. J. T. Wills.
Avoca	Lutheran	23	30	21	3	F. Aurand.
Avon	Central Pres	20	12	18	1	T. C. Davenport.
Baldwinsville	Methodist					Rev. Mr. Eastwood.
"	Presbyterian	83	23	89	10	Miss Mina Andrews.
Ballston Centre	Presbyterian					Nathan Curtis.
Ballston Spa	First Presbyterian	42	19	45	8	Carrie S. Gilchrist, Ballston ave.
" "	First Baptist	22		22		F. W. Patchen.
" "	Methodist Episcopal	24				
" Springs	Baptist					Sadie Winnie.
" "	First Methodist					Hattie Howland.
Bath	First Presbyterian	77	58	74	15	F. H. Hendryx.
Bay Shore	Congregational	18	1	15		A. M. Thompson.
Bayville, L. I.						Rev. Thomas Douglas.
Bedford Station						Willie B. Adams.
Bellport	First Presbyterian	20		15		Mrs. F. V. Frisbie.
Benton Centre	Baptist	10	3	11		Mary A. Campbell.
Berkshire	First Congregational	45	4	45		Cornelia W. Eldridge.
Bethany	Union					
Bethlehem	Ref	13	19	13		
Binghamton	First Baptist	82	9	79	9	Mrs. E. A. Goodrich, 7 S. Mary st.
"	Methodist Episcopal					
"	W. Presbyterian	66	25	84	20	A. B. Osgood, Jr., 78 Dickinson st.

OF CHRISTIAN ENDEAVOR. li

NEW YORK. — (Continued.)

CITY.	CHURCH.	Act. Memb.	Asso. Memb.	Ch. Memb.	United with C.	Secretary and Address.
Binghamton	Christian Chapel	20	2	....	....	M. J. H. Van Atta.
Boonville	Presbyterian	....	....	....	....	
Brainard	Methodist	21	16	11	....	Daniel E. Thomson.
Bridgewater	Congregational	15	10	13	....	Jennie E. Langworthy.
Bridgehampton	Methodist	41	2	39	....	E. R. Bishop, Box 33.
"		....	....	....	....	W. E. Overton.
Bridgeport	Baptist	10	18	10	....	Genevieve Bushnell.
Brier Hill	First Congregational	18	....	15	....	Luther I. Tilton.
Broadalbin	Baptist	20	....	20	....	Mamie E. James.
Brockport	First Baptist	45	10	48	5	M. G. Allen (Clarkson, N.Y.).
"	Methodist Episcopal	52	34	24	4	M. Ella Ball, 6 Clinton st.
"		....	....	....	4	
"	Presbyterian	....	....	....	....	Carrie Knowles.
"	Baptist	....	....	....	....	Rev. J. H. Mason.
Brookfield	Seventh Day Baptist	15	8	15	....	W. C. Whitford.
Brooklyn (E.D.)	Ainslie St. Presbyterian	61	62	65	28	Wm. B. Alford, 232 Ainslie st.
"	Memorial Presbyterian	65	7	50	5	W. J. Betts, 181 St. John pl.
"	Bedford Ref	23	7	23	3	Edith C. Dickie, 311 Lexington ave.
"	Pilgrim Congregational	23	12	28	....	Lucia A. Demond, 99 14th st.
"	Second Presbyterian	11	22	20	....	Eliza Keetels, 14 St. Felix st.
(E.D.)	Noble St. Presbyterian	68	26	....	....	Jessie Dickson, 121 Java st.
"	Clinton Ave. Cong	77	13	66	5	Otis W. Barker, 385 Adelphi st.
"	Classon Ave. Pres	....	....	....	....	G. N. Hart, 141 Gates ave.
"	Bedford Ave. Baptist	....	....	....	....	Rev. H. Hutchins.
"	Duryea Presbyterian	....	....	....	....	Rev. S. Halsey.
"	Immanuel Baptist	....	....	....	....	Rev. Mr. Humpstone.
"	Stuyvesant Ave. Cong	53	....	....	....	Annie Holywell, 419 Macon st.
"	Old Bushwick Ref	....	....	....	....	W. H. Ford, Humboldt st.
"	Sixth Ave. Baptist	....	....	....	....	Rev. R. B. Kelsey.
"	Centennial Chapel Ref	45	38	....	....	Emma A. Monroe, 219½ 11th st.
"	Strong Place Baptist	....	....	....	....	
"	Strong Place Baptist, Jr.	....	....	....	....	
"	Carroll Pk. Mission Bap	....	....	....	....	C. F. Bernhardt.
"	Greenpoint Pres	....	....	....	....	
"	Hanson Place Baptist	....	....	....	....	
"	Willoughby Ave. Chap. Congregational	16	9	....	2	Samuel Walton, 182 Steuben st.
"	Trinity Baptist	....	....	....	....	
"	Redemption Ref. Ep	12	12	13	....	E. J. Vass, 120 Oak st.
(E.D.)	Hope Baptist Miss	9	....	8	....	G. W. Powles, 380 Hooper st.
"	First Dutch Reformed	35	23	....	....	W. S. White, 430 W. Gold st.
"	Washington St. Meth	10	....	10	....	Frederick Brown.
"	Ocean Hill Baptist	....	....	....	....	J. P. Wheeler.
"	Central Baptist	....	....	....	....	
"	Gospel Chapel Cong	....	....	....	....	G. Schwab, 69 Walton st.
"	Reformed Episcopal	....	....	....	....	K. E. Aldrich, 665 Humboldt st.
"	Greenpoint Reformed	....	....	....	....	Mamie F. Ogden, 139 Kent st.
"	So. Reform	40	....	25	....	
Brookville (Oyster Bay)	Reform	....	....	....	....	Alice A. Smith (E. Harwich).
Brownville	Presbyterian	....	....	....	....	A. T. Vail.
Brushton	Christian	18	10	10	....	Rev. B. S. Crosby.
Bruynswick	Reformed	....	....	....	....	Aggie H. Decker.
Buffalo	First Presbyterian	28	25	43	2	W. B. Taylor, 114 Morgan st.
"	First Congregational	65	8	69	7	W. H. Grein, 117 Oak st.
"	Lafayette St. Pres	65	5	62	4	May E. Perry, 134 Richmond ave.
"	East Presbyterian	47	2	47	....	Anna J. Krummel, 224 Van Rensselaer st.
"	North Presbyterian	....	....	....	....	S. C. Butler, 263 Main st.
"	Calvary Presbyterian	....	....	....	....	Ed. Tanner.
"	Cedar St. Baptist	....	....	....	....	Emma M. Onskip.
"	Washington St. Baptist	....	....	....	....	Rev. Mr. Griffiths.
"	Wells St. Presbyterian	....	....	....	....	Rev. P. G. Cook.
"	Michigan St. Baptist	....	....	....	....	Rev. H. Powell.
"	Hudson St. Free Will Bt	....	....	....	....	T. R. Vaughan, 272 Prospect st.
"	Immanuel Baptist	....	....	....	....	

NEW YORK. — (*Continued.*)

CITY.	CHURCH.	Act. Memb.	Asso. Memb.	Ch. Memb.	United with C.	Secretary and Address.
Buffalo	Ch. of Covenant Pres...					Rev. W. A. Robinson, 918 W. Ferry st.
"	Dearborn St. Baptist....					Mrs. Wm. Hunt, 359 Dearborn st.
"	Delaware Ave. Baptist.	34				F. C. Scheffer, 1157 Main st.
"	Lutheran...............					Rev. F. A. Kahler.
"	Universalist...........	15	17	17	3	Marian I. Moore, 220 Hudson st.
"	First Free Baptist......	67	7	58		Louie H. Isham.
"	Pilgrim Congregational.	32	16	37		Lucia A. Demond, 99 14th st.
Buskirk	Reformed..............					J. L. Southard.
Caledonia	United Presbyterian....					Rev. Mr. Russell.
Caldwell						Hettie Harrison.
Cambria	Congregational........	40	10	40		C. F. Comstock.
Cambria Centre	First Congregational...	52	8	52		Lizzie Margetts.
Camden	First Congregational...	69	4	64	8	F. P. Barnes, Second st.
"	Presbyterian...........					Rev. A. W. Allen.
"	Congregational.........	42	9	35		Hattie S. Peters.
Camillus	Methodist Episcopal....	18	4	13	3	Mary E. Julian.
"	Baptist................					G. H. Hubbard.
"	Presbyterian...........					Celia B. Rowe.
Cambridge	Congregational........					Alice M. Robertson, 54 E. Main st.
Canajoharie	Methodist Episcopal...	39		39	7	Cora Miller, 4 Otsego st.
"	Reformed..............	45	47	56	13	J. D. McDiarmid.
"	St. Mark's Evan. Luth..	79	7	79	6	Ella Vosburgh (Palatine Bridge).
"	Baptist................					
Canaan 4 Corners	Congregational........					Rev. J. P. Beaver.
Canandaigua	First Baptist..........	75	9	66	42	Clara B. Howe, Chapin st.
"	First Presbyterian.....	71	8	71	21	Nettie B. Hall, Bristol st.
"	Methodist Episcopal...					Rev. Theron Cooper.
Canastota	Presbyterian..........	43	17	40	14	Gussie M. New.
"	Methodist Episcopal...	49	8	49	12	Mrs. Willis Phelps.
"	Baptist................					J. F. Acker.
Candor	Congregational........					Rev. Mr. Richardson.
Canisteo	Presbyterian..........					Rev. Duncan Campbell.
Canton	Presbyterian..........	40	16	46	7	Mrs. Horace Whitmarsh.
"	Methodist.............					Rev. L. T. Cole.
Cape Vincent	Presbyterian..........					Ida Horr.
"						
Carmel	Presbyterian..........	13	15	11		Clara Slawson.
"	Methodist.............					Mrs. J. C. Coleman, Mahopac Falls.
Carthage	Presbyterian..........	23	10			G. V. Eggleston.
"	Methodist.............					W. W. Sweet.
Castile	Presbyterian..........	28	20			Fannie Smith.
"	Christian..............					Frank C. Beaumont, Box 335.
Castleton Cor's (L.I.)	Moravian..............					Rev. C. E. Eberman.
Cate						
Catskill	Reformed..............	23	10	24		Libbie E. Burhams.
"	Baptist................					Dr. Baldwin.
Cazenovia	Second Baptist........					G. E. Loomis.
"	Methodist.............					E. L. Bradt, Box 229.
Ceres	Methodist.............	12		8	1	Marion L. Rose.
Champlain	Presbyterian..........	27		27		Mrs. L. G. Boardman.
Charleston						
Chatauqua	Methodist.............	18		18		Ella Beaujeau.
Chenango						F. I. Niles.
Chenango Bridge	Union.................	30	2	11		B. L. Parker.
Chenango Forks	Congregational........					Will H. Hoadley.
Chili	First Presbyterian.....	8		7		Elizabeth H. Hunt.
"	North Methodist.......					Rev. Mr. Hawkins.
Chittenango	Reformed..............	47	26	52	27	Mrs. A. E. Root.
"	Baptist................					Carrie Maffit, Box 343.
"	Methodist.............					Rev. J. B. Foote.
"	Presbyterian..........					
Churchville	Congregational........	54	70	50	12	F. E. Squires.
Cicero	Reformed..............					
Claverack	Dutch Reformed.......	30	14	35	7	L. A. Bristol.
"	College................					Prof. W. McAfee.

OF CHRISTIAN ENDEAVOR.   liii

NEW YORK.— (*Continued.*)

CITY.	CHURCH.	Act. Memb.	Asso. Memb.	Ch. Memb.	United with C.	Secretary and Address.
Clayville............	Presbyterian...........					Carrie Tompkins.
Clayton.............	Baptist................					F. C. Shaw.
Clifton Park........	Baptist................	35	1	35	14	J. P. Greene.
"	Methodist..............	30	20	30	....	John McDowell (Jonesville).
Clinton.............	Presbyterian...........					Rev. F. Hudson.
"	Methodist..............	34	12	34	6	Libbie Lawrence.
Clockville..........	Presbyterian...........					
"	Methodist..............					
Clyde...............	Presbyterian...........					Rev. W. H. Bates.
"	First Methodist........	44	4	43	....	Edith Schindler, 34 W. Genesee st.
Cohoes..............	First Presbyterian.....	85	40	107	30	Carrie B. Vail, 438 Saratoga st.
"	First Baptist..........					Clara Adams.
Conhocton...........	Presbyterian...........	21	7	21	....	F. A. Wygant, M. D.
Conklin Sta.........	Presbyterian...........	43	6	40	6	Nellie Van Wormer.
Coxsackie...........	Reform.................					
Cortland............	First Congregational...	41	9	41	....	Myron Norton, 26 R. R. ave.
"	First Baptist..........	67	21	61	....	R. B. Stone, 59 Elm st.
Corona..............	Evan. Union Cong......	29	29	28	6	Gustave J. Talleur.
Corinth.............	Presbyterian...........	20	11	20	....	M. E. White (Palmer).
Coventry............	First Congregational...	38	9	32	3	Carrie Williams (Coventryville).
"	Second Congregational.					Rev. Mr. Zanes.
Coventryville.......						Rev. A. Caldwell.
Cranesville.........	Reform.................					
Crescent............	Methodist..............	58	10	57	....	Jennie E. Haight.
Cuba................	First Presbyterian.....	34	29	26	....	Genevieve Taylor.
Croton Falls........	Presbyterian...........	12	16	17	5	Lizette A. Schroorm.
Crown Point.........	First Congregational...	36	28	33	8	Mrs. C. P. Nichols.
Dansville...........	Presbyterian...........	7	9	7	....	Florence W. Knapp.
Deansville..........	Congregational.........					Mary E. Lyman.
Delmar..............	Second Reformed	12	24	12	....	Gertrude C. Haswell.
Dempster............						Geo. Tremaine.
Deposit.............	First Presbyterian.....	64	13	50	....	Emily M. Austin.
Dexter..............	Presbyterian...........	20	8	15	3	G. E. Leonard.
Dryden..............	First Presbyterian.....	44	....	20	1	Frances M. Phillips.
Dunkirk.............	First Presbyterian.....					Henry H. Dickinson.
Eagle Mills.........	Methodist..............	19	....	19	....	Eunice A. Potter.
Earlville...........	Union..................					Rev. A. R. Moore.
"	Baptist................	21	14	20	....	E. May Williamson.
East Albany.........	Congregational.........	31	41	25	4	Ella E. Case, 13 Partition st.
" "	Methodist..............					W. A. Buckley.
" Aurora..........	First Presbyterian.....	18	12	20	....	Mrs. F. N. Spooner, Box 38.
" "	Baptist................					
" "	Disciples..............	12	4	12	....	Lucy Taber.
" Bloomfield......	Congregational.........	45	11	24	....	C. H. Mason, Jr.
" "	Presbyterian...........	33	4			W. E. French.
" Greenbush.......	Reform.................					Libbie S. Schermerhorn.
" Palmyra.........	Presbyterian...........					
" Patchogue						
" Syracuse........	Presbyterian...........	37	32	36	5	Lulu Swift.
" Webster.........						
{ East Williamsb'g. / Newton, L. I.	Reform................	20	....	17	2	F. Licht, 22 J st., New York City.
Eaton...............	Union..................	35	10		....	Chas. E. Hamilton.
Edmeston............	Second Baptist.........	21	21	16	....	Lulie M. Reed.
"	Methodist..............					Rev. Mr. Frisbie.
"	Presbyterian...........					
Elbridge............	First Baptist..........	31	14	29	....	Ella Crosman.
"	Congregational.........					
Ellenville..........						D. H. Yaird.
Ellisburg...........	Congregational.........	38	....	15	....	Mrs. M. J. Ashford.
Elmira..............	Hedding Methodist......	54	5	48	2	Marcia G. Derby, 459 West 2d st.
"	Park Ind. Cong.........	63	19	26	3	Carrie B. Fitch, 356 West 1st st.
"	First Baptist..........	156	....	120	....	Edna Squires, 221 Channing place.
"	First Presbyterian.....	56	34	60	15	Hattie B. Godfrey, 712 E. Church st.

NEW YORK.—(Continued.)

CITY.	CHURCH.	Act. Memb.	Asso. Memb.	Ch. Memb.	United with C.	Secretary and Address.
Elmira	First Methodist	...	...	...	...	Rev. C. C. Wilbur.
"	Lake St. Presbyterian	...	...	...	...	Libbie Bogardus.
"	Centenary Methodist	...	...	...	...	
"	Grace Episcopal	...	...	...	...	Rev. J. F. Herrlich.
"	Franklin St. Presbt	...	...	...	...	
"	Magee St. Chapel Pres.	...	...	...	...	Rev. J. R. Robinson.
"	Benton St. Baptist	...	...	...	...	
"	Trinity Episcopal	...	...	...	...	G. H. McKnight.
"	Park St. Baptist	...	...	...	...	
Esopus	Dutch Reformed	20	3	20	...	Lizzie Stryker (Ulster Park).
Fair Haven	First Presbyterian	15	5	15	3	A. Adelle Turner.
" "	Presbyterian	...	...	...	...	W. J. Sweet.
Fairport	Congregational	30	5	32	...	A. W. Palmer.
"	Methodist	...	...	...	...	
"	Baptist	...	...	...	...	Rev. W. H. Batson.
Fairville	Presbyterian	...	...	...	...	Rev. S. Nelson.
Far Rockaway, L.I.	Presbyterian	5	...	5	1	Margarita E. Schmuch.
Farmer's Village	Baptist	34	18	34	...	L. M. Rappleye.
Fayetteville	Baptist	87	6	81	0	Mrs. F. P. Carr.
Fishkill-on-Hudson	Dutch Reformed	42	10	42	...	May L. Crafts.
Flatbush, L. I.	Dutch Reformed	11	7	11	...	F. R. Bocock.
Fleming	Methodist	11	...	9	...	W. E. Mosher.
Flushing	Reformed	20	34	23	3	Eliza P. Cobb, 234 Amity st.
"	First Congregational	77	11	54	1	Isabelle Dykes, 176 Amity st.
"	First Baptist	36	11	32	...	C. A. Rhodes, Jamaica ave.
Fort Ann	Baptist	26	16	28	...	Mrs. J. D. Earle.
" Edward	Presbyterian	81	10	70	10	Mrs. S. W. McCoy.
" Plain	Reformed	38	70	73	9	Clarence Vosburgh, Upper Canal st.
" "	Methodist	...	...	...	...	
Fowlerville	Presbyterian	...	...	...	...	D. D. Sinclair.
Franklinville	Baptist	18	1	18	1	Mrs. Irene Bowen, McClouth ave.
"	First Presbyterian	...	...	...	...	Belle Kingsley.
"	Methodist	...	...	...	...	Rev. J. V. Lowell.
"	Presbyterian	31	7	29	16	Lizzie I. Wells (Mattituck, N. Y.).
Fredonia	First Presbyterian	52	9	...	...	Annie M. Tremaine.
Freeman	Presbyterian	...	...	...	...	Ogden Daly.
Freeport	Presbyterian	28	27	27	9	Mrs. A. F. Grafing, Box 102.
Friendship	First Baptist	32	1	32	...	Ella Miner.
Fulton	Methodist	72	23	75	29	E. E. Morrill.
"	Baptist	...	...	...	...	L. L. Green.
"	Presbyterian	41	39	53	...	
Fultonville	Reformed	23	13	22	4	Emma Craig.
Gaines	Congregational	29	77	24	2	C. H. Ross.
"	Baptist	...	...	...	...	Rev. A. C. Osborn.
Galway Village	Presbyterian	...	...	...	...	Hattie M. Helling.
Garrettsville	Baptist	...	...	...	...	Miss Ellenwood.
Gasport	Congregational	27	11	13	5	M. F. Mudge.
"	Christian	...	...	...	...	Rev. F. E. Marble.
Gifford		...	...	...	...	J. K. Rhinehart.
Genoa	Second Presbyterian	10	16	10	...	Estella Young.
Geneseo	Presbyterian	100	5	95	4	John Lincoln.
"	Baptist	...	...	...	...	
"	Methodist	...	...	...	...	Rev. Loren Stiles.
Geneva	First Baptist	42	5	40	...	Alice Gates, 56 William st.
"	First Presbyterian	...	...	...	...	Rev. H. B. Stevenson.
"	North Presbyterian	...	...	...	...	Rev. Paul VanDyke.
Glen	Reformed	14	12	14	...	H. M. Leach, M. D.
" Cove		...	...	...	...	W. B. Robinson.
Glens Falls	Presbyterian	...	...	...	...	
Glenville	Reformed	47	14	51	9	Jane DeGroot.
"	Dutch Reformed	...	...	...	...	Everett Groot.
Gloversville	Fremont St. Methodist	76	4	70	...	S. W. Fear, 25 Yale st.
"	Congregational	26	14	20	...	Hattie Hill.
Gorham		...	...	...	...	
Gouverneur	Methodist Episcopal	37	34	35	...	

NEW YORK. — (Continued.)

CITY.	CHURCH.	Act. Memb.	Asso. Memb.	Ch. Memb.	United with C.	Secretary and Address.
Gouverneur	Presbyterian					Arthur T. Johnson.
Graham	United Presbyterian					W. T. Skinner.
Granville	Presbyterian					Rev. J. E. Stewart.
"	Baptist	20	2	19		Minnie Bulkley.
Great Bend	Baptist					Nellie Dodge.
Green Island	Presbyterian	14	2	13		Mary A. Eggleston.
Greenpoint, L.I.	{ Redemption / Reformed Episcopal }	15	1	15	2	Mrs. G. L. Aldrich, 665 Humboldt st.
"	Dutch Reformed					Maria F. Ogden.
"	Presbyterian	44	11	23		Ella Voorhees, 587 Leonard st.
Greenport	Presbyterian	53	3	49	5	Harriet D. Hallock.
"	First Baptist	42	8	42	2	Ella G. Webb.
Greenwich	Dutch Reformed	24	9	24	2	Jessie B. Angell.
"	Baptist					Rev. Thos. Cull.
"	Presbyterian					
Groton	Congregational					Rev. W. A. Smith.
Guilderland						Webster Belden.
Guilford Centre	First Congregational	18		18		Augustus Hall.
Hamburg	Freewill Baptist	21	1	21		Amanda Michael.
Hamilton	Second Congregational	28		26	2	Chas. G. Simmons, Box 273.
"	Methodist					F. E. Arthur.
Hammond	Presbyterian	20	5	18		Maribel McGregor.
Hammondsport	Methodist	65	17	55	16	A. E. Chatten.
"	Presbyterian	30	34			Eloise S. Hobbs, 15 Vine st.
Hamlet	Baptist					Bessie Turner.
"	Methodist Episcopal	16	8	16		
Hannibal	Presbyterian	26	32	22	5	Amy Sykes.
" (Kinney's Corners)	Methodist	15	18	13		
Hannibal	Union	18	10	15		May Campbell.
Harlem	Mt. Morris Baptist					Chas. A. Strong, 158 E. 127th st.
Hartford	Baptist	74	44	06	31	A. J. Maynard.
"	Methodist	50	10	40	18	M. D. Atwood.
"	Presbyterian					
Havana	Presbyterian					E. G. Martin.
Herkimer	Reformed	45	15	45	26	E. Florence Cox.
"	Methodist					Dr. I. S. Bingham.
High Falls	Reformed	46	24	45	5	Debbie Snyder.
Holland Patent	Union					
Holley	Presbyterian	23	6	20	1	Sara Cook.
"	Baptist					Rev. A. D. Abrams.
Homer	Congregational					W. A. Robinson.
"	Baptist					Kate Chittenden.
"	Methodist	12	18			Alice White.
Honeoye	First Congregational	32	36	29	25	Alice Stevens.
" Falls						Rev. S. A. Freeman.
Hoosac "	Presbyterian					
Hornellsville	Park Methodist	94	5	92	15	Emma Santee.
"	Baptist					Rev. Mr. Whittaker.
"	Presbyterian					Wm. Walbridge.
Hulburton	Methodist					Rev. M. Maryott.
Hudson	Reform	66	10	66		Eva D. L. Macy, 63 No. 5th st.
"						L. A. Van Deusen, Jr., 7 No. 7th st.
"	Baptist					Rev. I. M. Bruce.
Huntington	First Presbyterian	42	15	49		Charlotte E. Lee.
"	Second Presbyterian					Jennie P. Woodend.
Ilion	First Baptist	57	21	58	5	Harry Hall.
"	First Presbyterian					J. C. Suits.
"	Methodist					
Ithaca	Methodist	46	3	44	8	Cornelia Williams, 53 Pleasant st.
"	First Congregational	28	1	3	1	R. B. Felton, Cornell Univ.
"	First Baptist	55	5	55	12	Nettie Thompson, 36 W. Buffalo st.
"	First Presbyterian					Rev. Mr. Fiske.

NEW YORK. — (Continued.)

CITY.	CHURCH.	Act. Memb.	Asso. Memb.	Ch. Memb.	United with C.	Secretary and Address.
Ithaca	Park Baptist	60	5	60	....	Rev. Mr. Janes.
Jamaica	Woodhaven Cong.	12	8	12	....	Frances E. Kirchmer.
Jamesport, L. I.	Congregational	11	....	6	....	Dora Albertson.
Jamestown	First Presbyterian	110	26	71	20	S. Winsor Baker, 503 E. 2d st.
"	First Congregational	32	1	18	....	W. B. Pitts, Prospect st.
Jeddo	Chapel Baptist	20	10	11	2	Anna M. Hall.
Johnsonville	Methodist	....	....	....	....	Anna M. Agan.
"	Presbyterian	....	....	....	....	Florence E. McRay.
Jonesville	Methodist	28	17	34	....	C. F. Burdick.
Jordan	Baptist	34	9	32	....	Ada L. Roger.
"	Presbyterian	....	....	....	....	Rev. Mr. Yergin.
Junius	Presbyterian	27	17	25	2	Clara Haight.
Keysville	First Baptist	33	18	35	5	J. A. Baber.
"	Congregational	....	....	....	....	Rev. A. C. Bishop.
Kinderhook	Reformed	....	....	....	....	Rev. E. I. Collier.
Kingston	Fair St. Reformed	....	....	....	....	Rev. S. D. Noyes.
"	First Baptist	35	18	42	....	Edward Snyder, Henry st.
Kirkland	Presbyterian	10	2	10	1	Matie French.
Knoxboro	Presbyterian	35	4	34	1	Ella B. Tubbs.
Knowlesville	Union	....	....	....	....	Rev. H. H. Thomas.
"	Baptist	....	....	....	....	L. R. Holroyd.
Kortright	Un. Presbyterian	7	1	7	....	Eva Sexsmith.
Kyserite		....	....	....	....	Grant Young.
Lake Geneva	First Congregational	18	2	12	4	Sarah L. E. Belcher.
" Mahopac	Methodist	....	....	....	....	Rev. Mr. Dutcher.
Lansingburg	First Presbyterian	65	36	62	5	J. E. Sipperly, 864 3d ave.
"	Olivet Chapel	....	....	....	....	James Lilley, 648 5th ave.
Lebanon Springs	Congregational	....	....	....	....	
Leroy	First Baptist	....	....	....	....	F. Glen Kenny.
Lima	Presbyterian	50	5	46	4	Mrs. H. H. Thompson.
Lisbon Centre	First Congregational	....	....	....	....	J. T. Stocking.
Lisle						
Livonia	Presbyterian	23	4	23	....	Ada Gibbs.
Little Falls	First Baptist	59	4	52	17	Mrs. A. C. Wheaton.
" "	Methodist	....	....	....	....	Rev. Samuel Call.
Little Valley	Congregational	....	....	....	....	H. G. Hall.
Liverpool	Union	20	27	20	2	Jessie McCord, Second st.
Locke	First Methodist	....	....	....	....	Rev. R. C. Herrick.
Lockport	First Congregational	40	107	....	....	Alice E. Crocker, 85 Walnut st.
"	First Presbyterian	....	....	....	....	
"	Methodist	....	....	....	....	
Lodi	Dutch Reformed	....	....	....	....	Judith Lott.
Long Island City	East Ave. Baptist	35	28	....	6	Alfred M. New, 44 East ave.
Lyons	Presbyterian	53	....	53	6	Mabel Hubbard.
Lyndonville	Presbyterian	32	21	24	2	E. C. Hard.
"	Baptist	....	....	....	....	Rev. F. Holt.
Lysander	Congregational	75	21	75	....	J. B. Gillette.
Madison	Baptist	....	....	....	....	A. R. Vose.
"	Methodist	....	....	....	....	
Mahopac Falls	Baptist	48	3	46	....	Emma J. Barrett.
" "	Presbyterian	....	....	....	....	Rev. Mr. Miller.
Maine		21	2	18	3	Fannie Dayton.
Malone	Congregational	....	....	....	....	J. H. King.
Manlius	Union	15	11	....	....	Mabel E. Candee.
Marathon	Baptist	....	....	....	....	Alice Norton.
"	Presbyterian	....	....	....	....	
Marcellus	Presbyterian	16	2	17	....	Mrs. G. A. DeCoudres.
Marbletown	Dutch Reformed	30	3	30	....	Deborah Smyth, High Falls.
Marlboro	Presbyterian	....	....	....	....	Rev. C. E. Bronson.
Martinsburg	Presbyterian	....	....	....	....	Anne Callahan.
Matteawan	First Presbyterian	24	2	21	8	Zenobia Porter.
McGrawville	Presbyterian	91	30	73	30	Fannie L. VanBuskirk, Box 395.
"	Baptist	34	3	25	1	S. H. White.
"	Methodist	....	....	....	....	Rev. A. C. Smith.
Mechanicville	First Baptist	49	33	43	17	Minnie Scolay.

NEW YORK.—(*Continued.*)

CITY.	CHURCH.	Act. Memb.	Asso. Memb.	Ch. Memb.	United with C.	Secretary and Address.
Mechanicville	Presbyterian	36	53	....	1	Rev. M. E. Hedding.
"	Methodist	....	....	....	....	Rev. Mr. Rulison.
Medina	Methodist	63	20	54	18	Kate L. Tucker, West st.
"	Baptist	....	....	....	....	
"	Presbyterian	50	20	....	....	Nettie M. Hubbard.
Melrose	Presbyterian	....	....	....	....	Rev. J. M. A. Denmar.
Meridian	First Presbyterian	25	27	18	....	Carrie J. Guppy.
"	First Baptist	25	19	24	5	M. E. Horigan.
"	Presbyterian	....	....	....	....	Julia Lawrence.
Mexico	First Presbyterian	39	15	37	1	Arthur Becker, Box 92. [Wash.
"	First Methodist	61	39	61	26	Mrs. D. H. Walton, cor. Main and
Middletown	Congregational	28	39	39	6	Alice B. Clark, 3 Spring st.
"	First Presbyterian	....	....	....	....	Helen M. Dorrance.
"	Second Presbyterian	....	....	....	....	Kate Harris.
"	Baptist	....	....	....	....	Rev. C. J. Page.
Milton	Presbyterian	13	2	13	....	Annie Clark.
Millville	Congregational	18	5	6	....	Oren Wyman.
"	Congregational	35	12	....	....	Robt. L. Ritchie.
Millport	Methodist	19	2	19	....	Harry B. Allen.
"		....	....	....	....	Rev. J. R. Drake.
Millbrook	Reformed	....	....	....	....	W. R. Anderson.
Millertown	Methodist	....	....	....	....	K. E. E. Munson.
Moravia	First Baptist	31	16	23	....	Alice Morton.
"	Congregational	....	....	....	....	May Murrow.
Morristown	Presbyterian	....	....	....	....	Rev. T. Lobbin.
"	First Congregational	22	3	20	....	Warren R. Moore.
Mt. Sinai	Congregational	....	....	....	....	Rev. E. A. Hazeltine.
Mt. Morris	First Presbyterian	....	....	....	....	Hattie L. Forest, Box 4258.
Mt. Vernon	Reformed	32	2	38	....	Mrs. C. K. Clearwater.
"	Baptist	....	....	....	....	Rev. F. M. Caldwell, D. D.
"	First Presbyterian	....	....	....	....	Rev. C. S. Lane.
Mt. Kisco		....	....	....	....	Lottie Hitchcock.
Mt. Upton	Baptist	....	....	....	....	Mrs. W. C. King.
Munnsville	Presbyterian	....	....	....	....	
"	First Congregational	21	16	14	....	O. A. Moore.
Murray	Free Baptist	31	26	20	....	Rev. H. Whitcher.
Navarino	Baptist	10	5	10	....	Mrs. Alice Haskins.
Newark	Presbyterian	53	4	39	13	Anna M. Blackmar.
"	First Baptist	12	1	10	....	Mary F. Fiske.
Newark Valley	First Congregational	70	5	69	35	Lilian Loveland, Whig st.
" "	First Methodist	....	....	....	....	Hallie Butler.
New Berlin	Presbyterian	32	7	28	3	Mrs. B. L. Card.
Newburgh	Calvary Presbyterian	42	7	42	1	Arabelle Chapman, 53 Chambers st.
"	United Presbyterian	67	....	....	....	Rev. F. B. Savage.
"	American Reformed	....	....	....	....	Nora B. Lowe, 147 Chambers st.
Newfield	Presbyterian	12	....	4	....	F. B. Hinds.
Newtown, L.I.	Presbyterian	22	10	25	3	Mrs. G. H. Payson.
" " (So. Bushwick)	Reformed	22	....	22	....	Rev. G. Hulst.
Newtown, L.I.	Reformed	....	....	....	....	Frederick Sicht, 22 J st., N. Y. City.
" "	Methodist	....	....	....	....	
New Berlin	Presbyterian	32	7	28	3	Mrs. B. L. Card.
" "	Methodist	....	....	....	....	Rev. W. Frisbie.
New Hartford	Presbyterian	59	37	69	9	Cecilia A. Sherrill.
" "	Baptist	....	....	....	....	Miss. P. J. Hutchinson.
" "	Methodist	....	....	....	....	M. D. Atwood.
New Haven	Methodist	40	10	....	....	George Tremaine (Dempster).
" "	Congregational	....	....	....	....	George Hale.
New Hurley	Reformed	....	....	....	....	M. C. Walker.
New Lebanon	Congregational	20	17	17	....	Lilian Potter.
New Paltz	Reformed	....	....	....	....	George Griffith.
New Rochelle	Presbyterian	53	14	....	8	Dr. R. C. Eddy.
" "	Methodist	....	....	....	....	
" "	Presbyterian	31	13	....	....	S. K. Phraner.

lviii   LIST OF SOCIETIES

NEW YORK. — (*Continued.*)

CITY.	CHURCH.	Act. Memb.	Asso. Memb.	Ch. Memb.	United with C.	Secretary and Address.
New York City	4th Germ. Ref.					Rev. J. H. Oerter, D. D.
" "	Mott Ave. Methodist	21	4	21		M. Jennie Rush.
" "	Second Presbyterian					
" "	Gospel Chapel					Peter Bruce.
" "	4th Ave. Presbyterian					C. F. Cutler.
" "	Tremont Baptist					Paul Brewer (Tremont).
" "	St. Paul's Reform					Geo. V. Ord, 625 E. 145th st.
" "	Bethany Cong.					Henry Plohr, 425 W. 36. [ham Road.
" "	Fordham Reform					M. B. Bussing, King's Bridge, Ford-
" "						Augustus V. Neely, 406 W. 24th st.
" "	Baptist					Rev. J. F. Elder, 49 E. 59th st.
" "	Clinton Ave.	67	10			C. E. Little, 59 Fulton st.
" "	Univ. Place Pres.					Rev. Geo. Alexander, Hotel Albert.
" "	Presbyterian					Sadie Scott, 180 E. 109th st.
" "	McDougall St. Bapt.	74	33	62		T. Munger, 48 Van Dam st.
" "	Ch. of the Saviour. } Methodist }	45		20		John S. Guest, { Wm. Boulevard, and 111th st.
" "	Grace Chapel Pres.	34	10	34		H. Jollenbeck, 407 1st ave.
" "	Tremont Baptist	19	3	19		Paul Bremer.
" "	Cent'y Presbyterian	49	1	46	2	C. W. Wheelock, 934 8th ave.
" "	(Mt. Morris) Baptist	56	9	56	4	Anna Smith, 264 Lenox ave.
" "	Ch. of the Strangers } Indep'd'nt Christian }	58	3	58		Chas. Ghetsch, 59 E. 8th st.
" "	14th St. Presbyterian	35	4	35	8	Sadie E. Naylor, 218 E. 15th st.
" "	Cornell Mem. Meth.	36	1			Miss A. N. Mills, 1181 3d ave.
" "	Ch. of Epiphany Bapt.	42	20	38		P. E. Cummings, 1 W. 27th st.
" "	Ch. of Redeemer Bapt.	27	10	29	10	Alice T. Shepard, 132 W. 126th st.
" "	First Un. Presbyterian	65	1			Miss A. E. Gunnell, 1809 2d ave.
" "	Wash. Heights Pres.	29	3			Rev. J. C. Bliss (Wash. Heights).
" "	13th St. Presbyterian	79	2			Lillie Dudley, 140 W. 11th st.
" "	Calvary Presbyterian	46		40		Lottie Lounsbury, 246 E. 111 st.
" "	(Tremont) First Pres.	16	12			H. Shelland (Tremont).
" "	West Farms Pres.	29				Rev. C. P. Mallery.
" "	North Presbyterian	10	4			Miss N. Van Oordt, 368 W. 31st st.
" "	Park Presbyterian	57	7			Martha Kennedy, 308 W. 84th st.
" "	Carmel Baptist	27	25			Ada E. Sprowl, 309 E. 116th st.
" "	Grace Baptist	28	1			Miss E. E. Rodman, 122 E. 91st st.
" "	Ascension Baptist	10	1			Miss B. Eisle, 688 E. 160th st.
" "	First Reform	27	15			Miss E. L. Cole (Fordham).
" "	Bloomingdale Ref.	47	10			Miss C. C. Watson, 345 5th ave.
" "	Norfolk St. Reform	35				F. E. Erhadt, 127 Norfolk st.
" "	Tremont Cong.	7	3			Miss F. E. Smart, 1648 Bathgate ave.
" "	Central Methodist					Rev. C. S. Hanover.
" "	Union	20	27	20		Jessie McCord, 2d st.
" "	E. Harlem Presbyterian	18		15		Miss Scott, 180 E. 109th st.
" "	23d St. Baptist	63	10	71		J. G. Robertson, 218 E. 28th st.
" "	German Presbyterian	12	6	16		G. C. Loeser, 209 E. 28th st.
" "	First Presbyterian	34	27	47		Hattie L. Forest, Box 258.
" "	7th Ave. U. P.	22	6	28		James Allen, 335 W. 12th st.
" "	East Side Chapel Union					Lizzie Glick. [Oneida.
" Mills	Methodist	33	37	34	20	W. J. Hepworth, 400 Main st.,
" "	Presbyterian					Rev. H. P. McAdam.
Niagara Falls	Baptist	21	7	22		Annie E. Simmons.
" "	First Presbyterian	32	22	32		Annie H. Sims.
North Arygle	Presbyterian					
Northampton	Presbyterian	9	4	8		Hattie Hinkley.
North Hebron	Baptist	15	9	15		Mary L. Braymer.
" Hector	Baptist	60	32	53	12	Maggie E. Swarthaut.
" "	Baptist					T. A. Hughes.
" Parma	Free Baptist	34	25	34		Jennie C. Fuller.
" "	First Methodist	30	4	28	15	W. J. Hawkins, Box 62.
" "	First Baptist					Ira Johnson.
" Ridge						
" Stockholm	Methodist	39	42	27		Gertie Knapp.
" Upton						Mrs. W. C. King.

NEW YORK.—(Continued.)

CITY.	CHURCH.	Act. Memb.	Asso. Memb.	Ch. Memb.	United with C.	Secretary and Address.
Northville	Baptist	15	1	9	3	G. L. Michaels.
Norwich	First Baptist	22	3	22	....	Laura S. Pratt, 15 Gold st.
"	Free Baptist	19	1	18	....	
"	Congregational	56	5	54	....	Agnes McCord.
Norwood	Congregational	34	35	33	2	W. D. Fuller.
"	First Methodist	....	....	....	....	Emma LaFontaine.
Nyack	First Reformed	53	7	55	1	Irving Hopper.
"	First Baptist	73	5	73	3	Sue C. Blauvelt, 30 Broadway.
Oak Hill	Methodist	30	....	....	....	F. T. Kenyon.
Ogden	Baptist	24	....	24	1	H. M. Hill.
"	Presbyterian	50	17	....	....	Rev. A. S. Hoyt.
Ogdensburg	First Congregational	....	....	....	....	Libbie McBane.
"	Baptist	....	....	....	....	A. Goodenough.
Ogden Centre	Presbyterian	....	....	....	....	
Olean	First Presbyterian	18	10	18	....	Rev. John Burrows, D. D.
"	First Baptist	11	13	....	....	Emma Ramsey, 11 Henry st.
Oneida	First Presbyterian	150	33	140	7	Wm. N. Baker, 73 Broad st.
"	Baptist	86	26	4	....	Hattie S. Coe, 35 Broad st.
"	First Methodist	81	16	76	....	J. P. Wildes, 74 Mulberry st.
" Castle	Presbyterian	....	....	....	....	Rev. A. S. Bacon.
Oneonta	Baptist	20	....	20	....	A. B. Costo.
"	Free Baptist	....	....	....	....	C. W. Wilson, 235 Main st. [cuse.
Onondaga	Methodist	69	17	....	....	Ada Andrews, 12 W. Castle st., Syra-
Orangeport	Christian	....	....	....	....	Mrs. Horace Sibley.
Orchard Park	Presbyterian	....	....	....	....	Rev. E. P. Robinson.
Oriskany Falls	Presbyterian	....	....	....	....	
Oswego, S. W.	Baptist	30	5	25	....	Lucy Hill.
" West	Baptist	118	19	118	15	W. L. Murdock, 225 Duer st.
"	Grace Presbyterian	....	....	....	....	U. Z. Maltby.
"	First Presbyterian	53	37	53	....	Mrs. J. H. Norris, 89 W. Seneca st.
"	First Baptist	....	....	....	....	Rev. W. H. Palmer.
"	First Methodist	....	....	....	....	R. W. Southurst.
"	Trinity Methodist	....	....	....	....	Rev. T. P. Shepard.
"	Free Methodist	....	....	....	....	Rev. Mr. Gibens.
"	Congregational	27	3	....	....	Morris Wall.
" Town	First Congregational	7	7	7	....	Hattie A. Brewster, Oswego Centre.
Otto	First Congregational	7	5	7	....	E. M. Pool.
Ovid	Presbyterian	36	38	43	5	Mrs. Seymour Wharton.
Oxford	Baptist	38	7	38	....	Hattie C. Jacobs.
"	Congregational	....	....	....	....	
Palatine Bridge	....	....	....	....	....	
Painted Post	Presbyterian	....	....	....	....	Minnie Burnett.
Palmyra	Presbyterian	75	28	65	....	Martha E. Root.
"	Baptist	....	....	....	....	Minnie Schofield.
Panama	....	....	....	....	....	Myrtle Cone.
Paris	Congregational	13	....	12	3	Nora Town, Sauquoit.
" Hill	Bethany	....	....	....	....	Lincoln Davis.
" "	Presbyterian	....	....	....	....	Rev. Mr. Mather.
Parishville	Methodist	39	12	49	....	Mrs. Chas. Green.
Palmer	Baptist	....	....	....	....	
Pattersonville	Reformed	....	....	....	....	Rev. E. Lowe.
Patchogue, L. I.	Congregational	28	....	20	....	Geo. E. Rowe, Box 61.
Penfield	School Dist. No. 9	27	....	27	....	W. H. Raymond.
Pennellsville	Union	....	....	....	....	Fred B. Foster.
Penn Yan	Presbyterian	....	....	....	....	C. P. St. John, Drawer 85.
" "	Baptist	....	....	....	....	Nettie Brown.
" "	First Methodist	37	17	34	3	Gertie Barden, Canal st.
Peekskill	Reformed	....	....	....	....	Eleanor Leavens.
Peterboro	Methodist Episcopal	....	....	....	....	Chas. P. McCurley.
Phelps	Baptist	....	....	....	....	
"	Methodist	60	5	60	....	Myron R. Boardman.
Philadelphia	Congregational	....	....	....	....	Rev. A. S. Wood.
Phœnicia	Methodist Episcopal	....	....	....	....	
Phœnix	Congregational	....	....	....	....	J. H. Buckley.
Perry	First Baptist	....	....	....	....	A. L. Aime.

NEW YORK. — (Continued.)

CITY.	CHURCH.	Act. Memb.	Asso. Memb.	Ch. Memb.	United with C.	Secretary and Address.
Pine Bush	Un. Presbyterian	16	3	16	....	Mrs. A. R. Armstrong.
Pine Plains	Methodist	22	7	22	....	G. Q. Johnson,
Piermont	Dutch Reformed	28	8	28	6	Venie R. Wood.
Plattsburg	Methodist	....	....	....	....	O. M. Tennant.
"	Baptist	17	13	18	....	E. L. Smith, 8 Lorraine st.
Pleasant Hill						
Pleasant Valley	Methodist	10	15	10	....	Mrs. W. A. Dalton.
Port Byron	Baptist	13	20	15	....	Lulu B. Hayden.
" "	Presbyterian	26	10	26	3	C. R. Hadden.
Port Chester	Baptist	....	....	....	....	Thos. Kirkland.
Port Jackson	Reformed	....	....	....	....	Elida A. Beebe.
Port Dickinson	Baptist	....	....	....	....	G. W. Adams.
Port Jervis	Hedding Baptist	23	4	23	....	C. G. Lockwood.
Port Leyden	Congregational	36	....	15	....	Rev. L. Williams.
Port Richmond	....	....	....	....	....	E. Bollger, Box 121.
Potsdam	Presbyterian	....	....	....	....	Mary E. Brown, 56 Main st.
Poughkeepsie	Second Reformed	45	24	45	....	Miss B. Van Vliet, 20 Conklin st.
"	Baptist	85	46	120	5	J. F. Lovejoy, 20 Noxon st.
"	First Baptist	....	....	....	....	E. G. Dean.
"	Presbyterian	....	....	....	....	F. J. Boyd.
"	Friends	75	2	9	2	Lavinia Cooley, 51 Carroll st.
"	Carmen St. Methodist	....	....	....	....	A. C. Lackey.
"	Hedding Methodist	35	5	25	....	Emma Buys.
"	First Methodist	....	....	....	....	A. B. Rockwell.
"	Congregational	....	....	....	....	Jennie A. Burgher.
"	Zion's Methodist	....	....	....	....	
Poultney	Union	6	11	....	....	Calvin McKinney.
Prattsburg	Union					
"	First Presbyterian	52	18	27	....	Mary Waldo.
Princeton'	Reformed	....	....	....	....	Rev. S. K. Rhinehart.
Prospect	Baptist					
Pulaski	Baptist	20	5	15	....	Rev. D. D. Owen.
"	Congregational	37	....	14	1	L. Grace Henderson.
Randolph	Congregational	25	37	15	....	Cary B. Rogers.
Rensselaer Falls	Congregational	24	13	22	....	May Chapman.
Richford	First Congregational	....	....	....	....	
Richville	Congregational	....	....	....	....	Willis B. Hendrick.
Ripley	Presbyterian	....	....	....	....	Rev. W. C. Macbeth.
River Head	Congregational	12	13	....	1	Ernest W. Tooker.
Rochester	Central Presbyterian	62	125	....	10	Alice Sutherland.
"	Brick Presbyterian	59	49	....	....	M. A. Sontag, 20 Upton Park.
"	Presbyterian	28	40	57	3	E. M. Walbridge, So. Fitzhugh st.
"	Calvary Presbyterian	17	9	24	4	Miss E. St. Jermain, 21 Hamilton pl.
"	Cornhill Methodist	60	24	70	....	Mary Pepper, 24 Mansion st.
"	So. Congregational	32	23	43	19	R. A. Ruddick, 23 E. Main st.
"	Second Baptist	72	21	79	10	Ada S. Terry, 59 Rowley st.
"	Westminster Pres	44	57	80	8	W. B. Gates, 15 St. Clair st.
"	North Presbyterian	25	54	63	11	Mrs. C. E. Colby, 112 Fulton ave.
"	Plymouth Ave. Baptist	....	....	....	....	
"	Alexander St. Methodist	....	....	....	....	
"	First Universalist	....	....	....	....	
"	Second Universalist	....	....	....	....	Rev. L. B. Fisher.
"	First Ch. of Christ	....	....	....	....	A. S. Burrows, 472 Exchange st.
"	North Congregational	....	....	....	....	Mrs. C. E. Colby, 112 Fulton ave.
"	Auburn Methodist	....	....	....	....	G. H. Jones.
"	Park Baptist	....	....	....	....	
"	Sommerfield Meth	....	....	....	....	Andrew Burns, Box 255.
"	St. Peter's	....	....	....	....	Katharine Lewis.
"	First Presbyterian	43	59	97	....	John C. Schroeder, 135 North ave.
Rockland	Methodist	19	6	17	3	John Albee.
"	....	....	....	....	....	Mrs. Temperance Gray.
Rockville Centre	Baptist	....	....	....	....	D. M. Bulson, M.D.
Rodman	Congregational	....	....	....	....	Rev. J. H. Griffith.
Round Lake	Methodist	15	3	15	9	Jessie A. Rose.
Romulus	First Presbyterian	23	5	26	....	Emma G. Updike.

NEW YORK.—(Continued.)

CITY.	CHURCH.	Act. Memb.	Asso. Memb.	Ch. Memb.	United with C.	Secretary and Address.
Rondout	Presbyterian					Rev. I. Mayer.
"	Wirt St. Methodist					T. Lamont.
"	First Baptist	54	2	55	8	Fred. Coy Kendall.
Royalton	Christian	23	10	22	10	Clara A. Weaver (Hartland).
Roscoe	(Rockland) 2d Pres	13	7	8		Mrs. Alice Seeley.
Rome	Baptist					
Sackett's Harbor	Presbyterian					Rev. L. R. Webber.
Salamanca	First Congregational	22	28	18	2	Maggie E. Hagadoon, 29 Maple st.
"	Baptist					Rev. R. H. Colby.
Salt Point	Presbyterian					
Sandy Hill	Baptist	40	16	40	2	Florence E. Dearstyne.
"	Presbyterian					Rev. C. D. Kellogg.
Saratoga Springs	First Methodist	81	52	117		Clarence S. Curtis, 77 Beekman st.
" "	First Presbyterian	47	20	47	6	Jessie L. Starr, 587 Broadway.
" "	N. E. Congregational	27	25	27	3	Lizzie G. Holmes, 107 Lawrence st.
" "	Second Presbyterian	45	23	40		Rev. W. R. Territt.
" "	First Baptist	50	30	50		J. V. Porter.
" "	North					
" "	Second Baptist	23	8			Hattie Brown.
" "		33	3	30		Louisa McLean, Circular st.
Sauquoit	Congregational					
"	Presbyterian	19	19	15		E. B. Mould.
Sayville	Congregational	74	36	67		A. R. Comstock.
Schaghticoke	Presbyterian	50	15	41	2	Addie A. Masters.
Schenectady	First Reformed	36	31	40	10	Ella McNee, 18 No. Church st.
"	Missionary Presbyterian					Robert Clemens, 512 Hamilton st.
"	First Baptist	38	3	38	8	Minnie Coffin, 206 Clinton st.
"	Park Pl. Presbyterian	40	10	40	20	R. H. Clemens, 512 Hamilton st.
"	East Ave. Presbyterian					Rev. Mr. Paxton.
"	Second Reformed					C. A. Rowe, Box 1057.
"	Congregational					Rev. Mr. Munsell.
"	Baptist	18	3	18		Cora F. Ketchum, 628 Hamilton st.
"	Union Presbyterian					J. E. Winnee.
Schodack Landing	Reformed					Sadie Martin.
Schuylerville	Reformed					Emma Jaquith.
Scipio	Baptist	34	9	30	21	Ada Lappeus.
Scott	Seventh Day Baptist	12	7	13	3	R. A. Clark
Scottsville	Presbyterian	45	31	47	5	Nellie Moon.
"						
Seneca Falls	First Congregational	32	26	27		H. DeLancey Knight, 92 State st.
" "	First Methodist	84	18	77		Samuel Kibbe, 110 State st.
" "	Presbyterian					L. H. Moray.
" "	First Presbyterian					Will Cole.
" "	Baptist	19	8	11		H. M. Lowe, 64 Bayard st.
Sennett	Baptist					Rev. Mr. Simmons.
Shortville	Presbyterian	40	13	31	7	Sarah L. Sheldon.
"	Presbyterian					Thos. Melvin, Jr.
Shushan	Union Presbyterian					G. N. Foster.
Sherburn	Baptist	40	7	35		Kittie Purdy.
" Four Corners	Union					
Skaneateles	Methodist	45	2	44		Minnie E. White, W. Genesee st.
"	Presbyterian	53	9	49	2	Mrs. Agnes G. Clark.
"	Congregational					
Smithtown	Presbyterian	35	13	32	5	Nellie N. Hunting (Smithtown Br.).
" Branch	Presbyterian	23	16	21		Annie W. Edwards.
Smyrna	Union	44	40			C. H. Hunt, Box 19.
Sodus	Presbyterian					May E. Danford.
Sodus Village	Presbyterian	38	23	38	8	F. L. Allen.
Southampton	So. Presbyterian					Rev. Walter Condict.
"	First Presbyterian	57		48		H. T. Thalsey.
Southport	Presbyterian	21	16	23	2	Mattie E. Miner.
So. Amsterdam	Reformed					Rev. J. Kyle.
"						Alida E. Beebe. [Ridge
So. Brooklyn	Reformed	32	5	31	4	Sarah A. Moore, Ovington Ave., Bay
So. Hartford	Congregational	17	21	23		Jennie M. Sweet.

LIST OF SOCIETIES

NEW YORK.—(Continued.)

CITY.	CHURCH.	Act. Memb.	Asso. Memb.	Ch. Memb.	United with C.	Secretary and Address.
So. Kortright	Union Presbyterian					Rev. F. B. Murch.
So. West Oswego	Baptist	45	9	32		Lucy L. Hill.
" "	Congregational					
South Wales	Presbyterian	12	4	12		G. J. Miller.
Spawangunk (New Hurley)	Reformed	44	46	42	23	Fannie R. Gale (Walkill).
Spencer	Methodist	27	1	25	12	Julia Moody.
"	Baptist	47	8	44	25	Lena Sager.
"	Presbyterian	26	10	28	10	Jennie Pray.
Spencerport	Presbyterian	49	32	57	14	John Kincaid.
"	White Ch. Cong.	56	40			Celia M. Day.
Sprakers	Presbyterian					Rev. J. A. Thomson.
Springville	Freewill Baptist	18	5	66	4	Etta A. Reynolds.
Stamfordville						
"	Christian	12	15	5		Minnie Bowman.
Stephentown	Presbyterian	18	5	17	4	Clara L. Cranston.
"	Calvary Baptist					Rev. H. W. Millington.
Sterling	United Presbyterian					Rev. Mr. Little.
Sterling Valley	Union	37	1	34	6	Grace E. Crosman.
Stillwater	Presbyterian	23	3	18	1	Louise J. Van De Mark.
"	First Presbyterian	30		30		Mary F. Tucker.
"	Baptist					Mollie E. Newland.
Stockbridge	Methodist					Rev. Mr. Williams.
Summer Hill	Congregational	32	8	26	2	Judson Van Martin.
Syracuse	Park Centre Pres.	75	62	125	11	Mrs. A. B. Chapman, 104 Hawley st.
"	Baptist	113	56	104	16	Mrs. Irving Holwell, 31 Kellogg st.
"	Emmanuel Baptist	35	20	36	7	Della Martin, 19 Gertrude st.
"	Westminster Pres.	41	21	41	8	Rev. A. E. Myers, 14 Highland pl.
"	Central Baptist	179	19	179		Elsie Schenck, 8 Holland st.
"	Memorial Presbyterian	47	14	40	12	Ella L. Kemp, 135 Almond st.
"	Fourth Presbyterian					Wm. A. Rice.
"	First Presbyterian					Grace W. Leslie.
"	Centenary Methodist	76	2	71	15	Carrie J. Thurston, 13 South ave.
"	First Baptist					Rev. H. M. Sherwood.
"	Goodwill Cong.	57	14	51	7	Bertha R. Markell, 9 Holland st.
"	Missionary Pres.	41	19			Ella Kemp, 135 Almond st.
"	First Ward Methodist.					
"	Freeman St. Methodist.	38	10			Jennie Webber.
"	Danford Congregational					Rev. D. F. Harris.
"	Ger. Baptist	17	2	17		Rev. C. H. Schmidt, 112 Catharine st.
"	Scattergood Pres.	38	21	27		Rev. A. E. Mayers, 617 Chestnut st.
"	So. Onondaga St. U. P.					Cora Ackley.
Tarrytown		74	26		21	J. A. Perrin, Box 310.
Thomson Ridge	Hopewell Pres.	23	18	22	9	Mrs. Alex. Thomson.
Thorn Hill	Baptist	14	19	14		Addie Chapman.
Ticonderoga						Kate B. LeLane.
"	First Congregational	17	18	20	2	E. T. Downs, Main st.
Tomhannock	Union					I. M. Hunt.
Tonawanda	First Presbyterian	38	2	38	1	E. F. Wilson.
"	Baptist					Rev. R. Otto.
Troy	Ninth Presbyterian	136	45	170	18	Frank Stevenson, 6 Harrison pl.
"	First Presbyterian	51	6	31	11	Lena B. Plum, 107 First st.
"	Vail Ave. Baptist					Wm. Swartwort.
"	Univ	43	9			Miss C. W. Safford, 108 Fourth st.
"	Church of Christ					W. H. Munn.
"	Sixth Avenue Baptist					Rev. C. F. Hahm.
"	Vail Ave. Presbyterian					E. H. Neal, 790 River st.
Trumansburg	Presbyterian	40	5	38		
"	Methodist					Rev. A. M. Damon.
Ulster Park	Reformed Episcopal					Annie Ellsworth.
Union Centre	Dutch Reformed					Rev. H. B. Vandoren.
" Springs	Baptist	17	6	17	7	Leon H. Cameron.
" "	First Presbyterian	40	34	50	8	Lillian Curry.
" "	Methodist					Rev. S. S. Barta.
Upper Red Hook	Dutch Reformed					G. D. Lydecker.

OF CHRISTIAN ENDEAVOR. lxiii

NEW YORK.—(Continued.)

CITY.	CHURCH.	Act. Memb.	Asso. Memb.	Ch. Memb.	United with C.	Secretary and Address.
Utica	Olivet Presbyterian	35	9	30	18	Pearl A. Bowden, 7 Rutger st.
"	South St. Methodist	47	7	45	....	G. E. Fairhead, 55 Eagle st.
"	Memorial Presbyterian	45	18	37	4	Mrs. E. A. Broadbent, 240 Court st.
"	Tabernacle Baptist	52	7	52	....	Wellington Williams, 179 Genesee st.
"	Park Baptist	....	....	....	....	Dr. E. T. Corey.
"	Centenary Methodist	....	....	....	....	Etta Davis, Kossuth ave.
"	Bethany Presbyterian	67	2	67	2	Robert McGregor, Jr., 158 Mary st.
"	Bleeker St. Baptist	44	10	44	....	Sarah E. McGucken, 19 Lansing st.
Valatie	Presbyterian	37	27	40	....	G. S. Becker, Box 201.
Verbank Village						
Vernon	Mt. Vernon Pres.	16	5	15	5	Miss G. C. Langford.
"	Baptist	....	....	....	....	W. Brewster.
"	Union	16	10	12	....	A. W. Barrows (Community).
" Centre	First Presbyterian	21	21	22	....	Merritt Smith.
" "	Methodist	....	....	....	....	Rev. Mr. Stanford.
Verona	Presbyterian	44	15	39	5	W. L. Crandall.
"	Methodist	....	....	....	....	
Vischer's Ferry	Reformed	15	6	....	....	Mrs. Alice Losee.
Walden	Reformed	42	56	53	10	J. C. C. Graham, cor. Orchard and Pine sts.
"	Methodist	59	17	....	....	H. J. Jones.
Walkill		....	....	....	....	Fannie R. Gale.
Walworth	Methodist	....	....	....	....	
Wampsville						
Warner	Baptist	....	....	....	....	
Wassaic	Presbyterian	13	4	13	....	Mrs. J. H. Smith.
Warsaw	West Branch Pres.	17	9	17	1	Mrs. J. H. Smith.
"	Congregational	56	5	49	....	Frank Relyea.
Washington	Reformed	8	....	8	....	Wm. R. Anderson.
Waterford	First Baptist	....	....	....	....	Rev. W. H. Main.
"	Methodist	....	....	....	....	Ada VanNorden.
" "	First Presbyterian	53	2	47	26	Mary M. Schofield.
Waterloo	First Methodist	50	....	34	16	Alida VanDenburg.
"	First Presbyterian	51	60	67	7	Kittie R. Fatzinger.
Water Mills	Presbyterian	26	7	22	....	Jas. Corwith.
Watertown	Stone Street Pres.	60	25	59	11	G. G. Lee, 43 Franklin st.
"	Baptist	....	....	....	....	Rev. L. J. Dean.
"	Univ	31	6	23	7	G. I. Woolley, 7 Ten Eyck st.
"	Immanuel	95	....	....	....	A. C. Rice, 13 Hawthorne st.
Waterville	Baptist	30	2	30	....	Alfred Stafford.
"	Presbyterian	....	....	....	....	Belle Benedict.
Watkins	Presbyterian	44	12	43	....	Nora M. Frost.
"	Baptist	30	....	22	....	Cora Sherman.
Webster's Corners	Union	21	1	10	....	Kate A. Trevett.
Weedsport	Baptist	....	....	....	....	Mrs. Arthur Putnam.
Wellsville	First Baptist	42	28	42	....	Ida L. Schnabel, 8 Harrison st.
"	Congregational	....	....	....	....	Rev. F. W. Beecher.
Westfield	First Presbyterian	....	....	....	....	H. N. Thompson.
"	Methodist	27	12	27	7	Lydia M. Culver, No. Portage st.
"	Baptist	....	....	....	....	G. W. Sawin.
West Moreland	Congregational	....	....	....	....	J. P. Beckwith.
Westernville	Presbyterian	....	....	....	....	
West Greece	Congregational	26	....	1	....	Chas. Spear (South Greece).
West Henrietta	Baptist	30	....	20	....	Cora Sherman.
W. New Brighton, L. I.	Presbyterian	40	20	40	....	Hattie P. Sexton, Box 21.
West Portland	Baptist	....	....	41	....	Rev. Alfred Knight.
West Troy	First Presbyterian	36	7	32	....	Fannie Lansing, 919 24th st.
" "	Wash. Methodist	....	....	....	....	Rev. B. B. Loomis.
" "	German Presbyterian L.	....	....	....	....	John Kennedy.
West Webster	Union	....	....	....	....	Jerome Hart.
West Winfield	Congregational	37	11	35	2	A. B. Park.
"		....	....	....	....	Roxanna Banfay.
White Church	Presbyterian	....	....	....	....	Rev. J. L. Harrington.
Whitesboro	Baptist	....	....	....	....	

lxiv   LIST OF SOCIETIES

NEW YORK.— (*Continued.*)

CITY.	CHURCH.	Act. Memb.	Asso. Memb.	Ch. Memb.	United with C.	Secretary and Address.
Whitehall	First Presbyterian	37	6	31	2	Ella Bascom.
Whitelake						R. A. Blackford.
White Plains	Methodist	55		55	1	Harry Romer.
" "	Presbyterian					
" "	Memorial					Rev. A. D. Vail.
Whitney's Point	Union	36	3	15	4	Mary Woughton.
Wolcott	First Presbyterian	40	11	36	3	Ella Peck.
"	Methodist					Benj. Talcott.
Wood Haven	First Congregational	14	11	17		F. E. Kitchmer.
Woodside, L. I.	Union	37				Geo. Jones, Jr., Cameron Terrace.
Woodville	Congregational					Julia Clark.
Wynantskill	Dutch Reformed					Cora M. Wolf.
Yonkers	Reformed	71	5	71	9	E. R. Cole.
"	Baptist					
"	Westminster Presb					

NORTH CAROLINA.

CITY.	CHURCH.	Act. Memb.	Asso. Memb.	Ch. Memb.	United with C.	Secretary and Address.
Charlotte	Baptist	31	19	49		
Clinton	Presbyterian					Miss Florence L. Jacobs.
Henderson	Baptist	14		14		S. S. Porham.
Pleasant Grove	Missionary Baptist	10	1			I. Richardson.
Wilmington	Christ Church, Cong.	19	1	19		Alice M. Beach, 613 Main st.
Wilmington	Baptist					Rev. Mr. Prichard.

OHIO.

CITY.	CHURCH.	Act. Memb.	Asso. Memb.	Ch. Memb.	United with C.	Secretary and Address.
Akron	First Congregational					Dr. H. W. Pierson, 14 Arcade blk.
"	First Methodist Ep					Rev. Mr. Vincent.
"	Second Methodist Ep					Rev. Mr. Condir.
"	First Presbyterian					Rev. Mr. Chapin.
"	First Baptist	35	9	34		Lulu Abbott, 537 E. Middlebury st.
"	Amherst Methodist Ep					Henry Wright.
Andover	Union					Ruth Bogue.
Ashtabula	First Congregational	44	8	38	3	Anna Burnett.
" Harbor	Second Congregational					Lillian L. Brigham
Belden	Congregational	16	4	16		Rev. Rose Schwartz.
Bellefontaine	Presbyterian					
Bellevue	Evan	16	5	16		Sallie Bowers.
"	Methodist Episcopal					
"	Congregational					Dr. H. M. Hoyt.
Belpré	Congregational					
Berlin Heights	Union	40	18	35	12	Dorrie Stahl.
" "	First Congregational	19	14	20		Miss Ida M. Hill.
Big Plain	California Methodist Ep.	19	4	19		Ella Noland.
Blanchester	Grace Methodist Ep	19	9	21		Rev. A. E. Price.
Bloomfield	Methodist Episcopal	13	2	14		Nora Duncanson.
Bridgeport	Kirkwood Presbyterian	30	4	30		Icie Wilson.
Bristolville	Congregational	18	6	18	0	Mellie Maltby.
Brownhelm	Congregational					
Burton	Congregational					
California						
Canton	Baptist	85	18	85		Jessie Roberts, 81 So. Plume st.
Cardington	Methodist Episcopal	25		25		DeWitt Wolfe.
Carroll	Methodist Episcopal					Alice Newman.
Centre Belpré	Congregational					
Central College	Presbyterian	26	16	26	0	Hannah Lind.

OF CHRISTIAN ENDEAVOR. lxv

OHIO. — (*Continued.*)

CITY.	CHURCH.	Act. Memb.	Asso. Memb.	Ch. Memb.	United with C.	Secretary and Address.
Ceylon.............						C. S. Ruggles.
Chardon...........	Disciples.............	40	50	40	6	Miss Emma J. Smith.
"	Congregational......	....	....	....	....	Rev. T. D. Phillips.
Chatham						
Chatham Centre....	Methodist............	21	0	21	8	O. G. Hubbard.
" "	Congregational......	....	....	....	....	Irene D. Dyer.
Chevoit............	Bethel Baptist........	23	....	20	....	Amos S. Goble.
Cincinnati.........	Central Congregational.	29	1	29	....	Chas. Meininger, Jr., Box 263.
"	Welsh Congregational..	43	3	42	....	Mrs. Elizabeth E. Morris, 171 Vine st.
"	Walnut Hill Cong.....	....	....	....	....	W. S. Truax, 91 Pearl st.
"	Storrs Congregational ..	20	10	20	....	Lou C. Judd, 35 Storrs st.
" Columbia	Baptist..............	18	....	17	....	
"	Riverside............	....	....	....	....	
" Price Hill	Westminster Pres.....	17	13	25	....	Miss M. Wilder, Warsaw ave.
"	First Presbyterian.....	52	....	52	....	William F. Schnelle.
Cleveland.........	First Baptist..........	34	18	42	7	Frances A. Adams, 419 Liberty st.
"	Euclid Ave. Cong......	44	4	42	11	J. H. Bryant, 15 Brookfield st.
"	Beckwith Chapel Pres..	....	....	....	....	Rev. J. D. Williamson.
"	Madison Ave. Cong....	....	....	....	....	L. Golden, 9 Townsend st.
"	Jennings Ave. Cong....	....	....	....	....	Rev. J. M. Sturtevant, Jr.
"	Wilson Ave. Baptist...	....	....	....	....	Rev. J. H. Hartman. [ire st.
"	Euclid Ave. Disciple...	....	....	....	....	H. L. McGregor Norman, 46 Chesh-
"	South Side Cong.......	....	....	....	....	Rev. Dr. Leavitt.
"	Olivet Chapel Cong....	20	2	15	....	Frank Taylor, 3 Pittsburgh st.
"	Scranton Ave. Free Bap.	40	10	....	....	J. V. Hitchcock, 87 Euclid ave.
"	Euclid Ave. Baptist....	106	14	100	80	Will A. Osborn, 694 Euclid ave.
"	Plym. Congregational ..	25	....	23	....	Miss Carrie E. Bassett, 29 Sibley st.
"	First Congregational...	45	2	39	....	Cora DeWitt, 258 Franklin ave.
"	Freewill Baptist.......	....	....	....	....	
"	Mt. Zion Cong.........	55	6	46	....	Nettie V. Jones, 23 Linden st.
College Hill.......						Sarah Dickinson.
Columbus.........	Eastwood Cong........	53	3	53	2	Ed. Dan, 30 North Twenty-second st.
"	Hildreth Baptist.......	20	3	20	....	Wm. O. Judd, 218 Washington ave.
"	Mt. Vernon Ave. M. E.	....	....	....	....	Rev. Jno. Rife.
"	Broad St. Presbyterian	....	....	....	....	Rev. Mr. Marston. [lin sts.
"	First Baptist..........	64	1	64	....	Lillian J. Wood, Monroe and Frank
"	First Congregational...	....	....	....	....	W. E. Jones, 190 Garfield ave.
Conneaut..........	Undenome...........	....	....	....	....	Fannie Hiler.
Conotton..........	Union Presbyterian....	15	18	11	....	Jno. Hough, Dell Roy.
Coolville..........	Congregational.......	....	....	....	....	Rev. Mr. Graham.
Cuyahoga Falls ...	First Congregational...	....	....	....	....	Rev. Mr. Danner.
Dayton...........	Grace Meth. Episcopal.	....	....	....	....	Emma L. Theobald, 375 N. 1st st.
"	Oak St. U. B..........	....	....	....	....	Rev. L. Brookwalter.
" (Miami City)	Broadway Meth. Epis...	....	....	....	....	Rev. Mr. Brown.
"	Linden Ave. Baptist...	....	....	....	....	Rev. Mr. Lounsbury. [5th st.
"	Memorial Presbyterian.	47	13	54	4	Miss Ottilie Pagenstecher, 1815 E.
"	United Brethren......	....	....	....	....	G. Fritz, 129 Bralham st.
Defiance..........	Baptist...............	....	....	....	....	J. N. Coolidge, Box 641.
Derby.............	Methodist Episcopal...	....	....	....	....	Rev. R. A. Lemaster.
Dover.............	Congregational........	46	2	46	....	Miss Marg. McCarty.
"	Methodist Episcopal...	....	....	....	....	
"	United...............	....	....	....	....	
E. Liverpool.......	United Presbyterian ...	....	....	....	....	Miss Becky A. Hart
Edison............	First Baptist..........	20	4	20	3	Miss Norma Tucker.
El Dorado.........						G. W. Arne.
Elmira............	Methodist Episcopal...	....	....	....	....	
Elyria.............	Methodist Episcopal...	88	21	88	....	Miss Frankie Bath.
"	First Baptist..........	56	....	46	....	Inez Peckham.
"	First Congregational...	40	6	35	....	Mary S. Williams. [st.
Findlay...........	First Congregational...	32	3	32	9	Emma L. Furnum, 129 E. Sandusky
"	First Meth. Epis.......	134	9	138	....	Paul A. Prentiss, 527 W. Sandusky st.
Fitchville.........						Rev. C. A. Rice.
Franklin..........	Presbyterian..........	25	10	16	....	Maggie Clark.
Fredericksburg....	Union................	36	40	50	....	Maggie Peppard.
"	United Presbyterian ...	....	....	....	....	Rev. W. P. Moore.

LIST OF SOCIETIES

OHIO. — (Continued.)

CITY.	CHURCH.	Act. Memb.	Asso. Memb.	Ch. Memb.	United with C.	Secretary and Address.
Freedom	Congregational	23	....	19	....	E. L. Babb.
Forest	Methodist Episcopal	30	5	40	....	Miss Eva Todd.
Galion	United Brethren	52	....	52	....	Erva Krohn, 17 Grand st.
"	Baptist	....	....	....	....	Anna Hart.
Galloway	Methodist Episcopal	....	....	....	....	Rev. W. F. Filler.
Garrettsville	Congregational	33	3	30	....	Miss Minnie Ellenwood.
Geneva	First Congregational	30	....	25	....	M. E. Votono.
Grafton	Congregational	12	18	15	....	Rev. Elisha Hoffman.
Granville	Baptist	60	....	60	17	Mary E. Talbot.
Greenfield	First Presbyterian	21	0	21	....	Alice Waddell.
Greenville	United Brethren	29	16	42	2	Deborah Norris, East Martin st.
"	Methodist Episcopal	....	....	....	....	Rev. Mr. Casset.
Hamlin	Methodist Episcopal	....	....	....	....	Mrs. Potts, Logan st.
"	United Presbyterian	....	....	....	....	George Fulton.
"	United Presbyterian	....	....	....	....	Lizzie Blackburn.
Harbor	....	....	....	....	....	Lillian L. Brigham.
Harmar	Congregational	27	3	21	....	Lida A. Moore.
Harrisburg	Methodist Episcopal	96	19	102	1	Ella M. Chenoweth.
Harshasville	....	....	....	....	....	Emma J. Patton.
Hicksville	Methodist Episcopal	26	3	26	....	W. S. Roop.
Hillsborough	First Presbyterian	51	3	51	17	Nannie Bowles.
Hudson	First Calvinistic Cong.	83	9	74	3	Ella J. Chapman, Box 40.
Ironton	Methodist Episcopal	....	....	....	....	John L. Layne.
"	Presbyterian	....	....	....	....	....
Jamestown	Methodist Episcopal	43	18	....	....	Mrs. C. C. Hosier.
Jefferson	Congregational	....	....	....	....	Rev. J. S. Edwards.
Kent	Congregational	....	....	....	....	....
Kenton	Presbyterian	46	6	46	....	Guy S. Dean.
Kingsville	First Baptist	38	12	36	3	Miss Victoria Crowther.
"	Presbyterian	....	....	....	....	Lida Kendall.
"	Methodist Episcopal	20	2	20	6	Lena Tisdale.
"	Presbyterian	....	....	....	....	Rev. Chas. Hitchcock.
Koch's	....	....	....	....	....	Wm. H. Beeler.
Lexington	Congregational	17	2	13	....	Cyrena M. Wolford.
Lilly Chapel	Methodist Episcopal	....	....	....	....	Rev. H. Carter.
Lindsay	....	....	....	....	....	Rev. J. S. Fitterer.
Lodi	Congregational	....	....	....	....	Rev. R. Chapin.
Lorraine	Methodist Episcopal	....	....	....	....	....
Loveland	Methodist Episcopal	6	....	6	....	....
Madison	Central Congregational	30	6	27	1	Mary Ensign, West Main st.
Mansfield	Congregational	....	....	....	....	Etta I. Gilkison, Box 195.
Marietta	First Congregational	70	34	....	13	Florence Curtis, 310 Fourth st.
"	Baptist	....	....	....	....	Rev. G. R. Gear.
Marshall	Presbyterian	....	....	....	....	Rev. J. G. Galbreath.
"	Union	....	....	....	....	Lizzie Watts.
Martin's Ferry	....	35	5	37	....	May Robinson.
Marysville	First Congregational	64	4	....	....	Winnie M. Reichert.
Mechanicsburg	....	....	....	....	....	Mrs. J. H. Alley.
Medina	Grange, Methodist Ep.	....	....	....	....	Lizzie M. Strong.
"	First Congregational	111	15	111	....	J. D. Dannley.
"	Congregational	....	....	....	....	Wm. H. Sipher.
Miamisburg	....	....	....	....	....	[Bank sts.
Milan	Methodist Episcopal	21	5	18	5	Miss Emma Lockwood, cor. Front &
Millersburg	Presbyterian	....	....	....	....	Mrs. F. W. Gasche.
Mt. Carmel	Presbyterian	16	....	....	....	Alice Perdrizet.
Mt. Gilead	First Baptist	32	15	32	8	Miss Alice Parsons.
Mt. Healthy	Un. Brethren	22	....	22	....	Becky A. Hoffner.
Mt. Liberty	....	....	....	....	....	....
Mt. Vernon	Presbyterian	46	5	46	3	Jennie E. Colville.
"	First Congregational	49	19	52	15	Kate B. Fordney.
"	First Baptist	22	11	23	....	Lois Bishop, Box 615.
"	Christian Church	....	....	....	....	....
Newark	Second Presbyterian	....	....	....	....	Rev. Mr. Walden.
New Carlisle	....	....	....	....	....	Mrs. Callie S. Gaddes.
North Amherst	Congregational	10	5	10	....	Hattie Kline.

OF CHRISTIAN ENDEAVOR. lxvii

OHIO.—(*Continued.*)

CITY.	CHURCH.	Act. Memb.	Asso. Memb.	Ch. Memb.	United with C.	Secretary and Address.
North Amherst	Methodist Episcopal	20	7	10		Cora Hulbert.
" Bloomfield	Congregational					William C. Savage.
Norwalk	Congregational					Amy Hayes.
Oberlin	First Congregational	145	6			Chas. K. Whiting, 12 Forest st.
"	Baptist					Stella Ralston.
Ottawa						Ida Gottschrus.
Paterson	Presbyterian					Rev. T. J. Cellar.
Paulding	First Presbyterian			5		Hattie Collins.
Piqua	Calvary Baptist	20	5	25		Hattie E. Manetta, Box 382.
Portsmouth	Second Presbyterian					
Ravenna	Congregational					Rev. Mr. Meek.
Reynoldsburg	Un. Presbyterain	35	15	40		Miss Maud Martin.
Ridgeville	Congregational					
Ripley	Presbyterian	41	4	41		Lillian E. Campbell.
RittmanCh.of Milton	Presbyterian	15	2	14		Mary Elliott.
Rome	Presbyterian					E. H. Stiles.
Rootstown	Congregational	20		18		Cora L. Clark.
Sandusky	First Presbyterian	31	3	31	9	Lizzie Converse, 918 Washington st.
"	First Congregational	61	37	74	35	Frank E. Davis, 134 Columbus ave.
"	Methodist	41	23	44	26	C. D. Lee, care W. U. Telegraph Co.
"	Wayne St. Baptist					Rev. G. W. Smith.
Savannah	Presbyterian	40	7	40	9	Mary McKibben.
Seaville	First Presbyterian	43	3	34		Miss. C. F. Noyes.
Springfield	Sinking Creek Baptist	15	6	14		J. A. Hedges, Box 556.
"	Lagonda Ave. Cong.	26	19	23	14	Alice W. Guthrie, 252 Lagonda ave.
"	First Congregational	59	36	37	13	Miss Hattie Mellen, So. Market st.
"	First Eng. Lutheran					Jessie Pretzman, W. High st.
"	Third Eng. Lutheran	21	5	21		Carrie Murray, East Pearl st.
"	Grace Methodist Epis					Lura P. Baker, Old Dayton Road.
Springhill	Presbyterian					Dr. H. S. Elliott.
Stanleyville	Congregational					
Steubenville	United Presbyterian	57	27	58	30	Georgia Fulton, 135 So. 6th st.
"	Second Congregational					Rev. C. W. Carroll.
"	First Presbyterian					Rev. O. V. Stewart.
"	Second Presbyterian					G. A. Gorlach.
"	Hamline Meth. Epis					Rev. Mr. Youman.
"	Fifth M. P.					Miss G. Fulton.
"	Second Methodist Epis					
So. Amherst	Methodist Episcopal					Edith Clark.
Sullivan						
Sylvania	Union	25	19	23	2	Miss Emma M. Comstock.
Tallmadge	First Congregational	55	19	68	24	Mrs. C. B. Skinner.
Tippin						W. F. McDowell.
"	Lutheran					Samuel Schwarm.
Toledo	First Congregational	40	30	42	5	Mabel Cronis, 320 12th st.
"	Congregational					
"	Presbyterian					
"	Methodist Episcopal					W. H. Bishop, Auburndale.
Troy	Methodist Episcopal	8	4			Will D. Cairns.
Twinsburgh	Congregational					Rev. Mr. Haines.
"	Union	69				Miss Mattie Stanley.
Unity	United Presbyterian	23	7	28		Emma Patten, Harshasville.
Urbana	Grace Meth. Epis	43	11	42		Epgar G. Banta.
"	First Presbyterian					Mattie Stanley.
"	First Baptist					Rev. Mr. Fields.
"	Lutheran					Rev. Mr. Iruhoff.
Vermillion	Congregational	24	6	22	1	Miss Lucy Morgan.
Warren	Presbyterian					Elizabeth Howard.
Wauseon	Congregational	24	1	24		Guy C. Marsh.
Wellington	Congregational	41	25	46		Eva Lang.
Wellsville	United Presbyterian	30	15	35		Susie Stevenson.
Welshfield						
Westerville	Methodist Episcopal					Edessa M. Kimball.
West Jefferson	Methodist Episcopal					Miss Etta Boyd.
West Liberty	First Presbyterian	36	6	39	10	Rus. Edwards.

LIST OF SOCIETIES

OHIO. — (Continued.)

CITY.	CHURCH.	Act. Memb.	Asso. Memb.	Ch. Memb.	United with C.	Secretary and Address.
West Liberty	Methodist Episcopal	....	....	....	....	Cora Davis, cor. Main and Delaware.
West Williamsfield.	Congregational	33	16	31	12	Bernie M. Hart.
Weymouth	First Congregational	28	13	25	6	E. C. Wallis.
Worcester	Bethany Baptist	41	16	....	....	E. A. Day.
Wyanet						
Wycliffe						
Xenia	Baptist					H. S. Taylor, Willoughby.
Xenia City	First United Pres	30	12	....	....	Leigh Galloway, Box 415.
" "	Trinity Methodist. E.	....	....	....	....	Rev. A. N. Spahr.
" "	First Methodist Epis	....	....	....	....	Gertrude Marley, 138 W. Market st.
" "	Presbyterian	....	....	....	....	Rev. J. C. Ely.
" "	Reformed	....	....	....	....	Rev. J. W. Smith.
Yellow Springs	Presbyterian	22	10	21	....	W. G. Rice.
Youngstown	Plymouth Cong	45	28	40	10	H. S. Evans, P. O. Box 491.
"	First Baptist	28	2	28	....	Minnie Williams, 941 Charles st.
"	United Presbyterian	....	....	....	....	E. McMillan.
"	First Presbyterian	....	....	....	....	Rev. D. H. Evans.
Zanesville	Market St. Baptist	32	7	32	....	Miss Ethelwyn Hopkins, 22 Elm st.
"	First Presbyterian	52	35	....	....	Lina Lazalere, Oak Ward.
"	Second Presbyterian	....	....	....	....	
"	Putnam Presbyterian	....	....	....	....	

OREGON.

CITY.	CHURCH.	Act. Memb.	Asso. Memb.	Ch. Memb.	United with C.	Secretary and Address.
Albany	First Congregational	12	7	12	....	C. B. Read.
Albina	First Presbyterian	....	....	....	....	
Astoria	Congregational	....	....	....	....	G. A. Charnock.
Baker City						
Corvallis						
Eugene City	First Presbyterian	45	10	45	3	Hattie I. Dunning, 11th st.
" "						
East Portland	First Congregational	36	9	16	3	Miss May Hardie, 430 Third st.,
" "	First Presbyterian	....	....	....	....	Rev. D. Ghormurly. [McMellin'sAca.
" "	First Methodist	....	....	....	....	Rev. I. D. Driver.
Forest Grove						
Marion	Presbyterian	....	....	....	....	Albert F. Robinson.
Oregon City	Baptist	39	....	39	7	Balfe De Vore Johnson.
" "	First Meth. Episcopal	....	....	....	....	Rev. W. A. Williams.
" "	First Congregational	....	....	....	....	W. T. Whitlock.
Portland	Calvary Presbyterian	24	40	22	....	Mrs. T. A. Stephens, 10 South 7th.
"	St. John's Presbyterian	....	....	....	....	
"	Fourth Presbyterian	....	....	....	....	
"	G. Methodist	....	....	....	....	Rev. Ross C. Houghton.
"	First Congregational	....	....	....	....	George N. Haines.
Salem	First Presbyterian	20	3	15	....	Mrs. H. A. Newell.
"	Congregational	....	....	....	....	Edith M. Harris.

PENNSYLVANIA.

CITY.	CHURCH.	Act. Memb.	Asso. Memb.	Ch. Memb.	United with C.	Secretary and Address.
Allegheny	United Presbyterian	....	....	....	....	Ella E. Crawford.
"	Third U. Presbyterian	43	11	40	....	A. L. Large.
"	First U. Presbyterian	....	....	....	....	Rev. W. P. Robinson.
"	North Ave. Meth. Ep	....	....	....	....	Rev. T. J. Leak.
"	Buena Vista Meth. Ep	25	15	8	....	G. L. Givichard, 51 Monterey st.
"	First Congregational	....	....	....	....	Rev. A. M. Hills, 138 Wash. ave.
"	Second Union Pres	....	....	....	....	Sadie Lyle.

PENNSYLVANIA. — (*Continued.*)

CITY.	CHURCH.	Act. Memb.	Asso. Memb.	Ch. Memb.	United with C.	Secretary and Address.
Allegheny City	Trinity Lutheran	40	135	50	....	Frank Kron, 48 Webster st.
Altoona	....					J. E. Wallace, 2015 2d ave.
Apollo	First Presbyterian	44	17	....	....	Minnie J. McIntire.
Arendtsville	....					Margaret Sanger.
Andenried	Presbyterian	15	2	13	....	Thomas Dougherty.
Bally	....	70	0	16	5	Hannah B. Yeakel.
Bangor	First Presbyterian	40	20	24	10	B. Haughwout.
Beaver Falls	Methodist Episcopal	50				Laurie Carson, 709 Seventh ave.
"	Presbyterian					Rev. J. D. Moorhead.
"	United Presbyterian					Nelson Spuncler, 1119 Fourth ave.
Bellefonte	Presbyterian					Geo. L. Hayes.
Bennet	Methodist Episcopal					
Bethlehem	Wesley M. E.	26	7	26	....	H. H. King.
"	Presbyterian		14		....	Geo. Barclay.
Blossburg	Second Congregational	27	10	27	....	G. W. Stott.
Bridgeville	Bethany Presbyterian					Rev. V. G. Sheely.
Brookville	....					S. Balten.
"	Union Presbyterian					George Monroe.
Bustleton	Lower Dublin Baptist	38	2	38	7	Gertrude C. McMillan. [phia.
Cambridgeboro	Union					Annie Ash, 614 Arch st., Philadel-
Carbondale	Presbyterian	24	3	24		Maggie Varnum.
Catasauqua	Methodist Episcopal					Rev. A. E. Anthon, Box 147.
Churchville	Second Reformed					Wm. D. Cornell.
Cochranville	Presbyterian					Rev. Joseph Polk.
Columbia	First Presbyterian	7	4	7		Rev. Geo. W. Ely.
Conshohockin	First Presbyterian	43	23	43	....	Anna E. Moore.
"	First Baptist	15		15		Chas. Crankshaw.
Cross Creek Village	Presbyterian	22	2	22	....	Nannie Bebout.
Danville	Mahoning Pres.	58	24	58	10	Bertha Wetzell, P. O. Box 247.
"	Grove Presbyterian	22	0	22	3	Alex. H. Grone, Spruce and Vine sts.
Dauphin	Presbyterian					Clara E. Bergstresser.
Downington	Presbyterian	18	18	18	..	Elizabeth Shelmire.
Dunmore	Presbyterian					Joseph Jeffrey, Box 106.
Easton	First Presbyterian	67	66	70	35	Eva F. Peters, College Hill.
East Mauch Chunck	Presbyterian					Carrie Leisenring.
East Smithfield	Baptist					Miss Lizzie Phelps.
Ebensburg	First Congregational	38	18	41	10	Mollie Evans.
Edwardsdale	Bethesda Cong.					E. R. Lewis.
Elizabeth	Baptist					Rev. A. B. Whitney.
Elkland	Presbyterian					Rev. S. H. Moon, D. D.
Erie	Park Presbyterian	58	43	51	4	Miss Kate Spencer, 155 W. 6th st.
"	First Baptist	37	3	37	3	Sarah E. Crouch, 320 E. 8th st.
"	United Presbyterian	55	15	53	6	Thos. Frater, 315 E. 8th st.
"	10th St. Methodist Epis.	20	11	27	6	Mrs. John L. Stratton, 538 E. 10th st.
"	Central Presbyterian					H. E. Mayer, 118 Sassafras st.
"	Chestnut St. Pres.					Rev. Mr. Vancleve.
"	8th St. United Pres.					Rev. Mr. Wilson.
"	Simpson Meth. Epis.					Rev. Mr. Espy.
"	Baptist					Rev. Mr. Thorns.
Factoryville	....					A. F. Gardner.
"	Baptist					J. H. Lewis.
Faggs Manor	....					Mamie Polk.
Fairview	Union					Retta E. Easton.
Franklin	Methodist Episcopal					Mrs. C. M. Sykes, 1227 Liberty st.
"	First Baptist	105		100	76	H. G. Reading, Box 778.
"	First Presbyterian	110	14	86	48	Miss Flora Black.
Germantown	First Presbyterian	65	35	61		Miss N. H. Partridge, Wayne st.
Glenolden	First Presbyterian	17	6	19	....	Annie Ash, 614 Arch st., Phil.
Greenville	Presbyterian	80	6	80	....	Sadie Leech.
"	Methodist Episcopal					
"	First Presbyterian	125		80		M. L. Hengist.
Grove City	Grace Methodist	68		68	....	Florence Perry.
Hatboro	Baptist					Rev. Oliver James.
"	Methodist Episcopal	21	13	24		Geo. Fisher, Willow Grove.
"	Baptist	29	11	27	....	Miss Angie Jones.

LIST OF SOCIETIES

PENNSYLVANIA. — (Continued.)

CITY.	CHURCH.	Act. Memb.	Asso. Memb.	Ch. Memb.	United with C.	Secretary and Address.
Harrisburgh	Fourth St. Ch. of God	73	15	62	2	Chas. S. Mech, P. O. Box 414.
"	Market Sq. Pres	136	30	120		M. Lizzie Bishop, 262 North st.
"						Geo. B. Stuart, 215 North 2d st.
Harrison Valley						S. M. Stevens.
Hawley	First Presbyterian	17		12	2	Sadie J. Bishop.
Hilltown	Baptist					Margaret Rice.
Jenkintown	Baptist					Miss Josie Harlow.
Jersey Shore	Baptist	36	1	36	6	Mattie Barnes.
" "	Presbyterian					Rev. J. G. Kohler.
Johnstown	Franklin St. Meth. Ep.	49	38		8	Ella Humphrey, 66 Livergood st.
Kingston	Presbyterian	90	30			J. F. Collins.
"	Congregational					Charlotte Davis, Slocum st.
"	Christian					
Lansford	Methodist Episcopal	55	6	55	25	E. N. Morsher.
Leaman Place						Rev. E. W. Gaylord.
Lehighton	Evan. Association					
Le Raysville	Congregational	16	22	16		Miss Fannie Payson.
"	Methodist Episcopal	14	1	14		Rev. D. D. King.
Lewisburgh	Baptist	26		26		Lillie J. Baker.
"	First Baptist	24		23		Rev. John T. Judd.
Lewiston	First Presbyterian	38	18	40	5	Miss Mary T. Elder.
Library						J. P. Wilson.
Lindsay	Baptist					
Lionville	St. Paul Lutheran					Rev. W. F. Rentz.
Manayunk	Presbyterian					Miss Martha Wermer.
Mansfield	Baptist					John Gwyne.
"	United Presbyterian					Rev. T. C. Atchinson.
" Valley	Mansfield Presbyterian	34	26	34	6	George A. Marsh.
Maplewood	Evangelical	32		32		S. Eugene Stevens.
Mauch Chunk	Presbyterian	58	59	36		Carrie B. Leonard.
" "	Methodist					
Meadville	Second Presbyterian	36	18	41		Nettie Smith, 400 North st.
Mechanicsville	Union					Jane B. Watson, Station O, Phila.
Media	Presbyterian	25	3	25		Mary G. Hough, Box 37.
Mifflintown	Lutheran					Rev. Philip Graif.
Milford	First Presbyterian	53	3	49		Miss Betty Cornelius.
"	Presbyterian					Emma McCarthy.
Millerstown	Presbyterian	20	11	26		Annie W. Bollinger.
Monongahela	First Presbyterian					Jennie S. Wilson, Box 16.
" City						Miss Jane McWilliams.
Moosic	Presbyterian	35	6	35		Mabel M. Olds.
Montrose	First Presbyterian	55	3	49		Fannie L. Read.
Mt. Jackson						Mrs. S. L. Taylor.
"	Westfield Presbyterian	49		36		Lizzie Paterson.
Murraysville	Presbyterian	13	1	14	1	Mintie M. Murray.
Nanticoke	First Presbyterian	50	20	20		G. M. Davis.
"	Congregational					Maggie Jacobs.
New Albany	Methodist Episcopal	16	9	15	2	Mrs. C. P. Garrison.
New Brighton						
New Castle	Second Presbyterian	42	1	39		Mary F. McConnell, 62 Crawford av.
"	United Presbyterian					Rev. J. Q. A. McDowell.
New Milford						
New Salem						R. D. Haslett.
Nicholson	Presbyterian	32	17	25		B. H. Cunningham.
Norristown	Cap. St. Methodist E.	35	7	35		J. Weir Crankshaw.
"	Central Presbyterian	68	37	74	28	W. H. Isett, 210 Main street.
"	Oak St. Methodist	27		27	1	Anna L. Long, 321 E. Acry st.
"	First Presbyterian					Rev. Mr. Becber.
"	Second Presbyterian					Rev. Mr. Queen.
Oil City	Baptist					
Oxford	First Presbyterian	99	23	101	10	Elva Alexander.
Paradise	Presbyterian					Clara Moore.
Peeksville	Baptist					Jennie Cadwallader.
Philadelphia	Spruce St. Baptist	30		29		E. E. Perry, 604 Arch st. [nut st.
"	Walnut St. Pres	118		76	5	Miss Alice G. Trumbull, 4103 Wal-

PENNSYLVANIA. — (Continued.)

CITY.	CHURCH.	Act. Memb.	Asso. Memb.	Ch. Memb.	United with C.	Secretary and Address.
Philadelphia........	W. Spruce St. Pres.....	59	42	61	8	G. S. Benson, Jr., 1515 Spruce st.
"	Powelton Ave. Baptist.	46	2	46	....	H. E. Moody, 837 Market st.
"	Columbia Ave. Pres....	29	8	29	3	John H. Beans, 1947 Uber st.
"	Arch St. Meth. Epis...	48	....	48	7	Miss E. L. Mink, 2108 Arch st.
"	Ch. of our Red'r Ref. E.	23	7	23	4	Ida V. Quigley,1703 N. 20th st. [st.
"	Temple Presbyterian..	42	4	2	....	Catherine D. Bowdle, 1238 Franklin
"	Atonement Pres........	13	13	14	1	Maggie R. Taylor, 1245 So. 18th st.
"	Green Hill Pres........	26	3	26	....	J. M. Brewer, 1333 North 12th st.
"	Patterson Mem. Pres...	31	4	31	9	Susie L. Smallwood, 6419 Vine st.
"	Memorial Baptist......	67	10	76	9	Marianne R. Young, 1715 Oxford st.
"	Centennial Baptist.....					Rev. James Lick. [1924 Gerard av.
"	Broad St. Baptist......					Wm. B. Davis,care Crew Lurick Co.,
"	Memorial Reformed....					Rev. Mr. Griffish.
"	Central Congregational.					Marion B. Heritage, 811 No. 21st st.
"	North Presbyterian....	86	12	87	....	Rev. Asbury C. Clark.
"	Spring Garden Meth...					Kev. Dr. Griffiths
"	West Arch St. Pres....					Rev. Dr. Hemphill.
"	Beth Eden Baptist.....	50	5	47	....	Rev. J. T. Beckley.
"	Ebenezer M. E.........					Rev. A. L. Urban.
"	Grace Baptist..........					Rev. R. H. Crowell.
"	Fifth Baptist..........					Rev. John Peddie.
"	No. Broad St. Pres.....					Rev. Dr. A. S. Mutchmore.
"	Northminster Pres.....					Rev. R. H. Fulton, D. D.
"	Westminster Pres......					Rev. John Kirkpatrick.
"	Holland Mem. Pres....					Rev. W. S. Padere.
"	Arch St. Pres..........					Rev. J. S. Sands, D. D.
"	Eighth United Pres.....					Rev. W. W. Barr, D. D.
"	Haddington M. E......					G. G. Rakestraw. [ave.
"	Spring Garden Bap....	35	4	35	....	Miss Emma Adams, 1345 Fairmount
"	Memorial Presbyterian.					Miss M.R.Young, 1544 Centennial av.
"	Protestant Episcopal...					Rev. Mr. Hubbard, 1600 Mosley st.
"	Torresdale Union......					Yates Hickey.
"	Presbyterian...........					Miss Adelaide Wood, 2231 Green st.
"	Marshallton M. E......					
"	Allegheny Ave. Baptist.					Rev. W. Hartley, 2060 E. Alleg'y av.
"	Presbyterian...........					W. H. McCutchen, 1736 Wellington
"	Baptist................					W. C. Geyer, 4810 Chester ave. [st.
"	Presbyterian...........					Fred Small, 812 Preston st., W. Phil.
"	First Reformed Dutch..					Matthew Walker, 400 Chestnut st.
"	Gaston Presbyterian...					
"	Belmont M. E..........	15	11	19	....	Benj. A. Francis, 702 No. 44th st.
"	Woodland Ave. M. E..					Geo. A. Crider, 329 Market st.
"	Tenth Presbyterian....					J. Allen Clapp, 1323 No. and 12th st.
"	Central Baptist........					
"	Bustleton Baptist......					Mamie DeKalb, Bustleton. [st.
"	Reformed Epis. Juv...					Miss Mary Summers,1706 Wellington
Phœnix						Amanda Hawke.
Phœnixville.........	Methodist Episcopal...					
"	First Presbyterian.....					Josephine R. Mellon.
Pittsburgh	Ruth St. M. E.........	185	16	188	26	H. N. Cameron, 256 44th st.
"	Third Union Pres......					Rev. J. T. McCrory.
"	Mt. Washington Pres...					Lee Digby, Joell's lane, 32 Ward.
"	Wylie Ave. Union Pres.					Rev. H. C. Knox.
"	Fifth Union Pres.......					Rev. Mr. Harsha.
"	Seminary M. E.........					Rev. Mr. Emerson.
"	Christ M. E					Rev. O. J. Cowles.
"	Eighth St. Reformed...					T. S. Duncan, 77 James st.
"	Eighth St. Un. Pres....					Ella M. Martin, 115 Erie st.
"	Trinity Congregational.					
Pittston............						
Pleasant Mt........						
Pleasant Valley.....	Primitive M. E.........	9	....	9	....	
Plymonth	Congregational........					Rev. R. T. Williams. [Phil.
Port Richmond.....	Philadelphia Baptist...	28	5	27	5	Chas. W. Cornell, 3188 Clifton st.,
Port Carbon........	First Presbyterian.....					Margaret Henderson.

lxxii LIST OF SOCIETIES

PENNSYLVANIA. — (Continued.)

CITY.	CHURCH.	Act. Memb.	Asso. Memb.	Ch. Memb.	United with C.	Secretary and Address.
Pottsville	Second Presbyterian	25	6	28	14	Belle Simmons, 1114 W. Market st.
"	Evan. Methodist					Rev. W. A. Leopold.
"	First Presbyterian					W. K. Woodbury.
Pottsdam	First Presbyterian					Walter C. Roe. [ton.
Providence	Congregational					Geo. W. Powell, Summit ave., Scran-
Scranton	Young Men					M. F. Hand, 315 Washington ave.
"	Plymouth Cong	30		30		Miss E.O.Evans,113 N.Hyde P'k ave.
"	Grace Reformed Epis.	40	35			Richard R. Weisenflue, 513 Webster
"	Jackson St. Baptist					John Lloyd. [ave.
"	Washburn St. Pres.	74	4	74		Lizzie G. Wade.
"	Second Presbyterian	54	19	52	8	Herbert E. Cox, 330 Wash'n ave.
"	Belleview C. M.					Rev. Mr. Morris.
"	Providence Baptist					Rev. I. N. Steelman.
"	First Presbyterian					Arthur R Foote,330 Washington ave.
"	Green Ridge Pres.					Rev. N. F. Stahl.
Sharpsburgh	Centenary M. E.					
Shinglehouse	Methodist Episcopal	9	3	4		Miss Millie Persott.
South Easton	Presbyterian					Rev. J. T. Sheppard.
South Williamsport						Bertha Steigelman.
Susquehanna	Presbyterian					W. H. Tucker, Box 749.
"	First Presbyterian	15	11	15		Sarah L. Bourne, Box 103.
Towersdale	(Phila.) Presbyterian					Jennie L. Hulme, Sta. O.
Titusville	First Baptist	54	10	47	2	Edna M. Murray, 12 W. Spring st.
"	Presbyterian					Rev. Dr. Kneeland.
Towanda	Presbyterian					Rev. J. S. Stewart.
Troy	First Presbyterian	52	15	45		Eloise DeWitt, Box 33.
Tyrone						James B. Grozier.
Union City	Presbyterian					Rev. E. P. Clark.
Uniontown	Baptist					Florence Wetner.
Wampum	Slippery Rock Pres.	23	8	25	10	Miss Effie E. Rice.
Warren	Presbyterian	21	5	21		P. V. Schermerhorn, 108 East st.
"	First Baptist	20		20	13	Miss Maggie D. Yuill.
West Chester	State Normal School	50	12			Carrie E. Bemus.
" "	Presbyterian					
West Mill Creek	Westminster Pres.					T. C. Miller.
West Philadelphia	Patterson Mem. Pres.					Geo. B. Bell.
West Pittston	Presbyterian Ind.					Thos. Nichols.
West Vincent	St. Matthew Lutheran					
Wilkesbarre	Cum. Presbyterian					
Williamsport	Baptist					Miss Jennie Heyman.
"	Second Presbyterian					E. F. Noble, Hepburn st.
York	First Presbyterian	29	17	30		Alexander McLean.

RHODE ISLAND.

Arnold's Mills	Methodist Episcopal					Rev. Lyman G. Horton.
Ashaway	Seventh Day Baptist	45	16	28	9	Mrs. I. L. Cottrell.
Auburn	Free Baptist	21	6	13		H. A. Potter, Drawer 31.
Barrington	Congregational	37	11	30	23	Mabel F. Peck, Drownville.
Bristol	Congregational					Rev. Mr. Stevens. [Pawtucket,R.I.
Central Falls	Broad St. Baptist	61	17	58	2	Miss J. Alice Davis, 166 Broad st.,
" "	Congregational	57	47	42	3	Miss Desda A. Allen.
" "	Lonsdale Baptist					Rev. Ross Matthews.
" "	Park Place Cong.					Rev. J. J. Woolley.
Crompton	First Baptist					Jno. Cameron.
East Providence	Newman Cong.	29	7	26		Harry B. Ellis, Rumford.
" "	Second Baptist					Rev. J. Stuart, Box 229.
" "	United Congregational					Wm. E. Zillson.
Hope Valley	Baptist	31	10	27	1	Mary S. Joslin.
Hopkinton	S. D. Baptist					Rev. Ira L. Cottrel.
Hughsdale	Congregational					

OF CHRISTIAN ENDEAVOR.   lxxiii

RHODE ISLAND. — (*Continued.*)

CITY.	CHURCH.	Act. Memb.	Asso. Memb.	Ch. Memb.	United with C.	Secretary and Address.
Johnston	Mt. Pleasant Cong					
Little Compton	Congregational	22	13	18	1	Mrs. Lydia G. Briggs.
Mystic Bridge	Congregational					Rev. H. S. Brown.
Newport	Second Baptist	28		27		Mrs. J. P. Leavard, Gould st.
Old Warwick	Shawmut Baptist	5	10	4		Lewis Gardner.
Olneyville	Free Baptist					Emma C. Gifford.
Pawtucket	First Free Baptist					Miss C. G. Wheeler, 22 Cherry st.
"	Park Place Cong	106	46	102	8	Frank O. Bishop, 115 Broad st.
"	Pawtucket Cong	30	12	30		Lyman C. Newell, 25 George st.
"	Broad St. Baptist					Rev. E. Bullen.
Pawtuxet	Baptist	36	7	29		Minnie C. Burlingame, Box 704.
Providence	Pilgrim Congregational	56	13	51	14	Ellen Snow, 195 Broadway.
"	Stewart St. Baptist	54	8	52	10	Alice M. Waldron, 21 Knight st.
"	Clifford St. First Pres	41	2	41	25	Z. T. Williams, 527 High st.
"	Elmwood Cong	31	7	29		Inez F. Atkins, 88 Mitchell st.
"	Broad St. Christian	23		19	4	C. A. Vaughn, 29 Benevolent st.
"	Park St. Free Baptist	46	4	27	7	Miss Ida Earle, 53 Douglas ave.
"	Plymouth Cong	76	7	69	13	Geo. E. Church, 15 Adelaide ave.
"	Chestnut St. Meth. Epis.	61	6	55	20	E. H. Tiffany, 209 Westminster st.
"	Yahveh Evang. Advent.	67	9	61	11	Mabel E. A. Waite, 226 Prairie ave.
"	Cranston St. Baptist	70	1	69	24	Emma A. Durfee, 10 Ringgold st.
"	North Congregational	48	19	44	18	Wm. O. Shurrocks, 127 Pleasant st.
"	Union Congregational					
"	Beneficient Cong					Rev. J. G. Vose.
"	Plainfield St. Free Bap.					
"	Academy Ave. Cong	19	12	19		Mrs. J. J. Anderson, 2 Hendricks st.
"	Friendship St. Baptist					Rev. E. Holyoke.
"	Mt. Pleasant Baptist					Rev. W. Smith.
"	Broadway Baptist					W. S. Clarke, City Hall.
"	Central Congregational	52	26	48	7	Miss F. H. Fowler, 236 Doyle ave.
"	Union Congregational	100	23	103		A. C. Day, Box 398.
"	Free Evang. Cong	33	13	33	7	Edith W. Larry, 20 Forest st.
"	Blackstone Park Chap. Cong.					
"	Broadway Meth. Epis.					Clarke Perry, 454 Pine st.
"	Central Baptist					W. J. Merrill.
Riverside	Congregational					Rev. Mr. Smiley.
Slatersville	Congregational	22	24	8		Lottie M. Colwell.
Valley Falls	Baptist					Mary H. Riley.
" "	Freewill Baptist					Rev. C. E. Frost.
Warren	Baptist					Rev. Mr. Pope.
Warwick	Shawmet Baptist	14	8	3	3	Louis Gardner, Warwick Neck.
Westerly	7th D. Baptist	34	7	34		N. A. Collins, 18 Moss st.
"	Congregational	32	23	29	3	Mrs. Geo. L. Clark, Dixon House.
"	First Baptist	83	42	83		Mrs. J. H. Hawk.
"	Congregational					L. D. B. Ashaway.
Woonsocket	Globe Congregational	23	9	21	2	Helen M. Cook, No. 9 Providence st.
"	Presbyterian					Jno. B. Griffith.
"	Baptist					Rev. Dr. S. W. Foljambe.
"	Presbyterian	25	11	30		Leander Fisher.

SOUTH CAROLINA.

Anderson	St. Paul Baptist	39	1	39		L. C. Smith, Box 304.
Ansel	Washington Baptist	12	3	11		J. D. Henerly.
Black Creek						
Clinton	Clinton Presbyterian	29	3	29		F. L. Jacobs.
Chalk Hill	Baptist					Gabriel Kendrich.
Chester	Baptist	29	10	30		Rev. R. W. Sanders.

SOUTH CAROLINA. — (Continued.)

CITY.	CHURCH.	Act. Memb.	Asso. Memb.	Ch. Memb.	United with C.	Secretary and Address.
Columbia						Rev. C. E. Becker.
Doverville	Antioch Baptist	7	47	39		J. F. Wilson.
" Black Creek		7	35	20		J. H. Gandy.
Florence						E. A. Roberts.
Hartsville	Baptist					A. F. Miller.
Hagood	Rafting Creek Baptist	48	21	52		Wm. Cohen.
Port Royal	Baptist					Rev. J. P. Jenkins.
Rock Hill	Baptist					James Gavison.
Spartanburg	Presbyterian					Rev. B. F. Wilson.
" Mt. Moriah						R. W. Baylor.
Society Hill	Baptist	43	20	38		Rev. Jno. Stout.
Welsh Neck	Baptist					Rev. J. Stout.
Winnsboro	Presbyterian					Rev. J. C. Wattsine.

TENNESSEE.

CITY.	CHURCH.	Act. Memb.	Asso. Memb.	Ch. Memb.	United with C.	Secretary and Address.
Chattanooga						Frestus B. Clark.
Clarksville	Methodist Episcopal	20	40	60		Miss Pearl Graham, Madison st.
Grand View	Congregational	20	9	20		
Hill City						Rev. W. A. Ervin.
Knoxville	Second Presbyterian					Rev. R. R. Sutherland.
"	Church St. M. E.					H. A. Ferguson, 38 Hill st.
Marysville						Mary T. Lord.
Nashville						Miss Mary Coffin, Fisk University.
"	First Cumberland Pres.					Rev. Wm. Graham.
"					6	Flora Farmer, 235½ No. Summer st.
Pleasant Hill	Union	5	13	16		Wm. Mair.
Skene	Methodist	12	18	11		T. C. Babcock.
Slades						Anna Cherry.
"	Congregational					Miss J. A. Calkins.
Wartburgh						

TEXAS.

CITY.	CHURCH.	Act. Memb.	Asso. Memb.	Ch. Memb.	United with C.	Secretary and Address.
Brownwood	First Presbyterian	27		27		Miss Mamie Hallum.
Calvert						
Dallas	Second Presbyterian	30		30	5	H. W. Burr, 1229 Elm st
"	First Congregational					Rev. C. I. Scofield.
Denison						Miss I. Walker.
Glen Rose	Presbyterian	13	6	11		Arthur Heatherty.
Groveton	Union	16	5	9		Alice M. Sloan.
Millwood						Rev. J. B. Kerr.
Paris	Cumberland Pres.	26	12	26	11	Miss Sallie Gibson, Clarksville st.
"	N. Main St. Cong.					Rev. Wm. LeBach.
San Antonio	First Presbyterian	11	7	11		Duncan Hensley, Box 586.
" "	Madison Square Pres.	34	12	20		Helen M. Hand.
Stephensonville						
Whitewright		38	15	36		Prof. James Anderson.

OF CHRISTIAN ENDEAVOR. lxxv

UTAH.

CITY.	CHURCH.	Act. Memb.	Asso. Memb.	Ch. Memb.	United with C.	Secretary and Address.
Coalville	First Congregational	17	5	6	4	Mrs. Mary E. Rhoades.
Logan	"Logan Brick" Pres.	36	1	36	21	Rev. E. N. Greene, P. O. Box 298.
Mt. Pleasant	Presbyterian	16		12		Mrs. N. J. Geyer.
Ogden	Congregational					Rev. A. J. Bailey.
" Academy						Alice B. Hamlin.
Salt Lake City	Presbyterian					Rev. R. G. McNair, D. D.
" "	Phillips Congregational					Anna Baker, 59 5th st.
" "	20th Ward Presbyterian					Prof. Milkpaugh. [So. st.
" "	Congregational	32	13	8		Edith L. Woodmansee, 648 E. 7th
" "	Miss. School, 10th Ward					Mrs. H. A. Newell, 438 E. 3d So. st.
" "	Westminster Pres.	24	20	17		C. H. Parsons.
" "	Burlington Society					
Springville	Presbyterian					Rev. Theo. Lee.

VERMONT.

CITY.	CHURCH.	Act. Memb.	Asso. Memb.	Ch. Memb.	United with C.	Secretary and Address.
Alburgh	Congregational					
Ascutneyville	Union					Mrs. E. F. Bristol.
Bakersfield						
Barnet	Congregational	27	7	19	3	Edith Wallace.
Barre	Congregational					John Hutcheon, Box 172.
Barton Landing	Congregational					Rev. M. A. Gates.
Bellows Falls	Baptist					
Benson	First Congregational	13	1	4		Jasper P. Newton.
Berkshire	Congregational					Rev. E. W. Hatch.
Berlin	First Congregational	11	12	9	7	Miss Irene W. Hubbard.
Bethel	Congregational	24	10	21	2	Lucy M. Graham.
Bradford	Congregational					Rev. J. W. Lee.
Brandon	Congregational	55		23		Erastus A. Dean.
Brattleboro						
Brookfield	Second Congregational					Rev. Wm. Carr.
Brownsville						
Burlington	Berean Baptist	17	4	18		Sarah A. Martin, 110 Pearl st.
"	First Congregational	100	17	108	12	May H. Lemon, 88 College st.
"	Methodist Episcopal					W. W. Weaver, 401 So. Union st.
"	First Baptist					F. J. Parry.
"	Methodist					Dr. H. Eaton.
"	Third Congregational	40	19	55		A. E. Willard, 244 Pearl st.
Charlotte	Congregational					Rev. A. W. Wilde.
Chester						
Colchester	Congregational	8		8	2	Rev. Mr. Holbrook.
Dorset	Congregational	23	8	21		Mrs. Marcia Dunning.
East Berkshire	Congregational	22	3	19	6	M. J. Olds.
East Fairfield	Union	14	24	9		Ernest A. Sturtevant.
East Montpelier	Union					Mary T. Foster.
East Swanton	Baptist	9	18	8	3	Lillie A. Brown.
Fairhaven						
Gaysville	Union	10	3	8		Kate Kimball.
Georgia	Congregational	19	5	15	5	Abbie L. Hurlburt.
Grand Isle	Congregational					Rev. F. J. Harris.
Greensboro	Congregational					Rev. Stephen Knowlton.
Groton	Baptist					Lizzie A. Nourse. [land, N. H.
Guildhall	Congregational	13	12	8		Mrs. F. A. Hannaford, Northumber-
Hartford	Congregational	70	31	60		Louis S. Newton, Box 74.
Hartland	Congregational	45	34	35	12	Clara A. Lamb.
Jamaica	Congregational	19	11	14		Mrs. W. H. Taft.
Jericho Corners	Union					Mr. C. W. Powell.
Johnson	Congregational					Genie B. Austin.
Lancaster	Congregational					Rev. S. A. Barnaby.
Lyndonville	Congregational					
Manchester	Congregational					Dr. E. P. Wild.

lxxvi   LIST OF SOCIETIES

VERMONT. — (Continued.)

CITY.	CHURCH.	Act. Memb.	Asso. Memb.	Ch. Memb.	United with C.	Secretary and Address.
Middlebury	Congregational					Edward E. Bond.
Middlet'wn(Spri'gs)	Union					W. P. Cary.
Milton	Congregational	36	31	31	2	Alice G. Jackson.
Montgomery	Methodist	22	2	12	1	Elma A. Davis.
Montpelier	Baptist	15	5	15	5	Helen S. Burpee, 15 Winter st.
"	Bethany Congregational	40	5			E. E. Townes, 39 So. Main st.
"	Trinity Methodist					Rev. J. O. Sherborn.
Morrisville	Congregational	40	14	29		May A. Merriam, Summer st.
Newbury	Congregational					Rev. S. L. Bates.
New Haven	Congregational					Mrs. L. S. Dowd.
Newport	Congregational	23	17	17		Miss Colby, 50 Main st.
North Bennington	First Congregational	16	18	16		Mrs. G. Hewitt.
" "	Second Congregational					
" "	Baptist					Mrs. C. A. Woodward.
Northfield	First Congregational	18	14	19		Fannie A. Brown.
North Pomfret	Congregational					
Norwich	Congregational					H. W. Hutchinson.
North Ferrisburg						Mrs. G. C. Martin.
Pawlet	Congregational					
Peacham	Congregational	74	0	68	11	Alice G. Blanchard.
Peru	Congregational	12		10		Rev. A. B. Peffers.
Pittsford	Baptist	11		10		Annie H. Steele.
Plainfield	Union	35	21	33	16	Laura Gale.
Pomfret	Union					
Post Mills	Union	45	5	20	4	Mrs. E. M. Gilman.
Poultney	Baptist	19	3	16		Hattie B. Angwine.
Putney						
Randolph	Congregational	56	15	48	5	Miss Anzonetta S. Murphy.
Rockingham	Congregational					
Royalton	Congregational	24	6	21		Inez E. Culver.
Royalton Centre	First Congregational	27	8	24		Mrs. Frank Rand.
Rupert	Congregational	12	2	11	1	Mrs. C. A. Perry.
Rutland	Congregational					Frances E. Cheney, 8 Pleasant st.
Rutland Valley	Presbyterian					Rev. Wm. Mead, Proctor, Vt.
St. Albans	First Congregational	90	25	78	11	W. W. Jennison.
"						
St. Johnsbury	North Congregational					Rev. C. M. Lamson.
"	South Congregational	76	15	62	6	Miss Etta A. Graham.
Saxtons River	Congregational	23	9	23	2	Edith M. Foster, Pleasant st.
Sharon	Congregational					Rev. Mr. Chamberlain.
So. Burlington	Eldridge S. S. Union					Henry Petty.
South Hero	Union	29	7	23		Mrs. H. D. Allen.
South Royalton	Union					Pearl Belknap.
Springfield						
Stowe						
Swanton	Congregational	47	19	30	3	Mrs. E. H. Martin.
Taftsville	Union	9	20	7	2	Mabel M. Tracy.
Townshend	Congregational	35	5	25		Anna W. Smith.
Underhill	Congregational					
Vergennes	Congregational	17	38	48		Miss M. Nellie Haven.
Waitsfield	Union	45	18	33	6	Abbie L. Jones.
West Brattleboro	Baptist	43	10	31		Wm. W. Plimpton, Box 150.
" "	Congregational	78	15	64	8	Miss Clara M. Stedman.
" Glover	Union	34	19	30	3	Delia L. Buswell.
" Hartford	Congregational					
" Lebanon						
" Randolph	Congregational					Rev. W. F. Peters.
" Rutland	Congregational	75	20	80	30	Frank Blanchard.
" "	Baptist					Rev. W. H. Walker.
" Windsor						
" Woodstock						Minora C. Joy.
Westminster, West.	Congregational	26	8	20	10	Miss Dell R. Ramsey.
"	First Congregational	58	32	44	12	S. Elizabeth Hills.
Winooski	Congregational	18	10	11		Sarah N. MacBride, 68 Main st.
Windsor	Congregational	51	44	35	11	Clayton C. Johnson.
"	Hartland St. Cong.					Rev. Mr. Noyes.
Woodstock	Union	59	14	52	12	Miss Lucia S. Ladd.

VIRGINIA.

CITY.	CHURCH.	Act. Memb.	Asso. Memb.	Ch. Memb.	United with C.	Secretary and Address.
Winchester........		....	....	....	....	

WEST VIRGINIA.

CITY.	CHURCH.	Act. Memb.	Asso. Memb.	Ch. Memb.	United with C.	Secretary and Address.
Charlestown......						
Morgantown.......	Presbyterian............	31	10	38	4	L. J. Corbly, Box 20.
"	Methodist Episcopal...	....	....	....	....	Miss Dora Dorsey.
New Richmond.....						
Parkersburg........	First Presbyterian......	16	11	16	6	C. M. Rittenhouse, 1048 Market st.
"	Baptist................	....	....	....	....	Rev. J. W. Carter.

WISCONSIN.

CITY.	CHURCH.	Act. Memb.	Asso. Memb.	Ch. Memb.	United with C.	Secretary and Address.
Appleton..........	First Congregational...	79	49	75	22	E. E. Dunn.
"	Memorial Presbyterian.	40	17	38	12	A. M. Smith, 509 South st.
"	Baptist................	25	6	25	11	Kittie Byrnes. [& Green Bay st.
"	First Methodist Epis...	40	2	40	....	Myrtie E. Thompson, cor. Col'ge av.
Antigo............	Congregational.........	23	4	22	5	George Petti.
"	Baptist................	....	....	....	....	Julia F. Bliss.
Baraboo...........	First Presbyterian......	30	20	....	....	Helen M. Holden.
"		....	....	....	....	Jessie Huntington.
"	Congregational.........	20	9	16	5	Edward Prouty.
Beaver Dam.......	Baptist................	30	10	30	6	Edw. P. Brown, Box 161.
" "	First Presbyterian......	....	....	....	....	
Beloit.............	First Congregational...	....	....	....	....	Miss Laura Cheny.
"	Second Congregational..	.	....	....	....	C. A. Osborn.
"	Presbyterian...........	....	....	....	....	Miss Dudley.
"	First Baptist...........	41	....	37	5	Lillian M. Dean.
Berlin............	Baptist................	....	....	....	....	
Black River Falls...		....	....	....	....	
Blake's............		....	....	....	....	
Boscobel..........	Congregational.........	20	17	17	....	Annie S. Young.
Brodhead..........		....	....	....	....	I. L. Hannaford.
Burlington.........	Congregational.........	48	18	26	10	Frank E. Norton, Box 75.
Centre............		....	....	....	....	Hattie E. Spoon.
Chippewa Falls....	Presbyterian...........	33	28	14	3	Barbara A. Greenwood.
" "	Baptist................	....	....	....	....	Emma Sellers, Box 431.
Clinton............	Congregational.........	35	14	33	3	L. L. Olds.
"	Baptist................	....	....	....	....	Rev. H. Happell.
"	Methodist Episcopal...	25	19	25	6	
Clintonville.......	Methodist..............	41	22	39	....	Cora M. Sackett.
"	First Congregational...	47	11	29	9	Alice H. Torrey.
Columbus.........	First Congregational...	36	28	25	9	F. W. Chadbourne.
De Pere...........	Congregational.........	....	....	....	....	Horace Van Galder.
Durand............	Pilgrim Congregational.	15	20	8	1	Jennie Atkins.
Eau Claire........	First Congregational...	38	9	29	3	Lillian Wilcox, 516 Menominis st.
" "	Second Congregational.	36	4	14	9	Ada Palmer, 417 Price st.
Elkhorn	First Congregational...	44	2	27	12	Charles Mayne.
Elroy	Congregational.........	29	11	9	2	Lewis Talbert.
Emerald Grove....	Congregational.........	....	....	....	....	Miss Nettie Jones.
Evansville.........	Congregational.........	30	....	30	5	Mary D. Backenstoe.
"	Methodist Episcopal...	....	....	....	....	Rev. Dr. Wheeler.
Florence	First Presbyterian......	16	5	3	1	V. E. Velie.
Fond du Lac	Congregational.........	42	19	41	11	Charles Low.
" "	Baptist................	....	....	....	....	Rev. G. A. Pettingill.

lxxviii LIST OF SOCIETIES

WISCONSIN. — (Continued.)

CITY.	CHURCH.	Act. Memb.	Asso. Memb.	Ch. Memb.	United with C.	Secretary and Address.
Fond du Lac	Methodist Episcopal					W. W. Painter.
Footville	Congregational	21	11	16	7	Effie L. Barlow.
Fort Atkinson	First Congregational	38	47	27	1	Ella L. Buck.
" "	Methodist					I. S. Leavitt.
Fort Howard	First Baptist	9	13	7		Daisy Barclay.
Fox Lake						Mary Lewis.
Genesee	Congregational	29		14	4	W. H. Hardy, Jr.
Geneva						
Grand Rapids	First Congregational	43	22	24	9	A. L. P. Loomis.
" "	Junior First Cong.					Florence Loomis.
Green Bay	First Presbyterian	39	38	8		Hattie Enoch.
Hammond						
Hayward	Congregational					Rev. A. D. Blakeslee.
Hudson	Baptist					Frankie Clark.
"	Presbyterian					L. A. Baker.
Ithaca	Union	10		7		O. B. Pickard.
Janesville	First Congregational	35	31	29	3	May Cunningham.
"	Presbyterian					E. M. Clark, Box 1186.
"	First Methodist					Ellis Sweet.
"	Baptist					Rev. M. D. Hodge.
Kaukauna	First Congregational	20	20	18		Geo. Fargo.
Kenosha	Methodist	51	23	47	29	H. C. Krook.
"	Congregational					Bessie Wells.
"	Baptist					I. A. Williams.
Koshkonong	Union Congregational	20	10	20		J. S. Leavitt, Whitewater, Box 454.
La Crosse	First Baptist	30	10	29	6	Hattie Mae Harrison, 525 Cass st.
Lake Geneva	First Congregational	14		12	2	Grace E. Kilmore.
Lake Mills	Congregational	28	32	14		Emmeline Joeckel.
Lancaster	Congregational					Fannie Smith.
Lodi	Union	30	3	28	2	W. E. Bartholemew.
Lynxville	Congregational					Rev. Mr. Teauber.
Madison	First Presbyterian	53		42	3	Florence E. Baker, 16 Langdon st.
"	First Congregational	93	20	69	9	Dr. C. H. Richards.
Manitowoc	First Presbyterian	45	29	29	5	Clara Filholm.
Mazo Marie	Congregational	21	20	9	4	Bella Knapp.
Menasha	First Congregational	36	24	31		Carrie Pheteplace.
Millsville	Presbyterian					E. B. Oakley.
Milton	Congregational	18	5			Miss Lucy Walker.
"	Methodist Episcopal					Rev. Mr. Robinson.
"	Seventh Day Baptist					W. Dell Burdick.
Milwaukee	Hanover St. Cong	71	6	48	25	Mattie Long, 419 National ave.
"	Asbury Methodist					Rev. Mr. Wharten.
"	South Side Baptist					Rev. Mr. Hurlburt.
"	Grand Ave. Cong	80	38	80	3	H. W. Nickerson, 1028 Wells st.
"	Pilgrim Cong.	10	13	12	3	Mrs. F. J. Ledyard, 220 33d st.
Neenah	Congregational					Rev. J. Rowland.
Neilsville	Presbyterian	29	15	15	3	E. B. Oakley.
New Cassel	Methodist Episcopal					Mrs. D. Orvis.
New London	Congregational	23	8	18	5	Mary Bradbury.
New Lisbon	Congregational	7	8	6		Annie Sandercook.
New Richmond	First Congregational	67	23	50	27	Miss Lovila M. Mosher.
North Bend						Annie Pryse.
North Lacrosse	Second Baptist	35	4	34	20	Ida Cotton, 1012 Rose st.
" "	First Baptist					Rev. Mr. Cheney.
Oak Creek	First Congregational	12	5	10		Frank L. Grover.
Omro	Presbyterian	16	19	15		Frank B. Sheerar.
Oregon	Presbyterian					Rev. Mr. Christieson.
Oshkosh	Algonia St. Methodist	32	11	33	11	Allie Waterman, 665 Algonia st.
"	Presbyterian					Rev. L. H. Morey.
"	First Congregational					Grace Morgan.
Ontario						Howard Miller.
Peshtigo	Pilgrim Congregational	14	7	14	11	Lucy B. Lamont.
Pewaukee	Methodist Episcopal	24	43	25	16	May Wildish.
Pine River	First Congregational	10	6	10	4	Jay S. Brown.
Platteville	Congregational	70	7	30		Will Hay.

WISCONSIN. — (*Continued.*)

CITY.	CHURCH.	Act. Memb.	Asso. Memb.	Ch. Memb.	United with C.	Secretary and Address.
Platteville	Branch Congregational	....	30	....	....	Richard Manuel.
Prairie du Chien	First Congregational	19	30	5	....	Ada Barnes.
Plymouth	Congregational	18	8	17	1	I. I. Jones.
Racine	Presbyterian	....	....	....	....	Dr. Corwin.
"	Congregational	....	....	....	....	Jessie Dorchester.
"	First Meth. Episcopal	76	....	62	6	Mary Gebhardt, 817 Union st.
Raymond		....	....	....	....	
Reedsburg	Union	17	....	15	6	M. E. Seymour.
Ripon	Congregational	26	10	26	2	Hattie E. Richardson.
"	First Baptist	29	2	20	....	Anna M. Hamilton.
River Falls	Methodist	....	....	....	....	
Roberts	Congregational	....	....	....	....	A. H. Aldridge.
Rosendale	Methodist	....	....	....	....	Rev. Mr. Cornell.
St. Croix Falls	Presbyterian	13	22	13	2	Mrs. E. Y. Arnold.
Seymour	Congregational	....	....	....	....	Sophia Strong.
Sharon	Congregational	18	2	12	....	Chas. H. Dickinson, Box 485.
Shawano	First Presbyterian	....	....	....	....	Rev. Mr. Hughs.
Sheboygan	Methodist Episcopal	....	....	....	....	Rev. C. E. Carpenter, 919 7th st.
Shopiere	Congregational	....	....	....	....	Miss L. Parker.
Stevens Point	First Presbyterian	37	8	32	....	Bertha Scott.
Stockbridge	Congregational	23	10	11	6	George Hicks.
Sun Prairie	Union	20	4	17	....	Mrs. I. M. Buell.
Sussex	Methodist Episcopal	....	....	....	....	Rev. Wm. Medland.
Taylor's Falls	Presbyterian	....	....	....	....	Rev. Irving P. Withington.
"	Methodist	....	....	....	....	Rev. E. E. Edward.
Turtle, Beloit P. O.	Union	....	....	....	....	Miss Kittie Gates.
Union Grove	First Congregational	27	....	21	....	Etta Bloxsidge.
Waukesha	Methodist Episcopal	....	....	....	....	Rev. Mr. Haylett.
Waupin		....	....	....	....	
Wausaw	First Baptist	22	4	21	9	Robert McConkey.
"	Methodist	....	....	....	....	Rev. Mr. Davis.
"	Presbyterian	....	....	....	....	Annie Burnet, M. D.
"	Universalist	....	....	....	....	Rev. B. F. Rogers.
Wauwatosa	Congregational	....	....	....	....	Carrie G. Warcen.
Whitewater	Baptist	33	2	33	4	D. A. Silliman.
"	Congregational	....	....	....	....	Emma L. Alexander, Box 454.
"	Methodist Episcopal	....	....	....	....	Rev. A. J. Benjamin.
Windsor	Congregational	11	12	8	....	Geo. C. Haswell.
Wyocena	First Congregational	14	4	14	....	Lewis Fenton.

WYOMING.

Cheyenne	First Congregational	27	5	29	....	P. F. Powelson, 2502 Thomes st.

FOREIGN MISSIONS.

CITY.	CHURCH.	Act. Memb.	Asso. Memb.	Ch. Memb.	United with C.	Secretary and Address.
Beirut, Syria		....	....	....	....	Mrs. Knapp.
Bitliss, Turkey		....	....	....	....	
Ceylon	Twenty Societies	....	....	....	....	
Foochow, China	Two Societies	....	....	....	....	Arthur B. Brown, 152 King st.
Honolulu	Hawaiian Isl'ds Cong	....	....	....	....	Ah Syoo.
Moulgren, Burma	Baptist	65	60	65	23	
San Sebastian, Spain		....	....	....	....	Mrs. Gulick.
Scotland, Dundee		....	....	....	....	
South Africa, Zulu Land		....	....	....	....	
Turkey	Three Societies	....	....	....	....	

WASHINGTON TERRITORY.

CITY.	CHURCH.	Act. Memb.	Asso. Memb.	Ch. Memb.	United with C.	Secretary and Address.
Colfax	Congregationalist	....	....	....	....	J. H. Sutherland.
Coupeville	Congregationalist	....	....	....	....	Edward Dew.
"	Puget Sd. Acad. Cong	....	....	....	....	Rev. Geo. Lindsay.
Ellensburgh	Pres	....	....	....	....	Dora McPherson.
Houghton	First Ch. of Christ	....	....	....	....	Amanda C. Nelson.
Seattle	Methodist	....	....	....	....	Rev. C. D. Davis.
"	Plymouth Cong	....	....	....	....	Everett Smith.
"	First Methodist	....	....	....	....	Rev. A. J. Hanson.
"	First Baptist	....	....	....	....	Rev. R. S. Green.
"	Pres	....	....	....	....	Dr. Price.
"	Battery St. M. E	....	....	....	....	John B. Denny.
"	Scandinavian Bap	....	....	....	....	Sam'l Houser.
"	Congregationalist	....	....	....	....	C. E. Kilbourne.
Spokane Falls	First Pres	....	....	....	....	F. J. Eaken.
" "	First Bap	....	....	....	....	Rev. J. F. Baker.
Tacoma	First Cong	....	....	....	....	J. W. Wood, 1515 Yakirna Ave.
"	First Pres	....	....	....	....	Eva Holgate.
Walla Walla	First Cong	....	....	....	....	Louise F. Anderson, P.O. Box 331
" "	Cumberland Pres	....	....	....	....	Lizzie Justice.
" "	Union	....	....	....	....	Abbie E. Cushman, P.O. Box 487

www.ingramcontent.com/pod-product-compliance
Lightning Source LLC
Chambersburg PA
CBHW022355040426
42450CB00005B/190